I0748956

THE LIMITS OF RELIGIOUS THOUGHT EXAMINED

IN

EIGHT LECTURES DELIVERED BEFORE THE UNIVERSITY OF OXFORD, IN THE YEAR MDCCCLVIII.,

ON

The Bampton Foundation.

BY

HENRY LONGUEVILLE MANSEL, B. D.,

READER IN MORAL AND METAPHYSICAL PHILOSOPHY AT MAGDALEN COLLEGE;
TUTOR AND LATE FELLOW OF ST. JOHN'S COLLEGE.

FIRST AMERICAN, FROM THE THIRD LONDON, EDITION.
WITH THE NOTES TRANSLATED.

BOSTON:
GOULD AND LINCOLN,
59 WASHINGTON STREET.
NEW YORK: SHELDON AND COMPANY.
CINCINNATI: GEORGE S. BLANCHARD.
1860.

ELECTROTYPED AND PRINTED

BY W. F. DRAPER, ANDOVER, MASS.

THE OBJECTIONS MADE TO FAITH ARE BY NO MEANS AN EFFECT OF KNOWLEDGE, BUT PROCEED RATHER FROM IGNORANCE OF WHAT KNOWLEDGE IS.

BISHOP BERKELEY.

NO DIFFICULTY EMERGES IN THEOLOGY, WHICH HAD NOT PREVIOUSLY EMERGED IN PHILOSOPHY.

SIR W. HAMILTON.

EXTRACT

FROM

THE LAST WILL AND TESTAMENT

OF THE

REV. JOHN BAMPTON,

CANON OF SALISBURY.

.... "I give and bequeath my Lands and Estates to the Chancellor, Masters, and Scholars of the University of Oxford for ever, to have and to hold all and singular the said Lands or Estates upon trust, and to the intents and purposes hereinafter mentioned; that is to say, I will and appoint that the Vice-Chancellor of the University of Oxford for the time being shall take and receive all the rents, issues, and profits thereof, and (after all taxes, reparations, and necessary deductions made) that he pay all the remainder to the endowment of eight Divinity Lecture Sermons, to be established for ever in the said University, and to be performed in the manner following:

"I direct and appoint, that, upon the first Tuesday in Easter Term, a Lecturer be yearly chosen by the Heads of Colleges only, and by no others, in the room adjoining to the Printing-House, between the hours of ten in the morning and two in the afternoon, to preach eight Divinity Lecture Sermons, the year following, at St. Mary's in Oxford, between the commencement of the last month in Lent Term, and the end of the third week in Act Term.

"Also I direct and appoint, that the eight Divinity Lecture Sermons shall be preached upon either of the following Subjects — to confirm and establish the Christian Faith, and to confute all heretics and schismatics — upon the divine authority of the holy Scriptures — upon the authority of the writings of the primitive Fathers, as to the faith and practice of the primitive Church — upon the Divinity of our Lord and Saviour Jesus Christ — upon the Divinity of the Holy Ghost — upon the Articles of the Christian Faith, as comprehended in the Apostles' and Nicene Creeds.

"Also I direct, that thirty copies of the eight Divinity Lecture Sermons shall be always printed, within two months after they are preached, and one copy shall be given to the Chancellor of the University, and one copy to the Head of every College, and one copy to the Mayor of the city of Oxford, and one copy to be put into the Bodleian Library; and the expense of printing them shall be paid out of the revenue of the Land or Estates given for establishing the Divinity Lecture Sermons; and the Preacher shall not be paid, nor be entitled to the revenue, before they are printed.

"Also I direct and appoint, that no person shall be qualified to preach the Divinity Lecture Sermons, unless he hath taken the degree of Master of Arts at least, in one of the two Universities of Oxford or Cambridge; and that the same person shall never preach the Divinity Lecture Sermons twice."

PUBLISHERS' ADVERTISEMENT

TO

THE AMERICAN EDITION.

The work, here offered to the American public, has been received with the most marked attention in England, and has already reached a third edition, though but few months have elapsed since the issue of the first. It is believed that its great merits will command for it a like attention wherever it is known; the rare learning and metaphysical ability with which it discusses problems, no less profound in their philosophical nature than practical in their religious applications; the devout reverence for the authority of the Bible, and the truly Christian spirit with which it is imbued, must gain for it a cherished place in the minds and hearts of all who wish well to a sound philosophy, and a pure, and we may add, a real, Christianity. In its more immediate aspect, it is eminently a work for the present times; so closely is it connected with the higher thinking of the present generation, and so boldly and triumphantly does it carry the Christian argument through the entire course of recent, and especially German, speculation. But rightly viewed, these Lectures of Mr. Mansel have a far wider scope than this; for, in unfolding his great theme, the author aims to lay the foundations of a sound religious philosophy in the laws of the human mind, and in the general conditions to which it is thereby necessarily subject in the attainment of all truth and knowledge; his work therefore belongs, in its principles and applications, to all periods of human inquiry, and is thus invested with a universal interest and a permanent value.

But without enlarging upon the general merits of this work, the Publishers have only to mention the single change of any importance, which it has undergone in the present reprint. This change is the *translation* in the author's learned NOTES — a most valuable portion of his work — of the numerous passages from foreign writers, Greek, Latin, French, and German, which in the English edition appear in the original languages. It has been thought best to translate these passages, in order to bring them within the reach of all general readers; and it is hoped that this proceeding will be regarded by scholars with indulgence at least, if not with entire approval.

The translations have been made by PROF. JOHN L. LINCOLN, of Brown University, whose reputation as a scholar is deemed by the Publishers a sufficient guaranty for the execution of the work. It has been the translator's endeavor to reproduce the original with as much fidelity as possible; and to make only such departures, even in the form of the thought, as the English idiom seemed to require. The difficulties belonging to the task of translating isolated passages from so many and so different writers, will doubtless be best understood by those who are most familiar with the languages in which they are written, and with the abstruse subjects which they discuss.

An INDEX OF THE AUTHORS, quoted in the work, has been also prepared for the American edition, which will be of great service to readers, and will indicate the wide and various range of Mr. Mansel's studies.

BOSTON, April 20, 1859.

PREFACE

TO

THE THIRD EDITION.

The various Criticisms to which these Lectures have been subjected since the publication of the last Edition, seem to call for a few explanatory remarks on the positions principally controverted. Such remarks may, it is hoped, contribute to the clearer perception of the argument in places where it has been misunderstood, and are also required in order to justify the republication, with little more than a few verbal alterations, of the entire work in its original form.

On the whole, I have no reason to complain of my Critics. With one or two exceptions, the tone of their observations has been candid, liberal, and intelligent, and in some instances more favorable than I could have ventured to expect. An argument so abstruse, and in some respects so controversial, must almost inevitably call forth a considerable amount of opposition; and such criticism is at least useful in stimulating further inquiry, and in pointing out to an author those among his statements which appear most to require explanation or defence. If it has not done more than this, it is because the original argument was not put forth without much previous consideration, nor without anticipation of many of the objections to which it was likely to be exposed.

At present, I must confine myself to those explanations which appear to be necessary to the right appreciation of the main purposes of the work, on the supposition that its fundamental principles may be admitted as tenable. To reärgue the whole question on first principles, or to reply minutely to the criticisms on subordinate details, would require a larger space than can be allotted to a preface, and would be at least premature at the present stage of the controversy, while the work has in all probability not yet completed the entire course of criticism which a new book is destined to undergo if it succeeds in attracting any amount of public attention.

In the first place, it may be desirable to obviate some misapprehensions concerning the design of the work as a whole. It should be remembered, that to answer the objections which have been urged against Christianity, or against any religion, is not to prove the religion to be true. It only clears the ground for the production of the proper evidences. It shows, so far as it is successful, that the religion *may be* true, notwithstanding the objections by which it has been assailed; but it cannot by itself convert this admission into a positive belief. It only calls for an impartial hearing of the other grounds on which the question must be decided.

When, therefore, a critic objects to the present argument, that "the presence of contradictions is no proof of the truth of a system;" that "we are not entitled to erect on this ethereal basis a superstructure of theological doctrine, only because it, too, possesses the same self-contradictions;" that "the argument places all religions and philosophies on precisely the same level;" — he merely charges it with accomplishing the very purpose which it was intended to accomplish. So far as certain difficulties are inherent in the constitution of the human mind itself, they must of necessity occupy the same position with respect to all religions,—the false no less than the true. It is sufficient if it can be shown that they have not, as is too often supposed, any peculiar force against Christianity alone. No sane man dreams of maintaining that a religion is true *because of* the difficulties which it involves: the utmost that can reasonably be maintained is that it may be true *in spite of* them. Such an argument of course requires, as its supplement, a further consideration of the direct evidences of Christianity; and this requirement is pointed out in the concluding Lecture. But it formed no part of my design to exhibit in detail the evidences themselves; — a task which the many excellent works already existing on that subject would have rendered wholly unnecessary, even if it could have been satisfactorily accomplished within the limits of the single Lecture which alone could have been given to it.

But granting for the present the main position of these Lectures, namely, that the human mind inevitably and by virtue of its essential constitution, finds itself involved in self-contradictions whenever it ventures on certain courses of speculation; it may be asked, in the next place, what conclusion does this admission warrant, as regards the respective positions of Faith and Reason in determining the religious convictions of men. These Lectures have been charged with condemning, under the name of Dogmatism, all Dogmatic Theology; with censuring "the exercise of Reason in defence and illustration of the truths of Revelation;" with including "schoolmen and saints and infidels alike" in one and the same condemnation. Such sweeping assertions are surely not warranted by anything that is maintained in the Lectures themselves. Dogmatism and Rationalism are contrasted with each other, not as employing reason for opposite purposes, but as employing it in extremes. The contrast was naturally suggested by the historical connection between the Wolfian philosophy and the Kantian, the one as the stronghold of Dogmatism, the other of Rationalism. The religious philosophy of Wolf and his followers, whose system, and not that of either "schoolmen or saints," is cited as the chief specimen of Dogmatism, was founded on the assumption that philosophical proofs of theological doctrines were *absolutely necessary* in *all* cases. "He maintained," says a writer quoted in the Notes, "that philosophy was indispensable to theology, and that, together with biblical proofs, a mathematical or strictly demonstrative dogmatical system, according to the principles of reason, was absolutely necessary." Dogmatism, as thus exemplified, is surely not the use of reason in theology, but its abuse. Unless a critic is prepared to accept, as legitimate reasoning, Canz's demonstration of the Trinity, cited at p. 232 of the present volume, or the more modern specimen of the same method noticed at p. 51, he must surely admit the conclusion which these instances were adduced to prove; namely, that the methods of the Dogmatist and the Rationalist are alike open to criticism, "in so far as they keep within or go beyond those limits of sound thought which the laws of man's mind, or the circumstances in which he is placed, have imposed upon him."

All Dogmatic Theology is not Dogmatism, nor all use of Reason Rationalism, any more than all drinking is drunkenness. The dogmatic or the rational method may be rightly or wrongly employed, and the question is to determine the limits of the legitimate or illegitimate use of each. It is expressly as extremes that the two systems are contrasted: each is described as leading to error in its *exclusive* employment, yet as being, in its utmost error, only a truth abused. If reason may not be

2

used *without restriction* in the defence any more than in the refutation of religious doctrines; if there are any mysteries of revelation which it is our duty to believe, though we cannot demonstrate them from philosophical premises, — this is sufficient to show that the provinces of Faith and Reason are not coëxtensive. But to assert this is surely not to deny that the dogmatic method may be and has been rightly used within certain limits. The dogmatism which is condemned is not system, but the extravagance of system. If systematic completeness is made the end which the theologian is bound to pursue, at every cost; if whatever is left obscure and partial in revealed truth is, as a matter of necessity, to be cleared and completed by definitions and inferences, certain or uncertain; if the declarations of Scripture are in all cases to be treated as conclusions to be supported by philosophical premises, or as principles to be developed into philosophical conclusions, — then indeed Dogmatic Theology is in danger of degenerating into mere Dogmatism. But it is only the indiscriminate use of the method which is condemned, and that not simply as an employment of reason in religious questions, but as an employment beyond its just limits. And if, in citing instances of this misuse, it has been occasionally necessary to point out the errors of writers whose names are justly honored in the Church, and whose labors, as a whole, are entitled to the reverence and gratitude of posterity, I wish distinctly to state, that the censure, such as it is, reaches only to the points directly indicated, by reference or quotation, and is not intended to apply further.

What, then, is the practical lesson which these Lectures are designed to teach concerning the right use of reason in religious questions? and what are the just claims of a reasonable faith, as distinguished from a blind credulity? In the first place, it is obvious that, if there is any object whatever of which the human mind is unable to form a clear and distinct conception, the inability equally disqualifies us for proving or disproving a given doctrine, in all cases in which such a conception is an indispensable condition of the argument. If, for example, we can form no positive notion of the Nature of God as an Infinite Being, we are not entitled either to demonstrate the mystery of the Trinity as a necessary property of that Nature, or to reject it as necessarily inconsistent therewith. Such mysteries clearly belong, not to Reason, but to Faith; and the preliminary inquiry which distinguishes a reasonable from an unreasonable belief, must be directed, not to the premises by which the doctrine can be proved or disproved as reasonable or unreasonable, but to the nature of the authority on which it rests, as revealed or unrevealed. The brief summary of Christian Evidences contained in my concluding Lecture,[1] and others which might be added to them, are

[1] See below, p. 214.

surely sufficient to form an ample field for the use of Reason, even in regard to those mysteries which it cannot directly examine. If to submit to an authority which can stand the test of such investigations, and to believe it when it tells us of things which we are unable to investigate, — if this be censured as a blind credulity, it is a blindness which in these things is a better guide than the opposite quality so justly described by the philosopher as "the sharp-sightedness of little souls."

In the second place, a caution is needed concerning the kind of evidence which reason is competent to furnish within the legitimate sphere of its employment. If we have not such a conception of the Divine Nature as is sufficient for the *a priori* demonstration of religious truth, our rational conviction in any particular case must be regarded, not as a *certainty*, but as a *probability*. We must remember the Aristotelian rule, to be content with such evidence as the nature of the object-matter allows. A single infallible criterion of all religious truth can be obtained only by the possession of a perfect Philosophy of the Infinite. If such a philosophy is unattainable; if the infinite can only be apprehended under finite symbols, and the authority of those symbols tested by finite evidences, — there is always room for error, in consequence of the inadequacy of the conception to express completely the nature of the object. In other words, we must admit that human reason, though not *worthless*, is at least *fallible*, in dealing with religious questions; and that the probability of error is always increased in proportion to the partial nature of the evidence with which it deals. Those who set up some one supreme criterion of religious truth, their "Christian consciousness," their "religious intuitions," their "moral reason," or any other of the favorite idols of the subjective school of theologians, and who treat with contempt every kind of evidence which does not harmonize with this, are especially liable to be led into error. They use the weight without the counterpoise, to the imminent peril of their mental equilibrium. This is the caution which it was the object of my concluding Lecture to enforce, principally by means of two practical rules; namely, first, that the true evidence, for or against a religion, is not to be found in any single criterion, but in the result of many presumptions examined and compared together; and, secondly, that in proportion to the weight of the counter-evidence in favor of a religion, is the probability that we may be mistaken in supposing a particular class of objections to have any real weight at all.

These considerations are no less applicable to moral than to speculative reasonings. The moral faculty, though furnishing undoubtedly some of the most important elements for the solution of the religious problem, is no more entitled than any other single principle of the human mind to be accepted as a sole and sufficient criterion. It is true that to our sense of moral obligation we owe our primary conception of God as a moral Governor; and it is also true that, were man left solely to *a priori* presumptions in forming his estimate of the nature and attributes of God, the moral sense, as being that one of all human faculties whose judgments are least dependent on experience, would furnish the principal, if not the only characteristics of his highest conception of God. But here, as elsewhere, the original presumption is modified and corrected by subsequent experience. It is a fact which experience forces upon us, and which it is useless, were it possible, to disguise, that the representation of God after the model of the highest human morality which we are capable of conceiving, is not sufficient to account for all the phenomena exhibited by the course of His natural Providence. The infliction of physical suffering, the permission of moral evil, the adversity of the good, the prosperity of the wicked, the crimes of the guilty involving the misery of the innocent, the tardy appearance and partial distribution of moral and religious knowledge in the world, — these are facts which no doubt are reconcilable, we know not how, with the Infinite Goodness of God; but which certainly are not to be explained on the supposition that its sole and sufficient type is to be found in the finite goodness of man. What right, then, has the philosopher to assume that a criterion which admits of so many exceptions in the facts of nature may be applied, without qualification or exception, to the statements of revelation?

The assertion that human morality contains in it a temporal and relative element, and cannot, in its highest manifestation, be regarded as a complete measure of the absolute Goodness of God, has been condemned by one critic as "rank Occamism,"[1] and contrasted with the teaching of "that marvellously profound, cautious, and temperate thinker," Bishop Butler; it has been denounced by another, of a very different school, as "destructive of healthful moral perception." That the doctrine in question, instead of being opposed to Butler, is directly taken from him, may be seen by any one who will take the trouble to read the extract from the *Analogy* quoted at p. 211. But it is of little importance

[1] It is in fact the very reverse of the doctrine usually attributed to Occam, which admits of no distinction between absolute and relative morality, but maintains that, as all distinction of right and wrong depends upon obedience or disobedience to a higher authority, therefore the Divine Nature must be morally indifferent, and all good and evil the result of God's arbitrary Will. The above assertion, on the other hand, expressly distinguishes absolute from relative morality, and regards human virtue and vice as combining an eternal and a temporal element, — the one an absolute principle grounded in the immutable nature of God; the other a relative application, dependent upon the created constitution of human nature. But I am by no means sure that the "Invincible Doctor" has been quite fairly dealt with in this matter.

by what authority an opinion is sanctioned, if it will not itself stand the test of sound criticism. The admission, that a divine command may, under certain circumstances, justify an act which would not be justifiable without it, is condemned by some critics as holding out an available excuse for any crime committed under any circumstances. If God can suspend, on any one occasion, the ordinary obligations of morality, how, it is asked, are we to know whether any criminal may not equally claim a divine sanction for his crimes? Now where, as in the present instance, the supposed exceptions are expressly stated as supernatural ones, analogous to the miraculous suspension of the ordinary laws of nature, this objection either proves too much, or proves nothing at all. If we believe in the possibility of a supernatural Providence at all, we may also believe that God is able to authenticate His own mission by proper evidences. The objection has no special relation to questions of moral duty. It may be asked, in like manner, how we are to distinguish a true from a false prophet, or a preacher sent by God from one acting on his own responsibility. The possibility of a special divine mission of any kind will of course be denied by those who reject the supernatural altogether; but this denial removes the question into an entirely different province of inquiry, where it has no relation to any peculiar infallibility supposed to attach to the moral reason, above the other faculties of the human mind.

Those who believe, with the Scriptures, that the Almighty has, at certain times in the world's history, manifested Himself to certain nations or individuals in a supernatural manner, distinct from His ordinary government of the world by the institutions of society, will scarcely be disposed to admit the assumption, that God could not on such occasions justify by His own authority such acts as are every day justified by the authority of the civil magistrate whose power is delegated from Him. To assert, with one of my critics, that upon this principle, "the deed which is criminal on earth may be praiseworthy in heaven," is to distort the whole doctrine and to beg the whole question. For we must first answer the previous inquiry: Does not a deed performed under such circumstances cease to be criminal at all, even upon earth? The question, so far as moral philosophy is concerned, is simply this: Is the moral quality of right or wrong an attribute so essentially adhering to acts as acts, that the same act can never vary in its character according to the motives by which it is prompted, or the circumstances under which it is committed? If we are compelled, as every moralist is compelled, to answer this question in the negative, we must then ask, in the second place, whether the existence of a direct command from the supreme Governor of the world, supposing such a command ever to have been given, is one of the circumstances which can in any degree affect the character of an act. On this question, to judge merely by the conflicting statements on opposite sides, men whose moral judgments are equally trustworthy may differ one from another; but that very difference is enough to show that the moral reason is not by itself a sufficient and infallible oracle on such questions. The further inquiry, whether such a command has ever, as a matter of fact, been given; and how, if given, it can be distinguished from counterfeits, is one which does not fall within the province of moral philosophy, in itself or in its relation to theology. The philosopher, as such, can at most only prepare the way for this inquiry, if he can succeed in showing that there is nothing in the moral reason of man which entitles it to pronounce on *a priori* grounds, that such a command is absolutely impossible.

It remains to make some remarks on another of the opinions maintained in the following Lectures, on which, to judge by the criticisms to which it has been subjected, a few words of explanation may be desirable. It has been objected by reviewers of very opposite schools, that to deny to man a knowledge of the Infinite is to make Revelation itself impossible, and to leave no room for evidences on which reason can be legitimately employed. The objection would be pertinent, if I had ever maintained that Revelation is or can be a direct manifestation of the Infinite Nature of God. But I have constantly asserted the very reverse. In Revelation, as in Natural Religion, God is represented under finite conceptions, adapted to finite minds; and the evidences on which the authority of Revelation rests are finite and comprehensible also. It is true that in Revelation, no less than in the exercise of our natural faculties, there is indirectly indicated the existence of a higher and more absolute truth, which, as it cannot be grasped by any effort of human thought, cannot be made the vehicle of any valid philosophical criticism. But the comprehension of this higher truth is no more necessary, either to a belief in the contents of Revelation or to a reasonable examination of its evidences, than a conception of the infinite divisibility of matter is necessary to the child before it can learn to walk.

But it is a great mistake to suppose, as some of my critics have supposed, that if the Infinite, as an object, is inconceivable, therefore the language which denotes it is wholly without meaning, and the corresponding state of mind one of complete quiescence. A negative idea by no means implies a negation of all mental activity.[1] It implies an attempt to think, and a failure in accomplishing the attempt. The language by which such ideas are indicated is not like a word in an unknown tongue, which excites no corresponding affection in the mind of the hearer. It indicates a relation, if only of difference, to that of which we are positively conscious, and a consequent effort to pass from the one to the other. This

[1] See Sir W. Hamilton's *Discussions*, p. 602.

is the case even with those more obvious negations of thought which arise from the union of two incongruous finite notions. We may attempt to conceive a space enclosed by two straight lines; and it is not till after the effort has been made that we become aware of the impossibility of the conception. And it may frequently happen, owing to the use of language as a substitute for thought, that a process of reasoning may be carried on to a considerable length, without the reasoner being aware of the essentially inconceivable character of the objects denoted by his terms. This is especially likely when the negative character of the notion depends, not, as in the above instance, on the union of two attributes which cannot be conceived in conjunction, but on the separation of those which cannot be conceived apart. We can analyze in language what we cannot analyze in thought; and the presence of the language often serves to conceal the absence of the thought. Thus, for example, it is impossible to conceive color apart from extension; an unextended color is therefore a purely negative notion. Yet many distinguished philosophers have maintained that the connection between these two ideas is one merely of association, and have argued concerning color apart from extension, with as much confidence as if their language represented positive thought. The speculations concerning the seat of the immaterial soul may be cited as another instance of the same kind. Forgetting that, to human thought, position in space and occupation of space are notions essentially bound together, and that neither can be conceived apart from the other, men have carried on various elaborate reasonings, and constructed various plausible theories, on the tacit assumption that it is possible to assign a local position to an unextended substance. Yet, considering that extension itself is necessarily conceived as a relation between parts exterior to each other, and that no such relation can be conceived as an ultimate and simple element of things, it would be the mere dogmatism of ignorance to assert that a relation between the extended and the unextended is in itself impossible; though assuredly we are unable to conceive how it is possible.

It is thus manifest that, even granting that all our positive consciousness is of the Finite only, it may still be possible for men to speculate and reason concerning the Infinite, without being aware that their language represents, not thought, but its negation. They attempt to separate the condition of finiteness from their conception of a given object; and it is not till criticism has detected the self-contradiction involved in the attempt, that we learn at last that all human efforts to conceive the infinite are derived from the consciousness, not of what it is, but only of what it is not.[1]

[1] A critic in the *National Review* is of opinion that "relative apprehension is always and necessarily of two terms together;" and "if of the finite, then also of the infinite." This is true as regards the

Whatever value may be attached, in different psychological theories, to that instinct or feeling of our nature which compels us to believe in the existence of the Infinite, it is clear that, so long as it remains a mere instinct or feeling, it cannot be employed for the purpose of theological criticism. The communication of mental phenomena from man to man must always be made in the form of thoughts conveyed through the medium of language. So long as the unbeliever can only say, "I feel that this doctrine is false, but I cannot say why;" so long as the believer can only retort, "I feel that it is true, but I can give no reason for my feeling,"—there is no common ground on which either can hope to influence the other. So long as a man's religion is a matter of feeling only, the feeling, whatever may be its influence on himself, forms no basis of argument for or against the truth of what he believes. But as soon as he interprets his feelings into thoughts, and proceeds to make those thoughts the instruments of criticism constructive or destructive, he is bound to submit them to the same logical criteria to which he himself subjects the religion on which he is commenting. In this relation, it matters not what may be

meaning of the words; but by no means as regards the conception of the corresponding objects. If extended to the latter, it should in consistency be asserted that the conception of that which is conceivable involves also the conception of that which is inconceivable; that the consciousness of anything is also a consciousness of nothing; that the intuition of space and time is likewise an intuition of the absence of both.

the character of our *feeling* of the infinite, provided our *conception* cannot be exhibited without betraying its own inherent weakness by its own self-contradictions. That such is the case with that philosophical conception of the Absolute and Infinite which has prevailed in almost every philosophy of note, from Parmenides to Hegel, it has been the aim of these Lectures to show. If a critic maintains that philosophy, notwithstanding its past failures, may possibly hereafter succeed in bringing the infinite within the grasp of reason, we may be permitted to doubt the assertion until the task has been actually accomplished.

The distinction between speculative and regulative truths, which has also been a good deal misapprehended, is one which follows inevitably from the abandonment of the philosophy of the Absolute. If human thought cannot be traced up to an absolutely first principle of all knowledge and all existence; if our highest attainable truths bear the marks of subordination to something higher and unattainable, — it follows, if we are to act or believe at all, that our practice and belief must be based on principles which do not satisfy all the requirements of the speculative reason. But it should be remembered that this distinction is not peculiar to the evidences of religion. It is shown that in all departments of human knowledge alike, — in the laws of thought, in the movement of our limbs, in the perception of our senses, the truths which guide our practice cannot be reduced to principles which satisfy our reason; and that, if religious thought is placed under the same restrictions, this is but in strict analogy to the general conditions to which God has subjected man in his search after truth. One half of the rationalist's objections against revealed religion would fall to the ground, if men would not commit the very irrational error of expecting clearer conceptions and more rigid demonstrations of the invisible things of God, than those which they are content to accept and act upon in all the concerns of their earthly life.

The above are all the explanations which, so far as I can at present judge, appear to be desirable, to obviate probable misapprehensions regarding the general principles advocated in these pages. Had I thought it worth while to enter into controversy on minute questions of detail, or to reply to misapprehensions which are due solely to the inadvertence of individual readers,[1] I might have extended these remarks

[1] A writer in the *Christian Observer* has actually mistaken the positions against which the author is contending for those which he maintains, and on the strength of this mistake has blundered through several pages of vehement denunciation of the monstrous consequences which follow from the assumption that the philosophical conception of the absolute is the true conception of God. The absolute and the infinite, he tells us (in opposition to the Lecturer ! ! !), "are names of God unknown to the Scriptures:" "The conception of infinity is plainly negative:" "the absolute and infinite, as defined in the Lectures after

to a considerably greater length. For the present I shall content myself with only two further observations; one on a single sentence, the language of which, having been misinterpreted in more than one quarter, may perhaps need a brief explanation; the other on a matter affecting, not the literary merit of these Lectures, but the personal honesty of their author.

The sentence occurs at p. 76, in the following words: "'What kind of an Absolute Being is that,' says Hegel, 'which does not contain in itself all that is actual, even evil included?' We may repudiate the conclusion with indignation; but the reasoning is unassailable. If the Absolute

the leaders of German metaphysics, is no synonym for the true and living God:" and "a philosophy of the so-called absolute is a spurious theology." *Est il possible?*

The same critic denounces, as "radically and thoroughly untrue," the distinction between speculative and regulative truths, and the consequent assertion that action, and not knowledge, is man's destiny and duty in this life, and that his highest principles, both in philosophy and in religion, have reference to this end. "On the contrary," he says, "all right action depends on right knowledge." As if this were not the very meaning of a regulative truth,—knowledge for the sake of action.

Another critic asserts that the author "sweeps down schoolmen and saints and infidels alike, with the assertion that dogmatism and rationalism equally assign to some superior tribunal the right of determining what is essential to religion and what is not." Had he looked a second time at the page which he quotes, he would have seen that this is said of rationalism alone.

and Infinite is an object of human conception at all, this, and none other, is the conception required."

This passage has been censured by more than one critic, as involving the skeptical admission that a false conclusion can be logically deduced from true premises. The concluding words may explain the real meaning. The whole argument is designed to show that to speak of a *conception of the Absolute* implies a self-contradiction at the outset, and that to reason upon such a conception involves *ab initio* a violation of the laws of human thought. That reasoning based on this assumption must end by annihilating itself, is surely no very dangerous concession to the skeptic. Suppose that an author had written such a sentence as the following:

"A circular parallelogram must have its opposite sides and angles equal, and must also be such that all lines drawn from the centre to the circumference shall be equal to each other. The conclusion is absurd; but the reasoning is unassailable, *supposing that a circular parallelogram can be conceived at all.*"

Would such a statement involve any formidable consequences either to geometry or to logic?

It remains only to say a few words on a question of fact,

involving one of the most serious accusations that can be brought against the character of an author. A writer in the *Rambler*, to whom in other respects I feel indebted for a liberal and kindly appreciation of my labors, has qualified his favorable judgment by the grave charge that the "whole gist of the book" is borrowed without acknowledgment from the teaching of Dr. Newman, as a preacher or as a writer. Against a charge of this kind there is but one possible defence. No obligation was acknowledged, simply because none existed. I say this, assuredly with no intention to speak slightingly of one whose transcendent gifts no differences should hinder me from acknowledging; but because it is necessary, in justice to myself, to state exactly the relation in which I stand towards him. Dr. Newman's teaching from the University pulpit was almost at its close before my connection with Oxford began: his parochial sermons I had very seldom an opportunity of hearing. His published writings might doubtless have given me much valuable assistance; but with these I was but slightly acquainted when these Lectures were first published; and the little that I knew contained nothing which appeared to bear upon my argument. This is but one out of many deficiencies, of which I have been painfully conscious during the progress of the work, and which I would gladly have endeavored to supply, had circumstances allowed me a longer time for direct preparation.

The point, indeed, on which the Reviewer lays the most stress, is one in which there was little room for originality, either in myself or in my supposed teacher. That Revelation is accommodated to the limitations of man's faculties, and is primarily designed for the purpose of practical religion, and not for those of speculative philosophy, has been said over and over again by writers of almost every age, and is indeed a truth so obvious that it might have occurred independently to almost any number of thinkers. Doubtless there is no truth, however trite and obvious, which may not assume a new and striking aspect in the hands of a great and original writer; and in this, as in other respects, a better acquaintance with Dr. Newman's works might have taught me a better mode of expressing many arguments to which my own language may have done but imperfect justice. Even at this late hour, I am tempted to subjoin, as a conclusion to these observations, one passage of singular beauty and truth, of which, had I known it earlier, I would gladly have availed myself, as pointing out the true spirit in which inquiries like these should be pursued, and the practical lesson which they are designed to teach.

"And should any one fear lest thoughts such as these should tend to a dreary and hopeless skepticism, let him take into account the Being and Providence of God, the Merciful and True; and he will at once be relieved of his anxiety. All is dreary till we believe, what our hearts tell us, that we are subjects of His Governance; nothing is dreary, all inspires hope and trust, directly we understand that we are under His hand, and that whatever comes to us is from Him, as a method of discipline and guidance. What is it to us whether the knowledge He gives us be greater or less, if it be He who gives it? What is it to us whether it be exact or vague, if He bids us trust it? What have we to care whether we are or are not given to divide substance from shadow, if He is training us heavenward by means of either? Why should we vex ourselves to find whether our deductions are philosophical or no, provided they are religious? If our senses supply the media by which we are put on trial, by which we are all brought together, and hold intercourse with each other, and are disciplined, and are taught, and enabled to benefit others, it is enough. We have an instinct within us, impelling us, we have external necessity forcing us, to trust our senses, and we may leave the question of their substantial truth for another world, 'till the day break, and the shadows flee away.' And what is true of reliance on our senses, is true of all the information which it has pleased God to vouchsafe to us, whether in nature or in grace."[1]

OXFORD, *February 18th*, 1859.

[1] *University Sermons*, p. 351.

CONTENTS.

LECTURE I.

LECTURE II.

LECTURE III.

LECTURE IV.

LECTURE V.

LECTURE VI.

LECTURE VII.

LECTURE VIII.

THE

LIMITS OF RELIGIOUS THOUGHT

EXAMINED.

LECTURE I.

YE SHALL NOT ADD UNTO THE WORD WHICH I COMMAND YOU, NEITHER SHALL YE DIMINISH AUGHT FROM IT.—DEUT. IV. 2.

DOGMATISM and Rationalism are the two extremes between which religious philosophy perpetually oscillates. Each represents a system from which, when nakedly and openly announced, the well regulated mind almost instinctively shrinks back; yet which, in some more or less specious disguise, will be found to underlie the antagonist positions of many a theological controversy. Many a man who rejects isolated portions of Christian doctrine, on the ground that they are repugnant to his reason, would hesitate to avow broadly and unconditionally that reason is the supreme arbiter of all religious truth; though at the same time he would find it hard to point out any particular in which the position of reason, in relation to the truths which he still retains, differs from that which it occupies in relation to those which he rejects. And on the other hand, there are many who, while they would by no means construct a dogmatic system on the assumption that the conclusions of reason may always be made to coincide with those of revelation, yet, for want of an accurate distinction between that which is within the province of human thought and that which is beyond it, are accustomed in practice to demand the assent of the reason to positions which it is equally incompetent to affirm or to deny. Thus they not only lessen the value of the service which it is capable of rendering within its legitimate sphere, but also indirectly countenance that very intrusion of the human intellect into sacred things, which, in some of its other aspects, they so strongly and so justly condemn.

In using the above terms, it is necessary to state at the outset the sense in which each is employed, and to emancipate them from the various and vague associations connected with their ordinary use. I do not include under the name of *Dogmatism* the mere enunciation of religious truths, as resting upon authority and not upon reasoning. The Dogmatist, as well as the Rationalist, is the constructor of a system; and in constructing it, however much the materials upon which he works may be given by a higher authority, yet in connecting them together and exhibiting their systematic form, it is necessary to call in the aid of human ability. Indeed, whatever may be their actual antagonism in the field of religious controversy, the two terms are in their proper sense so little exclusive of each other, that both were originally employed to denote the same persons;—the name *Dogmatists* or *Rationalists* being indifferently given to those medical theorists who insisted on the necessity of calling in the aid of rational principles, to support or correct the conclusions furnished by experience.(1) A like signification is to be found in the later language of philosophy, when the term *Dogmatists* was used to denote those philosophers who endeav-

(1) Numbers within brackets refer to Notes at the close of the volume.

ored to explain the phenomena of experience by means of rational conceptions and demonstrations; the intelligible world being regarded as the counterpart of the sensible, and the necessary relations of the former as the principles and ground of the observed facts of the latter.(2) It is in a sense analogous to this that the term may be most accurately used in reference to Theology. Scripture is to the theological Dogmatist what Experience is to the philosophical. It supplies him with the facts to which his system has to adapt itself. It contains in an unsystematic form the positive doctrines, which further inquiry has to exhibit as supported by reasonable grounds and connected into a scientific whole. Theological Dogmatism is thus an application of reason to the support and defence of preëxisting statements of Scripture.(3) Rationalism, on the other hand, so far as it deals with Scripture at all, deals with it as a thing to be adapted to the independent conclusions of the natural reason, and to be rejected where that adaptation cannot conveniently be made. By *Rationalism*, without intending to limit the name to any single school or period in theological controversy, I mean generally to designate that system whose final test of truth is placed in the direct assent of the human consciousness, whether in the form of logical deduction, or moral judgment, or religious intuition; by whatever previous process those faculties may have been raised to their assumed dignity as arbitrators. The Rationalist, as such, is not bound to maintain that a divine revelation of religious truth is impossible, nor even to deny that it has actually been given. He may admit the existence of the revelation as a fact: he may acknowledge its utility as a temporary means of instruction for a ruder age: he may even accept certain portions as of universal and permanent authority.(4) But he assigns to some superior tribunal the right of determining what is essential to religion and what is not: he claims for himself and his age the privilege of accepting or rejecting any given revelation, wholly or in part, according as it does or does not satisfy the conditions of some higher criterion to be supplied by the human consciousness.(5)

In relation to the actual condition of religious truth, as communicated by Holy Scripture, Dogmatism and Rationalism may be considered as severally representing, the one the spirit which adds to the word of God, the other that which diminishes from it. Whether a complete system of scientific Theology could or could not have been given by direct revelation, consistently with the existing laws of human thought and the purposes which Revelation is designed to answer, it is at least certain that such a system is not given in the Revelation which we possess, but, if it is to exist at all, must be constructed out of it by human interpretation. And it is in attempting such a construction that Dogmatism and Rationalism exhibit their most striking contrasts. The one seeks to build up a complete scheme of theological doctrine out of the unsystematic materials furnished by Scripture, partly by the more complete development of certain leading ideas; partly by extending the apparent import of the Revelation to ground which it does not avowedly occupy, and attempting by inference and analogy to solve problems which the sacred volume may indeed suggest, but which it does not directly answer. The other aims at the same end by opposite means. It strives to attain to unity and completeness of system, not by filling up supposed deficiencies, but by paring down supposed excrescences. Commencing with a preconceived theory of the purpose of a revelation and the form which it ought to assume, it proceeds to remove or reduce all that will not harmonize with this leading idea; sometimes explaining away in the interpretation that which it accepts as given in the letter; sometimes denying, on *a priori* grounds, the genuineness of this or that portion of the sacred text; sometimes pretending to distinguish between the several purposes of Revelation itself, and to determine what portions are intended to convey the elements of an absolute religion, valid in all countries and for all ages, and what must be regarded as relative and accidental features of the divine plan, determined by the local or temporal peculiarities of the individuals to whom it was first addressed.

The two methods thus contrasted may appear at first sight to represent the respective claims of Faith and Reason, each extended to that point at which it encroaches on the domain of the other. But in truth the contrast between Faith and Reason, if it holds good in this relation at all, does so merely by accident. It may be applicable in some instances to the disciples of the respective systems, but not to the teachers; and even as regards the former, it is but partially and occasionally true. The disciples of the Rationalist are not necessarily the disciples of reason. It is quite as possible to receive with unquestioning submission a system of religion or philosophy invented by a human teacher, as it is to believe, upon the authority of Revelation, doctrines which no human reason is competent to discover. The so-called freethinker is as often as any other man the slave of some self-chosen master; and many who scorn the imputation of believing anything merely because it is found in the Bible, would find it hard to give any better reason for their own unbelief than the *ipse dixit* of some infidel philosopher. But when we turn from the disciples to the teachers, and look to the origin of Dogmatism and Rationalism as systems, we find both alike to be the products of thought, operating in different ways upon the same materials. Faith, properly so called, is not constructive, but receptive. It cannot supply the missing portions of an incomplete system, though it may bid us remain content with the deficiency. It cannot of itself give harmony to the discordant voices of religious thought; it cannot reduce to a single focus the many-colored rays into which the light of God's presence is refracted in its passage through the human soul; though it may bid us look forward to a time when the eyes of the blind shall be opened, and the ears of the deaf shall be unstopped;[1] when that apparent discord shall be known but as the echo of a half-heard concert, and those diverging rays shall be blended once more in the pure white light of heaven. But Faith alone cannot suggest any actual solution of our doubts: it can offer no definite reconciliation of apparently conflicting truths; for in order to accomplish that end, the hostile elements must be examined, compared, accommodated, and joined together, one with another; and such a process is an act of thought, not of belief. Considered from this point of view, both Dogmatism and Rationalism may be regarded as emanating from the same source, and amenable to the same principles of criticism; in so far as they keep within or go beyond those limits of sound thought which the laws of man's mind, or the circumstances in which he is placed, have imposed upon him.

In fact the two systems may be considered as both aiming, though in different ways, at the same end; that end being to produce a coincidence between what we believe and what we think; to remove the boundary which sepa-

[1] Isaiah xxxv. 5.

rates the comprehensible from the incomprehensible. The Dogmatist employs reason to prove, almost as much as the Rationalist employs it to disprove. The one, in the character of an advocate, accepts the doctrines of revealed religion as conclusions, but appeals to the reason, enlightened, it may be, by Revelation, to find premises to support them. The other, in the character of a critic, draws his premises from reason in the first instance; and, adopting these as his standard, either distorts the revealed doctrine into conformity with them, or, if it obstinately resists this treatment, sets it aside altogether. The one strives to lift up reason to the point of view occupied by Revelation: the other strives to bring down Revelation to the level of reason. And both alike have prejudged or neglected the previous inquiry, — Are there not definite and discernible limits to the province of reason itself, whether it be exercised for advocacy or for criticism?

Thus, to select one example out of many, the revealed doctrine of Christ's Atonement for the sins of men has been alternately defended and assailed by some such arguments as these. We have been told, on the one hand, that man's redemption *could not* have been brought about by any other means (6): — that God could not, consistently with his own attributes, have suffered man to perish unredeemed, or have redeemed him by any inferior sacrifice (7): — that man, redeemed from death, must become the servant of him who redeems him; and that it was not meet that he should be the servant of any other than God (8): — that no other sacrifice could have satisfied divine justice (9): —that no other victim could have endured the burden of God's wrath. (10) These and similar arguments have been brought forward, as one of the greatest of their authors avows, to defend the teaching of the Catl olic Faith on the ground of a *reasonable necessity.*(11) While, on the other hand, it has been argued that the revealed doctrine itself cannot be accepted as literally true; because we cannot believe that God was angry, and needed to be propitiated(12): — because it is inconsistent with the Divine Justice that the innocent should suffer for the sins of the guilty(13): — because it is more reasonable to believe that God freely forgives the offences of his creatures(14): — because we cannot conceive how the punishment of one can do away with the guilt of another.(15)

I quote these arguments only as specimens of the method in which Christian doctrines have been handled by writers on opposite sides. To examine them more in detail would detain me too long from my main purpose. I shall not therefore at present consider whether the conclusions actually arrived at, on the one side or on the other, are in themselves reasonable or unreasonable, orthodox or heretical. I am concerned only with the methods respectively employed, and the need of some rule for their employment. May reason be used without restriction in defence or refutation of religious doctrines? And if not, what are the conditions of its legitimate use? It may be that this man has defended, on reasonable grounds, none but the most essential articles of the Christian Faith: but has he pointed out any rule which can hinder the same or similar reasoning from being advanced by another in support of the most dangerous errors? It may be that that man has employed the test of reasonableness, only in the refutation of opinions concerning which the church has pronounced no positive judgment: but has he fenced his method round with any cautions to prevent its being used for the overthrow of Christianity itself? If we can find no other ground than the arbitrary will of the man himself, why he should stop short at the particular point which he has chosen, we may not perhaps condemn the tenets of the individual, but we may fairly charge his method with the consequences to which it logically leads us.

Thus, we find a late lamented writer of our own day, and at that time of our own church, defending the doctrine of the Incarnation of Christ, on the metaphysical assumption of the real existence of an abstract humanity. "This," he tells us, "is why the existence of human nature is a thing too precious to be surrendered to the subtleties of logic, because, upon its existence depends that real manhood of Christ, which renders him a copartner with ourselves." And again: "To the reality of this work, the existence of that common nature is indispensable, whereby, as the children were partakers of flesh and blood, He Himself took part of the same. Else, how would the perfect assumption of humanity have consisted with His retaining that divine personality which it was impossible that He should surrender? Since it was no new person which He took, it can only have been the substratum, in which personality has its existence." (16) In this case, our belief in the undeniable truth of the doctrine defended may dispose us to overlook the questionable character of the defence. But if we are inclined for a moment to acquiesce in this unnatural union of metaphysical premises and theological conclusions, we are recalled to ourselves by the recollection of the fearful consequence which Occam deduces from the same hypothesis, of the assumption by Christ of a "substratum in which personality has its existence;" — a consequence drawn in language which we shudder to read, even as it is employed by its author, merely for the purpose of reducing to an absurdity the principles of his antagonists. (17)

There is an union of Philosophy with Religion in which each contributes to the support of the other; and there is also an union which, under the appearance of support, does but undermine the foundations and prey upon the life of both. To which of these two the above argument belongs, it needs but a bare statement of its assumption to determine. It tells us that our belief in the doctrine of God manifest in the flesh, indispensably depends upon our acceptance of the Realist theory of the nature of universal notions. Philosophy and Theology alike protest against such an outrage upon the claims, both of Reason and of Revelation, as is implied in this association of one of the most fundamental truths of the Christian Faith with one of the most questionable speculations of mediæval metaphysics. What does Theology gain by this employment of a weapon which may, at any moment, be turned against her? Does it make one whit clearer to our understandings that mysterious two-fold nature of one Christ, very God, and very Man? By no means. It was a truth above human comprehension before; and it remains a truth above human comprehension still. We believe that Christ is both God and Man; for this is revealed to us. We know not how He is so; for this is not revealed; and we can learn it in no other way. Theology gains nothing; but she is in danger of losing everything. Her most precious truths are cut from the anchor which held them firm, and cast upon the waters of philosophical speculation, to float hither and thither with the ever-shifting waves of thought. And what does Philosophy gain? Her just domains are narrowed, and her free limbs cramped in their onward course. The problems which she has a native right to sift to the uttermost, are taken out of the field of free discussion, and fenced about with religious doctrines which it is heresy to call in question. Neither Christian truth nor philosophical inquiry can be advanced by such a system as this, which revives and sanctifies, as essential to the Catholic Faith, the forgotten follies of Scholastic Realism, and endangers the cause of religion, by seeking to explain its greatest mysteries by the lifeless forms of a worn-out controversy. "Why seek ye the living among the dead? Christ is not here."[1]

But if the tendency of Dogmatism is to endanger the interests of religious truth, by placing that which is divine and unquestionable in too close an alliance with that which is human and doubtful, Rationalism, on the other hand, tends to destroy revealed religion altogether, by obliterating the whole distinction between the human and the divine. Rationalism, if it retains any portion of revealed truth as such, does so, not in consequence of, but in defiance of, its fundamental principle. It does so by virtually declaring that it will follow reason up to a certain point, and no further; though the conclusions which lie beyond that point are guaranteed by precisely the same evidence as those which fall short of it. We may select a notable example from the writings of a great thinker, who has contributed, perhaps, more than any other person to give a philosophical sanction to the rationalizing theories of his countrymen, yet from whose speculative principles, rightly employed, might be extracted the best antidote to his own conclusions, even as the body of the scorpion, crushed upon the wound, is said to be the best cure for its own venom.

Kant's theory of a rational religion is based upon the

[1] St. Luke xxiv. 5, 6.

assumption that the sole purpose of religion must be to give a divine sanction to man's moral duties.[(18)] He maintains that there can be no duties towards God, distinct from those which we owe towards men; but that it may be necessary, at certain times and for certain persons, to give to moral duties the authority of divine commands.[(19)] Let us hear then the philosopher's *rational* explanation, upon this assumption, of the duty of Prayer. It is a mere superstitious delusion, he tells us, to consider prayer as a service addressed to God, and as a means of obtaining His favor.[(20)] The true purpose of the act is not to alter or affect in any way God's relation towards us; but only to quicken our own moral sentiments, by keeping alive within us the idea of God as a moral Lawgiver.[(21)] He, therefore, neither admits the duty unconditionally, nor rejects it entirely; but leaves it optional with men to adopt that or any other means, by which, in their own particular case, this moral end may be best promoted; — as if any moral benefit could possibly accrue from the habitual exercise of an act of conscious self-deception.

The origin of such theories is of course to be traced to that morbid horror of what they are pleased to call Anthropomorphism, which poisons the speculations of so many modern philosophers, when they attempt to be wise above what is written, and seek for a metaphysical exposition of God's nature and attributes.[(22)] They may not, forsooth, think of the unchangeable God as if He were their fellow man, influenced by human motives, and moved by human supplications. They want a truer, a juster idea of the Deity as He is, than that under which He has been pleased to reveal Himself; and they call on their reason to furnish it. Fools, to dream that man can escape from himself, that human reason can draw aught but a human portrait of God! They do but substitute a marred and mutilated humanity for one exalted and entire: they add nothing to their conception of God as He is, but only take away a part of their conception of man. Sympathy, and love, and fatherly kindness, and forgiving mercy, have evaporated in the crucible of their philosophy; and what is the *caput mortuum* that remains, but only the sterner features of humanity exhibited in repulsive nakedness? The God who listens to prayer, we are told, appears in the likeness of human mutability. Be it so. What is the God who does not listen, but the likeness of human obstinacy? Do we ascribe to him a fixed purpose? our conception of a purpose is human. Do we speak of Him as continuing unchanged? our conception of continuance is human. Do we conceive Him as knowing and determining? what are knowledge and determination but modes of human consciousness? and what know we of consciousness itself, but as the contrast between successive mental states? But our rational philosopher stops short in the middle of his reasoning. He strips off from humanity just so much as suits his purpose; — "and the residue thereof he maketh a god;"[1] — less pious in his idolatry than the carver of the graven image, in that he does not fall down unto it and pray unto it, but is content to stand off and reason concerning it. And why does he retain any conception of God at all, but that he retains some portions of an imperfect humanity? Man is still the residue that is left; deprived indeed of all that is amiable in humanity, but, in the darker features which remain, still man. Man in his purposes; man in his inflexibility; man in that relation to time from which no philosophy, whatever its pre-

[1] Isaiah xliv. 17.

tensions, can wholly free itself; pursuing with indomitable resolution a preconceived design; deaf to the yearning instincts which compel his creatures to call upon him.(23) Yet this, forsooth, is a philosophical conception of the Deity, more worthy of an enlightened reason than the human imagery of the Psalmist: "The eyes of the Lord are over the righteous, and His ears are open unto their prayers."[1]

Surely downright idolatry is better than this *rational* worship of a fragment of humanity. Better is the superstition which sees the image of God in the wonderful whole which God has fashioned, than the philosophy which would carve for itself a Deity out of the remnant which man has mutilated. Better to realize the satire of the Eleatic philosopher, to make God in the likeness of man, even as the ox or the horse might conceive gods in the form of oxen or horses, than to adore some half-hewn Hermes, the head of a man joined to a misshapen block.(24) Better to fall down before that marvellous compound of human consciousness whose elements God has joined together, and no man can put asunder, than to strip reason of those cognate elements which together furnish all that we can conceive or imagine of conscious or personal existence, and to deify the emptiest of all abstractions, a something or a nothing, with just enough of its human original left to form a theme for the disputations of philosophy, but not enough to furnish a single ground of appeal to the human feelings of love, of reverence, and of fear. Unmixed idolatry is more religious than this. Undisguised atheism is more logical.

Throughout every page of Holy Scripture God reveals himself, not as a Law, but as a Person. Throughout the

[1] Psalm xxxiv. 15.

breadth and height and depth of human consciousness, Personality manifests itself under one condition, that of a Free Will, influenced, though not coerced, by motives. And to this consciousness God addresses Himself, when he adopts its attributes as the image under which to represent to man His own incomprehensible and ineffable nature. Doubtless in this there is much of accommodation to the weakness of man's faculties; but not more than in any other representation of any of the divine attributes. By what right do we say that the conception of the God who hears and answers prayer[1] is an accommodation, while that of Him in whom is no variableness nor shadow of turning[2] is not so? By what right do we venture to rob the Deity of half His revealed attributes, in order to set up the other half, which rests on precisely the same evidence, as a more absolute revelation of the truth? By what right do we enthrone, in the place of the God to whom we pray, an inexorable Fate or immutable Law?—a thing with less than even the divinity of a Fetish; since *that* may be at least conceived by its worshipper as capable of being offended by his crimes and propitiated by his supplications?

Yet surely there is a principle of truth of which this philosophy is the perversion. Surely there is a sense in which we may not think of God as though He were man; as there is also a sense in which we cannot help so thinking of Him. When we read in the same narrative, and almost in two consecutive verses of Scripture, "The Strength of Israel will not lie nor repent; for He is not a man that He should repent;" and again, "The Lord repented that He had made Saul king over Israel:"[3] we are imperfectly con-

[1] Psalm lxv. 2; St. James v. 16. [2] St. James i. 17. [3] 1 Sam. xv. 29, 35.

scious of an appeal to two different principles of representation, involving opposite sides of the same truth; we feel that there is a true foundation for the system which denies human attributes to God; though the superstructure, which has been raised upon it, logically involves the denial of His very existence.

What limits then can we find to determine the legitimate provinces of these two opposite methods of religious thought, each of which, in its exclusive employment, leads to errors so fatal; yet each of which, in its utmost error, is but a truth abused? If we may not, with the Dogmatist, force Philosophy into unnatural union with Revelation, nor yet, with the Rationalist, mutilate Revelation to make it agree with Philosophy, what guide can we find to point out the safe middle course? what common element of both systems can be employed to mediate between them? It is obvious that no such element can be found by the mere contemplation of the objects on which religious thought is exercised. We can adequately criticize that only which we know as a whole. The objects of Natural Religion are known to us in and by the ideas which we can form of them; and those ideas do not of themselves constitute a whole, apart from the remaining phenomena of consciousness. We must not examine them by themselves alone: we must look to their origin, their import, and their relation to the mind of which they are part. Revealed Religion, again, is not by itself a direct object of criticism: first, because it is but a part of a larger scheme, and that scheme one imperfectly comprehended; and secondly, because Revelation implies an accommodation to the mental constitution of its human receiver; and we must know what that constitution is, before we can pronounce how far the accommodation extends. But if partial knowledge must not be treated as if it were complete, neither, on the other hand, may it be identified with total ignorance. The false humility which assumes that it can know nothing, is often as dangerous as the false pride which assumes that it knows everything. The provinces of Reason and Faith, the limits of our knowledge and of our ignorance, must both be clearly determined: otherwise we may find ourselves dogmatically protesting against dogmatism, and reasoning to prove the worthlessness of reason.

There is one point from which all religious systems must start, and to which all must finally return; and which may therefore furnish a common ground on which to examine the principles and pretensions of all. *The primary and proper object of criticism is not Religion, natural or revealed, but the human mind in its relation to Religion.* If the Dogmatist and the Rationalist have heretofore contended as combatants, each beating the air in his own position, without being able to reach his adversary; if they have been prevented from taking up a common ground of controversy, because each repudiates the fundamental assumptions of the other; that common ground must be sought in another quarter; namely, in those laws and processes of the human mind, by means of which both alike accept and elaborate their opposite systems. If human philosophy is not a direct guide to the attainment of religious truth (and its entire history too truly testifies that it is not), may it not serve as an indirect guide, by pointing out the limits of our faculties, and the conditions of their legitimate exercise? Witnessing, as it does, the melancholy spectacle of the household of humanity divided against itself, the reason against the feelings and the feelings against the reason, and the dim half-consciousness of the shadow of the infinite frowning down upon both, may it not seek, with the heathen Philosopher of old, to find the reconciling and regulating principle in that justice, of which the essential character is, that every member of the system shall do his own duty, and forbear to intrude into the office of his neighbor? (25)

A criticism of the human mind, in relation to religious truth, was one of the many unrealized possibilities of philosophy, sketched out in anticipation by the far-seeing genius of Bacon. "Here therefore," he writes, "I note this deficiency, that there hath not been, to my understanding, sufficiently enquired and handled the true limits and use of reason in spiritual things, as a kind of divine dialectic: which for that it is not done, it seemeth to me a thing usual, by pretext of true conceiving that which is revealed, to search and mine into that which is not revealed; and by pretext of enucleating inferences and contradictories, to examine that which is positive: the one sort falling into the error of Nicodemus, demanding to have things made more sensible than it pleaseth God to reveal them, 'Quomodo possit homo nasci cum sit senex?' the other sort into the error of the disciples, which were scandalized at a show of contradiction, 'Quid est hoc quod dicit nobis, Modicum, et non videbitis me; et iterum, modicum, et videbitis me?'" (26)

An examination of the Limits of Religious Thought is an indispensable preliminary to all Religious Philosophy. And the limits of religious thought are but a special manifestation of the limits of thought in general. Thus the Philosophy of Religion, on its human side, must be subject to those universal conditions which are binding upon Philosophy in general. It has ever fared ill, both with Philosophy and with Religion, when this caution has been neglected. It was an evil hour for both, when Fichte made his first essay, as a disciple of the Kantian school, by an attempted criticism of all Revelation. (27) The very title of Kant's great work, and, in spite of many inconsistencies, the general spirit of its contents also, might have taught him a different lesson, — might have shown him that Reason, and not Revelation, was the primary object of criticism. If Revelation is a communication from an infinite to a finite intelligence, the conditions of a criticism of Revelation on philosophical grounds must be identical with those which are required for constructing a Philosophy of the Infinite. For Revelation can make known the Infinite Being only in one of two ways; by *presenting* him as he is, or by *representing* him under symbols more or less adequate. A presentative Revelation implies faculties in man which can receive the presentation; and such faculties will also furnish the conditions of constructing a philosophical theory of the object presented. If, on the other hand, Revelation is merely representative, the accuracy of the representation can only be ascertained by a knowledge of the object represented; and this again implies the possibility of a philosophy of the Infinite. Whatever impediments, therefore, exist to prevent the formation of such a philosophy, the same impediments must likewise prevent the accomplishment of a complete criticism of Revelation. Whatever difficulties or contradictions are involved in the philosophical idea of the Infinite, the same or similar ones must naturally be expected in the corresponding ideas which Revelation either exhibits or implies. And if an examination of the problems of Philosophy and the conditions of their solution should compel us to admit the existence of principles and modes of thought which must be accepted as true in practice, though they cannot be explained in theory; the same practical acceptance may be claimed, on philosophical grounds, in behalf of the corresponding doctrines of Revelation.

If it can be shown that the limits of religious and philosophical thought are the same; that corresponding difficulties occur in both, and, from the nature of the case, must occur, the chief foundation of religious Rationalism is cut away from under it. The difficulties which it professes to find in Revelation are shown to be not peculiar to Revelation, but inherent in the constitution of the human mind, and such as no system of Rationalism can avoid or overcome. The analogy, which Bishop Butler has pointed out, between Religion and the constitution and course of Nature, may be in some degree extended to the constitution and processes of the human mind. The representations of God which Scripture presents to us may be shown to be analogous to those which the laws of our minds require us to form; and therefore such as may naturally be supposed to have emanated from the same author. Such an inquiry occupies indeed but a subordinate place among the direct evidences of Christianity; nor is it intended to usurp the place of those evidences. But indirectly it may have its use, in furnishing an answer to a class of objections which were very popular a few years ago, and are not yet entirely extinguished. Even if it does not contribute materially to strengthen the position occupied by the defenders of Christianity, it may serve to expose the weakness of the assailants. Human reason may, in some respects, be weak as a supporter of Religion; but it is at least strong enough to repel an attack founded on the negation of reason.

"We know in part, and we prophesy in part. But when that which is perfect is come, then that which is in part shall be done away. For now we see through a glass, darkly; but then face to face: now I know in part; but then shall I know even as also I am known."[1] Such is the Apostle's declaration of the limits of human knowledge. "The logical conception is the absolute divine conception itself; and the logical process is the immediate exhibition of God's self-determination to Being."(28) Such is the Philosopher's declaration of the extent of human knowledge. On the first of these statements is founded the entire Theology of Scripture: on the second is founded the latest and most complete exposition of the Theology of Rationalism. The one represents God, not as He is in the brightness of His own glory, dwelling in the light which no man can approach unto;[2] but as He is reflected faintly in broken and fitful rays, glancing back from the restless waters of the human soul. The other identifies the shadow with the substance, not even shrinking from the confession that, to know God as He is, man must himself be God.(29) It turns from the feeble image of God in the soul of the individual man, to seek the entire manifestation of Deity in the collective consciousness of mankind. "Ye shall be as gods,"[3] was the earliest suggestion of the Tempter to the parents of the human race: "Ye are God," is the latest assurance of philosophy to the human race itself.(30) Revelation represents the infinite God under finite symbols, in condescension to the finite capacity of man; indicating at the same time the existence of a further reality beyond the symbol, and bidding us look forward in faith to the promise of a more perfect knowledge hereafter. Rationalism, in the hands of these expositors, adopts an opposite view of man's powers and duties. It claims to behold God as He is *now*: it finds a common object for Religion and Philosophy in the *explanation of*

[1] 1 Cor. xiii. 9, 10, 12. [2] 1 Tim. vi. 16. [3] Genesis iii. 5.

God.(31) It declares Religion to be *the Divine Spirit's knowledge of himself through the mediation of the finite Spirit.*(32)

"Beloved, now are we the sons of God; and it doth not yet appear what we shall be: but we know that, when He shall appear, we shall be like Him; for we shall see Him as He is. And every man that hath this hope in him purifieth himself, even as He is pure."[1] Philosophy too confesses that like must be known by like; but, reversing the hope of the Apostle, it finds God in the forms of human thought. Its kingdom is proclaimed to be Truth absolute and unveiled. It contains in itself the exhibition of God, as He is in His eternal essence, before the creation of a finite world.(33) Which of these two representations contains the truer view of the capacities of human reason, it will be the purpose of the following Lectures to inquire. Such an inquiry must necessarily, during a portion at least of its course, assume a philosophical, rather than a theological aspect; yet it will not perhaps on that account be less ultimately serviceable in theological controversy. It has been acutely said, that even if Philosophy is useless, it is still useful, as the means of proving its own uselessness.(34) But it is not so much the utility as the necessity of the study, which constitutes its present claim on our attention. So long as man possesses facts of consciousness and powers of reflection, so long he will continue to exercise those powers and study those facts. So long as human consciousness contains the idea of a God and the instincts of worship, so long mental philosophy will walk on common ground with religious belief. Rightly or wrongly, men will think of these things; and a knowledge of the laws under which they think is the only security for

[1] 1 St. John iii. 2, 3.

thinking soundly. If it be thought no unworthy occupation for the Christian preacher, to point out the evidences of God's Providence in the constitution of the sensible world and the mechanism of the human body; or to dwell on the analogies which may be traced between the scheme of revelation and the course of nature; it is but a part of the same argument to pursue the inquiry with regard to the structure and laws of the human mind. The path may be one which, of late years at least, has been less frequently trodden: the language indispensable to such an investigation may sound at times unwonted and uncouth; but the end is one with that of those plainer and more familiar illustrations which have taken their place among the acknowledged evidences of religion; and the lesson of the whole, if read aright, will be but to teach us that in mind, no less than in body, we are fearfully and wonderfully made[1] by Him whose praise both alike declare: that He who "laid the foundations of the earth, and shut up the sea with doors, and said, Hitherto shalt thou come, but no further," is also He who "hath put wisdom in the inward parts, and hath given understanding to the heart."[2]

[1] Psalm cxxxix. 14. [2] Job xxxviii. 4, 8, 11, 36.

LECTURE II.

KEEP THAT WHICH IS COMMITTED TO THY TRUST, AVOIDING PROFANE AND VAIN BABBLINGS, AND OPPOSITIONS OF SCIENCE FALSELY SO CALLED; WHICH SOME PROFESSING HAVE ERRED CONCERNING THE FAITH. — I TIMOTHY VI. 20, 21.

A PHILOSOPHY of Religion may be attempted from two opposite points of view, and by two opposite modes of development. It may be conceived either as a Philosophy of the Object of Religion; that is to say, as a scientific exposition of the nature of God; or as a Philosophy of the Subject of Religion; that is to say, as a scientific inquiry into the constitution of the human mind, so far as it receives and deals with religious ideas. The former is that branch of Metaphysics which is commonly known by the name of Rational Theology. Its general aim, in common with all metaphysical inquiries, is to disengage the real from the apparent, the true from the false: its special aim, as a Theology, is to exhibit a true representation of the Nature and Attributes of God, purified from foreign accretions, and displaying the exact features of their Divine Original. The latter is a branch of Psychology, which at its outset at least, contents itself with investigating the phenomena presented to it, leaving their relation to further realities to be determined at a later stage of the inquiry. Its primary concern is with the operations and laws of the human mind; and its special purpose is to ascertain the nature, the origin, and the limits of the religious element in man; postponing, till after that question has been decided, the further inquiry into the absolute nature of God.

As applied to the criticism of Revelation, the first method, supposing its end to be attained, would furnish an immediate and direct criterion by which the claims of any supposed Revelation to a divine origin might be tested; while at the same time it would enable those possessed of it to dispense with the services of any Revelation at all. For on the supposition that we possess an exact idea of any attribute of the Divine Nature, we are at liberty to reject at once any portion of the supposed Revelation which contradicts that idea; and on the supposition that we possess a complete idea of that Nature as a whole, we are at liberty to reject whatever goes beyond it. And as, upon either supposition, the highest praise to which Revelation can aspire is that of coinciding, partially or wholly, with the independent conclusions of Philosophy, it follows that, so far as Philosophy extends, Revelation becomes superfluous.(1) On the other hand, the second method of philosophical inquiry does not profess to furnish a direct criticism of Revelation, but only of the instruments by which Revelation is to be criticized. It looks to the human, not to the divine, and aspires to teach us no more than the limits of our own powers of thought, and the consequent distinction between what we may and what we may not seek to comprehend. And if, upon examination, it should appear that any portion of the contents of Revelation belongs to the latter class of truths, this method will enable us to reconcile with each other the conflicting claims of Reason and Faith, by showing that Reason itself, rightly interpreted, teaches the existence of truths that are above Reason.

Whatever may be the ultimate use of the first of these methods of criticism, it is obvious that the previous question, concerning our right to use it at all, can only be satisfactorily answered by the employment of the second method. The possibility of criticism at all implies that human reason is liable to error: the possibility of a valid criticism implies that the means of distinguishing between its truth and its error may be ascertained by a previous criticism. Let it be granted, for the moment, that a religion whose contents are irreconcilable with human reason is thereby proved not to have come from God, but from man, — still the reason which judges is at least as human as the religion which is judged; and if the human representation of God is erroneous in the latter, how can we assume its infallibility in the former? If we grant for the present the fundamental position of Rationalism, namely, that man by his own reason can attain to a right conception of God, we must at any rate grant also, what every attempt at criticism implies, that he may also attain to a wrong one. We have therefore still to ask by what marks the one is to be distinguished from the other; by what method we are to seek the truth; and how we are to assume ourselves that we have found it. And to answer this question, we need a preliminary examination of the conditions and limits of human thought. Religious criticism is itself an act of thought; and its immediate instruments must, under any circumstances, be thoughts also. We are thus compelled in the first instance to inquire into the origin and value of those thoughts themselves.

A Philosophy which professes to elicit from its own conceptions all the essential portions of religious belief, is bound to justify its profession, by showing that those conceptions themselves are above suspicion. The ideas thus exalted to the supreme criteria of truth must bear on their front unquestionable evidence that they are true and sufficient representations of the Divine Nature, such as may serve all the needs of human thought and human feeling, adequate alike for contemplation and for worship. They must manifest the clearness and distinctness which mark the strong vision of an eye gazing undazzled on the glory of Heaven, not the obscurity and confusion of one that turns away blinded from the glare, and gropes in its own darkness after the fleeting spectrum. The conviction which boasts itself to be superior to all external evidence must carry in its own inward constitution some sure indication of its truth and value.

Such a conviction may be possible in two different ways. It may be the result of a direct intuition of the Divine Nature; or it may be gained by inference from certain attributes of human nature, which, though on a smaller scale, are known to be sufficiently representative of the corresponding properties of the Deity. We may suppose the existence in man of a special faculty of knowledge, of which God is the immediate object, — a kind of religious sense or reason, by which the Divine attributes are apprehended in their own nature: (2) or we may maintain that the attributes of God differ from those of man in degree only, not in kind; and hence that certain mental and moral qualities, of which we are immediately conscious in ourselves, furnish at the same time a true and adequate image of the infinite perfections of God. (3) The first of these suppositions professes to convey a knowledge of God by direct apprehension, in a manner similar to the evidence of the senses: the second professes to convey the same knowledge by a logical process, similar to the demonstrations of science. The former is the method of Mysticism, and of that Rationalism which agrees with Mysticism, in referring the knowledge of divine things to an extraordinary and abnormal process of intuition or thought.(4) The latter is the method of the vulgar Rationalism, which regards the reason of man, in its ordinary and normal operation, as the supreme criterion of religious truth.

On the former supposition, a system of religious philosophy or criticism may be constructed by starting from the divine and reasoning down to the human: on the latter, by starting from the human and reasoning up to the divine. The first commences with a supposed immediate knowledge of God as He is in his absolute nature, and proceeds to exhibit the process by which that nature, acting according to its own laws, will manifest itself in operation, and become known to man. The second commences with an immediate knowledge of the mental and moral attributes of man, and proceeds to exhibit the manner in which those attributes will manifest themselves, when exalted to the degree in which they form part of the nature of God. If, for example, the two systems severally undertake to give a representation of the infinite power and wisdom of God, the former will profess to explain how the nature of the infinite manifests itself in the forms of power and wisdom; while the latter will attempt to show how power and wisdom must manifest themselves when existing in an infinite degree. In their criticisms of Revelation, in like manner, the former will rather take as its standard that absolute and essential nature of God, which must remain unchanged in every manifestation; the latter will judge by reference to those intellectual and moral qualities, which must exist in all their essential features in the divine nature as well as in the human.

Thus, for example, it has been maintained by a modern philosopher, that the absolute nature of God is that of a pure Will, determining itself solely by a moral law, and subject to no affections which can operate as motives. Hence it is inferred that the same law of action must form the rule of God's manifestation to mankind as a moral Governor; and therefore that no revelation can be of divine origin, which attempts to influence men's actions by the prospect of reward or punishment.(5) In this mode of reasoning, an abstract conception of the nature of God is made the criterion to determine the mode in which He must reveal Himself to man. On the other hand, we meet with an opposite style of criticism, which reasons somewhat as follows: All the excellences, it contends, of which we are conscious in the creature, must necessarily exist in the same manner, though in a higher degree, in the Creator. God is indeed more wise, more just, more merciful than man; but for that very reason, His wisdom and justice and mercy must contain nothing that is incompatible with the corresponding attributes in their human character.(6) Hence, if the certainty of man's knowledge implies the necessity of the events which he knows, the certainty of God's omniscience implies a like necessity of all things:(7) if man's justice requires that he should punish the guilty alone, it is inconsistent with God's justice to inflict the chastisement of sin upon the innocent:(8) if man's mercy finds its natural exercise in the free forgiveness of offences, God's mercy, too, must freely forgive the sins of His creatures.(9) From the same premises it is consistently concluded that no act which would be wrong, if performed by a man upon his own responsibility, can be justified by the plea of a direct command from God.(10) Abraham may not be praised for his readiness to slay his son in obedience to God's command; for the internal prohibition must always be more certain than the external precept.(11) Joshua cannot be warranted in obeying the Divine injunction to exterminate the Canaanites, unless he would be equally warranted in destroying them of his own accord.(12) And, as the issuing of such commands is contrary to the moral nature of God, therefore the Book which represents them as so issued is convicted of falsehood, and cannot be regarded as a Divine Revelation.(13) In this mode of reasoning, the moral or intellectual nature of man is made the rule to determine what ought to be the revealed attributes of God, and in what manner they must be exercised.

Within certain limits, both these arguments may have their value; but each is chiefly useful as a check upon the exclusive authority of the other. The philosophy which reasons downwards from the infinite, is but an exaggeration of the true conviction that God's thoughts are not our thoughts, nor His ways our ways:[1] the philosophy which reasons upwards from the human, bears witness, even in its perversion, to the unextinguishable consciousness, that man, however fallen, was created in the image of God.[2] But this admission tends rather to weaken than to strengthen the claims of either to be received as the supreme criterion of religious truth. The criticisms of rationalism exhibit the weakness as well as the strength of reason; for the representations which it rejects, as dishonoring to God, are, on its own showing, the product of human thought, no less than the principle by which they are judged and condemned. If the human mind has passed through successive stages of religious cultivation, from the grovelling superstition of the savage to the intellectual elevation of the critic of all possible revelations, who shall assure the critic that the level on which he now

[1] Isaiah lv. 8. [2] Genesis i. 27.

stands is the last and highest that can be attained? If reason is to be the last court of appeal in religious questions, it must find some better proof of its own infallibility than is to be found in its own progressive enlightenment. Its preëminence must be shown, not by successive approximations to the truth, but by the possession of the truth itself. Of the limits within which reason may be legitimately employed, I shall have occasion to speak hereafter. At present, I am concerned only with its pretensions to such a knowledge of the Divine Nature, as can constitute the foundation of a Rational Theology.

There are three terms, familiar as household words, in the vocabulary of Philosophy, which must be taken into account in every system of Metaphysical Theology. To conceive the Deity as He is, we must conceive Him as First Cause, as Absolute, and as Infinite. By the *First Cause*, is meant that which produces all things, and is itself produced of none. By the *Absolute*, is meant that which exists in and by itself, having no necessary relation to any other Being.(14) By the *Infinite*, is meant that which is free from all possible limitation; that than which a greater is inconceivable; and which, consequently, can receive no additional attribute or mode of existence, which it had not from all eternity.

The Infinite, as contemplated by this philosophy, cannot be regarded as consisting of a limited number of attributes, each unlimited in its kind. It cannot be conceived, for example, after the analogy of a line, infinite in length, but not in breadth; or of a surface, infinite in two dimensions of space, but bounded in the third; or of an intelligent being, possessing some one or more modes of consciousness in an infinite degree, but devoid of others. Even if it be granted, which is not the case, that such a partial infinite may without contradiction be conceived, still it will have a relative infinity only, and be altogether incompatible with the idea of the Absolute.[15] The line limited in breadth is thereby necessarily related to the space that limits it: the intelligence endowed with a limited number of attributes, coëxists with others which are thereby related to it, as cognate or opposite modes of consciousness.[16] The metaphysical representation of the Deity, as absolute and infinite, must necessarily, as the profoundest metaphysicians have acknowledged, amount to nothing less than the sum of all reality.[17] "What kind of an Absolute Being is that," says Hegel, "which does not contain in itself all that is actual, even evil included?"[18] We may repudiate the conclusion with indignation; but the reasoning is unassailable. If the Absolute and Infinite is an object of human conception at all, this, and none other, is the conception required. That which is conceived as absolute and infinite must be conceived as containing within itself the sum, not only of all actual, but of all possible, modes of being. For if any actual mode can be denied of it, it is related to that mode, and limited by it;[19] and if any possible mode can be denied of it, it is capable of becoming more than it now is, and such a capability is a limitation. Indeed, it is obvious that the entire distinction between the possible and the actual can have no existence as regards the absolutely infinite; for an unrealized possibility is necessarily a relation and a limit. The scholastic saying, *Deus est actus purus*,[20] ridiculed as it has been by modern critics, is in truth but the expression, in technical language, of the almost unanimous voice of philosophy, both in earlier and later times.[21]

But these three conceptions, the Cause, the Absolute,

the Infinite, all equally indispensable, do they not imply contradiction to each other, when viewed in conjunction, as attributes of one and the same Being? A Cause cannot, as such, be absolute: the Absolute cannot, as such, be a cause. The cause, as such, exists only in relation to its effect: the cause is a cause of the effect; the effect is an effect of the cause. On the other hand, the conception of the Absolute implies a possible existence out of all relation.(22) We attempt to escape from this apparent contradiction, by introducing the idea of succession in time. The Absolute exists first by itself, and afterwards becomes a Cause. But here we are checked by the third conception, that of the Infinite. How can the Infinite become that which it was not from the first? If Causation is a possible mode of existence, that which exists without causing is not infinite; that which becomes a cause has passed beyond its former limits. Creation at any particular moment of time being thus inconceivable, the philosopher is reduced to the alternative of Pantheism, which pronounces the effect to be mere appearance, and merges all real existence in the cause.(23) The validity of this alternative will be examined presently.

Meanwhile, to return for a moment to the supposition of a true causation. Supposing the Absolute to become a cause, it will follow that it operates by means of free will and consciousness. For a necessary cause cannot be conceived as absolute and infinite. If necessitated by something beyond itself, it is thereby limited by a superior power; and if necessitated by itself, it has in its own nature a necessary relation to its effect. The act of causation must, therefore, be voluntary; and volition is only possible in a conscious being. But consciousness, again, is only conceivable as a relation. There must be a conscious subject, and an object of which he is conscious. The subject is a subject to the object; the object is an object to the subject; and neither can exist by itself as the absolute. This difficulty, again, may be for the moment evaded, by distinguishing between the absolute as related to another, and the absolute as related to itself. The Absolute, it may be said, may possibly be conscious, provided it is only conscious of itself.(24) But this alternative is, in ultimate analysis, no less self-destructive than the other. For the object of consciousness, whether a mode of the subject's existence or not, is either created in and by the act of consciousness, or has an existence independent of it. In the former case, the object depends upon the subject, and the subject alone is the true absolute. In the latter case, the subject depends upon the object, and the object alone is the true absolute. Or, if we attempt a third hypothesis, and maintain that each exists independently of the other, we have no absolute at all, but only a pair of relatives; for coëxistence, whether in consciousness or not, is itself a relation.(25)

The corollary from this reasoning is obvious. Not only is the Absolute, as conceived, incapable of a necessary relation to anything else; but it is also incapable of containing, by the constitution of its own nature, an essential relation within itself; as a whole, for instance, composed of parts, or as a substance consisting of attributes, or as a conscious subject in antithesis to an object.(26) For if there is in the absolute any principle of unity, distinct from the mere accumulation of parts or attributes, this principle alone is the true absolute. If, on the other hand, there is no such principle, then there is no absolute at all, but only a plurality of relatives.(27) The almost unanimous voice of philosophy, in pronouncing that the absolute is both one and simple, must be accepted as the voice of reason also, so far as reason has any voice in the matter.(28) But this absolute unity, as indifferent and containing no attributes, can neither be distinguished from the multiplicity of finite beings by any characteristic feature, nor be identified with them in their multiplicity.(29) Thus we are landed in an inextricable dilemma. The Absolute cannot be conceived as conscious, neither can it be conceived as unconscious: it cannot be conceived as complex, neither can it be conceived as simple: it cannot be conceived by difference, neither can it be conceived by the absence of difference: it cannot be identified with the universe, neither can it be distinguished from it. The One and the Many, regarded as the beginning of existence, are thus alike incomprehensible.

The fundamental conceptions of Rational Theology being thus self-destructive, we may naturally expect to find the same antagonism manifested in their special applications. These naturally inherit the infirmities of the principle from which they spring. If an absolute and infinite consciousness is a conception which contradicts itself, we need not wonder if its several modifications mutually exclude each other. A mental attribute, to be conceived as infinite, must be in actual exercise on every possible object: otherwise it is potential only with regard to those on which it is not exercised; and an unrealized potentiality is a limitation. Hence every infinite mode of consciousness must be regarded as extending over the field of every other; and their common action involves a perpetual antagonism. How, for example, can Infinite Power be able to do all things, and yet Infinite Goodness be unable to do evil? How can infinite Justice exact the utmost penalty for every sin, and yet Infinite Mercy pardon the sinner? How can Infinite Wisdom know all that is to come, and yet Infinite Freedom be at liberty to do or to forbear? (30) How is the existence of Evil compatible with that of an infinitely perfect Being; for if he wills it, he is not infinitely good; and if he wills it not, his will is thwarted and his sphere of action limited? Here, again, the Pantheist is ready with his solution. There is in reality no such thing as evil: there is no such thing as punishment: there is no real relation between God and man at all. God is all that really exists: He does, by the necessity of His nature, all that is done: all acts are equally necessary and equally divine: all diversity is but a distorted representation of unity: all evil is but a delusive appearance of good. (31) Unfortunately, the Pantheist does not tell us whence all this delusion derives its seeming existence.

Let us however suppose for an instant that these difficulties are surmounted, and the existence of the Absolute securely established on the testimony of reason. Still we have not succeeded in reconciling this idea with that of a Cause: we have done nothing towards explaining how the absolute can give rise to the relative, the infinite to the finite. If the condition of causal activity is a higher state than that of quiescence, the absolute, whether acting voluntarily or involuntarily, has passed from a condition of comparative imperfection to one of comparative perfection; and therefore was not originally perfect. If the state of activity is an inferior state to that of quiescence, the Absolute, in becoming a cause, has lost its original perfection. (32) There remains only the supposition that the two states are equal, and the act of creation one of complete indifference. But this supposition annihilates the unity of the absolute, or it annihilates itself. If the act of creation is real, and yet indifferent, we must admit the possibility of two conceptions of the absolute, the one as productive, the other as non-productive. If the act is not real, the supposition itself vanishes, and we are thrown once more on the alternative of Pantheism.

Again, how can the Relative be conceived as coming into being? If it is a distinct reality from the absolute, it must be conceived as passing from non-existence into existence. But to conceive an object as non-existent, is again a self-contradiction; for that which is conceived exists, as an object of thought, in and by that conception. We may abstain from thinking of an object at all; but, if we think of it, we cannot but think of it as existing. It is possible at one time not to think of an object at all, and at another to think of it as already in being; but to think of it in the act of becoming, in the progress from not being into being, is to think that which, in the very thought, annihilates itself. Here again the Pantheistic hypothesis seems forced upon us. We can think of creation only as a change in the condition of that which already exists; and thus the creature is conceivable only as a phenomenal mode of the being of the Creator. (33)

The whole of this web of contradictions (and it might be extended, if necessary, to a far greater length) is woven from one original warp and woof; — namely, the impossibility of conceiving the coëxistence of the infinite and the finite, and the cognate impossibility of conceiving a first commencement of phenomena, or the absolute giving birth to the relative. The laws of thought appear to admit of no possible escape from the meshes in which thought is entangled, save by destroying one or the other of the cords of which they are composed. Pantheism or Atheism are thus the alternatives offered to us, according as we prefer to save the infinite by the sacrifice of the finite, or to maintain the finite by denying the existence of the infinite. Pantheism thus presents itself, as to all appearance the only logical conclusion, if we believe in the possibility of a Philosophy of the Infinite. But Pantheism, if it avoids self-contradiction in the course of its reasonings, does so only by an act of suicide at the outset. It escapes from some of the minor incongruities of thought, only by the annihilation of thought and thinker alike. It is saved from the necessity of demonstrating its own falsehood, by abolishing the only conditions under which truth and falsehood can be distinguished from each other. The only conception which I can frame of substantive existence at all, as distinguished from the transient accidents which are merely modes of the being of something else, is derived from the immediate knowledge of my own personal unity, amidst the various affections which form the successive modes of my consciousness. The Pantheist tells me that this knowledge is a delusion; that I am no substance, but a mode of the absolute substance, even as my thoughts and passions are modes of me; and that in order to attain to a true philosophy of being, I must begin by denying my own being. And for what purpose is this act of self-destruction needed? In order to preserve inviolate certain philosophical conclusions, which I, the non-existent thinker, have drawn by virtue of my non-existent powers of thought. But if my personal existence, the great primary fact of all consciousness, is a delusion, what claim have the reasonings of the Pantheist himself to be considered as anything better than a part of the universal falsehood? If I am mistaken in supposing myself to have a substantial existence at all, why is that existence more true when it is presented to me under the particular form of apprehending and accepting the arguments of the pantheistic philosophy? Nay, how do I know that there is any argument at all? For if my consciousness is mistaken in testifying to the fact of my own existence, it may surely be no less mistaken in testifying to my apparent apprehension of an apparent reasoning. Nay, the very arguments which appear to prove the Pantheist's conclusion to be true, may in reality, for aught I know, prove it to be false. Or rather, no Pantheist, if he is consistent with himself, can admit the existence of a distinction between truth and falsehood at all. For if God alone exists, in whatever way that existence may be explained, He alone is the immediate cause of all that takes place. He thinks all that is thought, He does all that is done. There can be no difference between truth and falsehood; for God is the only thinker; and all thoughts are equally necessary and equally divine. There can be no difference between right and wrong; for God is the only agent; and all acts are equally necessary and equally divine. (34) How error and evil, even in appearance, are possible, — how the finite and the relative can appear to exist, even as a delusion, — is a problem which no system of Pantheism has made the slightest approach towards solving. (35)

Pantheism thus failing us, the last resource of Rationalism is to take refuge in that which, with reference to the highest idea of God, is speculative Atheism, and to deny that the Infinite exists at all. (36) And it must be admitted that, so long as we confine ourselves to one side only of the problem, that of the inconceivability of the Infinite, this is the only position logically tenable by those who would make man's power of thought the exact measure of his duty of belief. For the infinite, as inconceivable, is necessarily shown to be non-existent; unless we renounce the claim of reason to supreme authority in matters of faith, by admitting that it is our duty to believe what we are altogether unable to comprehend. But the logical advantage of the atheistic alternative vanishes, as soon as we view the question from the other side, and endeavor positively to represent in thought the sum total of existence as a limited quantity. A limit is itself a relation; and to conceive a limit as such, is virtually to acknowledge the existence of a correlative on the other side of it. (37) By a law of thought, the significance of which has perhaps not yet been fully investigated, it is impossible to conceive a finite object of any kind, without conceiving it as one out of many, — as related to other objects, coëxistent and antecedent. A first moment of time, a first unit of space, a definite sum of all existence, are thus as inconceivable as the opposite suppositions of an infinity of each. (38) While it is impossible to represent in thought any object, except as finite, it is equally impossible to represent any finite object, or any aggregate of finite objects, as exhausting the universe of being. Thus the hypothesis which would annihilate the Infinite is itself shattered to pieces against the rock of the Absolute; and we are involved in the self-contradictory assumption of a limited universe, which yet can neither contain a limit in itself, nor be limited by anything beyond itself. For if it contains a limit in itself, it is both limiting and limited, both beyond the limit, and within it; and if it is limited by anything else, it is not the universe. (39)

To sum up briefly this portion of my argument. The conception of the Absolute and Infinite, from whatever side we view it, appears encompassed with contradictions. There is a contradiction in supposing such an object to exist, whether alone or in conjunction with others; and there is a contradiction in supposing it not to exist. There is a contradiction in conceiving it as one; and there is a contradiction in conceiving it as many. There is a contradiction in conceiving it as personal; and there is a contradiction in conceiving it as impersonal. It cannot without contradiction be represented as active; nor, without equal contradiction, be represented as inactive. It cannot be conceived as the sum of all existence; nor yet can it be conceived as a part only of that sum. A contradiction thus thoroughgoing, while it sufficiently shows the impotence of human reason as an *a priori* judge of all truth, yet is not in itself inconsistent with any form of religious belief. For it tells with equal force against all belief and all unbelief, and therefore necessitates the conclusion that belief cannot be determined solely by reason. No conclusion can be drawn from it in favor of universal skepticism; first, because universal skepticism equally destroys itself; and secondly, because the contradictions thus detected belong not to the use of reason in general, but only to its exercise on one particular object of thought. It may teach us that it is our duty, in some instances, to believe that which we cannot conceive; but it does not require us to disbelieve anything which we are capable of conceiving.

What we have hitherto been examining, be it remembered, is not the nature of the Absolute in itself, but only our own conception of that nature. The distortions of the image reflected may arise only from the inequalities of the mirror reflecting it. And this consideration leads us naturally back to the second of the two methods of religious philosophy which were mentioned at the beginning of the present Lecture. If the attempt to grasp the absolute nature of the Divine Object of religious thought thus fails us on every side, we have no resource but to recommence our inquiry by the opposite process, that of investigating the nature of the human Subject. Such an investigation will not, indeed, solve the contradictions which our previous attempt has elicited; but it may serve to show us why they are insoluble. If it cannot satisfy to the full the demands of reason, it may at least enable us to lay a reasonable foundation for the rightful claims of belief. If, from an examination of the laws and limits of human consciousness, we can show that thought is not, and cannot be, the measure of existence; if it can be shown that the contradictions which arise in the attempt to conceive the infinite, have their origin, not in the nature of that which we would conceive, but in the constitution of the mind conceiving; that they are such as must necessarily accompany every form of religion, and every renunciation of religion; we may thus prepare the way for a recognition of the separate provinces of Reason and Faith. This task I shall endeavor to accomplish in my next Lecture. Meanwhile, I would add but a few words, to point out the practical lesson to be drawn from our previous inquiry. It is this: that so far is human reason from being able to construct a scientific Theology, independent of and superior to Revelation, that it cannot even read the alphabet out of which that Theology must be framed. It has not been without much hesitation that I have ventured to address you in language seldom heard in this place,— to transport to the preacher's pulpit the vocabulary of metaphysical speculation. But it was only by such a course that I could hope to bring the antagonist principles of true and false religious philosophy face to face with each other. It needs but a slight acquaintance with the history of opinions, to show how intimately, in various ages, the current forms of religious belief or unbelief have been connected with the prevailing systems of speculative philosophy. It was in no small degree because the philosophy of Kant identified religion with morality, and maintained that the supernatural and the historical were not necessary to belief;[40] that Paulus explained away the miracles of Christ, as misrepresentations of natural events;[41] and Wegscheider claimed for the moral reason supreme authority in the interpretation of Scripture;[42] and Röhr promulgated a new Creed, from which all the facts of Christianity are rejected, to make way for ethical precepts.[43] It was in like manner because the philosophy of Hegel was felt to be incompatible with the belief in a personal God, and a personal Christ, and a supernatural revelation;[44] that Vatke rejected the Old Testament history, as irreconcilable with the philosophical law of religious development;[45] and Strauss endeavored by minute cavils to invalidate the Gospel narrative, in order to make way for the theory of an ideal Christ, manifested in the whole human race;[46] and Feuerbach maintained that the Supreme Being is but humanity deified, and that the belief in a superhuman God is contradictory in itself, and pernicious in its consequences.[47] And if, by wandering for a little while in the tangled mazes of metaphysical speculation, we can test the worth of the substitute which this philosophy offers us in the place of the faith which it rejects; if we can show how little such a substitute can satisfy even the intellect of man (to the heart it does not pretend to appeal), the inquiry may do some service, slight and indirect though it be, to the cause of Christian Truth, by suggesting to the wavering disciple, ere he quits the Master with whom he has hitherto walked, the pregnant question of the

Apostle, "Lord, to whom shall we go?"[1] When Philosophy succeeds in exhibiting in a clear and consistent form the Infinite Being of God; when her opposing schools are agreed among themselves as to the manner in which a knowledge of the Infinite takes place, or the marks by which it is to be discerned when known; then, and not till then, may she claim to speak as one having authority in controversies of Faith. But while she speaks with stammering lips, and a double tongue; while she gropes her way in darkness, and stumbles at every step; while she has nothing to offer us but the alternative of principles which abjure consciousness, or a consciousness which contradicts itself, we may well pause before we appeal to her decisions as the gauge and measure of religious truth.

In one respect, indeed, I have perhaps departed from the customary language of the pulpit, to a greater extent than was absolutely necessary; — namely, in dealing with the ideas common to Theology and Metaphysics in the terms of the latter, rather than in those of the former. But there is a line of argument, in which the vague generalities of the Absolute and the Infinite may be more reverently and appropriately employed than the sacred names and titles of God. For we almost instinctively shrink back from the recklessness which thrusts forward, on every occasion, the holiest names and things, to be tossed to and fro, and trampled under foot, in the excitement of controversy. We feel that the name of Him whom we worship may not lightly be held up as a riddle for prying curiosity to puzzle over: we feel that the Divine Personality of our Father in Heaven is not a thing to be pitted in the arena of disputation, against the lifeless abstractions and sophistical word-jugglings of Pantheism.

[1] St. John vi. 68.

We feel that, though God is indeed, in His incomprehensible Essence, absolute and infinite, it is not as the Absolute and Infinite that He appeals to the love and the fear and the reverence of His creatures. We feel that the life of religion lies in the human relations in which God reveals Himself to man, not in the divine perfection which those relations veil and modify, though without wholly concealing. We feel that the God to whom we pray, and in whom we trust, is not so much the God eternal and infinite, without body, parts, or passions (though we acknowledge that He is all these), as the God who is "gracious and merciful, slow to anger, and of great kindness, and repenteth Him of the evil."[1] (48) Those who have observed the prevailing character of certain schools of religious thought, in that country which, more than any other, has made Religion speak the language of Metaphysics; those who have observed how often, in modern literature, both at home and abroad, the most sacred names are played with, in familiar, almost in contemptuous intimacy, will need no other proof to convince them that we cannot attach too much importance to the duty of separating, as far as it can be effected, the language of prayer and praise from the definitions and distinctions of philosophy.

The metaphysical difficulties which have been exhibited in the course of this Lecture almost suggest of themselves the manner in which they should be treated. We must begin with that which is within us, not with that which is above us; with the philosophy of Man, not with that of God. Instead of asking, what are the facts and laws in the constitution of the universe, or in the Divine Nature, by virtue of which certain conceptions present certain

[1] Joel ii. 13.

anomalies to the human mind, we should rather ask, what are the facts and laws in the constitution of the human mind, by virtue of which it finds itself involved in contradictions, whenever it ventures on certain courses of speculation. Philosophy, as well as Scripture, rightly employed, will teach a lesson of humility to its disciple; exhibiting, as it does, the spectacle of a creature of finite intuitions, surrounded by partial indications of the Unlimited; of finite conceptions, in the midst of partial manifestations of the Incomprehensible. Questioned in this spirit, the voice of Philosophy will be but an echo of the inspired language of the Psalmist: "Thou hast beset me behind and before, and laid thine hand upon me. Such knowledge is too wonderful for me: it is high; I cannot attain unto it."[1]

[1] Psalm cxxxix. 5, 6.

LECTURE III.

AND HE SAID, THOU CANST NOT SEE MY FACE; FOR THERE SHALL NO MAN SEE ME, AND LIVE. AND THE LORD SAID, BEHOLD, THERE IS A PLACE BY ME, AND THOU SHALT STAND UPON A ROCK: AND IT SHALL COME TO PASS, WHILE MY GLORY PASSETH BY, THAT I WILL PUT THEE IN A CLEFT OF THE ROCK, AND WILL COVER THEE WITH MY HAND WHILE I PASS BY: AND I WILL TAKE AWAY MINE HAND, AND THOU SHALT SEE MY BACK PARTS; BUT MY FACE SHALL NOT BE SEEN.—EXODUS XXXIII. 20–23.

MY last Lecture was chiefly occupied with an examination of the ideas of the Absolute and the Infinite,—ideas which are indispensable to the foundation of a metaphysical Theology, and of which a clear and distinct consciousness must be acquired, if such a Theology is to exist at all. I attempted to show the inadequacy of these ideas for such a purpose, by reason of the contradictions which to our apprehension they necessarily involve from every point of view. The result of that attempt may be briefly summed up as follows. We are compelled, by the constitution of our minds, to believe in the existence of an Absolute and Infinite Being,—a belief which appears forced upon us, as the complement of our consciousness of the relative and the finite. But the instant we attempt to analyze the ideas thus suggested to us, in the hope of attaining to an intelligible conception of them, we are on every side involved in inextricable confusion and contradiction. It is no matter from what point of view we commence our examination;—whether, with the Theist, we admit the coëxistence of the Infinite and the Finite, as distinct realities; or, with the Pantheist, deny the real existence of the Finite; or, with the Atheist, deny the real existence of the Infinite; — on each of these suppositions alike, our reason appears divided against itself, compelled to admit the truth of one hypothesis, and yet unable to overcome the apparent impossibilities of each. The philosophy of Rationalism, thus traced upwards to its highest principles, finds no legitimate resting-place, from which to commence its deduction of religious consequences.

In the present Lecture, it will be my endeavor to offer some explanation of the singular phenomenon of human thought, which is exhibited in these results. I propose to examine the same ideas of the Absolute and the Infinite from the opposite side, in order to see if any light can be thrown on the anomalies which they present to us, by a reference to the mental laws under which they are formed. Contradiction, whatever may be its ultimate import, is in itself not a quality of things, but a mode in which they are viewed by the mind; and the inquiry which it most immediately suggests is, not an investigation of the nature of things in themselves, but an examination of those mental conditions under which it is elicited in thought. Such an examination, if it does not enable us to extend the sphere of thought beyond a certain point, may at least serve to make us more distinctly conscious of its true boundaries.

The much-disputed question, to what class of mental phenomena the religious consciousness belongs, must be postponed to a later stage of our inquiry. At present, we are concerned with a more general investigation, which the answer to that question will in nowise affect. Whether the relation of man to God be primarily presented to the human mind in the form of knowledge, or of feeling, or of practical impulse, it can be given only as a mode of consciousness, subject to those conditions under which alone consciousness is possible. Whatever knowledge is imparted, whatever impulse is communicated, whatever feeling is excited, in man's mind, must take place in a manner adapted to the constitution of its human recipient, and must exhibit such characteristics as the laws of that constitution impose upon it. A brief examination of the conditions of human consciousness in general will thus form a proper preliminary to any inquiry concerning the religious consciousness in particular.

Now, in the first place, the very conception of Consciousness, in whatever mode it may be manifested, necessarily implies *distinction between one object and another.* To be conscious, we must be conscious of something; and that something can only be known as that which it is, by being distinguished from that which it is not.(1) But distinction is necessarily limitation; for, if one object is to be distinguished from another, it must possess some form of existence which the other has not, or it must not possess some form which the other has. But it is obvious that the Infinite cannot be distinguished, as such, from the Finite, by the absence of any quality which the Finite possesses; for such absence would be a limitation. Nor yet can it be distinguished by the presence of an attribute which the Finite has not; for, as no finite part can be a constituent of an infinite whole, this differential characteristic must itself be infinite; and must at the same time have nothing in common with the finite. We are thus thrown back upon our former impossibility; for this second infinite will be distinguished from the finite by the absence of qualities which the latter possesses. A consciousness of the Infinite as such thus necessarily involves a self-contradiction; for it implies the recognition, by limitation and difference, of that which can only be given as unlimited and indifferent. (2)

That man can be conscious of the Infinite, is thus a supposition which, in the very terms in which it is expressed, annihilates itself. Consciousness is essentially a limitation; for it is the determination of the mind to one actual out of many possible modifications. But the Infinite, if it is to be conceived at all, must be conceived as potentially everything and actually nothing; for if there is anything in general which it cannot become, it is thereby limited; and if there is anything in particular which it actually is, it is thereby excluded from being any other thing. But again, it must also be conceived as actually everything and potentially nothing; for an unrealized potentiality is likewise a limitation. (3) If the infinite can be that which it is not, it is by that very possibility marked out as incomplete, and capable of a higher perfection. If it is actually everything, it possesses no characteristic feature, by which it can be distinguished from anything else, and discerned as an object of consciousness.

This contradiction, which is utterly inexplicable on the supposition that the infinite is a positive object of human thought, is at once accounted for, when it is regarded as the mere negation of thought. If all thought is limitation, — if whatever we conceive is, by the very act of conception, regarded as finite, — *the infinite*, from a human point of view, is merely a name for the absence of those conditions under which thought is possible. To speak of a *Conception of the Infinite* is, therefore, at once to affirm those conditions and to deny them. The contradiction, which we discover in such a conception, is only that which we have ourselves placed there, by tacitly assuming the conceivability of the inconceivable. The condition of consciousness is distinction; and the condition of distinction is limitation. We have no consciousness of Being in general which is not some Being in particular; a *thing*, in consciousness, is one thing out of many. In assuming the possibility of an infinite object of consciousness, I assume, therefore, that it is at the same time limited and unlimited; — actually something, without which it could not be an object of consciousness, and actually nothing, without which it could not be infinite.(4)

Rationalism is thus only consistent with itself, when it refuses to attribute consciousness to God. Consciousness, in the only form in which we can conceive it, implies limitation and change, — the perception of one object out of many, and a comparison of that object with others. To be always conscious of the same object, is, humanly speaking, not to be conscious at all;(5) and, beyond its human manifestation, we can have no conception of what consciousness is. Viewed on the side of the object of consciousness, the same principle will carry us further still. Existence itself, that so-called highest category of thought, is only conceivable in the form of existence modified in some particular manner. Strip off its modification, and the apparent paradox of the German philosopher becomes literally true; — pure being is pure nothing.(6) We have no conception of existence which is not existence in some particular manner; and if we abstract from the manner, we have nothing left to constitute the existence. Those who, in their horror of what they call anthropomorphism, or anthropopathy, refuse to represent the Deity under symbols borrowed from the limitations of human consciousness, are bound, in consistency, to deny that God exists; for the conception of existence is as human and as limited as any other. The conclusion which Fichte boldly announces, awful as it is, is but the legitimate consequence of his premises. "The moral order of the universe is itself God: we need no other, and we can comprehend no other." (7)

A second characteristic of Consciousness is, that it is only possible in the form of a *relation*. There must be a Subject, or person conscious, and an Object, or thing of which he is conscious. There can be no consciousness without the union of these two factors; and, in that union, each exists only as it is related to the other. (8) The subject is a subject, only in so far as it is conscious of an object: the object is an object, only in so far as it is apprehended by a subject: and the destruction of either is the destruction of consciousness itself. It is thus manifest that a consciousness of the Absolute is equally self-contradictory with that of the Infinite. To be conscious of the Absolute as such, we must know that an object, which is given in relation to our consciousness, is identical with one which exists in its own nature, out of all relation to consciousness. But to know this identity, we must compare the two together; and such a comparison is itself a contradiction. We are in fact required to compare that of which we are conscious with that of which we are not conscious; the comparison itself being an act of consciousness, and only possible through the consciousness of both its objects. It is thus manifest that, even if we could be conscious of the absolute, we could not possibly know that it *is* the absolute: and, as we can be conscious of an object as such, only by knowing it to be what it is, this is equivalent to an admission that we cannot be conscious of the absolute at all. As an object of consciousness, everything is necessarily relative; and what a thing may be out of consciousness, no mode of consciousness can tell us.

This contradiction, again, admits of the same explanation as the former. Our whole notion of existence is necessarily relative; for it is existence as conceived by us. But *Existence*, as we conceive it, is but a name for the several ways in which objects are presented to our consciousness, — a general term, embracing a variety of relations. *The Absolute*, on the other hand, is a term expressing no object of thought, but only a denial of the relation by which thought is constituted. To assume absolute existence as an object of thought, is thus to suppose a relation existing when the related terms exist no longer. An object of thought exists, as such, in and through its relation to a thinker; while the Absolute, as such, is independent of all relation. The *Conception of the Absolute* thus implies at the same time the presence and the absence of the relation by which thought is constituted; and our various endeavors to represent it are only so many modified forms of the contradiction involved in our original assumption. Here, too, the contradiction is one which we ourselves have made. It does not imply that the Absolute cannot exist; but it implies, most certainly, that we cannot conceive it as existing. (9)

Philosophers who are anxious to avoid this conclusion have sometimes attempted to evade it, by asserting that we may have in consciousness a partial, but not a total knowledge of the infinite and the absolute. (10) But here again the supposition refutes itself. To have a partial knowledge of an object, is to know a part of it, but not the whole. But the part of the infinite which is supposed to be known must be itself either infinite or finite. If it is infinite, it presents the same difficulties as before. If it is finite, the point in question is conceded, and our consciousness is allowed to be limited to finite objects. But in truth it is obvious, on a moment's reflection, that neither the Absolute nor the Infinite can be represented in the form of a whole composed of parts. Not the Absolute; for the existence of a whole is dependent on the existence of its parts. Not the Infinite; for if any part is infinite, it cannot be distinguished from the whole; and if each part is finite, no number of such parts can constitute the Infinite.

It would be possible, did my limits allow, to pursue the argument at length, through the various special modifications which constitute the subordinate forms of consciousness. But with reference to the present inquiry, it will be sufficient to notice two other conditions, under which all consciousness is necessarily manifested; both of which have a special bearing on the relation of philosophy to theological controversy.

All human consciousness, as being a change in our mental state, is necessarily subject to the law of *Time*, in its two manifestations of *Succession* and *Duration*. Every object, of whose existence we can be in any way conscious, is necessarily apprehended by us as succeeding in time to some former object of consciousness, and as itself occupying a certain portion of time. In the former point of view, it is manifest, from what has been said before, that whatever succeeds something else, and is distinguished from it, is necessarily apprehended as finite; for distinction is itself a limitation. In the latter point of view, it is no less manifest that whatever is conceived as having a continuous existence in time is equally apprehended as finite. For continuous existence is necessarily conceived as divisible into successive moments. One portion has already gone by; another is yet to come; each successive moment is related to something which has preceded, and to something which is to follow: and out of such relations the entire existence is made up. The acts, by which such existence is manifested, being continuous in time, have, at any given moment, a further activity still to come: the object so existing must therefore always be regarded as capable of becoming something which it is not yet actually, — as having an existence incomplete, and receiving at each instant a further completion. It is manifest therefore that, if all objects of human thought exist in time, no such object can be regarded as exhibiting or representing the true nature of an Infinite Being.

As a necessary consequence of this limitation, it follows, that an act of *Creation*, in the highest sense of the term, — that is to say, an absolutely first link in the chain of phenomena, preceded by no temporal antecedent, — is to human thought inconceivable. To represent in thought the first act of the first cause of all things, I must conceive myself as placed in imagination at the point at which temporal succession commences, and as thus conscious of the relation between a phenomenon in time and a reality out of time. But the consciousness of such a relation implies a consciousness of both the related members; to realize which, the mind must be in and out of time at the same moment. Time, therefore, cannot be regarded as limited; for to conceive a first or last moment of time would be to conceive a consciousness into which time enters, preceded or followed by one from which it is absent. But, on the other hand, an infinite succession in time is equally inconceivable; for this succession also cannot be bounded by time, and therefore can only be apprehended by one who is himself free from the law of conceiving in time. From a human point of view, such a conception could only be formed by thrusting back the boundary forever; — a process which itself would require an infinite time for its accomplishment.[(11)] Clogged by these counter impossibilities of thought, two opposite speculations have in vain struggled to find articulate utterance, the one for the hypothesis of an endless duration of finite changes, the other for that of an existence prior to duration itself. It is perhaps another aspect of the same difficulty, that, among various theories of the generation of the world, the idea of a creation out of nothing seems to have been altogether foreign to ancient philosophy.[(12)]

The limited character of all existence which can be conceived as having a continuous duration, or as made up of successive moments, is so far manifest, that it has been assumed, almost as an axiom, by philosophical theologians, that in the existence of God there is no distinction between past, present, and future. "In the changes of things," says Augustine, there is a past and a future: in God there is a present, in which neither past nor future can be."[(13)] "Eternity," says Boethius, "is the perfect possession of interminable life, and of all that life at once:"[(14)] and Aquinas, accepting the definition, adds, "Eternity has no succession, but exists all together."[(15)] But, whether this assertion be literally true or not (and this we have no means of ascertaining), it is clear that such a mode of existence is altogether inconceivable by us, and that the words in which it is described represent not thought, but the refusal to think at all. It is impossible that man, so long as he exists in time, should contemplate an object in whose existence there is no time. For the thought by which he contemplates it must be one of his own mental states: it must have a beginning and an end: it must occupy a certain portion of duration, as a fact of human consciousness. There is therefore no manner of resemblance or community of nature between the representative thought and that which it is supposed to represent; for the one cannot exist out of time, and the other cannot exist in it.(16) Nay, more: even were a mode of representation out of time possible to a man, it is utterly impossible that he should know it to be so, or make any subsequent use of the knowledge thus conveyed to him. To be conscious of a thought as *mine*, I must know it as a present condition of my consciousness: to know that it *has been mine*, I must remember it as a past condition; and past and present are alike modes of time. It is manifest, therefore, that a knowledge of the infinite, as existing out of time, even supposing it to take place at all, cannot be known to be taking place, cannot be remembered to have taken place, and cannot be made available for any purpose at any period of our temporal life.(17)

The command, so often urged upon man by philosophers and theologians of various ages and schools, "In contemplating God, transcend time,"(18) if meant for anything more than a figure of rhetoric, is equivalent to saying, "Be man no more; be thyself God." It amounts to the admission that, to know the infinite, the human mind must itself be infinite; because an object of consciousness, which is in any way limited by the conditions of human thought, cannot be accepted as a representation of the unlimited. But two infinites cannot be conceived as existing together; and if the mind of man must become infinite to know God, it must itself be God.(19) Pantheism, or self-acknowledged falsehood, are thus the only alternatives possible under this precept. If the human mind, remaining in reality finite, merely fancies itself to be infinite in its contemplation of

God, the knowledge of God is itself based on a falsehood. If, on the other hand, it not merely imagines itself to be, but actually is, infinite, its personality is swallowed up in the infinity of the Deity; its human existence is a delusion: God is, literally and properly, all that exists; and the Finite, which appears to be, but is not, vanishes before the single existence of the One and All.

Subordinate to the general law of Time, to which all consciousness is subject, there are two inferior conditions, to which the two great divisions of consciousness are severally subject. Our knowledge of body is governed by the condition of *space;* our knowledge of mind by that of *personality.* I can conceive no qualities of body, save as having a definite local position; and I can conceive no qualities of mind, save as modes of a conscious self. With the former of these limitations our present argument is not concerned; but the latter, as the necessary condition of the conception of spiritual existence, must be taken into account in estimating the philosophical value of man's conception of an infinite Mind.

The various mental attributes which we ascribe to God — Benevolence, Holiness, Justice, Wisdom, for example — can be conceived by us only as existing in a benevolent and holy and just and wise Being, who is not identical with any one of his attributes, but the common subject of them all; in one word, in a *Person.* But Personality, as we conceive it, is essentially a limitation and a relation. [20] Our own personality is presented to us as relative and limited; and it is from that presentation that all our representative notions of personality are derived. Personality is presented to us as a relation between the conscious self and the various modes of his consciousness. There is no personality in abstract thought without a thinker:

there is no thinker, unless he exercises some mode of thought. Personality is also a limitation; for the thought and the thinker are distinguished from and limit each other; and the several modes of thought are distinguished each from each by limitation likewise. If I am any one of my own thoughts, I live and die with each successive moment of my consciousness. If I am not any one of my own thoughts, I am limited by that very difference, and each thought, as different from another, is limited also. This, too, has been clearly seen by philosophical theologians; and accordingly, they have maintained that in God there is no distinction between the subject of consciousness and its modes, nor between one mode and another. "God," says Augustine, "is not a Spirit as regards substance, and good as regards quality; but both as regards substance. The justice of God is one with his goodness and with his blessedness; and all are one with his spirituality." (21) But this assertion, if it be literally true (and of this we have no means of judging), annihilates Personality itself, in the only form in which we can conceive it. We cannot transcend our own personality, as we cannot transcend our own relation to time: and to speak of an Absolute and Infinite Person, is simply to use language to which, however true it may be in a superhuman sense, no mode of human thought can possibly attach itself.

But are we therefore justified, even on philosophical grounds, in denying the Personality of God? or do we gain a higher or a truer representation of Him, by asserting, with the ancient or the modern Pantheist, that God, as absolute and infinite, can have neither intelligence nor will? (22) Far from it. We dishonor God far more by identifying Him with the feeble and negative impotence of thought, which we are pleased to style the Infinite, than by remaining content within those limits which He for his own good purposes has imposed upon us, and confining ourselves to a manifestation, imperfect indeed and inadequate, and acknowledged to be so, but still the highest idea that we can form, the noblest tribute that we can offer. Personality, with all its limitations, though far from exhibiting the absolute nature of God as He is, is yet truer, grander, more elevating, more religious, than those barren, vague, meaningless abstractions in which men babble about nothing under the name of the Infinite. Personal, conscious existence, limited though it be, is yet the noblest of all existences of which man can dream; for it is that by which all existence is revealed to him: it is grander than the grandest object which man can know; for it is that which knows, not that which is known. (23) "Man," says Pascal, "is but a reed, the frailest in nature; but he is a reed that thinks. It needs not that the whole universe should arm itself to crush him; — a vapor, a drop of water, will suffice to destroy him. But should the universe crush him, man would yet be nobler than that which destroys him; for he knows that he dies; while of the advantage which the universe has over him, the universe knows nothing." (24) It is by consciousness alone that we know that God exists, or that we are able to offer Him any service. It is only by conceiving Him as a Conscious Being, that we can stand in any religious relation to Him at all; that we can form such a representation of Him as is demanded by our spiritual wants, insufficient though it be to satisfy our intellectual curiosity.

It is from the intense consciousness of our own real existence as Persons, that the conception of reality takes its rise in our minds: it is through that consciousness alone that we can raise ourselves to the faintest image of the supreme reality of God. What is reality, and what is appearance, is the riddle which Philosophy has put forth from the birthday of human thought; and the only approach to an answer has been a voice from the depths of the personal consciousness: "I think; therefore I am." (25) In the antithesis between the thinker and the object of his thought, — between myself and that which is related to me, — we find the type and the source of the universal contrast between the one and the many, the permanent and the changeable, the real and the apparent. That which I see, that which I hear, that which I think, that which I feel, changes and passes away with each moment of my varied existence. I, who see, and hear, and think, and feel, am the one continuous self, whose existence gives unity and connection to the whole. Personality comprises all that we know of that which exists: relation to personality comprises all that we know of that which seems to exist. And when, from the little world of man's consciousness and its objects, we would lift up our eyes to the inexhaustible universe beyond, and ask, to whom all this is related, the highest existence is still the highest personality; and the Source of all Being reveals Himself by His name, I AM.[1] (26)

If there is one dream of a godless philosophy to which, beyond all others, every moment of our consciousness gives the lie, it is that which subordinates the individual to the universal, the person to the species; which deifies kinds and realizes classifications; which sees Being in generalization, and Appearance in limitation; which regards the living and conscious man as a wave on the ocean of

[1] Exodus iii. 14.

the unconscious infinite; his life, a momentary tossing to and fro on the shifting tide; his destiny, to be swallowed up in the formless and boundless universe.(27) The final conclusion of this philosophy, in direct antagonism to the voice of consciousness, is, "I think; therefore I am not." When men look around them in bewilderment for that which lies within them; when they talk of the enduring species and the perishing individual, and would find, in the abstractions which their own minds have made, a higher and truer existence than in the mind which made them;—they seek for that which they know, and know not that for which they seek.(28) They would fain lift up the curtain of their own being, to view the picture which it conceals. Like the painter of old, they know not that the curtain *is* the picture.(29)

It is our duty, then, to think of God as personal; and it is our duty to believe that He is infinite. It is true that we cannot reconcile these two representations with each other; as our conception of personality involves attributes apparently contradictory to the notion of infinity. But it does not follow that this contradiction exists any where but in our own minds: it does not follow that it implies any impossibility in the absolute nature of God. The apparent contradiction, in this case, as in those previously noticed, is the necessary consequence of an attempt on the part of the human thinker to transcend the boundaries of his own consciousness. It proves that there are limits to man's power of thought; and it proves no more.

The preceding considerations are equally conclusive against both the methods of metaphysical theology described in my last Lecture,—that which commences with the divine to reason down to the human, and that which commences with the human to reason up to the divine.

For though the mere abstract expression of *the infinite*, when regarded as indicating nothing more than the negation of limitation, and, therefore, of conceivability, is not contradictory in itself, it becomes so the instant we attempt to apply it in reasoning to any object of thought. A thing — an object — an attribute — a person — or any other term signifying one out of many possible objects of consciousness, is by that very relation necessarily declared to be finite. An infinite thing, or object, or attribute, or person, is, therefore, in the same moment declared to be both finite and infinite. We cannot, therefore, start from any abstract assumption of the divine infinity, to reason downwards to any object of human thought. And, on the other hand, if all human attributes are conceived under the conditions of difference, and relation, and time, and personality, we cannot represent in thought any such attribute magnified to infinity; for this, again, is to conceive it as finite and infinite at the same time. We can conceive such attributes, at the utmost, only *indefinitely:* that is to say, we may withdraw our thought, for the moment, from the fact of their being limited; but we cannot conceive them as *infinite:* that is to say, we cannot positively think of the absence of the limit; for, the instant we attempt to do so, the antagonist elements of the conception exclude one another, and annihilate the whole.

There remains but one subterfuge to which Philosophy can have recourse, before she is driven to confess that the Absolute and the Infinite are beyond her grasp. If consciousness is against her, she must endeavor to get rid of consciousness itself. And, accordingly, the most distinguished representatives of this philosophy in recent times, however widely differing upon other questions, agree in maintaining that the foundation for a knowledge of the infinite must be laid in a point beyond consciousness.(30) But a system which starts from this assumption postulates its own failure at the outset. It attempts to prove that consciousness is a delusion; and consciousness itself is made the instrument of proof; for by consciousness its reasonings must be framed and apprehended. It is by reasonings, conducted in conformity to the ordinary laws of thought, that the philosopher attempts to show that the highest manifestations of reason are above those laws. It is by representations, exhibited under the conditions of time and difference, that the philosopher endeavors to prove the existence, and deliver the results, of an intuition in which time and difference are annihilated. They thus assume, at the same moment, the truth and the falsehood of the normal consciousness; they divide the human mind against itself; and by that division prove no more than that two supposed faculties of thought mutually invalidate each other's evidence. Thus, by an act of reason, philosophy destroys reason itself: it passes at once from rationalism to mysticism, and makes inconceivability the criterion of truth. In dealing with religious truths, the theory which repudiates with scorn the notion of believing a doctrine *although* it is incomprehensible, springs at one desperate bound clear over faith into credulity, and proclaims that its own principles must be believed *because* they are incomprehensible. The rhetorical paradox of the fervid African is adopted in cold blood as an axiom of metaphysical speculation: "It is certain, because it is impossible."(31) Such a theory is open to two fatal objections, — it cannot be communicated, and it cannot be verified. It cannot be communicated; for the communication must be made in words; and the meaning of those words must be understood; and the understanding is a state of the normal consciousness. It cannot be verified; for, to verify, we must compare the author's experience with our own; and such a comparison is again a state of consciousness. Let it be granted for a moment, though the concession refutes itself, that a man may have a cognizance of the infinite by some mode of knowledge which is above consciousness. He can never say that the idea thus acquired is like or unlike that possessed by any other man; for likeness implies comparison; and comparison is only possible as a mode of consciousness, and between objects regarded as limited and related to each other. That which is out of consciousness cannot be pronounced true; for truth is the correspondence between a conscious representation and the object which it represents. Neither can it be pronounced false; for falsehood consists in the disagreement between a similar representation and its object. Here, then, is the very suicide of Rationalism. To prove its own truth and the falsehood of antagonistic systems, it postulates a condition under which neither truth nor falsehood is possible.

The results, to which an examination of the facts of consciousness has conducted us, may be briefly summed up as follows. Our whole consciousness manifests itself as subject to certain limits, which we are unable, in any act of thought, to transgress. That which falls within these limits, as an object of thought is known to us as *relative* and *finite*. The existence of a limit to our powers of thought is manifested by the consciousness of *contradiction*, which implies at the same time an attempt to think and an inability to accomplish that attempt. But a limit is necessarily conceived as a relation between something within and something without itself; and thus the consciousness of a limit of thought implies, though it does not directly present to us, the existence of something of which we do not and cannot think. When we lift up our eyes to that blue vault of heaven, which is itself but the limit of our own power of sight, we are compelled to suppose, though we cannot perceive, the existence of space beyond, as well as within it; we regard the boundary of vision as parting the visible from the invisible. And when, in mental contemplation, we are conscious of relation and difference, as the limits of our power of thought, we regard them, in like manner, as the boundary between the conceivable and the inconceivable; though we are unable to penetrate, in thought, beyond the nether sphere, to the unrelated and unlimited which it hides from us.(32) The *Absolute* and the *Infinite* are thus, like the *Inconceivable* and the *Imperceptible*, names indicating, not an object of thought or of consciousness at all, but the mere absence of the conditions under which consciousness is possible. The attempt to construct in thought an object answering to such names, necessarily results in contradiction; — a contradiction, however, which we have ourselves produced by the attempt to think; — which exists in the act of thought, but not beyond it; — which destroys the conception as such, but indicates nothing concerning the existence or non-existence of that which we try to conceive. It proves our own impotence, and it proves nothing more. Or rather, it indirectly leads us to believe in the existence of that Infinite which we cannot conceive; for the denial of its existence involves a contradiction, no less than the assertion of its conceivability. We thus learn that the provinces of Reason and Faith are not coëxtensive; — that it is a duty, enjoined by Reason itself, to believe in that which we are unable to comprehend.

I have now concluded that portion of my argument in which it was necessary to investigate in abstract terms the limits of human thought in general, as a preliminary to the examination of religious thought in particular. As yet, we have viewed only the negative side of man's consciousness; — we have seen how it *does not* represent God, and why it does not so represent Him. There remains still to be attempted the positive side of the same inquiry, — namely, what does our consciousness actually tell us concerning the Divine Existence and Attributes; and how does its testimony agree with that furnished by Revelation. In prosecuting this further inquiry, I hope to be able to confine myself to topics more resembling those usually handled in this place, and to language more strictly appropriate to the treatment of Christian Theology. Yet there are advantages in the method which I have hitherto pursued, which may, I trust, be accepted as a sufficient cause for whatever may have sounded strange and obscure in its phraseology. So long as the doubts and difficulties of philosophical speculation are familiar to us only in their religious aspect and language, so long we may be led to think that there is some peculiar defect or perplexity in the evidences of religion, by which it is placed in apparent antagonism to the more obvious and unquestionable conclusions of reason. A very brief examination of cognate questions in their metaphysical aspect, will suffice to dissipate this misapprehension, and to show that the philosophical difficulties, which rationalists profess to discover in Christian doctrines, are in fact inherent in the laws of human thought, and must accompany every attempt at religious or irreligious speculation.

There is also another consideration, which may justify the Christian preacher in examining, at times, the thoughts and language of human philosophy, apart from their special application to religious truths. A religious association may sometimes serve to disguise the real character of a line of thought which, without that association, would have little power to mislead. Speculations which end in unbelief are often commenced in a believing spirit. It is painful, but at the same time instructive, to trace the gradual progress by which an unstable disciple often tears off strip by strip the wedding garment of his faith,—scarce conscious the while of his own increasing nakedness,—and to mark how the language of Christian belief may remain almost untouched, when the substance and the life have departed from it. While Philosophy speaks nothing but the language of Christianity, we may be tempted to think that the two are really one; that our own speculations are but leading us to Christ by another and a more excellent way. Many a young aspirant after a philosophical faith, trusts himself to the trackless ocean of rationalism in the spirit of the too-confident Apostle: "Lord, bid me to come unto thee on the water."[1] And for a while he knows not how deep he sinks, till the treacherous surface on which he treads is yielding on every side, and the dark abyss of utter unbelief is yawning to swallow him up. Well is it indeed with those who, even in that last fearful hour, can yet cry, "Lord, save me!" and can feel that supporting hand stretched out to grasp them, and hear that voice, so warning, yet so comforting, "O thou of little faith, wherefore didst thou doubt?"

But who that enters upon this course of mistrust shall dare to say that such will be the end of it? Far better is it to learn at the outset the nature of that unstable surface on which we would tread, without being tempted by the phantom of religious promise, which shines delusively over it. He who hath ordered all things in measure and number and weight,[2] has also given to the reason of man, as to his life, its boundaries, which it cannot pass.[3] And if, in the

[1] St. Matthew xiv. 28. [2] Wisdom xi. 20. [3] Job xiv. 5.

investigation of those boundaries, we have turned for a little while, to speak the language of human philosophy, the result will but be to show that philosophy, rightly understood, teaches one lesson with the sacred volume of Revelation. With that lesson let us conclude, as it is given in the words of our own judicious divine and philosopher. "Dangerous it were for the feeble brain of man to wade far into the doings of the Most High; whom although to know be life, and joy to make mention of His name; yet our soundest knowledge is to know that we know Him not as indeed He is, neither can know Him: and our safest eloquence concerning Him is our silence, when we confess without confession that His glory is inexplicable, His greatness above our capacity and reach. He is above, and we upon earth; therefore it behoveth our words to be wary and few." (33)

LECTURE IV.

O THOU THAT HEAREST PRAYER, UNTO THEE SHALL ALL FLESH COME. — PSALM LXV. 2.

THAT the Finite cannot comprehend the Infinite, is a truth more frequently admitted in theory than applied in practice. It has been expressly asserted by men who, almost in the same breath, have proceeded to lay down canons of criticism, concerning the purpose of Revelation, and the truth or falsehood, importance or insignificance, of particular doctrines, on grounds which are tenable only on the supposition of a perfect and intimate knowledge of God's Nature and Counsels. (1) Hence it becomes necessary to bring down the above truth from general to special statements; — to inquire more particularly wherein the limitation of man's faculties consists, and in what manner it exhibits itself in the products of thought. This task I endeavored to accomplish in my last Lecture. To pursue the conclusion thus obtained to its legitimate consequences in relation to Theology, we must next inquire how the human mind, thus limited, is able to form the idea of a relation between man and God, and what is the nature of the conception of God which arises from the consciousness of this relation. The purpose of our inquiry is to ascertain the limits of religious thought; and, for this purpose, it is necessary to proceed from the limits of thought and of human consciousness in general, to those particular forms of consciousness which, in thought, or in some other mode, especially constitute the essence of Religion.

Reasonings, probable or demonstrative, in proof of the being and attributes of God, have met with a very different reception at different periods. Elevated at one time, by the injudicious zeal of their advocates, to a certainty and importance to which they have no legitimate claim, at another, by an equally extravagant reäction, they have been sacrificed in the mass to some sweeping principle of criticism, or destroyed piecemeal by minute objections in detail. While one school of theologians has endeavored to raise the whole edifice of the Christian Faith on a basis of metaphysical proof,(2) others have either expressly maintained that the understanding has nothing to do with religious belief, or have indirectly attempted to establish the same conclusion by special refutations of the particular reasonings.(3)

An examination of the actual state of the human mind, as regards religious ideas, will lead us to a conclusion intermediate between these two extremes. On the one hand, it must be allowed that it is not through reasoning that men obtain the first intimation of their relation to the Deity; and that, had they been left to the guidance of their intellectual faculties alone, it is possible that no such intimation might have taken place; or at best, that it would have been but as one guess, out of many equally plausible and equally natural. Those who lay exclusive stress on the proof of the existence of God from the marks of design in the world, or from the necessity of supposing a first cause of all phenomena, overlook the fact that man learns to pray before he learns to reason, — that he feels within him the consciousness of a Supreme Being, and the instinct of worship, before he can argue from effects to causes, or estimate the traces of wisdom and benevolence scattered through the creation. But, on the other hand, arguments which would be insufficient to create the notion of a Supreme Being in a mind previously destitute of it, may have great force and value in enlarging or correcting a notion already existing, and in justifying to the reason the unreasoning convictions of the heart. The belief in a God, once given, becomes the nucleus round which subsequent experiences cluster and accumulate; and evidences which would be obscure or ambiguous, if addressed to the reason only, become clear and convincing, when interpreted by the light of the religious consciousness.

We may therefore, without hesitation, accede to the argument of the great critic of metaphysics, when he tells us that the speculative reason is unable to prove the existence of a Supreme Being, but can only correct our conception of such a Being, supposing it to be already obtained. (4) But, at the same time, it is necessary to protest against the pernicious extent to which the reäction against the use of the reason in theology has in too many instances been carried. When the same critic tells us that we cannot legitimately infer, from the order and design visible in the world, the omnipotence and omniscience of its Creator, because a degree of power and wisdom short of the very highest might possibly be sufficient to produce all the effects which we are able to discern; (5) or when a later writer, following in the same track, condemns the argument from final causes, because it represents God exclusively in the aspect of an artist; (6) or when a third writer, of a different school, tells us that the processes of thought have nothing to do with the soul, the organ of religion; (7) — we feel that systems which condemn the use of reasoning in sacred things may be equally one-sided and extravagant with those which assert its supreme authority. Reasoning must not be condemned for failing to accomplish what no possible mode of human consciousness ever does or can accomplish. If consciousness itself is a limitation; if every mode of consciousness is a determination of the mind in one particular manner out of many possible; —it follows indeed that the infinite is beyond the reach of man's arguments; but only as it is also beyond the reach of his feelings or his volitions. We cannot indeed reason to the existence of an infinite Cause from the presence of finite effects, nor contemplate the infinite in a finite mode of knowledge; but neither can we feel the infinite in the form of a finite affection, nor discern it as the law of a finite action. If our whole consciousness of God is partial and incomplete, composed of various attributes manifested in various relations, why should we condemn the reasoning which represents Him in a single aspect, so long as it neither asserts nor implies that that aspect is the only one in which He can be represented? If man is not a creature composed solely of intellect, or solely of will, why should any one element of his nature be excluded from participating in the pervading consciousness of Him in whom we live, and move, and have our being?[1] A religion based solely on the reason may starve on barren abstractions, or bewilder itself with inexplicable contradictions; but a religion which repudiates thought to take refuge in feeling, abandons itself to the wild follies of fanaticism, or the diseased ecstasies of mysticism; while one which acknowledges the practical energies alone, may indeed attain to Stoicism, but will fall far short of Christianity. It is our duty indeed to pray with the spirit; but it is no less our duty to pray with the understanding also.[2]

Taking, then, as the basis of our inquiry, the admission

[1] Acts xvii. 28. [2] 1 Corinthians xiv. 15.

that the whole consciousness of man, whether in thought, or in feeling, or in volition, is limited in the manner of its operation and in the objects to which it is related, let us endeavor, with regard to the religious consciousness in particular, to separate from each other the complicated threads which, in their united web, constitute the conviction of man's relation to a Supreme Being. In distinguishing, however, one portion of these as forming the origin of this conviction, and another portion as contributing rather to its further development and direction, I must not be understood to maintain or imply that the former could have existed and been recognized, prior to and independently of the coöperation of the latter. Consciousness, in its earliest discernible form, is only possible as the result of an union of the reflective with the intuitive faculties. A state of mind, to be known at all as existing, must be distinguished from other states; and, to make this distinction, we must think of it, as well as experience it. Without thought as well as sensation, there could be no consciousness of the existence of an external world: without thought as well as emotion and volition, there could be no consciousness of the moral nature of man. Sensation without thought would at most amount to no more than an indefinite sense of uneasiness or momentary irritation, without any power of discerning in what manner we are affected, or of distinguishing our successive affections from each other. To distinguish, for example, in the visible world, any one object from any other, to know the house as a house, or the tree as a tree, we must be able to refer them to distinct notions; and such reference is an act of thought. The same condition holds good of the religious consciousness also. In whatever mental affection we become conscious of our relation to a Supreme Being, we can discern that consciousness, as such, only by reflecting upon it as conceived under its proper notion. Without this, we could not know our religious consciousness to be what it is; and, as the knowledge of a fact of consciousness is identical with its existence, — without this, the religious consciousness, as such, could not exist.

But, notwithstanding this necessary coöperation of thought in every manifestation of human consciousness, it is not to the reflective faculties that we must look, if we would discover the origin of religion. For, to the exercise of reflection, it is necessary that there should exist an object on which to reflect; and though, in the order of time, the distinct recognition of this object is simultaneous with the act of reflecting upon it, yet, in the order of nature, the latter presupposes the former. Religious thought, if it is to exist at all, can only exist as representative of some fact of religious intuition, — of some individual state of mind, in which is presented, as an immediate fact, that relation of man to God, of which man, by reflection, may become distinctly and definitely conscious.

Two such states may be specified, as dividing between them the rude material out of which Reflection builds up the edifice of Religious Consciousness. These are the *Feeling of Dependence* and the *Conviction of Moral Obligation.* To these two facts of the inner consciousness may be traced, as to their sources, the two great outward acts by which religion in various forms has been manifested among men; — *Prayer*, by which they seek to win God's blessing upon the future, and *Expiation*, by which they strive to atone for the offences of the past. (8) The feeling of Dependence is the instinct which urges us to pray. It is the feeling that our existence and welfare are in the hands of a superior Power; — not of an inexorable Fate or immutable Law; but of a Being having at least so far the attributes of Personality, that He can show favor or severity to those dependent upon Him, and can be regarded by them with the feelings of hope, and fear, and reverence, and gratitude. It is a feeling similar in kind, though higher in degree, to that which is awakened in the mind of the child towards his parent, who is first manifested to his mind as the giver of such things as are needful, and to whom the first language he addresses is that of entreaty. It is the feeling so fully and intensely expressed in the language of the Psalmist: "Thou art he that took me out of my mother's womb: thou wast my hope, when I hanged yet upon my mother's breasts. I have been left unto thee ever since I was born: thou art my God even from my mother's womb. Be not thou far from me, O Lord: thou art my succour; haste thee to help me. I will declare thy Name unto my brethren: in the midst of the congregation will I praise thee."[1] With the first development of consciousness, there grows up, as a part of it, the innate feeling that our life, natural and spiritual, is not in our power to sustain or to prolong; — that there is One above us, on whom we are dependent, whose existence we learn, and whose presence we realize, by the sure instinct of Prayer. We have thus, in the Sense of Dependence, the foundation of one great element of Religion, — the Fear of God.

But the mere consciousness of dependence does not of itself exhibit the character of the Being on whom we depend. It is as consistent with superstition as with religion; — with the belief in a malevolent, as in a benevolent Deity: it is as much called into existence by the severities, as by the mercies of God; by the suffering which we are unable to avert, as by the benefits which we did not ourselves pro-

[1] Psalm xxii. 9, 10, 19, 22.

cure. (9) The Being on whom we depend is, in that single relation, manifested in the infliction of pain, as well as in the bestowal of happiness. But in order to make suffering, as well as enjoyment, contribute to the religious education of man, it is necessary that he should be conscious, not merely of *suffering*, but of *sin*; — that he should look upon pain not merely as *inflicted*, but as *deserved*; and should recognize in its Author the justice that punishes, not merely the anger that harms. In the feeling of dependence, we are conscious of the Power of God, but not necessarily of His Goodness. This deficiency, however, is supplied by the other element of religion, — the Consciousness of Moral Obligation, — carrying with it, as it necessarily does, the Conviction of Sin. It is impossible to establish, as a great modern philosopher has attempted to do, the theory of an absolute Autonomy of the Will; that is to say, of an obligatory law, resting on no basis but that of its own imperative character. (10) Considered solely in itself, with no relation to any higher authority, the consciousness of a law of obligation is a fact of our mental constitution, and it is no more. The fiction of an absolute law, binding on all rational beings, has only an apparent universality; because we can only conceive other rational beings by identifying their constitution with our own, and making human reason the measure and representative of reason in general. Why then has one part of our constitution, merely as such, an imperative authority over the remainder? What right has one portion of the human consciousness to represent itself as *duty*, and another merely as *inclination*? There is but one answer possible. The moral Reason, or Will, or Conscience, of Man, call it by what name we please, can have no authority, save as implanted in him by some higher Spiritual Being, as a *Law* emanating from a *Lawgiver*.

Man can be a law unto himself, only on the supposition that he reflects in himself the Law of God; — that he shows, as the Apostle tells us, the works of that law written in his heart.[1] If he is absolutely a law unto himself, his duty and his pleasure are undistinguishable from each other; for he is subject to no one, and accountable to no one. Duty, in this case, becomes only a higher kind of pleasure, — a balance between the present and the future, between the larger and the smaller gratification. We are thus compelled, by the consciousness of moral obligation, to assume the existence of a moral Deity, and to regard the absolute standard of right and wrong as constituted by the nature of that Deity.(11) The conception of this standard, in the human mind, may indeed be faint and fluctuating, and must be imperfect: it may vary with the intellectual and moral culture of the nation or the individual: and in its highest human representation, it must fall far short of the reality. But it is present to all mankind, as a basis of moral obligation and an inducement to moral progress: it is present in the universal consciousness of sin; in the conviction that we are offenders against God; in the expiatory rites by which, whether inspired by some natural instinct, or inherited from some primeval tradition, divers nations have, in their various modes, striven to atone for their transgressions, and to satisfy the wrath of their righteous Judge.(12) However erroneously the particular acts of religious service may have been understood by men: yet, in the universal consciousness of innocence and guilt, of duty and disobedience, of an appeased and offended God, there is exhibited the instinctive confession of all mankind, that the moral nature of man, as subject to a law of obligation, reflects and represents, in some degree, the moral nature of a Deity by whom that obligation is imposed.

[1] Romans ii. 15.

But these two elements of the religious consciousness, however real and efficient within their own limits, are subject to the same restrictions which we have before noticed as binding upon consciousness in general. Neither in the feeling of dependence, nor in that of obligation, can we be directly conscious of the Absolute or the Infinite, as such. And it is the more necessary to notice this limitation, inasmuch as an opposite theory has been maintained by one whose writings have had perhaps more influence than those of any other man, in forming the modern religious philosophy of his own country; and whose views, in all their essential features, have been ably maintained and widely diffused among ourselves. According to Schleiermacher, the essence of Religion is to be found in a feeling of absolute and entire dependence, in which the mutual action and reäction of subject and object upon each other, which constitutes the ordinary consciousness of mankind, gives way to a sense of utter, passive helplessness, — to a consciousness that our entire personal agency is annihilated in the presence of the infinite energy of the Godhead. In our intercourse with the world, he tells us, whether in relation to nature or to human society, the feeling of freedom and that of dependence are always present in mutual operation upon each other; sometimes in equilibrium; sometimes with a vast preponderance of the one or the other feeling; but never to the entire exclusion of either. But in our communion with God, there is always an accompanying consciousness that the whole activity is absolutely and entirely dependent upon Him; that, whatever amount of freedom may be apparent in the individual moments of life, these are but detached and isolated portions of a passively dependent whole.(13) The theory is carried still further, and expressed in more positive terms, by an English disciple, who says that,

"Although man, while in the midst of finite objects, always feels himself to a certain extent independent and free; yet in the presence of that which is self-existent, infinite, and eternal, he may feel the sense of freedom utterly pass away, and become absorbed in the sense of absolute dependence." "Let the relation," he continues, "of subject and object in the economy of our emotions become such that the whole independent energy of the former merges in the latter as its prime cause and present sustainer; let the subject become as nothing, — not, indeed, from its intrinsic insignificance or incapacity of moral action, but by virtue of the infinity of the object to which it stands consciously opposed: and the feeling of dependence *must* become *absolute;* for all finite power is as *nothing* in relation to the Infinite." (14)

Of this theory it may be observed, in the first place, that it contemplates God chiefly in the character of an *object of infinite magnitude.* The relations of the object to the subject, in our consciousness of the world, and in that of God, differ from each other in degree rather than in kind. The Deity is manifested with no attribute of personality: He is merely the world magnified to infinity: and the feeling of absolute dependence is in fact that of the annihilation of our personal existence in the Infinite Being of the Universe. Of this feeling, the intellectual exponent is pure Pantheism; and the infinite object is but the indefinite abstraction of Being in general, with no distinguishing characteristic to constitute a Deity. For the distinctness of an object of consciousness is in the inverse ratio to the intensity of the passive affection. As the feeling of dependence becomes more powerful, the knowledge of the character of the object on which we depend must necessarily become less and less; for the discernment of any object as such is a state of mental energy and reäction of thought upon that object.

Hence the feeling of absolute dependence, supposing it possible, could convey no consciousness of God as God, but merely an indefinite impression of dependence upon something. Towards an object so vague and meaningless, no real religious relation is possible.(15)

In the second place, the consciousness of an absolute dependence in which our activity is annihilated, is a contradiction in terms; for consciousness itself is an activity. We can be conscious of a state of mind as such, only by attending to it; and attention is in all cases a mode of our active energy. Thus the state of absolute dependence, supposing it to exist at all, could not be distinguished from other states; and, as all consciousness is distinction, it could not, by any mode of consciousness, be known to exist.

In the third place, the theory is inconsistent with the duty of Prayer. Prayer is essentially a state in which man is in active relation towards God; in which he is intensely conscious of his personal existence and its wants; in which he endeavors by entreaty to prevail with God. Let any one consider for a moment the strong energy of the language of the Apostle: "Now I beseech you, brethren, for the Lord Jesus Christ's sake, and for the love of the Spirit, that ye strive together with me in your prayers to God for me;"[1] or the consciousness of a personal need, which pervades that Psalm in which David so emphatically declares his dependence upon God: "My God, my God, look upon me; why hast thou forsaken me, and art so far from my health, and from the words of my complaint? O my God, I cry in the day-time, but thou hearest not; and in the night season also I take no rest;"[2]—let him ponder the words of our Lord himself: "Shall not God avenge his own elect, which cry day and night unto him:"[3]—and then

[1] Romans xv. 30. [2] Psalm xxii. 1, 2. [3] St. Luke xviii. 7.

let him say if such language is compatible with the theory which asserts that man's personality is annihilated in his communion with God. (16)

But, lastly, there is another fatal objection to the above theory. It makes our moral and religious consciousness subversive of each other, and reduces us to the dilemma that either our faith or our practice must be founded on a delusion. The actual relation of man to God is the same, in whatever degree man may be conscious of it. If man's dependence on God is not really destructive of his personal freedom, the religious consciousness, in denying that freedom, is a false consciousness. If, on the contrary, man is in reality passively dependent upon God, the consciousness of moral responsibility, which bears witness to his free agency, is a lying witness. Actually, in the sight of God, we are either totally dependent, or, partially at least, free. And as this condition must be always the same, whether we are conscious of it or not, it follows, that, in proportion as one of these modes of consciousness reveals to us the truth, the other must be regarded as testifying to a falsehood. (17)

Nor yet is it possible to find in the consciousness of moral obligation any immediate apprehension of the Absolute and Infinite. For the free agency of man, which in the feeling of dependence is always present as a subordinate element, becomes here the centre and turning-point of the whole. The consciousness of the Infinite is necessarily excluded; first, by the mere existence of a relation between two distinct agents; and, secondly, by the conditions under which each must necessarily be conceived in its relation to the other. The moral consciousness of man, as subject to law, is, by that subjection, both limited and related; and hence it cannot in itself be regarded as a representation of the Infinite. Nor yet can such a representation be furnished by the other term of the relation, — that of the Moral Lawgiver, by whom human obligation is enacted. For, in the first place, such a Lawgiver must be conceived as a Person; and the only human conception of Personality is that of limitation. In the second place, the moral consciousness of such a Lawgiver can only be conceived under the form of a variety of attributes; and different attributes are, by that very diversity, conceived as finite. Nay, the very conception of a moral nature is in itself the conception of a limit; for morality is the compliance with a law; and a law, whether imposed from within or from without, can only be conceived to operate by limiting the range of possible actions.

Yet along with all this, though our positive religious consciousness is of the finite only, there yet runs through the whole of that consciousness the accompanying conviction that the Infinite does exist, and must exist; — though of the manner of that existence we can form no conception; and that it exists along with the Finite; — though we know not how such a coëxistence is possible. We cannot be conscious of the Infinite; but we can be and are conscious of the limits of our own powers of thought; and therefore we know that the possibility or impossibility of conception is no test of the possibility or impossibility of existence. We know that, unless we admit the existence of the Infinite, the existence of the Finite is inexplicable and self-contradictory; and yet we know that the conception of the Infinite itself appears to involve contradictions no less inexplicable. In this impotence of Reason, we are compelled to take refuge in Faith, and to believe that an Infinite Being exists, though we know not how; and that He is the same with that Being who is made known in consciousness as our Sustainer and our Lawgiver. For to deny that an Infinite Being exists, because we cannot comprehend the manner of His existence, is, of two equally inconceivable alternatives, to accept the one which renders that very inconceivability itself inexplicable. If the Finite is the universe of existence, there is no reason why that universe itself should not be as conceivable as the several parts of which it is composed. Whence comes it then that our whole consciousness is compassed about with restrictions, which we are ever striving to pass, and ever failing in the effort? Whence comes it that the Finite cannot measure the Finite? The very consciousness of our own limitations of thought bears witness to the existence of the Unlimited, who is beyond thought. The shadow of the Infinite still broods over the consciousness of the finite; and we wake up at last from the dream of absolute wisdom, to confess, "Surely the Lord is in this place; and I knew it not."[1]

We are thus compelled to acquiesce in at least one portion of Bacon's statement concerning the relation of human knowledge to its object: "Natura percutit intellectum radio directo; Deus autem, propter medium inæquale (creaturas scilicet), radio refracto."(18) To have sufficient grounds for believing in God is a very different thing from having sufficient grounds for reasoning about Him. The religious sentiment, which compels men to believe in and worship a Supreme Being, is an evidence of His existence, but not an exhibition of His nature. It proves *that* God is, and makes known some of His relations to us; but it does not prove *what* God is in His own Absolute Being.(19) The natural senses, it may be, are diverted and colored by the medium through which they pass to reach the intellect, and present to us, not things in themselves, but things as

1 Genesis xxviii. 16.

they appear to us. And this is manifestly the case with the religious consciousness, which can only represent the Infinite God under finite forms. But we are compelled to believe, on the evidence of our senses, that a material world exists, even while we listen to the arguments of the idealist, who reduces it to an idea or a nonentity; and we are compelled, by our religious consciousness, to believe in the existence of a personal God; though the reasonings of the Rationalist, logically followed out, may reduce us to Pantheism or Atheism. But to preserve this belief uninjured, we must acknowledge the true limits of our being: we must not claim for any fact of human consciousness the proud prerogative of revealing God as He is; for thus we throw away the only weapon which can be of avail in resisting the assaults of Skepticism. We must be content to admit, with regard to the internal consciousness of man, the same restrictions which the great philosopher just now quoted has so excellently expressed with reference to the external senses. "For as all works do show forth the power and skill of the workman, and not his image; so it is of the works of God, which do show the omnipotency and wisdom of the maker, but not his image . . . . . . Wherefore by the contemplation of nature to induce and inforce the acknowledgment of God, and to demonstrate his power, is an excellent argument; . . . . . but on the other side, out of the contemplation of nature, or ground of human knowledge, to induce any verity or persuasion concerning the points of faith, is in my judgment not safe . . . . For the heathens themselves conclude as much in that excellent and divine fable of the golden chain: That men and gods were not able to draw Jupiter down to the earth; but contrariwise, Jupiter was able to draw them up to heaven." (20)

One feature deserves especial notice, as common to both of those modes of consciousness which primarily exhibit our relation towards God. In both, we are compelled to regard ourselves as *Persons related to a Person.* In the feeling of dependence, however great it may be, the consciousness of *myself*, the dependent element, remains unextinguished; and, indeed, without that element there could be no consciousness of a relation at all. In the sense of moral obligation, I know *myself* as the agent on whom the law is binding: I am free to choose and to act, as a person whose principle of action is in himself. And it is important to observe that it is only through this consciousness of personality that we have any ground of belief in the existence of a God. If we admit the arguments by which this personality is annihilated, whether on the side of Materialism or on that of Pantheism, we cannot escape from the consequence to which those arguments inevitably lead, — the annihilation of God himself. If, on the one hand, the spiritual element within me is merely dependent on the corporeal, — if *myself* is a result of my bodily organization, and may be resolved into the operation of a system of material agents, — why should I suppose it to be otherwise in the great world beyond me? If I, who deem myself a spirit distinct from and superior to matter, am but the accident and product of that which I seem to rule, why may not all other spiritual existence, if such there be, be dependent upon the constitution of the material universe? (21) Or if, on the other hand, I am not a distinct substance, but a mode of the infinite, — a shadow passing over the face of the universe, — what is that universe which you would have me acknowledge a God? It is, says the Pantheist, the One and All. (22) By no means: it is the Many, in which is neither All nor One. You have taught me that within the little world of my own consciousness there is no relation between the one and the many; but that all is transient and accidental alike. If I accept your conclusion, I must extend it to its legitimate consequence. Why should the universe itself contain a principle of unity? why should the Many imply the One? All that I see, all that I know, are isolated and unconnected phenomena; I myself being one of them. Why should the Universe of Being be otherwise? It cannot be All; for its phenomena are infinite and innumerable; and *all* implies unity and completeness. It need not be One; for you have yourself shown me that I am deceived in the only ground which I have for believing that a plurality of modes implies an unity of substance. If there is no Person to pray; if there is no Person to be obedient; — what remains but to conclude that He to whom prayer and obedience are due, — nay, even the mock-king who usurps His name in the realms of philosophy, — is a shadow and a delusion likewise?

The result of the preceding considerations may be summed up as follows. There are two modes in which we may endeavor to contemplate the Deity: the one negative, based on a vain attempt to transcend the conditions of human thought, and to expand the religious consciousness to the infinity of its Divine Object; the other positive, which keeps within its proper limits, and views the object in a manner accommodated to the finite capacities of the human thinker. The first aspires to behold God in His absolute nature: the second is content to view Him in those relations in which he has been pleased to manifest Himself to his creatures. The first aims at a *speculative* knowledge of God as He is; but, bound by the conditions of finite thought, even in the attempt to transgress them, obtains nothing more than a tissue of ambitious self-contradictions, which indicate only what He is not. (23) The second, abandoning the speculative knowledge of the infinite, as only possible to the Infinite Intelligence itself, is content with those *regulative* ideas of the Deity, which are sufficient to guide our practice, but not to satisfy our intellect; (24) — which tell us, not what God is in Himself, but how He wills that we should think of Him. (25) In renouncing all knowledge of the Absolute, it renounces at the same time all attempts to construct *a priori* schemes of God's Providence as it ought to be: it does not seek to reconcile this or that phenomenon, whether in nature or in revelation, with the absolute attributes of Deity; but confines itself to the actual course of that Providence as manifested in the world; and seeks no higher internal criterion of the truth of a religion, than may be derived from its analogy to other parts of the Divine Government. Guided by this, the only true Philosophy of Religion, man is content to practise where he is unable to speculate. He acts, as one who must give an account of his conduct: he prays, believing that his prayer will be answered. He does not seek to reconcile this belief with any theory of the Infinite; for he does not even know how the Infinite and the Finite can exist together. But he feels that his several duties rest upon the same basis: he knows that, if human action is not incompatible with Infinite Power, neither is human worship with Infinite Wisdom and Goodness: though it is not as the Infinite that God reveals Himself in His moral government; nor is it as the Infinite that he promises to answer prayer.

"O Thou that hearest prayer, unto Thee shall all flesh come." Sacrifice, and offering, and burnt-offerings, and offering for sin, Thou requirest no more; for He whom these prefigured has offered Himself as a sacrifice once for all.[1] But He who fulfilled the sacrifice, commanded the prayer, and Himself taught us how to pray. He tells us that we are dependent upon God for our daily bread, for forgiveness of sins, for deliverance from evil; — and how is that dependence manifested? Not in the annihilation of our personality; for we appeal to Him under the tenderest of personal relations, as the children of Our Father who is in heaven. Not as passive in contemplation, but as active in service; for we pray, "Thy will be done, as in heaven, so in earth." In this manifestation of God to man, alike in Consciousness as in Scripture, under finite forms to finite minds, as a Person to a Person, we see the root and foundation of that religious service, without which belief is a speculation, and worship a delusion; which, whatever would-be philosophical theologians may say to the contrary, is the common bond which unites all men to God. All are God's creatures, bound alike to reverence and obey their Maker. All are God's dependents, bound alike to ask for his sustaining bounties. All are God's rebels, needing daily and hourly to implore His forgiveness for their disobedience. All are God's redeemed, purchased by the blood of Christ, invited to share in the benefits of His passion and intercession. All are brought by one common channel into communion with that God to whom they are related by so many common ties. All are called upon to acknowledge their Maker, their Governor, their Sustainer, their Redeemer; and the means of their acknowledgment is Prayer.

And, apart from the fact of its having been God's good pleasure so to reveal Himself, there are manifest, even to human understanding, wise reasons why this course should have been adopted, benevolent ends to be answered by this

[1] Hebrews x. 8, 10.

gracious condescension. We are not called upon to live two distinct lives in this world. It is not required of us that the household of our nature should be divided against itself; — that those feelings of love, and reverence, and gratitude, which move us in a lower degree towards our human relatives and friends, should be altogether thrown aside, and exchanged for some abnormal state of ecstatic contemplation, when we bring our prayers and praises and thanks before the footstool of our Father in heaven. We are none of us able to grasp in speculation the nature of the Infinite and Eternal; but we all live and move among our fellow-men, at times needing their assistance, at times soliciting their favors, at times seeking to turn away their anger. We have all, as children, felt the need of the supporting care of parents and guardians: we have all, in the gradual progress of education, required instruction from the wisdom of teachers: we have all offended against our neighbors, and known the blessings of forgiveness, or the penalty of unappeased anger. We can all, therefore, taught by the inmost consciousness of our human feelings, place ourselves in communion with God, when He manifests Himself under human images. "He that loveth not his brother whom he hath seen," says the Apostle St. John, "how can he love God whom he hath not seen?"[1] Our heavenly affections must in some measure take their source and their form from our earthly ones: our love towards God, if it is to be love at all, must not be wholly unlike our love towards our neighbor: the motives and influences which prompt us, when we make known our wants and pour forth our supplications to an earthly parent, are graciously permitted by our heavenly Father to be the type and symbol of those by which our intercourse with Him is to be regulated, — with

[1] St. John iv. 20.

which He bids us "come boldly unto the throne of grace, that we may obtain mercy, and find grace to help in time of need."[1]

So should it be during this transitory life, in which we see through a glass, darkly;[2] in which God reveals Himself in types and shadows, under human images and attributes, to meet graciously and deal tenderly with the human sympathies of His creatures. And although, even to the sons of God, it doth not yet appear what we shall be, when we shall be like him, and shall see Him as He is;[3] yet, if it be true that our religious duties in this life are a training and preparation for that which is to come; — if we are encouraged to look forward to and anticipate that future state, while we are still encompassed with this earthly tabernacle; — if we are taught to look, as to our great Example, to One who in love and sympathy towards His brethren was Very Man; — if we are bidden not to sorrow without hope concerning them which are asleep,[4] and are comforted by the promise that the ties of love which are broken on earth shall be united in heaven, — we may trust that not wholly alien to such feelings will be our communion with God face to face, when the redeemed of all flesh shall approach once more to Him that heareth prayer; — no longer in the chamber of private devotion; no longer in the temple of public worship; but in that great City where no temple is; "for the Lord God Almighty and the Lamb are the temple of it."[5]

[1] Hebrews iv. 16. [2] 1 Corinthians xiii. 12. [3] 1 St. John iii. 2.
[4] Thessalonians iv. 13. [5] Revelation xxi. 22.

LECTURE V.

FOR AFTER THAT IN THE WISDOM OF GOD THE WORLD BY WISDOM KNEW NOT GOD, IT PLEASED GOD BY THE FOOLISHNESS OF PREACHING TO SAVE THEM THAT BELIEVE. FOR THE JEWS REQUIRE A SIGN, AND THE GREEKS SEEK AFTER WISDOM: BUT WE PREACH CHRIST CRUCIFIED, UNTO THE JEWS A STUMBLINGBLOCK, AND UNTO THE GREEKS FOOLISHNESS; BUT UNTO THEM WHICH ARE CALLED, BOTH JEWS AND GREEKS, CHRIST THE POWER OF GOD, AND THE WISDOM OF GOD. — 1 CORINTHIANS I. 21–24.

"THOUGH it were admitted," says Bishop Butler, "that this opinion of Necessity were speculatively true; yet, with regard to practice, it is as if it were false, so far as our experience reaches; that is, to the whole of our present life. For the constitution of the present world, and the condition in which we are actually placed, is as if we were free. And it may perhaps justly be concluded that, since the whole process of action, through every step of it, suspense, deliberation, inclining one way, determining, and at last doing as we determine, is as if we were free, therefore we are so. But the thing here insisted upon is, that under the present natural government of the world, we find we are treated and dealt with as if we were free, prior to all consideration whether we are or not." (1)

That this observation has in any degree settled the speculative difficulties involved in the problem of Liberty and Necessity, will not be maintained by any one who is acquainted with the history of the controversy. Nor was it intended by its author to do so. But, like many other pregnant sentences of that great thinker, it introduces a principle capable of a much wider application than to the inquiry which originally suggested it. The vexed question of Liberty and necessity, whose counter-arguments have become a by-word for endless and unprofitable wrangling, is but one of a large class of problems, some of which meet us at every turn of our daily life and conduct, whenever we attempt to justify in theory that which we are compelled to carry out in practice. Such problems arise inevitably, whenever we attempt to pass from the sensible to the intelligible world, from the sphere of action to that of thought, from that which appears to us to that which is in itself. In religion, in morals, in our daily business, in the care of our lives, in the exercise of our senses, the rules which guide our practice cannot be reduced to principles which satisfy our reason. (2)

The very first Law of Thought, and, through Thought, of all Consciousness, by which alone we are able to discern objects as such, or to distinguish them one from another, involves in its constitution a mystery and a doubt, which no effort of Philosophy has been able to penetrate: — How can the One be many, or the Many one? (3) We are compelled to regard ourselves and our fellow-men as *persons*, and the visible world around us as made up of *things:* but what is *personality*, and what is *reality*, are questions which the wisest have tried to answer, and have tried in vain. Man, as a Person, is one, yet composed of many elements; — not identical with any one of them, nor yet with the aggregate of them all; and yet not separable from them by any effort of abstraction. Man is one in his thoughts, in his actions, in his feelings, and in the responsibilities which these involve. It is *I* who think, *I* who act, *I* who feel; yet I am not thought, nor action, nor feeling, nor a combination of thoughts and actions and feelings heaped together. Extension, and resistance, and shape, and the various sensible qualities, make up my conception of each individual body as such; yet *the body* is not its extension, nor its shape, nor its hardness, nor its color, nor its smell, nor its taste; nor yet is it a mere aggregate of all these with no principle of unity among them. If these several parts constitute a single whole, the unity, as well as the plurality, must depend upon some principle which that whole contains: if they do not constitute a whole, the difficulty is removed but a single step; for the same question, — what constitutes individuality? — must be asked in relation to each separate part. The actual conception of every object, as such, involves the combination of the One and the Many; and that combination is practically made every time we think at all. But at the same time, no effort of reason is able to explain how such a relation is possible; or to satisfy the intellectual doubt which necessarily arises on the contemplation of it.

As it is with the first law of Thought, so it is with the first principle of Action and of Feeling. All action, whether free or constrained, and all passion, implies and rests upon another great mystery of Philosophy, — the Commerce between Mind and Matter. The properties and operations of matter are known only by the external senses: the faculties and acts of the mind are known only by the internal apprehension. The energy of the one is motion: the energy of the other is consciousness. What is the middle term which unites these two? and how can their reciprocal action, unquestionable as it is in fact, be conceived as possible in theory? (4) How can a contact between body and body produce consciousness in the immaterial soul? How can a mental self-determination produce the motion of material organs? (5) How can mind, which is neither extended nor figured nor colored itself, represent by its ideas the extension and figure and color of bodies? How can the body be determined to a new position in space by an act of thought, to which space has no relation? How can thought itself be carried on by bodily instruments, and yet itself have nothing in common with bodily affections? What is the relation between the last pulsation of the material brain and the first awakening of the mental perception? How does the spoken word, a merely material vibration of the atmosphere, become echoed, as it were, in the silent voice of thought, and take its part in an operation wholly spiritual? Here again we acknowledge, in our daily practice, a fact which we are unable to represent in theory; and the various hypotheses to which Philosophy has had recourse, — the Divine Assistance, the Preëstablished Harmony, the Plastic Medium, and others, (6) are but so many confessions of the existence of the mystery, and of the extraordinary, yet wholly insufficient efforts made by human reason to penetrate it. (7)

The very perception of our senses is subject to the same restrictions. "No priestly dogmas," says Hume, "ever shocked common sense more than the infinite divisibility of extension, with its consequences." (8) He should have added, that the antagonist assumption of a finite divisibility is equally incomprehensible; it being as impossible to conceive an ultimate unit, or least possible extension, as it is to conceive the process of division carried on to infinity. Extension is presented to the mind as a relation between parts exterior to each other, whose reality cannot consist merely in their juxtaposition. We are thus compelled to believe that extension itself is dependent upon some higher law; — that it is not an original principle of things in themselves, but a derived result of their connection with each other. But to conceive how this generation of space is possible, — how unextended objects can by their conjunction produce extension, — baffles the utmost efforts of the wildest imagination or the profoundest reflection.(9) We cannot conceive how unextended matter can become extended; for of unextended matter we know nothing, either in itself or in its relations; though we are apparently compelled to postulate its existence, as implied in the appearances of which alone we are conscious. The existence of mental succession in time is as inexplicable as that of a material extension in space; — a first moment and an infinite regress of moments being both equally inconceivable, no less than the corresponding theories of a first atom and an infinite division.

The difficulty which meets us in these problems may help to throw some light on the purposes for which human thought is designed, and the limits within which it may be legitimately exercised. The primary fact of consciousness, which is accepted as regulating our practice, is in itself *inexplicable*, but not *inconceivable*. There is *mystery;* but there is not yet *contradiction.* Thought is baffled, and unable to pursue the track of investigation; but it does not grapple with an idea and destroy itself in the struggle. Contradiction does not begin till we direct our thoughts, not to the fact itself, but to that which it suggests as beyond itself. This difference is precisely that which exists between following the laws of thought, and striving to transcend them; — between leaving the mystery of Knowing and Being unsolved, and making unlawful attempts to solve it. The facts, — that all objects of thought are conceived as wholes composed of parts; that mind acts upon matter, and matter upon mind; that bodies are extended in space, and thoughts successive in time, — do not, in their own statement, severally contain elements repulsive of each other. As mere facts, they are so far from being inconceivable, that they embody the very laws of conception itself, and are experienced at every moment as true: but though we are able, nay, compelled to conceive them as *facts*, we find it impossible to conceive them as *ultimate facts*. They are made known to us as *relations;* and all relations are in themselves complex, and imply simpler principles; — objects to be related, and a ground by which the relation is constituted. The conception of any such relation as a fact thus involves a further inquiry concerning its existence as a consequence; and to this inquiry no satisfactory answer can be given. Thus the highest principles of thought and action, to which we can attain, are *regulative*, not *speculative;* — they do not serve to satisfy the reason, but to guide the conduct; they do not tell us what things are in themselves, but how we must conduct ourselves in relation to them.

The conclusion which this condition of human consciousness almost irresistibly forces upon us, is one which equally exhibits the strength and the weakness of the human intellect. We are compelled to admit that the mind, in its contemplation of objects, is not the mere passive recipient of the things presented to it; but has an activity and a law of its own, by virtue of which it reäcts upon the materials existing without, and moulds them into that form in which consciousness is capable of apprehending them. The existence of modes of thought, which we are compelled to accept as at the same time relatively ultimate and absolutely derived, — as limits beyond which we cannot penetrate, yet which themselves proclaim that there is a further truth behind and above them, — suggests, as its obvious explanation, the hypothesis of a mind cramped by its own laws, and bewildered in the contemplation of its own forms. If the mind, in the act of consciousness, were merely blank and inert; — if the entire object of its contemplation came from without, and nothing from within; — no fact of consciousness would be inexplicable; for everything would present itself as it is. No reality would be suggested, beyond what is actually given: no question would be asked which is not already answered. For how can doubt arise, where there is no innate power in the mind to think beyond what is placed before it, — to reäct upon that which acts upon it? But upon the contrary supposition, all is regular, and the result such as might naturally be expected. If thought has laws of its own, it cannot by its own act go beyond them; yet the recognition of law, as a restraint, implies the existence of a sphere of liberty beyond. If the mind contributes its own element to the objects of consciousness, it must, in its first recognition of those objects, necessarily regard them as something complex, something generated partly from without and partly from within. Yet in that very recognition of the complex, as such, is implied an impossibility of attaining to the simple; for to resolve the composition is to destroy the very act of knowledge, and the relation by which consciousness is constituted. The object of which we are conscious is thus, to adopt the well-known language of the Kantian philosophy, a *phenomenon*, not a *thing in itself*; — a product, resulting from the twofold action of the thing apprehended, on the one side, and the faculties apprehending it, on the other. The perceiving subject alone, and the perceived object alone, are two unmeaning elements, which first acquire a significance in and by the act of their conjunction. (10)

It is thus strictly in analogy with the method of God's Providence in the constitution of man's mental faculties, if we believe that, in Religion also, He has given us truths which are designed to be regulative, rather than speculative; intended, not to satisfy our reason, but to guide our practice; not to tell us what God is in His absolute nature, but how He wills that we should think of Him in our present finite state.(11) In my last Lecture, I endeavored to show that our knowledge of God is not a consciousness of the Infinite as such, but that of the relation of a Person to a Person;—the conception of personality being, humanly speaking, one of *limitation.* This amounts to the admission that, in natural religion at least, our knowledge of God does not satisfy the conditions of speculative philosophy, and is incapable of reduction to an ultimate and absolute truth. And this, as we now see, is in accordance with the analogy which the character of human philosophy in other provinces would naturally lead us to expect.(12) It is reasonable also that we should expect to find, as part of the same analogy, that the revealed manifestation of the Divine nature and attributes should also carry on its face the marks of subordination to some higher truth, of which it indicates the existence, but does not make known the substance. It is to be expected that our apprehension of the revealed Deity should involve mysteries inscrutable and doubts insoluble by our present faculties: while, at the same time, it inculcates the true spirit in which such doubts should be dealt with; by warning us, as plainly as such a warning is possible, that we see a part only, and not the whole; that we behold effects only, and not causes; that our knowledge of God, though revealed by Himself, is revealed in relation to human faculties, and subject to the limitations and imperfections inseparable from the constitution of the human mind.(13) We may neglect this warning if we please: we may endeavor to supply the imperfection, and thereby make it more imperfect still: we may twist and torture the divine image on the rack of human philosophy, and call its mangled relics by the high-sounding titles of the Absolute and the Infinite; but these ambitious conceptions, the instant we attempt to employ them in any act of thought, manifest at once, by their inherent absurdities, that they are not that which they pretend to be;—that in the place of the Absolute and Infinite manifested in its own nature, we have merely the Relative and Finite contradicting itself.

We may indeed believe, and ought to believe, that the knowledge which our Creator has permitted us to attain to, whether by Revelation or by our natural faculties, is not given to us as an instrument of deception. We may believe, and ought to believe, that, intellectually as well as morally, our present life is a state of discipline and preparation for another; and that the conceptions which we are compelled to adopt, as the guides of our thoughts and actions now, may indeed, in the sight of a higher Intelligence, be but partial truth, but cannot be total falsehood. But in thus believing, we desert the evidence of Reason, to rest on that of Faith; and of the principles on which Reason itself depends, it is obviously impossible to have any other guarantee. But such a Faith, however well founded, has itself only a regulative and practical, not a speculative and theoretical application. It bids us rest content within the limits which have been assigned to us; but it cannot enable us to overleap those limits, nor exalt to a more absolute character the conclusions obtained by finite thinkers under the conditions of finite thought. But, on the other hand, we must beware of the opposite extreme,—that of mistaking the inability to affirm for the ability to deny. We cannot say that our conception of the Divine Nature exactly resembles that Nature in its absolute existence; for we know not what that absolute existence is. But, for the same reason, we are equally unable to say that it does not resemble; for, if we know not the Absolute and Infinite at all, we cannot say how far it is or is not capable of likeness or unlikeness to the Relative and Finite. We must remain content with the belief that we have that knowledge of God which is best adapted to our wants and training. How far that knowledge represents God as He is, we know not, and we have no need to know.

The testimony of Scripture, like that of our natural faculties, is plain and intelligible, when we are content to accept it as a fact intended for our practical guidance: it becomes incomprehensible, only when we attempt to explain it as a theory capable of speculative analysis. We are distinctly told that there is a mutual relation between God and man, as distinct agents; — that God influences man by His grace, visits him with rewards or punishments, regards him with love or anger; — that man, within his own limited sphere, is likewise capable of "prevailing with God;"[1] that his prayers may obtain an answer, his conduct call down God's favor or condemnation. There is nothing self-contradictory or even unintelligible in this, if we are content to believe *that* it is so, without striving to understand *how* it is so. But the instant we attempt to analyze the ideas of God as infinite and man as finite; — to resolve the scriptural statements into the higher principles on which their possibility apparently depends; — we are surrounded on every side by contradictions of our own raising; and, unable to comprehend how the Infinite and the Finite can exist in mutual

[1] Genesis xxxii. 28.

relation, we are tempted to deny the fact of that relation altogether, and to seek a refuge, though it be but insecure and momentary, in Pantheism, which denies the existence of the Finite, or in Atheism, which rejects the Infinite. And here, again, the parallel between Religion and Philosophy holds: the same limits of thought are discernible in relation to both. The mutual intercourse of mind and matter has been explained away by rival theories of Idealism on the one side and Materialism on the other. The unity and plurality, which are combined in every object of thought, have been assailed, on this side by the Eleatic, who maintains that all things are one, and variety a delusion; (14) on that side by the Skeptic, who tells us that there is no unity, but merely a mixture of differences; that nothing is, but all things are ever becoming; that mind and body, as substances, are mere philosophical fictions, invented for the support of isolated impressions and ideas. (15) The mystery of Necessity and Liberty has its philosophical as well as its theological aspect: and a parallel may be found to both, in the counter-labyrinth of Continuity in Space, whose mazes are sufficiently bewildering to show that the perception of our bodily senses, however certain as a fact, reposes, in its ultimate analysis, upon a mystery no less insoluble than that which envelops the free agency of man in its relation to the Divine Omniscience. (16)

Action, and not knowledge, is man's destiny and duty in this life; and his highest principles, both in philosophy and in religion, have reference to this end. But it does not follow, on that account, that our representations are untrue, because they are imperfect. To assert that a representation is *untrue*, because it is relative to the mind of the receiver, is to overlook the fact that truth itself is nothing more than a relation. Truth and falsehood are not properties of things in themselves, but of our conceptions, and are tested, not by the comparison of conceptions with things in themselves, but with things as they are given in some other relation. My conception of an object of sense is *true*, when it corresponds to the characteristics of the object as I perceive it; but the perception itself is equally a relation, and equally implies the coöperation of human faculties. Truth in relation to no intelligence is a contradiction in terms: our highest conception of absolute truth is that of truth in relation to all intelligences. But of the consciousness of intelligences different from our own we have no knowledge, and can make no application. Truth, therefore, in relation to man, admits of no other test than the harmonious consent of all human faculties; and, as no such faculty can take cognizance of the Absolute, it follows that correspondence with the Absolute can never be required as a test of truth.(17) The utmost deficiency that can be charged against human faculties amounts only to this:—that we cannot say that we know God as God knows himself;(18)—that the truth of which our finite minds are susceptible may, for aught we know, be but the passing shadow of some higher reality, which exists only in the Infinite Intelligence.

That the true conception of the Divine Nature, so far as we are able to receive it, is to be found in those regulative representations which exhibit God under limitations accommodated to the constitution of man; not in the unmeaning abstractions which, aiming at a higher knowledge, distort, rather than exhibit, the Absolute and the Infinite; is thus a conclusion warranted, both deductively, from the recognition of the limits of human thought, and inductively, by what we can gather from experience and analogy concerning God's general dealings with mankind. There remains yet a third indispensable probation, to which the same conclusion must be subjected; namely, how far does it agree with the teaching of Holy Scripture?

In no respect is the Theology of the Bible, as contrasted with the mythologies of human invention, more remarkable, than in the manner in which it recognizes and adapts itself to that complex and self-limiting constitution of the human mind, which man's wisdom finds so difficult to acknowledge. To human reason, the personal and the infinite stand out in apparently irreconcilable antagonism; and the recognition of the one in a religious system almost inevitably involves the sacrifice of the other. The Personality of God disappears in the Pantheism of India; His Infinity is lost sight of in the Polytheism of Greece. (19) In the Hebrew Scriptures, on the contrary, throughout all their variety of Books and Authors, one method of Divine teaching is constantly manifested, appealing alike to the intellect and to the feelings of man. From first to last we hear the echo of that first great Commandment: "Hear, O Israel: The Lord our God is one Lord: and thou shalt love thy God with all thine heart, and with all thy soul, and with all thy might."[2] God is plainly and uncompromisingly proclaimed as the One and the Absolute: "I am the first, and I am the last; and beside me there is no God:"[2] yet this sublime conception is never for an instant so exhibited as to furnish food for that mystical contemplation to which the Oriental mind is naturally so prone. On the contrary, in all that relates to the feelings and duties by which religion is practically to be regulated, we cannot help observing how the Almighty, in communicating with His people, condescends to place Himself on what may, humanly speaking, be called a lower level than that on which the natural

[1] Deuteronomy vi. 4, 5. St. Mark xii. 29, 30. [2] Isaiah xliv. 6.

reason of man would be inclined to exhibit Him. While His Personality is never suffered to sink to a merely human representation; while it is clearly announced that His thoughts are not our thoughts, nor His ways our ways,[1] yet His Infinity is never for a moment so manifested as to destroy or weaken the vivid reality of those human attributes, under which He appeals to the human sympathies of His creature. "The Lord spake unto Moses face to face, as a man speaketh unto his friend."[2] He will listen to our supplications:[3] He will help those that cry unto Him:[4] He reserveth wrath for His enemies:[5] He is appeased by repentance:[6] He showeth mercy to them that love Him.[7] As a King, He listens to the petitions of His subjects:[8] as a Father, He pitieth His own children.[9] It is impossible to contemplate this marvellous union of the human and divine, so perfectly adapted to the wants of the human servant of a divine Master, without feeling that it is indeed the work of Him who formed the spirit of man, and fitted him for the service of His Maker. "He showeth His word unto Jacob, His statutes and ordinances unto Israel. He hath not dealt so with any nation; neither have the heathen knowledge of His laws."[10]

But if this is the lesson taught us by that earlier manifestation in which God is represented under the likeness of human attributes, what may we learn from that later and fuller revelation which tells us of One who is Himself both God and Man? The Father has revealed Himself to

1 Isaiah lv. 8. 2 Exodus xxxiii. 11. 3 Psalm cxlii. 1, 2.
4 Psalm cii. 17, 18; cxlv. 19. Isaiah lviii. 9. 5 Nahum i. 2.
6 1 Kings xxi. 19. Jeremiah xviii. 8. Ezekiel xviii. 23, 30. Jonah iii. 10.
7 Exodus xx. 6. 8 Psalm v. 2; lxxiv. 12. Isaiah xxxiii. 22.
9 Psalm ciii. 13. 10 Psalm cxlvii. 19, 20.

mankind under human types and images, that He may appeal more earnestly and effectually to man's consciousness of the human spirit within him. The Son has done more than this: He became for our sakes very Man, made in all things like unto His brethren;[1] the Mediator between God and men,[2] being both God and Man. (20) Herein is our justification, if we refuse to aspire beyond those limits of human thought in which He has placed us. Herein is our answer, if any man would spoil us through philosophy and vain deceit.[3] Is it irrational to contemplate God under symbols drawn from the human consciousness? Christ is our pattern: "for in Him dwelleth all the fulness of the Godhead bodily."[4] (21) Is it unphilosophical that our thoughts of God should be subject to the law of time? It was when the fulness of the time was come, that God sent forth his Son.[5] (22) Does the philosopher bid us strive to transcend the human, and to annihilate our own personality in the presence of the Infinite? The Apostle tells us to look forward to the time when we shall "all come in the unity of the faith, and of the knowledge of the Son of God, unto a perfect man, unto the measure of the stature of the fulness of Christ."[6] Does human wisdom seek, by some transcendental form of intuition, to behold God as He is in his infinite nature; repeating in its own manner the request of Philip, "Lord, show us the Father, and it sufficeth us?" Christ Himself has given the rebuke and the reply: "He that hath seen me hath seen the Father; and how sayest thou then, Show us the Father?"[7]

[1] Hebrews ii. 17. [2] 1 Timothy ii. 5. [3] Colossians ii. 8.
[4] Colossians ii. 9. [5] Galatians iv. 4. [6] Ephesians iv. 13.
[7] St. John xiv. 8, 9.

The doctrine of a personal Christ, very God and very Man, has indeed been the great stumblingblock in the way of those so-called philosophical theologians who, in their contempt for the historical and temporal, would throw aside the vivid revelation of a living and acting God, to take refuge in the empty abstraction of an impersonal idea. And accordingly, they have made various elaborate attempts to substitute in its place a conception more in accordance with the supposed requirements of speculative philosophy. Let us hear on this point, and understand as we best may, the language of the great leader of the chief modern school of philosophical rationalists. "To grasp rightly and definitely in thought," says Hegel, "the nature of God as a Spirit, demands profound speculation. These propositions are first of all contained therein: God is God only in so far as He knows Himself: His own self-knowledge is moreover His self-consciousness in man, and man's knowledge *of* God, which is developed into man's self-knowledge *in* God." . . . "The Form of the Absolute Spirit," he continues, "separates itself from the Substance, and in it the different phases of the conception part into separate spheres or elements, in each of which the Absolute Substance exhibits itself, first as an eternal substance, abiding in its manifestation with itself; secondly, as a distinguishing of the eternal Essence from its manifestation, which through this distinction becomes the world of appearance, into which the substance of the absolute Spirit enters; thirdly, as an endless return and reconciliation of the world thus projected with the eternal Essence, by which that Essence goes back from appearance into the unity of its fulness." (23) The remainder of the passage carries out this metaphysical caricature of Christian doctrine into further details, bearing on my present argument, but with even additional obscurity; — an obscurity so great, that the effect of a literal translation would be too ludicrous for an occasion like the present. But enough has been quoted to show that if rationalizing philosophers have not made much progress, since the days of Job, in the ability to find out the Almighty unto perfection,[1] they have at least not gone backwards in the art of darkening counsel by words without knowledge.[2]

What is the exact meaning of this profound riddle, which the author has repeated in different forms in various parts of his writings; (24) — whether he really means to assert or to deny the existence of Christ as a man; — whether he designs to represent the Incarnation and earthly life of the Son of God as a fact, or only as the vulgar representation of a philosophical idea, — is a point which has been stoutly disputed among his disciples, and which possibly the philosopher himself did not wish to see definitely settled. (25) But there is another passage, in which he has spoken somewhat more plainly, and which, without being quite decisive, may be quoted as throwing some light on the tendency of his thought. "Christ," says this significant passage, "has been called by the church the God-Man. This monstrous combination is to the understanding a direct contradiction; but the unity of the divine and human nature is in this respect brought into consciousness and certainty in man; in that the Diversity, or, as we may also express it, the Finiteness, Weakness, Frailty of human nature, is not incompatible with this Unity, as in the eternal Idea Diversity in nowise derogates from the Unity which is God. This is the monstrosity whose necessity we have seen. It is therein implied that the divine and human nature are not in themselves different. God in human form. The

[1] Job xi. 7. [2] Job xxxviii. 2.

truth is, that there is but one Reason, one Spirit; that the Spirit as finite has no real existence." (26)

The dark sentences of the master have been, as might naturally be expected, variously developed by his disciples. Let us hear how the same theory is expressed in the language of one who is frequently commended as representing the orthodox theology of this school, and who has striven hard to reconcile the demands of his philosophy with the belief in a personal Christ. Marheineke assures us, that "the possibility of God becoming Man shows in itself that the divine and human nature are in themselves not separate:" that, "as the truth of the human nature is the divine, so the reality of the divine nature is the human." (27) And towards the conclusion of a statement worthy to rank with that of his master for grandiloquent obscurity, he says, "As Spirit, by renouncing Individuality, Man is in truth elevated above himself, without having abandoned the human nature: as Spirit renouncing Absoluteness, God has lowered Himself to human nature, without having abandoned his existence as Divine Spirit. The unity of the divine and human nature is but the unity in that Spirit whose existence is the knowledge of the truth, with which the doing of good is identical. This Spirit, as God in the human nature and as Man in the divine nature, is the God-Man. The man wise in divine holiness, and holy in divine wisdom, is the God-Man. As a historical fact," he continues, "this union of God with man is manifest and real in the Person of Jesus Christ: in Him the divine manifestation has become perfectly human. The conception of the God-Man in the historical Person of Jesus Christ, contains in itself two phases in one; first, that God is manifest only through man; and in this relation Christ is as yet placed on an equality with all other men: He is the Son of Man, and therein at first represents only the possibility of God becoming Man: secondly, that in this Man, Jesus Christ, God is manifest, as in none other: this manifest Man is the manifest God; but the manifest God is the Son of God; and in this relation, Christ is God's Son; and this is the actual fulfilment of the possibility or promise; it is the reality of God becoming Man." (28)

But this kind of halting between two opinions, which endeavors to combine the historical fact with the philosophical theory, was not of a nature to satisfy the bolder and more logical minds of the same school. In the theory of Strauss, we find the direct antagonism between the historical and the philosophical Christ fairly acknowledged; and the former is accordingly set aside entirely, to make way for the latter. And here we have at least the advantage, that the trumpet gives no uncertain sound; — that we are no longer deluded by a phantom of Christian doctrine enveloped in a mist of metaphysical obscurity; but the two systems stand out sharply and clearly defined, in their utter contrariety to each other. "In an individual, a God-Man," he tells us, "the properties and functions which the church ascribes to Christ contradict themselves; in the idea of the race, they perfectly agree. Humanity is the union of the two natures — God become Man, the infinite manifesting itself in the finite, and the finite Spirit remembering its infinitude: it is the child of the visible Mother and the invisible Father, Nature and Spirit: it is the worker of miracles, in so far as in the course of human history the spirit more and more completely subjugates nature, both within and around man, until it lies before him as the inert matter on which he exercises his active power: it is the sinless one, for the course of its development is a blameless one; pollution cleaves to the individual only, but in the race and its history it is taken away. It is Humanity that dies, rises, and ascends to heaven; for from the negation of its natural state there ever proceeds a higher spiritual life; from the suppression of its finite character as a personal, national, and terrestrial Spirit, arises its union with the infinite Spirit of the heavens. By faith in this Christ, especially in his death and resurrection, man is justified before God: that is, by the kindling within him of the idea of Humanity, the individual man participates in the divinely human life of the species. Now the main element of that idea is, that the negation of the merely natural and sensual life, which is itself the negation of the spirit (the negation of negation, therefore), is the sole way to true spiritual life." (29)

These be thy gods, O Philosophy: these are the Metaphysics of Salvation. (30) This is that knowledge of things divine and human, which we are called upon to substitute for the revealed doctrine of the Incarnation of the eternal Son in the fulness of time. It is for this philosophical idea, so superior to all history and fact, — this necessary process of the unconscious and impersonal Infinite, — that we are to sacrifice that blessed miracle of Divine Love and Mercy, by which the Son of God, of His own free act and will, took man's nature upon Him for man's redemption. It is for this that we are to obliterate from our faith that touching picture of the pure and holy Jesus, to which mankind for eighteen centuries has ever turned, with the devotion of man to God rendered only more heartfelt by the sympathy of love between man and man: which from generation to generation has nurtured the first seeds of religion in the opening mind of childhood, by the image of that Divine Child who was cradled in the manger of Bethlehem, and was subject to His parents at Nazareth: which has checked the fiery temptations of youth, by the thought of Him who "was in all points tempted like as we are, yet without sin:"[1] which has consoled the man struggling with poverty and sorrow, by the pathetic remembrance of Him who on earth had not where to lay his head:[2] which has blended into one brotherhood the rich and the poor, the mighty and the mean among mankind, by the example of Him who, though He was rich, yet for our sakes became poor;[3] though He was equal with God, yet took upon Him the form of a servant:[4] which has given to the highest and purest precepts of morality an additional weight and sanction, by the records of that life in which the marvellous and the familiar are so strangely yet so perfectly united; — that life so natural in its human virtue, so supernatural in its divine power: which has robbed death of its sting, and the grave of its victory, by faith in Him who "was delivered for our offences, and was raised again for our justification:"[5] which has ennobled and sanctified even the wants and weaknesses of our mortal nature, by the memory of Him who was an hungered in the wilderness and athirst upon the cross; who mourned over the destruction of Jerusalem, and wept at the grave of Lazarus.

Let Philosophy say what she will, the fact remains unshaken. It is the consciousness of the deep wants of our human nature, that first awakens God's presence in the soul; it is by adapting His Revelation to those wants that God graciously condescends to satisfy them. The time may indeed come, though not in this life, when these various manifestations of God, "at sundry times and in divers manners,"[6] may be seen to be but different sides and partial

[1] Hebrews iv. 15. [2] St. Luke ix. 58. [3] 2 Corinthians viii. 9.
[4] Philippians ii. 6, 7. [5] Romans iv. 25. [6] Hebrews i. 1.

representations of one and the same Divine Reality;—when the light which now gleams in restless flashes from the ruffled waters of the human soul, will settle into the steadfast image of God's face shining on its unbroken surface. But ere this shall be, that which is perfect must come, and that which is in part must be done away.[1] But as regards the human wisdom which would lead us to this consummation now, there is but one lesson which it can teach us; and *that* it teaches in spite of itself. It teaches the lesson which the wise king of Israel learned from his own experience: "I gave my heart to seek and search out by wisdom concerning all things that are done under heaven: I have seen all the works that are done under the sun: and, behold, all is vanity and vexation of spirit. And I gave my heart to know wisdom, and to know madness and folly: I perceived that this also is vexation of spirit."[2] And if ever the time should come to any of us, when, in the bitter conviction of that vanity and vexation, we, who would be as gods in knowledge, wake up only to the consciousness of our own nakedness, happy shall we be, if then we may still hear, ringing in our ears and piercing to our hearts, an echo from that personal life of Jesus which our philosophy has striven in vain to pervert or to destroy: "Lord, to whom shall we go? thou hast the words of eternal life: and we believe and are sure that thou art that Christ, the Son of the living God."[3]

[1] 1 Corinthians xiii. 10. [2] Ecclesiastes i. 13, 14, 17.
[3] St. John vi. 68, 69.

LECTURE VI.

FOR WHAT MAN KNOWETH THE THINGS OF A MAN, SAVE THE SPIRIT OF MAN WHICH IS IN HIM? EVEN SO THE THINGS OF GOD KNOWETH NO MAN, BUT THE SPIRIT OF GOD. — 1 CORINTHIANS II. 11.

THE conclusion to be drawn from our previous inquiries is, that the doctrines of Revealed Religion, like all other objects of human thought, have a relation to the constitution of the thinker to whom they are addressed; within which relation their practical application and significance is confined. At the same time, this very relation indicates the existence of a higher form of the same truths, beyond the range of human intelligence, and therefore not capable of representation in any positive mode of thought. Religious ideas, in short, like all other objects of man's consciousness, are composed of two distinct elements, — a Matter, furnished from without, and a Form, imposed from within by the laws of the mind itself. The latter element is common to all objects of thought as such: the former is the peculiar and distinguishing feature, by which the doctrines of Revelation are distinguished from other religious representations, derived from natural sources; or by which, in more remote comparison, religious ideas in general may be distinguished from those relating to other objects. Now it is indispensable, before we can rightly estimate the value of the various objections which are adduced against this or that representation of Christian doctrine, to ascertain which of these elements it is, against which the force of the objection really makes itself felt. There may be objections whose force, such as it is, tells against the revealed doctrine alone, and which are harmless when directed against any other mode of religious representation. And there may also be objections which are applicable to the form which revealed religion shares in common with other modes of human thinking, and whose force, if they have any, is in reality directed, not against Revelation in particular, but against all Religion, and indeed against all Philosophy also. Now if, upon examination, it should appear that the principal objections which are raised on the side of Rationalism properly so called, — those, namely, which turn on a supposed incompatibility between the doctrine of Scripture and the deductions of human reason, are of the latter kind, and not of the former, Christianity is at least so far secure from any apprehension of danger from the side of rational philosophy. For the weapon with which she is assailed exhibits its own weakness in the very act of assailing. If there is error or imperfection in the essential forms of human thought, it must adhere to the thought criticizing, no less than to the thought criticized; and the result admits of but two legitimate alternatives. Either we must abandon ourselves to an absolute Skepticism, which believes nothing and disbelieves nothing, and which thereby destroys itself in believing that nothing is to be believed; or we must confess that reason, in thus criticizing, has transcended its legitimate province: that it has failed, not through its inherent weakness, but through being misdirected in its aim. We must then shift the inquiry to another field, and allow our belief to be determined, not solely by the internal character of the doctrines themselves, as reasonable or unreasonable, but partly at least, by the evidence which can be produced in favor of their asserted origin as a fact. The reasonable believer, in short, must abstain from pronouncing judgment on the nature of the message, until he has fairly examined the credentials of the messenger.

There are two methods by which such an examination of objections may be conducted. We may commence by an analysis of thought in general, distinguishing the Form, or permanent element, from the Matter, or variable element; and then, by applying the results of that analysis to special instances, we may show, upon deductive grounds, the formal or material character of this or that class of objections. Or we may reverse the process, commencing by an examination of the objections themselves; and, by exhibiting them in their relation to other doctrines besides those of Revelation, we may arrive at the same conclusion as to their general or special applicability. The former method is perhaps the most searching and complete, but could hardly be adequately carried out within my present limits, nor without the employment of a language more technical than would be suitable on this occasion. In selecting the latter method, as the more appropriate, I must request my hearers to bear in mind the general principles which it is proposed to exhibit in one or two special instances. These are, first, that there is no rational difficulty in Christian Theology which has not its corresponding difficulty in human Philosophy: and, secondly, that therefore we may reasonably conclude that the stumblingblocks which the rationalist professes to find in the doctrines of revealed religion arise, not from defects peculiar to revelation, but from the laws and limits of human thought in general, and are thus inherent in the method of rationalism itself, not in the objects which it pretends to criticize.

But, before applying this method to the peculiar doctrines of the Christian revelation, it will be desirable to say a few words on a preliminary condition, on which our belief in the possibility of any revelation at all is dependent. We must justify, in the first instance, the limitations which have been assigned to human reason in relation to the great foundation of all religious belief whatsoever: we must show how far the same method warrants the assertion which has been already made on other grounds; namely, that we may and ought to believe in the existence of a God whose nature we are unable to comprehend; that we are bound to believe *that* God exists; and to acknowledge Him as our Sustainer and our Moral Governor: though we are wholly unable to declare *what* He is in His own Absolute Essence. (1)

Many philosophical theologians, who are far from rejecting any of the essential doctrines of revelation, are yet unwilling to ground their acceptance of them on the duty of believing in the inconceivable. "The doctrine of the incognizability of the Divine essence," says the learned and deep-thinking Julius Müller, "with the intention of exalting God to the highest, deprives Him of the realities, without which, as it is itself obliged to confess, we cannot really think of Him. That this negative result, just as decidedly as the assumption of an absolute knowledge of God, contradicts the Holy Scriptures, which especially teach that God becomes revealed in Christ, as it does that of the simple Christian consciousness, may be too easily shown for it to be requisite that we should here enter upon the same: it is also of itself clear into what a strange position theology must fall by the renunciation of the knowledge of its essential object." (2) As regards the former part of this objection, I endeavored, in my last Lecture, to show that a full belief in God, as revealed in Christ, is not incompatible with a speculative inability to apprehend the Divine Essence. As regards the latter part, it is important to observe the exact parallel which in this respect exists between the fundamental conception of Theology and that of Philosophy. The Principle of Causality, the father, as it has been called, of metaphysical science, (3) is to the philosopher what the belief in the existence of God is to the theologian. Both are principles inherent in our nature, exhibiting, whatever may be their origin, those characteristics of universality and certainty which mark them as part of the inalienable inheritance of the human mind. Neither can be reduced to a mere logical inference from the facts of a limited and contingent experience. Both are equally indispensable to their respective sciences: without Causation, there can be no Philosophy; as without God there can be no Theology. Yet to this day, while enunciating now, as ever, the fundamental axiom, that for every event there must be *a Cause*, Philosophy has never been able to determine what Causation is; to analyze the elements which the causal nexus involves; or to show by what law she is justified in assuming the universal postulate upon which all her reasonings depend. (4) The Principle of Causality has ever been, and probably ever will be, the battle ground on which, from generation to generation, Philosophy has struggled for her very existence in the death-gripe of Skepticism; and at every pause in the contest, the answer has been still the same: "We *cannot* explain it, but we *must* believe it." Causation is not the mere invariable association of antecedent and consequent: we feel that it implies something more than this. (5) Yet, beyond the little sphere of our own volitions, what more can we discover? and within that sphere, what do we discover that we can explain? (6) The unknown something, call it by what name you will,— power, effort, tendency, — still remains absolutely concealed, yet is still conceived as absolutely indispensable. Of Causality, as of Deity, we may almost say, in the emphatic language of Augustine, "Cujus nulla scientia est in anima, nisi scire quomodo eum nesciat." (7) We can speak out boldly and clearly of each, if we are asked, what it is not: we are silent only when we are asked, what it is. The eloquent words of the same great father are as applicable to human as to divine Philosophy:[1] "Deus ineffabilis est: facilius dicimus quid non sit, quam quid sit. Terram cogitas; non est hoc Deus: mare cogitas; non est hoc Deus: omnia quæ sunt in terra, homines et animalia; non est hoc Deus: omnia quæ sunt in mari, quæ volant per aerem; non est hoc Deus: quidquid lucet in cœlo, stellæ, sol et luna; non est hoc Deus: ipsum cœlum; non est hoc Deus. Angelos cogita, Virtutes, Potestates, Archangelos, Thronos, Sedes, Dominationes; non est hoc Deus. Et quid est? Hoc solum potui dicere, quid non sit." (8)

1 "God is ineffable; more easily do we tell what He is not, than what He is. You think of earth; this is not God: of the sea; this is not God: of all things that are on the earth, men and animals; these are not God: of all that are in the sea, that fly through the air; these are not God: of whatever shines in heaven, stars, sun, and moon; these are not God: the heaven itself; this is not God. Think of Angels, Virtues, Powers, Archangels, Thrones, Seats, Dominations; these are not God. And what is He? This only can I tell, what He is not."

From the fundamental doctrine of Religion in general, let us pass on to that of Christianity in particular. "The Catholic Faith is this: that we worship one God in Trinity, and Trinity in Unity." How, asks the objector, can the One be Many, or the Many One? or how is a distinction of Persons compatible with their perfect equality? (9) It is not a contradiction to say, that we are compelled by the Christian Verity to acknowledge every Person by Himself to be God and Lord; and yet are forbidden by the Catholic Religion to say, There be three Gods, or three Lords. (10)

To exhibit the philosophical value of this objection, we need only make a slight change in the language of the doctrine criticized. Instead of a plurality of persons in the Divine Unity, we have only to speak of a plurality of Attributes in the Divine Essence. How can there be a variety of Attributes, each infinite in its kind, and yet all together constituting but one Infinite? or how, on the other hand, can the Infinite be conceived as existing without diversity at all? We know, indeed, that various attributes exist in man constituting in their plurality one and the same conscious self. Even here, there is a mystery which we cannot explain; but the fact is one which we are compelled, by the direct testimony of consciousness, to accept without explanation. But in admitting, as we are compelled to do, the coëxistence of many attributes in one person, we can conceive those attributes only as distinct from each other, and as limiting each other. Each mental attribute is manifested as a separate and determinate mode of consciousness, marked off and limited, by the very fact of its manifestation as such. Each is developed in activities and operations from which the others are excluded. But this type of the conscious existence fails us altogether, when we attempt to transfer it to the region of the Infinite. That there can be but one Infinite, appears to be a necessary conclusion of reason; for diversity is itself a limitation: yet here we have many Infinites, each distinct from the other, yet all constituting one Infinite, which is neither identical with them nor distinguishable from them. If Reason, thus baffled, falls back on the conception of a simple Infinite Nature, composed of no attributes, her case is still more hopeless. That which has no attributes is nothing conceivable; for things are conceived by their attributes. Strip the Infinite of the Attributes by which it is distinguished as infinite, and the Finite of those by which it is distinguished as finite; and the residue is neither the Infinite as such, nor the Finite as such, nor any one being as distinguished from any other being. It is the vague and empty conception of Being in general, which is no being in particular, — a shape,

> "If Shape it might be called, that shape had none
> Distinguishable in member, joint, or limb,
> Or Substance might be called, that Shadow seemed,
> For each seemed either." (11)

The objection, "How can the One be Many, or the Many One?" is thus so far from telling with peculiar force against the Catholic doctrine of the Holy Trinity, that it has precisely the same power or want of power, and may be urged with precisely the same effect, or want of effect, against any conception, theological or philosophical, in which we may attempt to represent the Divine Nature and Attributes as infinite, or, indeed, to exhibit the Infinite at all. The same argument applies with equal force to the conception of the Absolute. If the Divine Nature is conceived as being nothing more than the sum of the Divine Attributes, it is not

Absolute; for the existence of the whole, will be dependent on the existence of its several parts. If, on the other hand, it is something distinct from the Attributes, and capable of existing without them, it becomes, in its absolute essence, an absolute void, — an existence manifested by no characteristic features, — a conception constituted by nothing conceivable. (12)

The same principle may be also applied to another portion of this great fundamental truth. The doctrine of the Son of God, begotten of the Father, and yet coëternal with the Father, is in nowise more or less comprehensible by human reason, than the relation between the Divine Essence and its Attributes. (13) In the order of Thought, or of Nature, the substance to which attributes belong has a logical priority to the attributes which exist in relation to it. The Attributes are attributes *of a Substance*. The former are conceived as the dependent and derived; the latter as the independent and original existence. Yet in the order of Time (and to the order of Time all human thought is limited), it is as impossible to conceive the Substance existing before its Attributes, as the Attributes before the Substance. (14) We cannot conceive a being originally simple, developing itself in the course of time into a complexity of attributes; for absolute simplicity cannot be conceived as containing within itself a principle of development, nor as differently related to different periods of time, so as to commence its development at any particular moment. (15) Nor yet can we conceive the attributes as existing prior to the substance; for the very conception of an attribute implies relation to a substance. Yet the third hypothesis, that of their coëxistence in all time, is equally incomprehensible; for this is to merge the Absolute and Infinite in an eternal relation and difference. We cannot conceive God as first existing, and then as creating His own attributes; for the creative power must then itself be created. Nor yet can we conceive the Divine Essence as constituted by the eternal coëxistence of attributes; for then we have many Infinites, with no bond of unity between them. The mystery of the Many and the One, which has baffled philosophy ever since philosophy began, meets it here, as everywhere, with its eternal riddle. Reason gains nothing by repudiating Revelation; for the mystery of Revelation is the mystery of Reason also.

I should not for an instant dream of adducing this metaphysical parallel as offering the slightest approach to a *proof* of the Christian doctrine of the Trinity in Unity. What it really illustrates is, not God's Nature, but man's ignorance. Without an Absolute Knowing there can be no comprehension of Absolute Being.(16) The position of human reason, with regard to the ideas of the Absolute and the Infinite, is such as equally to exclude the Dogmatism which would demonstrate Christian Doctrine from philosophical premises, and the Rationalism which rejects it on the ground of philosophical difficulties, as well as that monstrous combination of both, which distorts it in pretending to systematize it. The Infinite is known to human reason, merely as the negation of the Finite: we know what it is not; and that is all. The conviction, *that* an Infinite Being exists, seems forced upon us by the manifest incompleteness of our finite knowledge; but we have no rational means whatever of determining *what* is the nature of that Being.(17) The mind is thus perfectly blank with regard to any speculative representation of the Divine Essence; and for that very reason, Philosophy is not entitled, on internal evidence, to accept any, or to reject any. The only question which we are reasonably at liberty to ask in this matter, relates to the evidences of the Revelation as a fact. If there is sufficient evidence, on other grounds, to show that the Scripture, in which this doctrine is contained, is a Revelation from God, the doctrine itself must be unconditionally received, not as reasonable, nor as unreasonable, but as scriptural. If there is not such evidence, the doctrine itself will lack its proper support; but the Reason which rejects it is utterly incompetent to substitute any other representation in its place.

Let us pass on to the second great doctrine of the Catholic Faith, — that which asserts the union of two Natures in the Person of Christ. "The right Faith is, that we believe and confess, that our Lord Jesus Christ, the Son of God, is God and Man: God of the Substance of the Father, begotten before the worlds; and Man, of the Substance of His Mother, born in the world." (18)

Our former parallel was drawn from the impossibility of conceiving, in any form, a relation between the Infinite and the Infinite. Our present parallel may be found in the equal impossibility of conceiving, by the natural reason, a relation between the Infinite and the Finite; — an impossibility equally insurmountable, whether the two natures are conceived as existing in one Being, or in divers. Let us attempt, if we can, to conceive, at any moment of time, a finite world coming into existence by the fiat of an Infinite Creator. Can we conceive that the amount of existence is thereby increased, — that the Infinite and the Finite together contain more reality than formerly existed in the Infinite alone? The supposition annihilates itself; for it represents Infinite Existence as capable of becoming greater still. But, on the other hand, can we have recourse to the opposite alternative, and conceive the Creator as evolving the world out of His own Essence; the amount of Being remaining as before, yet the Infinite and the Finite both existing? This supposition also annihilates itself; for if the Infinite suffer diminution by that portion of it which becomes the Finite, it is infinite no longer; and if it suffers no diminution, the two together are but equal to the Infinite alone, and the Finite is reduced to absolute nonentity.[19] In any mode whatever of human thought, the coëxistence of the Infinite and the Finite is inconceivable; and yet the non-existence of either is, by the same laws of consciousness, equally inconceivable. If Reason is to be the supreme Judge of Divine Truths, it will not be sufficient to follow its guidance up to a certain point, and to stop when it is inconvenient to proceed further. There is no logical break in the chain of consequences, from Socinianism to Pantheism, and from Pantheism to Atheism, and from Atheism to Pyrrhonism; and Pyrrhonism is but the suicide of Reason itself. "Nature," says Pascal, "confounds the Pyrrhonists, and reason confounds the Dogmatists. What then becomes of man, if he seeks to discover his true condition by his natural reason? He cannot avoid one of these sects, and he cannot subsist in either."[20]

Let Religion begin where it will, it must begin with that which is above Reason. What then do we gain by that parsimony of belief, which strives to deal out the Infinite in infinitesimal fragments, and to erect the largest possible superstructure of deduction upon the smallest possible foundation of faith? We gain just this: that we forsake an incomprehensible doctrine, which rests upon the word of God, for one equally incomprehensible, which rests upon the word of man. Religion, to be a relation between God and man at all, must rest on a belief in the Infinite, and also on a belief in the Finite; for if we deny the first, there is no God; and if we deny the second, there is no Man. But the coëxistence of the Infinite and the

Finite, in any manner whatever, is inconceivable by reason; and the only ground that can be taken for accepting one representation of it rather than another, is that one is revealed, and another is not revealed. We may seek as we will for a "Religion within the limits of the bare Reason;" and we shall not find it; simply because no such thing exists; and if we dream for a moment that it does exist, it is only because we are unable or unwilling to pursue reason to its final consequences. But if we do not, others will; and the system which we have raised on the shifting basis of our arbitrary resting-place, waits only till the wind of controversy blows against it, and the flood of unbelief descends upon it, to manifest itself as the work of the "foolish man which built his house upon the sand."[1]

Having thus endeavored to exhibit the limits of human reason in relation to those doctrines of Holy Scripture which reveal to us the nature of God, I shall next attempt briefly to apply the same argument to those representations which more directly declare His relation to the world.

The course of Divine Providence, in the government of the world, is represented in Scripture under the twofold aspect of *General Law* and *Special Interposition.* Not only is God the Author of the universe, and of those regular laws by which the periodical recurrence of its natural phenomena is determined;[2] but He is also exhibited as standing in a special relation to mankind; as the direct cause of events by which their temporal or spiritual welfare is affected: as accessible to the prayers of His servants; as to be praised for His special mercies towards

[1] St. Matthew vii. 26.

[2] Genesis i. 14; viii. 22; Job xxxviii. xxxix; Psalm xix. 1—6; lxxiv. 17; civ. 5—31; cxxxv. 7; cxlviii. 6.

each of us in particular.[1] But this scriptural representation has been discovered by Philosophy to be irrational. God is unchangeable; and therefore He cannot be moved by man's entreaty. He is infinitely wise and good; and therefore He ought not to deviate from the perfection of His Eternal Counsels. "The religious man," says a writer of the present day, "who believes that all events, mental as well as physical, are preördered and arranged according to the decrees of infinite wisdom, and the philosopher, who knows that, by the wise and eternal laws of the universe, cause and effect are indissolubly chained together, and that one follows the other in inevitable succession, — equally feel that this ordination — this chain — cannot be changeable at the cry of man. . . . If the purposes of God were not wise, they would not be formed; — if wise, they cannot be changed, for then they would become unwise. . . . The devout philosopher, trained to the investigation of universal system, — the serene astronomer, fresh from the study of the changeless laws which govern innumerable worlds, — shrinks from the monstrous irrationality of asking the great Architect and Governor of all to work a miracle in his behalf, — to interfere, for the sake of *his* convenience or *his* plans, with the sublime order conceived by the Ancient of Days in the far Eternity of the Past; for what is a special providence but an interference with established laws? and what is such interference but a miracle?" (21)

Now here, as in the objections previously noticed, the rationalist mistakes a general difficulty of all human thought for a special difficulty of Christian belief. The really insoluble problem is, how to conceive God as acting at all; not how to conceive Him as acting in this way, rather

[1] Psalm lxv. 2; cii. 17, 18; ciii. 1, 3; cxliii. 1, 2; cxlv. 19.

than in that. The creation of the world at *any* period of time; — the establishment, at *any* moment, of immutable laws for the future government of that world; — this is the real mystery which reason is unable to fathom, this is the representation which seems to contradict our conceptions of the Divine Perfection. To that pretentious perversion of the finite which philosophy dignifies with the name of the Infinite, it is a contradiction to suppose that any change can take place at any moment; — that any thing can begin to exist, which was not from all eternity. To conceive the Infinite Creator, at any moment of time, calling into existence a finite world, is, in the human point of view, to suppose an imperfection, either before the act, or after it. It is to suppose the development of a power hitherto unexercised, or the limiting to a determinate act that which was before general and indeterminate.

May we not then repeat our author's objection in another form? How can a Being of Infinite Wisdom and Goodness, without an act of self-deterioration, change the laws which have governed His own solitary existence in the far Eternity when the world was not? Or rather, may we not ask what these very phrases of "changeless laws" and "far Eternity" really mean? Do they not represent God's existence as manifested under the conditions of duration and succession, — conditions which necessarily involve the conception of the imperfect and the finite? They have not emancipated the Deity from the law of Time: they have only placed Him in a different relation to it. They have merely substituted, for the revealed representation of the God who from time to time vouchsafes His aid to the needs of His creatures, the rationalizing representation of the God who, throughout all time, steadfastly refuses to do so. (22)

If, then, the condition of Time is inseparable from all human conceptions of the Divine Nature, what advantage do we gain, even in philosophy, by substituting the supposition of immutable order in time for that of special interposition in time? Both of these representations are doubtless *speculatively* imperfect: both depict the Infinite God under finite symbols. But for the *regulative* purposes of human conduct in this life, each is equally necessary: and who may dare, from the depths of his own ignorance, to say that each may not have its prototype in the ineffable Being of God? (23) We are sometimes told that it gives us a more elevated idea of the Divine Wisdom and Power, to regard the Creator as having finished His work once for all, and then abandoned it to its own unerring laws, than to represent Him as interfering, from time to time, by the way of direct personal superintendence;—just as it implies higher mechanical skill to make an engine which shall go on perpetually by its own motion, than one which requires to be continually regulated by the hand of its maker. (24) This ingenious simile fails only in the important particular, that both its terms are utterly unlike the objects which they profess to represent. The world is not a machine; and God is not a mechanic. The world is not a machine; for it consists, not merely of wheels of brass, and springs of steel, and the fixed properties of inanimate matter; but of living and intelligent and free-acting persons, capable of personal relations to a living and intelligent and free-acting Ruler. And God is not a mechanic; for the mechanic is separated from his machine by the whole diameter of being; as mind, giving birth to material results; as the conscious workman, who meets with no reciprocal consciousness in his work. It may be a higher evidence of mechanical skill, to abandon brute matter once for all to its own laws; but to take this as the analogy of God's dealings with His living creatures — as well tell us that the highest image of parental love and forethought is that of the ostrich, "which leaveth her eggs in the earth, and warmeth them in dust."[1] (25)

But if such conclusions are not justified by our *a priori* knowledge of the Divine nature, are they borne out empirically by the actual constitution of the world? Is there any truth in the assertion, so often put forth as an undeniable discovery of modern science, "that cause and effect are indissolubly chained together, and that one follows the other in inevitable succession?" There is just that amount of half-truth which makes an error dangerous; and there is no more. Experience is of two kinds, and Philosophy is of two kinds; — that of the world of matter, and that of the world of mind, — that of physical succession, and that of moral action. In the material world, if it be true that the researches of science *tend towards* (though who can say that they will ever reach?) the establishment of a system of fixed and orderly recurrence; in the mental world, we are no less confronted, at every instant, by the presence of contingency and free will. (26) In the one we are conscious of a chain of phenomenal effects; in the other of *self*, as an acting and originating cause. Nay, the very conception of the immutability of the law of cause and effect, is not so much derived from the positive evidence of the former, as from the negative evidence of the latter. We believe the succession to be necessary, because nothing but mind can be conceived as interfering with the successions of matter; and, where mind is excluded, we are unable to imagine contingence. (27) But what right has this so-called philosophy

[1] Job xxxix. 14.

to build a theory of the universe on material principles alone, and to neglect what experience daily and hourly forces upon our notice, — the perpetual interchange of the relations of matter and mind? In passing from the material to the moral world, we pass at once from the phenomenal to the real; from the successive to the continuous; from the many to the one; from an endless chain of mutual dependence to an originating and self-determining source of power. That mysterious, yet unquestionable presence of *Will;* — that agent, uncompelled, yet not uninfluenced, whose continuous existence and productive energy are summoned up in the word *Myself;* — that perpetual struggle of good with evil; — those warnings and promptings of a Spirit, striving with our spirit, commanding, yet not compelling; acting upon us, yet leaving us free to act for ourselves; — that twofold consciousness of infirmity and strength in the hour of temptation; — that grand ideal of what we ought to be, so little, alas! to be gathered from the observation of what we are; — that overwhelming conviction of Sin in the sight of One higher and holier than we; — that irresistible impulse to Prayer, which bids us pour out our sorrows and make our wants known to One who hears and will answer us; — that indefinable yet inextinguishable consciousness of a direct intercourse and communion of man with God, of God's influence upon man, yea, and (with reverence be it spoken) of man's influence upon God: — these are facts of experience, to the full as real and as certain as the laws of planetary motions and chemical affinities; — facts which Philosophy is bound to take into account, or to stand convicted as shallow and one-sided; — facts which can deceive us, only if our whole Consciousness is a liar, and the boasted voice of Reason itself but an echo of the universal lie.

Even within the domain of Physical Science, however much analogy may lead us to conjecture the universal prevalence of law and orderly sequence, it has been acutely remarked, that the phenomena which are most immediately important to the life and welfare of man, are precisely those which he never has been, and probably never will be, able to reduce to a scientific calculation. (28) The astronomer, who can predict the exact position of a planet in the heavens a thousand years hence, knows not what may be his own state of health to-morrow, nor how the wind which blows upon him will vary from day to day. May we not be permitted to conclude, with a distinguished Christian philosopher of the present day, that there is a Divine Purpose in this arrangement of nature; that, while enough is displayed to stimulate the intellectual and practical energies of man, enough is still concealed to make him feel his dependence upon God? (29)

For man's training in this life, the conceptions of General Law and of Special Providence are both equally necessary; the one, that he may labor for God's blessings, and the other, that he may pray for them. He sows, and reaps, and gathers in his produce, to meet the different seasons, as they roll their unchanging course: he acknowledges also that "neither is he that planteth anything, neither he that watereth; but God that giveth the increase."[1] He labors in the moral training of himself and others, in obedience to the general laws of means and ends, of motives and influences; while he asks, at the same time, for wisdom from above to guide his course aright, and for grace to enable him to follow that guidance. Necessary alike during this our state of trial, it may be that both conceptions alike are but shadows of

[1] 1 Corinthians iii. 7.

some higher truth, in which their apparent oppositions are merged in one harmonious whole. But when we attempt, from our limited point of view, to destroy the one, in order to establish the other more surely, we overlook the fact that our conception of General Law is to the full as human as that of Special Interposition; — that we are not really thereby acquiring a truer knowledge of the hidden things of God, but are measuring Him by a standard derived from the limited representations of man. (30)

Subordinate to the Conception of Special Providence, and subject to the same laws of thought in its application, is that of *Miraculous Agency*. I am not now going to waste an additional argument in answer to that shallowest and crudest of all the assumptions of unbelief, which dictatorially pronounces that Miracles are impossible; — an assumption which is repudiated by the more philosophical among the leaders of Rationalism itself; (31) and which implies, that he who maintains it has such a perfect and intimate acquaintance with the Divine Nature and Purposes, as to warrant him in asserting that God cannot or will not depart from the ordinary course of His Providence on any occasion whatever. If, as I have endeavored to show, the doctrine of Divine Interposition is not in itself more opposed to reason than that of General Law; and if the asserted immutability of the laws of nature is, at the utmost, tenable only on the supposition that material nature alone is spoken of, — we are not warranted, on any ground, whether of deduction from principles or of induction from experience, in denying the possible suspension of the Laws of Matter by the will of the Divine Mind. But the question on which it may still be desirable to say a few words, before concluding this portion of my argument, is one which is disputed, not necessarily between the believer and the unbeliever, but often between believers equally sincere and equally pious, differing only in their modes of representing to their own minds the facts and doctrines which both accept. Granting, that is to say, that variations from the established sequence of physical phenomena may take place, and have taken place, as Scripture bears witness; — are such variations to be represented as departures from or suspensions of natural law; or rather, as themselves the result of some higher law to us unknown, and as miraculous only from the point of view of our present ignorance? (32)

Which of these representations, or whether either of them, is the true one, when such occurrences are considered in their relation to the Absolute Nature of God, our ignorance of that Nature forbids us to determine. Speculatively, to human understanding, it appears as little consistent with the nature of the Absolute and Infinite, to be subject to universal law, as it is to act at particular moments. But as a regulative truth, adapted to the religious wants of man's constitution, the more natural representation, that of a departure from the general law, seems to be also the more accurate. We are liable, in considering this question, to confound together two distinct notions under the equivocal name of *Law*. The first is a positive notion, derived from the observation of facts, and founded, with various modifications, upon the general idea of the *periodical recurrence of phenomena*. The other is a merely negative notion, deduced from a supposed apprehension of the Divine Nature, and professing to be based on the idea of the eternal Purposes of God. Of the former, the ideas of *succession* and *repetition* form an essential part. To the latter, the idea of Time, in any form, has no legitimate application; and it is thus placed beyond the sphere of human thought. Now, when we speak of a Miracle as the possible result of some higher law, do we employ the term *law* in the former sense, or in the latter? do we mean, a law which actually exists in the knowledge of God; or one which, in the progress of science, may come to the knowledge of man? — one which might be discovered by a better acquaintance with the Divine Counsels, or one which might be inferred from a larger experience of natural phenomena? If we mean the former, we do not know that a more perfect acquaintance with the Divine Counsels, implying, as it does, the elevation of our faculties to a superhuman level, might not abolish the conception of Law altogether. If we mean the latter, we assume that which no experience warrants us in assuming; we endanger the religious significance and value of the miracle, only for the sake of removing God a few degrees further back from that chain of phenomena which is admitted ultimately to depend upon Him. A miracle, in one sense, need not be necessarily a violation of the laws of nature. God may make use of natural instruments, acting after their kind; as man himself, within his own sphere, does in the production of artificial combinations. The great question, however, still remains: Has God ever, for religious purposes, exhibited phenomena in certain relations, which the observed course of nature, and the artistic skill of man, are unable to bring about, or to account for?

I have thus far endeavored to apply the principle of the Limits of Religious Thought to some of these representations which are usually objected to by the Rationalist, as in apparent opposition to the Speculative Reason of Man. In my next Lecture, I shall attempt to pursue the same argument, in relation to those doctrines which are sometimes regarded as repugnant to man's Moral Reason. The lesson to be derived from our present inquiry may be given in the pregnant sentence of a great philosopher, but recently taken from us: "No difficulty emerges in Theology, which had not previously emerged in Philosophy." (33) The intellectual stumblingblocks, which men find in the doctrines of Revelation, are not in consequence of any improbability or error peculiar to the things revealed; but are such as the thinker brings with him to the examination of the question; —such as meet him on every side, whether he thinks with or against the testimony of Scripture; being inherent in the constitution and laws of the Human Mind itself. But must we therefore acquiesce in the melancholy conclusion, that self-contradiction is the law of our intellectual being;—that the light of Reason, which is God's gift, no less than Revelation, is a delusive light, which we follow to our own deception? Far from it: the examination of the Limits of Thought leads to a conclusion the very opposite to this. Reason does not deceive us, if we will only read her witness aright; and Reason herself gives us warning, when we are in danger of reading it wrong. The light that is within us is not darkness; only it cannot illuminate that which is beyond the sphere of its rays. The self-contradictions, into which we inevitably fall, when we attempt certain courses of speculation, are the beacons placed by the hand of God in the mind of man, to warn us that we are deviating from the track that He designs us to pursue; that we are striving to pass the barriers which He has planted around us. The flaming sword turns every way against those who strive, in the strength of their own reason, to force their passage to the tree of life. Within her own province, and among her own objects, let Reason go forth, conquering and to conquer. The finite objects, which she can clearly and distinctly conceive, are her lawful empire and her true glory. The countless phenomena of the visible world; the unseen things which lie in the depths of the human soul;—these are given into her hand; and over them she may reign in unquestioned dominion. But when she strives to approach too near to the hidden mysteries of the Infinite;—when, not content with beholding afar off the partial and relative manifestations of God's presence, she would "turn aside and see this great sight," and know why God hath revealed Himself thus;—the voice of the Lord Himself is heard, as it were, speaking in warning from the midst: "Draw not nigh hither: put off thy shoes from off thy feet; for the place whereon thou standest is holy ground."[1]

[1] Exodus iii. 5.

LECTURE VII.

YET YE SAY, THE WAY OF THE LORD IS NOT EQUAL. HEAR NOW, O HOUSE OF ISRAEL; IS NOT MY WAY EQUAL? ARE NOT YOUR WAYS UNEQUAL?—EZEKIEL XVIII. 25.

"IF I build again the things which I destroyed, I make myself a transgressor."[1] This text might be appropriately prefixed to an examination of that system of moral and religious criticism which, at the close of the last century, succeeded for a time in giving a philosophical connection to the hitherto loose and floating theological rationalism of its age and country. (1) It was indeed a marvellous attempt to send forth from the same fountain sweet waters and bitter, to pull down and to build up by the same act and method. The result of the Critical Philosophy, as applied to the speculative side of human Reason, was to prove beyond all question the existence of certain necessary forms and laws of Intuition and thought, which impart a corresponding character to all the objects of which Consciousness, intuitive or reflective, can take cognizance. Consciousness was thus exhibited as a Relation between the human mind and its object; and this conclusion, once established, is fatal to the very conception of a Philosophy of the Absolute. But by an inconsistency scarcely to be paralleled in the history of philosophy, the author of this comprehensive criticism attempted to deduce a partial conclusion from universal premises, and to

[1] Galatians ii. 18.

exempt the speculations of moral and religious thought from the relative character with which, upon his own principles, all the products of human consciousness were necessarily invested. The Moral Law, and the ideas which it carries with it, are, according to this theory, not merely facts of human consciousness, conceived under the laws of human thought, but absolute, transcendental realities, implied in the conception of all Reasonable Beings as such, and therefore independent of the law of time, and binding, not on man as man, but on all possible intelligent beings, created or uncreated. (2) The Moral Reason is thus a source of absolute and unchangeable realities; while the Speculative Reason is concerned only with phenomena, or things modified by the constitution of the human mind. (3) As a corollary to this theory, it follows, that the law of human morality must be regarded as the measure and adequate representative of the moral nature of God;—in fact, that our knowledge of the Divine Being is identical with that of our own moral duties;—for God is made known to us, as existing at all, only in and by the moral reason: we do not look upon actions as binding because they are commanded by God; but we know them to be divine commands because we are bound by them. (4) Applying these principles to the criticism of Revealed Religion, the philosopher maintains that no code of laws claiming divine authority can have any religious value, except as approved by the moral reason; (5) that there can be no duties of faith or practice towards God, distinct from the moral obligations which reason enjoins; (6) and that, consequently, every doctrine to which this test is inapplicable is either no part of revelation at all, or at best can only be given for local and temporary purposes, of which the enlightened reason need no longer take any account. (7)

Amid much that is true and noble in this teaching when confined within its proper limits, its fundamental weakness as an absolute criterion of religious truth is so manifest as hardly to need exposure. The fiction of a moral law binding in a particular form upon all possible intelligences, acquires this seeming universality, only because human intelligence is made the representative of all. I can conceive moral attributes only as I know them in consciousness: I can imagine other minds only by first assuming their likeness to my own. To construct a theory, whether of practical or of speculative reason, which shall be valid for other than human intelligences, it is necessary that the author should himself be emancipated from the conditions of human thought. Till this is done, the so-called Absolute is but the Relative under another name: the universal consciousness is but the human mind striving to transcend itself.

The very characteristics of Universality and Necessity, with which our moral obligations are invested, point to an origin the very reverse of that which the above theory supposes. For these characteristics are in all cases due to the presence of the formal and personal element in the phenomena of consciousness, and appear most evidently in those conceptions in which the matter as well as the manner of thinking is drawn from the laws or formal conditions of experience. Of these conditions, I have in a former Lecture enumerated three — Time, Space, and Personality; the first as the condition of human consciousness in general: the second and third as the conditions of the same consciousness in relation to the phenomena of matter and of mind respectively.(8) From these are derived three corresponding systems of *necessary truths* in the highest human sense of the term: the science of Numbers being connected with the condition of Time; that of Magnitudes with Space; and that of Morals with Personality. These three sciences rest on similar bases, and are confined within the same limits: all being equally necessary and valid within the legitimate bounds of human intelligence; and all equally negative and self-contradictory, when we attempt to pass beyond those bounds. The contradictions involved in the conceptions of Infinite Number and Infinite Magnitude find their parallel when we attempt to conceive the attributes of an Infinite Morality: the necessity which is manifested in the finite relations of the two former is the counterpart of that which accompanies those of the latter.[9] That Moral Obligation, conceived as a law binding upon man, must be regarded as immutable so long as man's nature remains unchanged, is manifest from the character of the conception itself, and follows naturally from a knowledge of its origin. An act of Duty is presented to my consciousness as enjoined by a Law whose obligation upon myself is directly and intuitively discerned. It thus differs essentially from the phenomena of external nature, whose laws are not immediately perceived, but inferred from the observed recurrence of facts. The immediate consciousness of Law unavoidably carries with it the conviction of necessity and immutability in relation to the agent who is subject to it. For to suppose that a moral law can be reversed or suspended in relation to *myself;* — to suppose a conviction of *right* unaccompanied by an obligation to act, or a conviction of *wrong* unaccompanied by an obligation to forbear, — is to suppose a reversal of the conditions of my personal existence; — a supposition which annihilates itself; since those conditions are implied in the attempt to conceive my personal existence at all. The Moral Sense is thus, like the intuitions of Time and Space, an *a priori* law of the human mind, not determined by experience as it is, but determining beforehand what experience ought to be. But it is not thereby elevated above the conditions of human intelligence; and the attempt so to elevate it is especially inadmissible in that philosophy which resolves Time and Space into forms of the human consciousness, and limits their operation to the field of the phenomena and the relative.

That there is an Absolute Morality, based upon, or rather identical with, the Eternal Nature of God, is indeed a conviction forced upon us by the same evidence as that on which we believe that God exists at all. But *what* that Absolute Morality is, we are as unable to fix in any human conception, as we are to define the other attributes of the same Divine Nature. To human conception it seems impossible that absolute morality should be manifested in the form of a *law of obligation;* for such a law implies relation and subjection to the authority of a lawgiver. And as all human morality is manifested in this form, the conclusion seems unavoidable, that human morality, even in its highest elevation, is not identical with, nor adequate to measure, the Absolute Morality of God. (10)

A like conclusion is forced upon us by a closer examination of human morality itself. To maintain the immutability of moral principles in the abstract is a very different thing from maintaining the immutability of the particular acts by which those principles are manifested in practice. The parallel between the mathematical and the moral sciences, as systems of necessary truth, holds good in this respect also. As principles in the abstract, the laws of morality are as unchangeable as the axioms of geometry. That duty ought in all cases to be followed in preference to inclination, is as certain a truth as that two straight lines cannot enclose a space. In their concrete application, both principles are equally liable to error; — we may err in supposing a particular visible line to be perfectly straight; as we may err in supposing a particular act to be one of duty. (11) But the two errors, though equally possible, are by no means equally important. For mathematical science, as such, is complete in its merely theoretical aspect; while moral science is valuable chiefly in its application to practice. It is in their concrete form that moral principles are adopted as guides of conduct and canons of judgment; and in this form they admit of various degrees of uncertainty or of positive error. But the difference between the highest and the lowest conception of moral duty is one of degree, not of kind; the interval between them is occupied by intermediate stages, separated from each other by minute and scarcely appreciable differences; and the very conception of a gradual progress in moral enlightenment implies the possibility of a further advance, of a more exalted intellect, and a more enlightened conscience. While we repudiate, as subversive of all morality, the theory which maintains that each man is the measure of his own moral acts; we must repudiate also, as subversive of all religion, the opposite theory, which virtually maintains that man may become the measure of the absolute Nature of God.

God did not *create* Absolute Morality: it is coëternal with Himself; and it were blasphemy to say that there ever was a time when God was and Goodness was not. But God did create the human manifestation of morality, when He created the moral constitution of man, and placed him in those circumstances by which the eternal principles of right and wrong are modified in relation to the present life. (12) For it is manifest, to take the simplest instances, that the sixth Commandment of the Decalogue, in its literal obligation, is relative to that state of things in which men are subject to death; and the seventh, to which there is marrying and giving in marriage; and the eighth, to that in which men possess temporal goods. It is manifest, to take a more general ground, that the very conception of moral obligation implies a superior authority, and an ability to transgress what that authority commands; that it implies a complex, and therefore a limited nature in the moral agent; the intellect, which apprehends the duty, being distinct from the will, which obeys or disobeys. That there is a higher and unchangeable principle embodied in these forms, we have abundant reason to believe; and yet we cannot, from our present point of view, examine the same duties apart from their human element, and separate that which is relative and peculiar to man in this life from that which is absolute and common to all moral beings. In this respect, again, our moral conceptions offer a remarkable analogy to the cognate phenomena on which other systems of necessary truth are based. Take, for example, the idea of Time, the foundation of the science of Number. We find no difficulty in conceiving that this present world was created at some definite point of time; but we are unable to conceive the same moment as the creation of Time itself. On the contrary, we are compelled to believe that there was a time before as well as after the creation of the world: that the being of God reaches back in boundless duration beyond the moment when He said, Let there be light; and there was light. But when we attempt to unite this conviction with another, necessary to the completion of the thought; — when we try to conceive God as an Infinite Being, existing in continuous duration, — the contradictions, which beset us on every side, admonish us that we have transcended the boundary within which alone human thought is possible. And so, too, while we are competent to believe that the creation of man's moral nature was not identical with the creation of morality itself; — that the great principles of all that is holy and righteous existed in God, before they assumed their finite form in the heart of man; — we still find ourselves baffled in every attempt to conceive an infinite moral nature, or its condition, an infinite personality: we find ourselves compelled to walk by faith, and not by sight; — to admit that we have knowledge enough to guide us in our moral training here; but not enough to unveil the hidden things of God.(13)

In so far, then, as Morality, in its human character, depends upon conditions not coëternal with God, but created along with man, in so far we are not justified in regarding the occasional suspension of human duties, by the same authority which enacted them, as a violation of the immutable principles of morality itself. That there are limits, indeed, within which alone this rule can be safely applied; — that there are doctrines and practices which carry on their front convincing proof that they cannot have been revealed or commanded by God; — that there are systems of religion which by this criterion may be shown to have sprung, not from divine appointment, but from human corruption, — is not for an instant denied. In my concluding Lecture, I shall endeavor to point out some of the conditions under which this kind of evidence is admissible. For the present, my argument is concerned, not with special and occasional commands, but with universal and perpetual doctrines; not with isolated facts recorded in sacred history, but with revealed truths, forming an integral portion of religious belief. In this point of view, I propose to apply the principle hitherto maintained, of the Limits of Religious Thought, to the examination of those doctrines of the Christian Faith which are sometimes regarded as containing something repugnant to the Moral Reason of man.

The Atoning Sacrifice of Christ has been the mark assailed by various attacks of this kind; some of them not very consistent with each other, but all founded on some supposed incongruity between this doctrine and the moral attributes of the Divine Nature. By one critic, the doctrine is rejected because it is more consistent with the infinite mercy of God to pardon sin freely, without any atonement whatsoever. (14) By another, because, from the unchangeable nature of God's laws, it is impossible that sin can be pardoned at all. (15) A third maintains that it is unjust that the innocent should suffer for the sins of the guilty. (16) A fourth is indignant at the supposition that God can be angry; (17) while a fifth cannot see by what moral fitness the shedding of blood can do away with sin or its punishment. (18) The principle which governs these and similar objections is, that we have a right to assume that there is, if not a perfect identity, at least an exact resemblance between the moral nature of man and that of God; that the laws and principles of infinite justice and mercy are but magnified images of those which are manifested on a finite scale; — that nothing can be compatible with the boundless goodness of God, which is incompatible with the little goodness of which man may be conscious in himself.

The value of this principle, as an absolute criterion of religious truth, may be tested by the simple experiment of applying the same reasoning to an imaginary revelation constructed on the rational principles of some one of the objectors. Let us suppose, then, that, instead of the Christian doctrine of the Atonement, the Scriptures had told us of an absolute and unconditional pardon of sin, following upon the mere repentance of the sinner. It is easy to imagine how ready our reasoning theologians would be with their philosophical criticism, speculative or moral. Does it not, they might say, represent man as influencing God, — the Finite as controlling, by the act of repentance, the unchangeable self-determinations of the Infinite? Does it not depict the Deity as acting in time, as influenced by motives and occasions, as subject to human feelings? Does it not tend to weaken our impression of the hatefulness of sin, and to encourage carelessness in the sinner, by the easy terms on which he is promised forgiveness? (19) If it is unworthy of God to represent Him as angry and needing to be propitiated, how can philosophy tolerate the conception that He is placable, and to be softened by repentance? And what moral fitness has repentance to do away with the guilt or punishment of a past transgression? Whatever moral fitness there exists between righteousness and God's favor, the same must exist between sin and God's anger: in whatever degree that which deserves punishment is not punished, in that degree God's justice is limited in its operation. A strictly moral theory requires, therefore, not free forgiveness, but an exactly graduated proportion between guilt and suffering, virtue and happiness. (20) If, on the other hand, we maintain that there is no moral fitness in either case, we virtually deny the existence of a moral Deity at all: we make God indifferent to good and evil as such: we represent Him as rewarding and punishing arbitrarily and with respect of persons. The moral objection, in truth, so far as it has any weight at all, has no special application to the Christian doctrine: it lies against the entire supposition of the remission of sins on any terms and by any means: and if it has been more strongly urged by Rationalists against the Christian representation than against others, this is merely because the former has had the misfortune to provoke hostility by being found in the Bible.

It is obvious indeed, on a moment's reflection, that the duty of man to forgive the trespasses of his neighbor, rests precisely upon those features of human nature which cannot by any analogy be regarded as representing an image of God.(21) Man is not the author of the moral law: he is not, as man, the moral governor of his fellows: he has no authority, merely as man, to punish moral transgressions as such. It is not as sin, but as injury, that vice is a transgression against man: it is not that his holiness is outraged, but that his rights or his interests are impaired. The duty of forgiveness is imposed as a check, not upon the justice, but upon the selfishness of man: it is not designed to extinguish his indignation against vice, but to restrain his tendency to exaggerate his own personal injuries.(22) The reasoner maintains, "it is a duty in man to forgive sins, therefore it must be morally fitting for God to forgive them also," overlooks the fact that this duty is binding upon man on account of the weakness and ignorance and sinfulness of his nature; that he is bound to forgive, as one who himself needs forgiveness; as one whose weakness renders him liable to suffering; as one whose self-love is ever ready to arouse his passions and pervert his judgment.

Nor yet would the advocates of the Moral Reason gain anything in Theology by the substitution of a rigid system of reward and punishment, in which nothing is forgiven, but every act meets with its appropriate recompense. We have only to suppose that this were the doctrine of Revelation, to imagine the outcry with which it would be assailed. "It is moral," the objector might urge, "only in the harsher and less amiable features of human morality: it gives us a God whom we may fear, but whom we cannot love;

who has given us affections with which He has no sympathy, and passions for whose consequences He allows no redress: who created man liable to fall, and placed him in a world of temptations, knowing that he would fall, and purposing to take advantage of his frailty to the utmost." Criticisms of this kind may be imagined without number; —nay, they are actually found in more than one modern work, the writers of which have erroneously imagined that they were assailing the real teaching of Scripture. (23) Verily, this vaunted Moral Reason is a "Lesbian rule." (24) It may be applied with equal facility to the criticism of every possible scheme of Divine Providence; and therefore we may be permitted to suspect that it is not entitled to implicit confidence against any. (25)

The endless controversy concerning Predestination and Free Will, whether viewed in its speculative or in its moral aspect, is but another example of the hardihood of human ignorance. The question, as I have observed before, has its philosophical as well as its theological aspect: it has no difficulties peculiar to itself: it is but a special form of the fundamental mystery of the coëxistence of the Infinite and the Finite. Yet, with this mystery meeting and baffling human reason at every turn, theologians have not scrupled to trace in their petty channels the exact flow and course of Infinite wisdom; one school boldly maintaining that even Omniscience itself has no knowledge of contingent events; another asserting, with equal confidence, that God's knowledge must be a restraint on man's freedom. (26) If philosophy offers for the moment an apparent escape from the dilemma, by suggesting that God's knowledge is not properly *foreknowledge*, as having no relation to time; (27) the suggestion itself is one which can neither be verified as a truth, nor even intelligibly exhibited as a thought; and the

Rationalist evades the solution by shifting the ground of attack, and retorts that Prophecy at least is anterior to the event which it foretells; and that a prediction of human actions is irreconcilable with freedom. (28) But the whole meaning of the difficulty vanishes, as soon as we acknowledge that the Infinite is not an object of human thought at all. There can be no consciousness of a relation, whether of agreement or of opposition, where there is not a consciousness of both the objects related. That a man, by his own power, should be able with certainty to foretell the future, implies that the laws of that future are fixed and unchangeable; for man can only foresee particular occurrences through a knowledge of the general law on which they depend. But is this relation of cause to effect, of law to its consequences, really a knowledge or an ignorance? Is the causal relation itself a law of things, or only a human mode of representing phenomena? Supposing it were possible for man, in some other state of intelligence, to foresee a future event without foreseeing it as the result of a law, — would that knowledge be a higher or a lower one than he at present possesses? — would it be the removal of some reality which he now sees, or only of some limitation under which he now sees it? (29) Man can only foresee what is certain; and from his point of view, the foreknowledge depends upon the certainty. But, apart from the human conditions of thought, in relation to a more perfect intelligence, can we venture to say, even as regards temporal succession, whether necessity is the condition of foreknowledge, or foreknowledge of necessity, or whether indeed necessity itself has any existence at all? (30) May not the whole scheme of Law and Determinism indicate a weakness, rather than a power of the human mind; and are there not facts of consciousness which give some support to this conjecture? (31) Can anything be *necessary* to an intellect whose thought creates its own objects? Can any necessity of things determine the cognitions of the Absolute Mind, even if those cognitions take place in succession to each other? These questions admit of no certain answer; but the very inability to answer them proves that dogmatic decisions on either side are the decisions of ignorance, not of knowledge.

But the problem, be its difficulties and their origin what they may, is not peculiar to Theology, and receives no additional complication from its position in Holy Writ. The very same question may be discussed in a purely metaphysical form, by merely substituting the universal law of causation for the universal knowledge of God. What is the meaning and value of that law of the human mind which apparently compels us to think that every event whatever has its determining cause? And how is that conviction reconcilable with a liberty in the human will to choose between two alternatives? The answer is substantially the same as before. The freedom of the will is a positive fact of our consciousness: as for the principle of causality, we know not whence it is, nor what it is. We know not whether it is a law of things, or a mode of human representation; whether it denotes an impotence or a power; whether it is innate or acquired. We know not in what the causal relation itself consists; nor by what authority we are warranted in extending its significance beyond the temporal sequence which suggests it and the material phenomena in which that sequence is undisturbed.

And is not the same conviction of the ignorance of man, and of his rashness in the midst of ignorance, forced upon us by the spectacle of the arbitrary and summary decisions of human reason on the most mysterious as well as the most awful of God's revealed judgments against sin, — the sentence of Eternal Punishment? We know not what is the relation of Sin to Infinite Justice. We know not under what conditions, consistently with the freedom of man, the final restoration of the impenitent sinner is possible; nor how, without such a restoration, guilt and misery can ever cease. We know not whether the future punishment of sin will be inflicted by way of natural consequence or of supernatural visitation; whether it will be produced from within or inflicted from without. We know not how man can be rescued from sin and suffering without the coöperation of his own will; nor what means can coöperate with that will, beyond those which are offered to all of us during our state of trial. (32) It becomes us to speak cautiously and reverently on a matter of which God has revealed so little, and that little of such awful moment; but if we may be permitted to criticize the arguments of the opponents of this doctrine with the same freedom with which they have criticized the ways of God, we may remark that the whole apparent force of the moral objection rests upon two purely gratuitous assumptions. It is assumed, in the first place, that God's punishment of sin in the world to come is so far analogous to man's administration of punishment in this world, that it will take place as a special infliction, not as a natural consequence. And it is assumed, in the second place, that punishment will be inflicted solely with reference to the sins committed during the earthly life; — that the guilt will continue finite, while the misery is prolonged to infinity. (33) Are we then so sure, it may be asked, that there can be no sin beyond the grave? Can any immortal soul incur God's wrath and condemnation, only so long as it is united to a mortal body? With as much reason might we assert that the angels are incapable of obedience to God, that the devils are incapable of rebellion. What if the sin perpetuates itself, — if the prolonged misery be the offspring of the prolonged guilt? (34)

Against this it is urged that sin cannot forever be triumphant against God. (35) As if the whole mystery of iniquity were contained in the words *for ever!* The real riddle of existence — the problem which confounds all philosophy, aye, and all religion too, so far as religion is a thing of man's reason — is the fact that evil exists *at all;* not that it exists for a longer or a shorter duration. Is not God infinitely wise and holy and powerful *now?* and does not sin exist along with that infinite holiness and wisdom and power? Is God to become more holy, more wise, more powerful hereafter; and must evil be annihilated to make room for His perfections to expand? Does the infinity of His eternal nature ebb and flow with every increase or diminution in the sum of human guilt and misery? Against this immovable barrier of the existence of evil, the waves of philosophy have dashed themselves unceasingly since the birthday of human thought, and have retired broken and powerless, without displacing the minutest fragment of the stubborn rock, without softening one feature of its dark and rugged surface. (36) We may be told that evil is a privation, or a negation, or a partial aspect of the universal good, or some other equally unmeaning abstraction; whilst all the while our own hearts bear testimony to its fearful reality, to its direct antagonism to every possible form of good. (37) But this mystery, vast and inscrutable as it is, is but one aspect of a more general problem; it is but the moral form of the ever-recurring secret of the Infinite. How the Infinite and the Finite, in any form of antagonism or other relation, can exist together; how infinite power can coëxist with finite activity; how infinite wisdom can coëxist with finite contingency; how infinite goodness can coëxist with finite evil; how the Infinite can exist in any manner without exhausting the universe of reality; — this is the riddle which Infinite Wisdom alone can solve, the problem whose very conception belongs only to that Universal Knowing which fills and embraces the Universe of Being. When philosophy can answer this question; when she can even state intelligibly the notions which its terms involve, — then, and not till then, she may be entitled to demand a solution of the far smaller difficulties which she finds in revealed religion; — or rather, she will have solved them already; for from this they all proceed, and to this they all ultimately return.

The reflections which this great and terrible mystery of Divine Judgment have suggested, receive perhaps some further support when we contemplate it in another aspect, and one more legitimately within the province of human reason; that is to say, in its analogy to the actual constitution and course of nature. "The Divine moral government which religion teaches us," says Bishop Butler, "implies that the consequence of vice shall be misery, in some future state, by the righteous judgment of God. That such consequent punishment shall take effect by His appointment, is necessarily implied. But, as it is not in any sort to be supposed that we are made acquainted with all the ends or reasons, for which it is fit future punishment should be inflicted, or why God has appointed such and such consequent misery should follow vice; and as we are altogether in the dark, how or in what manner it shall follow, by what immediate occasions, or by the instrumentality of what means, — there is no absurdity in supposing it may follow in a way analogous to that in which many miseries follow such and such courses of action at present: poverty, sickness, infamy, untimely death from diseases, death from the hands of civil justice. There is no absurdity in supposing future punishment may follow wickedness of course, as we speak, or in the way of natural consequence from God's original constitution of the world; from the nature He has given us, and from the condition in which He places us; or in a like manner as a person rashly trifling upon a precipice, in the way of natural consequence, falls down; in the way of natural consequence, breaks his limbs, suppose; in the way of natural consequence of this, without help perishes." (38)

And if we may be permitted to extend the same analogy from the constitution of external nature to that of the human mind, may we not trace something not wholly unlike the irrevocable sentence of the future, in that dark and fearful, yet too certain law of our nature, by which sin and misery ever tend to perpetuate themselves; by which evil habits gather strength with every fresh indulgence, till it is no longer, humanly speaking, in the power of the sinner to shake off the burden which his own deeds have laid upon him? In that mysterious condition of the depraved will, compelled, and yet free, — the slave of sinful habit, yet responsible for every act of sin, and gathering deeper condemnation as the power of amendment grows less and less, — may we not see some possible foreshadowing of the yet deeper guilt and the yet more hopeless misery of the worm that dieth not, and the fire that is not quenched? The fact, awful as it is, is one to which our every day's experience bears witness: and who shall say that the invisible things of God may not, in this as in other instances, be shadowed forth to us in the things that are seen?

The same argument from analogy is indeed applicable to every one of the difficulties which Rationalism professes to discover in the revealed ways of God's dealings with man. The Fall of Adam, and the inherited corruption of his posterity, find their parallel in the liability to sin which remains unextinguished throughout man's moral progress; and in that mysterious, though certain dispensation of Providence, which ordains that not only bodily taints and infirmities, but even moral dispositions and tendencies should, in many instances, descend from father to son; and which permits the child of sinful parents to be depraved by evil example, before he knows how, by his own reason, clearly to discern between right and wrong; before he has strength, of his own will, to refuse the evil and choose the good (39) There is a parallel, too, in that strange, yet too familiar fact, of vice persisted in, with the clearest and strongest conviction of its viciousness and wretchedness; and the skepticism which denies that man, if created sinless, could so easily have fallen from innocence, finds its philosophical counterpart in the paradox of the ancient moralist, who maintained that conscious sin is impossible, because nothing can be stronger than knowledge. (40) Justification by faith through the merits of Christ is at least in harmony with that course of things established by Divine Providence in this world; in which so many benefits, which we cannot procure for ourselves or deserve by any merit of our own, are obtained for us by the instrumentality of others; and in which we are so often compelled, as an indispensable condition of obtaining the benefit, to trust in the power and good-will of those whom we have never tried, and to believe in the efficacy of means whose manner of working we know not. (41) The operations of Divine Grace, influencing, yet not necessitating, the movements of the human soul, find their corresponding fact and their corresponding mystery in the determinations of the Will;—in that Freedom to do or leave undone, so certain in fact, so inexplicable in theory, which consists neither in absolute indifference nor in absolute subjection; which is acted upon and influenced by motives, yet in its turn acts upon and controls their influences, prevented by them, and yet working with them. (42) But it is unnecessary to pursue further an argument which, in all its essential features, has already been fully exhibited by a philosopher whose profound and searching wisdom has answered by anticipation nearly every cavil of the latest form of Rationalism, no less than those of his own day. We may add here and there a detail of application, as the exigencies of controversy may suggest; but the principle of the whole, and its most important consequences, have been established and worked out more than a century ago, in the unanswerable argument of Butler.

The warning which his great work contains against "that idle and not very innocent employment of forming imaginary models of a world, and schemes of governing it," (43) is as necessary now as then, as applicable to moral as to speculative theories. Neither with regard to the physical nor to the moral world, is man capable of constructing a Cosmogony; and those Babels of Reason, which Philosophy has built for itself, under the names of Rational Theories of Religion, and Criticisms of every Revelation, are but the successors of those elder children of chaos and night, which, with no greater knowledge, but with less presumption, sought to describe the generation of the visible universe. It is no disparagement of the value and authority of the Moral Reason in its regulative capacity, within its proper sphere of human action, if we refuse to exalt it to the measure and standard of the Absolute and Infinite Goodness of God. The very Philosopher whose writings have most contributed to establish the supreme authority of Conscience in man, is also the one who has pointed out most clearly the existence of analogous moral difficulties in nature and in religion, and the true answer to both, — the admission that God's Government, natural as well as spiritual, is a scheme imperfectly comprehended.

In His Moral Attributes, no less than in the rest of His Infinite Being, God's judgments are unsearchable, and His ways past finding out.[1] While He manifests Himself clearly as a Moral Governor and Legislator, by the witness of the Moral Law which He has established in the hearts of men, we cannot help feeling, at the same time, that that Law, grand as it is, is no measure of His Grandeur, that He Himself is beyond it, though not opposed to it, distinct, though not alien from it. We feel that He who planted in man's conscience that stern, unyielding Imperative of Duty, must Himself be true and righteous altogether; that He from whom all holy desires, all good counsels, and all just works do proceed, must Himself be more holy, more good, more just than these. But when we try to realize in thought this sure conviction of our faith, we find that here, as everywhere, the Finite cannot fathom the Infinite; that, while in our hearts we believe, yet our thoughts at times are sore troubled. It is consonant to the whole analogy of our earthly state of trial, that, in this as in other features of God's Providence, we should meet with things impossible to understand and difficult to believe; by which reason is baffled and faith tried; — acts whose purpose we see not; dispensations whose wisdom is

[1] Romans xi. 33.

above us; thoughts which are not our thoughts, and ways which are not our ways. In these things we hear, as it were, the same loving voice which spoke to the wondering disciple of old: "What I do, thou knowest not now; but thou shalt know hereafter."[1] The luminary by whose influence the ebb and flow of man's moral being is regulated, moves around and along with man's little world, in a regular and bounded orbit; one side, and one side only, looks downward upon its earthly centre; the other, which we see not, is ever turned upwards to the all-surrounding Infinite. And those tides have their seasons of rise and fall, their places of strength and weakness; and that light waxes and wanes with the growth or decay of man's mental and moral and religious culture; and its borrowed rays seem at times to shine as with their own lustre, in rivalry, even in opposition, to the source from which they emanate. Yet is that light still but a faint and partial reflection of the hidden glories of the Sun of Righteousness, waiting but the brighter illumination of His presence, to fade and be swallowed up in the full blaze of the heaven kindling around it; — not cast down indeed from its orbit, nor shorn of its true brightness and influence, but still felt and acknowledged in its real existence and power, in the memory of the past discipline, in the product of the present perfectness, though now distinct no more, but vanishing from sight to be made one with the Glory that beams from the "Father of lights, with whom is no variableness, neither shadow of turning."[2]

[1] St. John xiii. 7. [2] St. James i. 17.

LECTURE VIII.

THE WORKS WHICH THE FATHER HATH GIVEN ME TO FINISH, THE SAME WORKS THAT I DO, BEAR WITNESS OF ME, THAT THE FATHER HATH SENT ME. — ST. JOHN V. 36.

To construct a complete Criticism of any Revelation, it is necessary that the Critic should be in possession of a perfect Philosophy of the Infinite. For, except on the supposition that we possess an exact knowledge of the whole Nature of God, such as only that Philosophy can furnish, we cannot know for certain what are the purposes which God intends to accomplish by means of Revelation, and what are the instruments by which those purposes may be best carried out. If then it can be shown, as I have attempted to show in the previous Lectures, that the attainment of a Philosophy of the Infinite is utterly impossible under the existing laws of human thought, it follows that it is not by means of philosophical criticism that the claims of a supposed Revelation can be adequately tested. We are thus compelled to seek another field for the right use of Reason in religious questions; and what that field is, it will not be difficult to determine. To Reason, rightly employed, within its proper limits and on its proper objects, our Lord himself and his Apostles openly appealed in proof of their divine mission; and the same proof has been unhesitatingly claimed by the defenders of Christianity in all subsequent ages. In other words, the legitimate object of a rational criticism of revealed religion, is not to be found in the *contents* of that religion, but in its *evidences*.

At first sight it may appear as if this distinction involved no real difference; for the contents of a revelation, it might be objected, are included among its evidences. In one sense, no doubt they are; but that very inclusion gives them a totally different significance and weight from that to which they lay claim when considered as the basis of a philosophical criticism. In the one case, they are judged by their conformity to the supposed nature and purposes of God; in the other, by their adaptation to the actual circumstances and wants of man. In the one case they are regarded as furnishing a single and a certain criterion; for on the supposition that our reason is competent to determine, from our knowledge of the Divine Nature, what the characteristics of a true Revelation ought to be, we are entitled, by virtue of that criterion alone, to reject without hesitation whatever does not satisfy its requirements. In the other case, they are regarded as furnishing only one probable presumption out of many; — a presumption which may confirm and be confirmed by coinciding testimony from other sources, or, on the contrary, may be outweighed, when we come to balance probabilities, by conflicting evidence on the other side.

The practical conclusion, which may be deduced from the whole previous survey of the Limits of Religious Thought, is this: that if no one faculty of the human mind is competent to convey a direct knowledge of the Absolute and the Infinite, no one faculty is entitled to claim preëminence over the rest, as furnishing especially *the criterion* of the truth or falsehood of a supposed Revelation. There are presumptions to be drawn from the internal character of the doctrines which the revelation contains: there are presumptions to be drawn from the facts connected with its first promulgation: there are presumptions to be drawn from its subsequent history and the effects which it has produced among mankind. But the true evidence, for or against the religion, is not to be found in any one of these taken singly and exclusively; but in the resultant of all, fairly examined and compared together; the apparently conflicting evidences being balanced against each other, and the apparently concurring evidences estimated by their united efficacy.

A truth so obvious as this may be thought hardly worth announcing as the result of an elaborate inquiry. But the whole history of religious controversy bears witness that, however evident in theory, there is no truth more liable to be neglected in practice. The defenders of Christianity are not altogether free from the charge of insisting exclusively or preëminently upon some one alone of its evidences: the assailants, under the influence of a still more exclusive reäction, have assumed that a method which fails to accomplish everything has succeeded in accomplishing nothing; and, flying at once to the opposite extreme, have in their turn appealed to some one infallible criterion, as constituting a royal road to philosophical unbelief.

In the present day we are feeling the pernicious effects of a reäction of this kind. Because the writings of Paley and his followers in the last generation laid a principal stress on the direct historical evidences of Christianity, we meet now with an antagonist school of writers, who perpetually assure us that history has nothing whatever to do with religion; (1) that an external revelation of religious truth is impossible; (2) that we may learn all that is essential to the Gospel by inward and spiritual evidence only. (3) In the spirit of the Pharisees of old, who said, "This man is not of God, because he keepeth not the Sabbath day,"[1] we are now told that the doctrine must in all cases prove the miracles, and not the miracles the doctrine; (4) that the external evidence of miracles is entirely useless for the support of the religious philosophy of Christ; (5) that man no more needs a miraculous revelation of things pertaining to religion than of things pertaining to agriculture or manufactures. (6) And, as is usually the case in such reäctions, the last state has become worse than the first; — a slight comparative neglect of the internal evidence on the one side has been replaced by an utter repudiation of all external evidence on the other; a trifling disproportion in the edifice of the Christian Faith has been remedied by the entire removal of some of its main pillars of support. The crying evil of the present day in religious controversy is the neglect or contempt of the external evidences of Christianity: the first step towards the establishment of a sound religious philosophy must consist in the restoration of those evidences to their true place in the Theological system.

The evidence derived from the internal character of a religion, whatever may be its value within its proper limits, is, as regards the divine origin of the religion, purely negative. It may prove in certain cases (though even here the argument requires much caution in its employment) that a religion *has not* come from God; but it is in no case sufficient to prove that it *has* come from Him. (7) For the doctrines revealed must either be such as are within the power of man's natural reason to verify, or such as are beyond it. In the former case, the reason which is competent to verify may also be competent to discover: the doctrine is tested by its conformity to the conclusions of

[1] St. John ix. 16.

human philosophy; and the wisdom which sits in judgment on the truth of a doctrine must itself be presumed to have an equal power of discerning the truth. In the latter case, where the doctrine is beyond the power of human reason to discover, it can be accepted only as resting on the authority of the teacher who proclaims it; and that authority itself must then be guaranteed by the external evidence of a superhuman mission. To advance a step beyond the merely negative argument, it is necessary that the evidence contained in the character of the doctrine itself should be combined with that derived from the exterior history. When, for example, the Divine Origin of Christianity is maintained, on the ground of its vast moral superiority to all Heathen systems of Ethics; or on that of the improbability that such a system could have been conceived by a Galilean peasant among the influences of the contemporary Judaism; the argument is legitimate and powerful: but its positive force depends not merely on the internal character of the doctrine, but principally on its relation to certain external facts.(8)

And even the negative argument, which concludes from the character of the contents of a religion that it *cannot* have come from God, however legitimate within its proper limits, is one which requires considerable caution in the application. The lesson to be learnt from an examination of the Limits of Religious Thought, is not that man's judgments are *worthless* in relation to divine things, but that they are *fallible;* and the probability of error in any particular case can never be fairly estimated, without giving their full weight to all collateral considerations. We are indeed bound to believe that a Revelation given by God can never contain anything that is really unwise or unrighteous; but we are not always capable of estimating exactly the wisdom or righteousness of particular doctrines or precepts. And we are bound to bear in mind that *exactly in proportion to the strength of the remaining evidence for the divine origin of a religion, is the probability that we may be mistaken in supposing this or that portion of its contents to be unworthy of God.* Taken in conjunction, the two arguments may confirm or correct each other: taken singly and absolutely, each may vitiate the result which should follow from their joint application. We do not certainly know the exact nature and operation of the moral attributes of God; we can but infer and conjecture from what we know of the moral attributes of man: and the analogy between the Finite and the Infinite can never be so perfect as to preclude all possibility of error in the process. But the possibility becomes almost a certainty, when any one human faculty is elevated by itself into an authoritative criterion of religious truth, without regard to those collateral evidences by which its decisions may be modified and corrected.

"The human mind," says a writer of the present day, "is competent to sit in *moral* and *spiritual* judgment on a professed revelation; and to decide, if the case seems to require it, in the following tone: This doctrine attributes to God, that which we should all call harsh, cruel, or unjust in man: it is therefore intrinsically inadmissible." ... "In fact," he continues, "all Christian apostles and missionaries, like the Hebrew prophets, have always refuted Paganism by direct attacks on its immoral and unspiritual doctrines; and have appealed to the consciences of heathens, as competent to decide in the controversy." (9) Now, an appeal of this kind may be legitimate or not, according to the purpose for which it is made, and the manner in which it is applied. The primary and proper employment of man's moral sense, as of his other faculties, is not *speculative*, but *regulative*. It is not designed to tell us what are the absolute and immutable principles of Right, as existing in the eternal nature of God; but to discern those relative and temporary manifestations of them, which are necessary for human training in this present life. But if morality, in its human manifestation, contains a relative and temporary, as well as an absolute and eternal element, an occasional suspension of the human Law is by no means to be confounded with a violation of the divine Principle. We can only partially judge of the Moral government of God, on the assumption that there is an analogy between the divine nature and the human: and in proportion as the analogy recedes from perfect likeness, the decisions of the human reason necessarily become more and more doubtful. The primary and direct inquiry, which human reason is entitled to make concerning a professed revelation is, — how far does it tend to promote or to hinder the moral discipline of man. It is but a secondary and indirect question, and one very liable to mislead, to ask how far it is compatible with the Infinite Goodness of God.

Thus, for example, it is one thing to condemn a religion on account of the habitual observance of licentious or inhuman rites of worship, and another to pronounce judgment on isolated acts, historically recorded as having been done by divine command, but not perpetuated in precepts for the imitation of posterity. The former are condemned for their regulative character, as contributing to the perpetual corruption of mankind; the latter are condemned on speculative grounds, as inconsistent with our preconceived notions of the character of God. "There are some particular precepts in Scripture," says Bishop Butler, "given to particular persons, requiring actions, which would be immoral and vicious, were it not for such precepts. But it is easy to see, that all these are of such a kind, as that the precept changes the whole nature of the case and of the action; and both constitutes and shows that not to be unjust or immoral, which, prior to the precept, must have appeared, and really have been so: which may well be, since none of these precepts are contrary to immutable morality. If it were commanded to cultivate the principles and act from the spirit of treachery, ingratitude, cruelty; the command would not alter the nature of the case or of the action, in any of these instances. But it is quite otherwise in precepts which require only the doing an external action; for instance, taking away the property or life of any. For men have no right to either life or property, but what arises solely from the grant of God: when this grant is revoked, they cease to have any right at all in either: and when this revocation is made known, as surely it is possible it may be, it must cease to be unjust to deprive them of either. And though a course of external acts, which without command would be immoral, must make an immoral habit; yet a few detached commands have no such natural tendency. . . . There seems no difficulty at all in these precepts, but what arises from their being offences: *i. e.* from their being liable to be perverted, as indeed they are, by wicked designing men, to serve the most horrid purposes; and, perhaps, to mislead the weak and enthusiastic. And objections from this head are not objections against revelation; but against the whole notion of religion, as a trial; and against the general constitution of nature." (10)

There is indeed an obvious analogy between these temporary suspensions of the laws of moral obligation and that corresponding suspension of the laws of natural phenomena which constitutes our ordinary conception of a Miracle. So much so, indeed, that the former might without impropriety be designated as *Moral Miracles.* In both, the Almighty is regarded as suspending, for special purposes, not the eternal laws which constitute His own absolute Nature, but the created laws, which he imposed at a certain time upon a particular portion of his creatures. Both are isolated and rare in their occurrence; and apparently, from the nature of the case, must be so, in order to unite harmoniously with the normal manifestations of God's government of the world. A perpetual series of physical miracles would destroy that confidence in the regularity of the course of nature, which is indispensable to the cultivation of man's intellectual and productive energies: a permanent suspension of practical duties would be similarly prejudicial to the cultivation of his moral character. But the isolated character of both classes of phenomena removes the objection which might otherwise be brought against them on this account: and this objection is the only one which can legitimately be urged, on philosophical grounds, against the *conception* of such cases as *possible;* as distinguished from the historical evidence, which may be adduced for or against their *actual occurrence.*

Even within its own legitimate province, an argument of this kind may have more or less weight, varying from the lowest presumption to the highest moral certainty, according to the nature of the offence which we believe ourselves to have detected, and the means which we possess of estimating its character or consequences. It is certain that we are not competent judges of the Absolute Nature of God: it is not certain that we are competent judges, in all cases, of what is best fitted for the moral discipline of man. But granting to the above argument its full value in this relation, it is still important to remember that we are dealing, not with demonstrative but with probable evidence; not with a single line of reasoning, but with a common focus, to which many and various rays converge; that we have not solved the entire problem, but only obtained one of the elements contributing to its solution. And the combined result of all these elements is by no means identical with the sum of their separate effects. The image, hitherto employed, of a balance of probabilities, is, in one respect at least, very inadequate to express the character of Christian evidence. It may be used with some propriety to express the provisional stage of the inquiry, while we are still uncertain to which side the evidence inclines; but it becomes inapplicable as soon as our decision is made. For the objections urged against a religion are not like the weights in a scale, which retain their full value, even when outweighed on the other side; — on the contrary, they become absolutely worthless, as soon as we are convinced that there is superior evidence to prove that the religion is true. We may not say, for example, that certain parts of the Christian scheme are unwise or unrighteous, though outweighed by greater acts of righteousness and wisdom; — we are bound to believe that we were mistaken from the first in supposing them to be unwise or unrighteous at all. In a matter of which we are so ignorant and so liable to be deceived, the objection which fails to prove everything proves nothing: from him that hath not, is taken away even that which he seemeth to have. And on the other hand, the objection which really proves anything proves everything. If the teaching of Christ is in any one thing not the teaching of God, it is in all things the teaching of man: its doctrines are subject to all the imperfections inseparable from man's sinfulness and ignorance: its effects must be such as can fully be accounted for as the results of man's wisdom, with all its weakness and all its error.

Here then is the issue, which the wavering disciple is bound seriously to consider. Taking into account the various questions whose answers, on the one side or the other, form the sum total of Evidences for or against the claims of the Christian Faith; — the genuineness and authenticity of the documents; the judgment and good faith of the writers; the testimony to the actual occurrence of prophecies and miracles, and their relation to the religious teaching with which they are connected; the character of the Teacher Himself, that one protrait, which, in its perfect purity and holiness and beauty, stands alone and unapproached in human history or human fiction; those rites and ceremonies of the elder Law, so significant as typical of Christ, so strange and meaningless without Him; those predictions of the promised Messiah, whose obvious meaning is rendered still more manifest by the futile ingenuity which strives to pervert them;(11) the history of the rise and progress of Christianity, and its comparison with that of other religions; the ability or inability of human means to bring about the results which it actually accomplished; its antagonism to the current ideas of the age and country of its origin; its effects as a system on the moral and social condition of subsequent generations of mankind; its fitness to satisfy the wants and console the sufferings of human nature; the character of those by whom it was first promulgated and received; the sufferings which attested the sincerity of their convictions; the comparative trustworthiness of ancient testimony and modern conjecture; the mutual contradictions of conflicting theories of unbelief, and the inadequacy of all of them to explain the facts for which they are bound to account; —

taking all these and similar questions into full consideration, are you prepared to affirm, as the result of the whole inquiry, that Jesus of Nazareth was an impostor, or an enthusiast, or a mythical figment; and his disciples crafty and designing, or well-meaning, but deluded men? For be assured, that nothing short of this is the conclusion which you must maintain, if you reject one jot or one tittle of the whole doctrine of Christ. Either He was what He proclaimed Himself to be, — the incarnate Son of God, the Divine Saviour of a fallen world — and if so, we may not divide God's Revelation, and dare to put asunder what He has joined together, — or the civilized world for eighteen centuries has been deluded by a cunningly devised fable; and He from whom that fable came has turned that world from darkness to light, from Satan to God, with a lie in His right hand.

Many who would shrink with horror from the idea of rejecting Christ altogether, will yet speak and act as if they were at liberty to set up for themselves an eclectic Christianity; separating the essential from the superfluous portions of Christ's teaching; deciding for themselves how much is permanent and necessary for all men, and how much is temporary and designed only for a particular age and people. (12) Yet if Christ is indeed God manifest in the flesh, it is surely scarcely less impious to attempt to improve His teaching, than to reject it altogether. Nay, in one respect it is more so; for it is to acknowledge a doctrine as the revelation of God, and at the same time to proclaim that it is inferior to the wisdom of man. That it may indeed come, and has come, within the purposes of God's Providence, to give to mankind a Revelation partly at least designed for a temporary purpose, and for a limited portion of mankind; — a Law in which something was permitted to the hardness of men's hearts,[1] and much was designed but as a shadow of things to come;[2]—this we know, to whom a more perfect Revelation has been given. But to admit that God may make His own Revelation more perfect from time to time, is very different from admitting that human reason, by its own knowledge, is competent to separate the perfect from the imperfect, and to construct for itself an absolute religion out of the fragments of an incomplete Revelation. The experiment has been tried under the elder and less perfect dispensation; but the result can hardly be considered so successful as to encourage a repetition of the attempt. The philosophical improvement of the Hebrew Scriptures produced, not the Sermon on the Mount, but the Creed of the Sadducee. The ripened intelligence of the Jewish people, instructed, as modern critics would assure us, by the enlightening influence of time, and by intercourse with foreign nations, bore fruit in a conclusion singularly coinciding with that of modern rationalism: "The Sadducees say that there is no resurrection, neither angel, nor spirit."[3] (13) And doubtless there were many then, as now, to applaud this wonderful discovery, as a proof that "religious truth is necessarily progressive, because our powers are progressive;" (14) and to find a mythical or critical theory, to explain or to set aside those passages of Scripture which appeared to inculcate a contrary doctrine. Unfortunately for human wisdom, Prometheus himself needs a Prometheus. The lapse of time, as all history bears witness, is at least as fruitful in corruption as in enlightenment; and reason, when it has done its best, still needs a higher reason to decide between its conflicting theories, and to tell us which is the advanced, which the retrograde Theology. (15)

1 St. Matthew xix. 8. 2 Hebrews x. 1. 3 Acts xxiii. 8.

In one respect, indeed, this semi-rationalism, which admits the authority of Revelation up to a certain point and no further, rests on a far less reasonable basis than the firm belief which accepts the whole, or the complete unbelief which accepts nothing. For whatever may be the antecedent improbability which attaches to a miraculous narrative, as compared with one of ordinary events, it can affect only the narrative taken as a whole, and the entire series of miracles from the greatest to the least. If a single miracle is once admitted as supported by competent evidence, the entire history is at once removed from the ordinary calculations of more or less probability. One miracle is sufficient to show that the series of events, with which it is connected, is one which the Almighty has seen fit to mark by exceptions to the ordinary course of His Providence: and this being once granted, we have no *a priori* grounds to warrant us in asserting that the number of such exceptions ought to be larger or smaller. If any one miracle recorded in the Gospels — the Resurrection of Christ, for example — be once admitted as true, the remainder cease to have any antecedent improbability at all, and require no greater evidence to prove them than is needed for the most ordinary events of any other history. For the improbability, such as it is, reaches no further than to show that it is unlikely that God should work miracles at all; not that it is unlikely that He should work more than a certain number.

Our right to criticize at all depends upon this one question: "What think ye of Christ? whose Son is He?"[1] What is it that constitutes our need of Christ? Is it a conviction of guilt and wretchedness, or a taste for Philosophy? Do we want a Redeemer to save us from our sins,

[1] St. Matthew xxii. 42.

or a moral Teacher to give us a plausible theory of human duties? Christ can be our Redeemer only if He is what He proclaims himself to be, the Son of God, sent into the world, that the world through Him might be saved.[1] If He is not this, His moral teaching began with falsehood, and was propagated by delusion. And if He is this, what but contempt and insult can be found in that half-allegiance which criticizes while it bows; which sifts and selects while it submits; which approves or rejects as its reason or its feelings or its nervous sensibilities may dictate; which condescends to acknowledge Him as the teacher of a dark age and an ignorant people; bowing the knee before Him, half in reverence, half in mockery, and crying, "Hail, King of the Jews!" If Christ is a mere human teacher, we of this nineteenth century can no more be Christians than we can be Platonists or Aristotelians. He belongs to that past which cannot repeat itself; His modes of thought are not ours; His difficulties are not ours; His needs are not ours. He may be our Teacher, but not our Master; for no man is master over the free thoughts of his fellow-men: we may learn from him, but we sit in judgment while we learn; we modify his teaching by the wisdom of later ages; we refuse the evil and choose the good. But remember that we can do this, only if Christ is a mere human teacher, or if we of these latter days have received a newer and a better revelation. If now, as of old, He speaks as never man spake;[2]—if God, who at sundry times and in divers manners spake in time past unto the fathers by the prophets, hath in these last days spoken unto us by His Son,[3]—what remains for us to do but to cast down imaginations, and every high thing that exalteth itself against the knowledge of God, and to bring into

1 St. John iii. 17. 2 St. John vii. 46. 3 Hebrews i. 1, 2.

captivity every thought to the obedience of Christ?[1] The witness which Christ offers of Himself either proves every thing or it proves nothing. No man has a right to say, "I will accept Christ as I like, and reject him as I like; I will follow the holy Example; I will turn away from the atoning Sacrifice; I will listen to His teaching; I will have nothing to do with His mediation; I will believe Him when He tells me that He came from the Father, because I feel that His doctrine has a divine beauty and fitness; but I will not believe Him when He tells me that He is one with the Father, because I cannot conceive how this unity is possible." This is not philosophy, which thus mutilates man; this is not Christianity, which thus divides Christ. (16) If Christ is no more than one of us, let us honestly renounce the shadow of allegiance to an usurped authority, and boldly proclaim that every man is his own Redeemer. If Christ is God, no less than man, let us beware, lest haply we be found even to fight against God.[2]

Beyond question, every doubt which our reason may suggest in matters of religion is entitled to its due place in the examination of the evidences of religion; if we will treat it as a part only and not the whole; if we will not insist on a positive solution of that which, it may be, is given us for another purpose than to be solved. It is reasonable to believe that, in matters of belief as well as of practice, God has not thought fit to annihilate the free will of man; but has permitted speculative difficulties to exist as the trial and the discipline of sharp and subtle intellects, as he has permitted moral temptations to form the trial and the discipline of strong and eager passions. (17) Our passions are not annihilated when we resist the temptation to sin: why should we expect that our

[1] 2 Corinthians x. 5. [2] Acts v. 39.

doubts must be annihilated if we are to resist the temptation to unbelief? This correspondence of difficulties is so far from throwing doubt on the divine origin of Revelation, that it rather strengthens the proof that it has emanated from that Giver whose other gifts are subject to like conditions. We do not doubt that the conditions of our moral trial tend towards good and not towards evil; that human nature, even in its fallen state, bears traces of the image of its Maker, and is fitted to be an instrument in His moral government. And we believe this, notwithstanding the existence of passions and appetites which, isolated and uncontrolled, appear to lead in an opposite direction. Is it then more reasonable to deny that a system of revealed religion, whose unquestionable tendency as a whole is to promote the glory of God and the welfare of mankind, can have proceeded from the same Author, merely because we may be unable to detect the same character in some of its minuter features, viewed apart from the system to which they belong?

It would of course be impossible now to enter upon any detailed examination of the positive Evidences of Christianity. The purpose of the foregoing Lectures will have been answered, if they can only succeed in clearing the way for a candid and impartial inquiry; by showing what are the limits within which it must be confined, and what kind of reasoning is inadmissible, as transgressing those limits. The conclusion, which an examination of the conditions of human thought unavoidably forces upon us, is this: There can be no such thing as a positive science of Speculative Theology; for such a science must necessarily be based on an apprehension of the Infinite; and the Infinite, though we are compelled to believe in its existence, cannot be positively apprehended in any mode of the human Consciousness. The same impediment which prevents the *formation* of Theology as a science, is also manifestly fatal to the theory which asserts its *progressive development.* We can test the progress of knowledge, only by comparing its successive representations with the objects which they profess to represent: and as the object in this case is inaccessible to human faculties, we have no criterion by which to distinguish between progress and mere fluctuation. The so-called progress in Theology is in truth only an advance in those conceptions of man's moral and religious duties which form the basis of natural religion; — an advance which is regulative and not speculative; which is primarily and properly a knowledge, not of God's nature, but of man's obligations; and which is the result, not of an immediate intuition of the Nature of the Infinite, but of a closer study of the Laws of the Finite. A progress of this kind can obviously have no place in relation to those truths, if such there be, which human reason is incapable of discovering for itself: and to assert its applicability to the criticism of Revealed Religion, is to beg the entire question in dispute, by assuming, without the slightest authority, that Revelation *cannot be* anything more than a republication of Natural Religion. (18)

But, on the other hand, there is an opposite caution no less needed, in making use of the counter-theory, which regards the doctrines of Revelation as truths accommodated to the finite capacities of man; as serving for regulative, not for speculative knowledge; and as not amenable to any criticism based on human representations of the Infinite. This theory is useful, not as explaining the difficulties involved in religious thought, but as showing why we must leave them unexplained; not as removing the mysteries of revelation, but as showing why such mysteries must exist. This caution has not always been sufficiently observed, even by those theologians who have shown the most just appreciation of the limits of man's faculties in the comprehension of divine things. Thus, to mention an example of an ancient method of interpretation which has been revived with considerable ability and effect in modern times, — the rule, that the Attributes ascribed to God in Scripture must be understood as denoting correspondence in Effects, but not similarity of Causes, is one which is liable to considerable misapplication: it contains indeed a portion of truth, but a portion which is sometimes treated as if it were the whole. "Affectus in Deo," says Aquinas, "denotat effectum:" (19) and the canon has been applied by a distinguished Prelate of our own Church, in language probably familiar to many of us. "The meaning," says Archbishop King, "confessedly is, that He will as certainly punish the wicked as if He were inflamed with the passion of anger against them; that He will as infallibly reward the good, as we will those for whom we have a particular and affectionate love; that when men turn from their wickedness, and do what is agreeable to the divine command, He will as surely change His dispensations towards them, as if He really repented, and had changed His mind." (20)

This is no doubt a portion of the meaning; but is it the whole? Does Scripture intend *merely* to assert a resemblance in the effects and none at all in the causes? If so, it is difficult to see why the natural rule of accommodation should have been reversed; why a plain and intelligible statement concerning the Divine Acts should have been veiled under an obscure and mysterious image of the Divine Attributes. If God's Anger means no more than His infliction of punishments; if His Love means no more than His bestowal of rewards; it would surely have been sufficient to have told us that God punishes sin and rewards obedience, without the interposition of a fictitious feeling as the basis of the relation. The conception of a God who acts, is at least as human as that of a God who feels; and though both are but imperfect representations of the Infinite under finite images, yet, while both rest upon the same authority of Scripture, it is surely going beyond the limits of a just reserve in speaking of divine mysteries, to assume that the one is merely the symbol, and the other the interpretation. It is surely more reasonable, as well as more reverent, to believe that these partial representations of the Divine Consciousness, though, as finite, they are unable speculatively to represent the Absolute Nature of God, have yet each of them a regulative purpose to fulfil in the training of the mind of man: that there is a religious influence to be imparted to us by the thought of God's Anger, no less than by that of His Punishments; by the thought of His Love, no less than by that of His Benefits: that both, inadequate and human as they are, yet dimly indicate some corresponding reality in the Divine Nature; and that to merge one in the other is not to gain a purer representation of God as He is, but only to mutilate that under which He has been pleased to reveal Himself. (21)

It is obvious indeed that the theory of an adaptation of divine truths to human faculties, entirely changes its significance, as soon as we attempt to give a further adaptation to the adapted symbol itself; to modify into a still lower truth that which is itself a modification of a higher. The instant we undertake to say that this or that speculative or practical interpretation is the *only real meaning* of that which Scripture represents to us under a different image, we abandon at once the supposition of an accommodation to the necessary limits of human thought, and virtually admit that the ulterior significance of the representation falls as much within those limits as the representation itself. (22) Thus interpreted, the principle no longer offers the slightest safeguard against Rationalism; — nay, it becomes identified with the fundamental vice of Rationalism itself, — that of explaining away what we are unable to comprehend.

The adaptation for which I contend is one which admits of no such explanation. It is not an adaptation to the ignorance of one man, to be seen through by the superior knowledge of another; but one which exists in relation to the whole human race, as men, bound by the laws of man's thought; as creatures of time, instructed in the things of eternity; as finite beings, placed in relation to and communication with the Infinite. I believe that Scripture teaches, to each and all of us, the lesson which it was designed to teach, so long as we are men upon earth, and not as the angels in heaven. (23) I believe that "now we see through a glass darkly," — in an enigma; — but that *now* is one which encompasses the whole race of mankind, from the cradle to the grave, from the creation to the day of judgment: that dark enigma is one which no human wisdom can solve; which Reason is unable to penetrate; and which Faith can only rest content with here, in hope of a clearer vision to be granted hereafter. If there be any who think that the Laws of Thought themselves may change with the changing knowledge of man; that the limitations of Subject and Object, of Duration and Succession, of Space and Time, belong to the vulgar only, and not to the philosopher; — if there be any who believe that they can think without the consciousness of themselves as thinking, or of anything about which they think; that they can be in such or such a mental state, and yet for no period of duration; that they can remember this state and make subsequent use of it, without conceiving it as antecedent, or as standing in any order of time to their present consciousness; that they can reflect upon God without their reflections following each other, without their succeeding to any earlier or being succeeded by any later state of mind; — if there be any who maintain that they can conceive Justice and Mercy and Wisdom, as neither existing in a merciful and just and wise Being, nor in any way distinguishable from each other, — if there be any who imagine that they can be conscious without variety, or discern without differences; — these, and these alone, may aspire to correct Revelation by the aid of Philosophy; for such alone are the conditions under which Philosophy can attain to a rational knowledge of the Infinite God.

The intellectual difficulties which Rationalism discovers in the contents of Revelation (I do not now speak of those which belong to its external evidences) are such as no system of Rational Theology can hope to remove; for they are inherent in the constitution of Reason itself. Our mental laws, like our moral passions, are designed to serve the purposes of our earthly culture and discipline; both have their part to perform in moulding the intellect and the will of man through the slow stages of that training here, whose completion is to be looked for hereafter. Without the possibility of temptation, where would be the merit of obedience? Without room for doubt, where would be the righteousness of faith? (24) But there is no temptation which taketh us, as Christians, but such as is common to man;[1] and there is no doubt that taketh us but such as is common to man also. It is the province of Philosophy to teach us this; and it is the province of Religion to turn the lesson to account. The proud definition of ancient sages, which bade the philosopher, as a lover of wisdom, strive after the knowledge of things divine and human, would speak more soberly and more truly by enjoining a Knowledge of things human, as subservient and auxiliary to Faith in things divine. (25) Of the Nature and Attributes of God in His Infinite Being, Philosophy can tell us nothing: of man's inability to apprehend that Nature, and why he is thus unable, she tells us all that we can know, and all that we need to know. "Know thyself," was the precept inscribed in the Delphic Temple, as the best lesson of Heathen wisdom. (26) "Know thyself," was the exhortation of the Christian Teacher to his disciple, adding, "if any man know himself, he will also know God." (27) He will at least be content to know so much of God's nature as God Himself has been pleased to reveal; and, where Revelation is silent, to worship without seeking to know more.

Know thyself in the various elements of thy intellectual and moral being: all alike will point reverently upward to the throne of the Invisible; but none will scale that throne itself, or pierce through the glory which conceals Him that sitteth thereon. Know thyself in thy powers of Thought, which, cramped and confined on every side, yet bear witness, in their very limits, to the Illimitable beyond. Know thyself in the energies of thy Will, which, free and yet bound, the master at once and the servant of Law, bows itself under the imperfect consciousness of a higher Lawgiver, and asserts its freedom but by the permission of the

[1] Corinthians x. 13.

Almighty. Know thyself in the yearnings of thy Affections, which, marvellously adapted as they are to their several finite ends, yet testify in their restlessness to the deep need of something better. (28) Know thyself in that fearful and wonderful system of Human Nature as a whole, which is composed of all these, and yet not one with any nor with all of them; — that system to whose inmost centre and utmost circumference the whole system of Christian Faith so strangely yet so fully adapts itself. It is to the whole Man that Christianity appeals: it is as a Whole and in relation to the whole Man that it must be judged. (29) It is not an object for the thought alone, nor for the will alone, nor for the feelings alone. It may not be judged by reference to this petty cavil or that minute scruple: it may not be cut down to the dimensions and wants of any single ruling principle or passion. We have no right to say that we will be Christians as far as pleases us, and no further; that we will accept or reject, according as our understanding is satisfied or perplexed. (30) The tree is not then most flourishing, when its branches are lopped, and its trunk peeled, and its whole body cut down to one hard, unyielding mass; but when one principle of life pervades it throughout; when the trunk and the branches claim brotherhood and fellowship with the leaf that quivers, and the twig that bends to the breeze, and the bark that is delicate and easily wounded, and the root that lies lowly and unnoticed in the earth. And man is never so weak as when he seems to be strongest, standing alone in the confidence of an isolated and self-sufficing Intellect: he is never so strong as when he seems to be weakest, with every thought and resolve, and passion and affection, from the highest to the lowest, bound together in one by the common tie of a frail and feeble Humanity. He is never so weak as when he casts off his burdens, and stands upright and unincumbered in the strength of his own will; he is never so strong as when, bowed down in his feebleness, and tottering under the whole load that God has laid upon him, he comes humbly before the throne of grace, to cast his care upon the God who careth for him.[1] The life of man is one, and the system of Christian Faith is one; each part supplying something that another lacks; each element making good some missing link in the evidence furnished by the rest. But we may avail ourselves of that which satisfies our own peculiar needs, only by accepting it as part and parcel of the one indivisible Whole. Thus only shall we grow in our Christian Life in just proportion of every part; the intellect instructed, the will controlled, the affections purified, "till we all come, in the unity of the faith and of the knowledge of the Son of God, unto a perfect man, unto the measure of the stature of the fulness of Christ: that we henceforth be no more children, tossed to and fro, and carried about with every wind of doctrine, by the sleight of men, and cunning craftiness, whereby they lie in wait to deceive; but speaking the truth in love, may grow up into Him in all things, which is the Head, even Christ; from whom the whole body, fitly joined together and compacted by that which every joint supplieth, according to the effectual working in the measure of every part, maketh increase of the body unto the edifying of itself in love."[2]

[1] 1 St. Peter v. 7. [2] Ephesians iv. 13—16.

NOTES.

NOTES.

LECTURE I.

NOTE I., p. 46.

SEE Galen, *De Sectis*, c. I. In this sense, the *Dogmatists* or *Rationalists* were distinguished from the *Empirics*. For the corresponding philosophical sense of the term, see Sextus Empiricus, *Pyrrh. Hyp.* I. § 1—3.

NOTE II., p. 47.

"Dogmatism has its name from this, — that it professes to demonstrate, i. e. to establish dogmatically, as a causal nexus, the relation between things *per se* and phenomena; and maintains that things *per se* contain the ground of all that we observe in man and in the world of nature."— Poelitz, *Kant's Vorlesungen über die Metaphysik. Einleitung*, p. xxi.

NOTE III., p. 47.

Of the theological method of Wolf, the leader of philosophical dogmatism in the eighteenth century, Mr. Rose observes: "He maintained that philosophy was indispensable to theology, and that, together with biblical proofs, a mathematical or strictly demonstrative dogmatical system, according to the principles of reason, was absolutely necessary. His own works carried this theory into practice, and after the first clamors against them had subsided, his opinions gained more attention, and it was not long before he had a school of vehement admirers who far outstripped him in the use of his own principles. We find some of them not content with applying demonstration to the truth of the system, but endeavoring to establish each separate dogma, the Trinity, the nature of the Redeemer, the Incarnation, the eternity of punishment, on philosophical, and, strange as it may appear, some of those truths on mathematical grounds."[1]

1 *State of Protestantism in Germany*, p. 54. Second edition.

The language of Wolf himself may be quoted as expressing exactly the relation between Scripture and human reason mentioned in the text. "*Sacred Scripture serves as an aid to natural theology.* For in the Scripture those things also are taught concerning God, which can be demonstrated from principles of reason; a thing which no one denies, who is versed in the reading of Scripture. It therefore furnishes natural theology with propositions, which ought to be demonstrated; consequently the philosopher is bound, not to invent, but to demonstrate them." [1]

The writings of Canz, a disciple of the Wolfian philosophy, are mentioned by Mr. Rose and by Dr. Pusey (*Historical Inquiry*, p. 116), as exemplifying the manner in which this philosophy was applied to doctrinal theology. The following extracts from his attempted demonstration of the doctrine of the Trinity may be interesting to the reader, not only on account of the extreme rarity of the work from which they are taken, but also as furnishing a specimen of the dogmatic method, and showing the abuse to which it is liable in injudicious hands.

"Since the character of every substance lies in some power of action, we must form our judgment of God from a power of action infinite and general. This power being infinite, embraces all perfections, and therefore, does not lie in a bare faculty, which sometimes ceases from activity; for that would imply imperfection; nor in the power of doing this thing only, or only that, for that in like manner would betray limitations; but in an ever-during act of working all things whatsoever in the most perfect and therefore the wisest manner. He is therefore a substance entirely singular.

"Moreover, since God is pure actuality, working all in all, it follows that finite things, which may be and may not be, do not find the ground of their existence in themselves, but in Him who works all things, i. e. in God. There is therefore in God — and this we observe in the first place — an infinite Creative Power.

"But since all created things relate to one another as means and ends, yet are themselves, in the ultimate scope, referred to the glory of God, it is plain that there is in God an infinite Faculty of Wisdom. . . . . .

"Finally, inasmuch as there is infinite good in created things, and God, who works all, must be judged to have furnished forth all this good; it is not difficult to understand that there is in God an infinite Power of Love. For he loves, who increases, as far as possible, with various blessings, the happiness of others.

* * * * * * * * *

"That which exists, is said to subsist, when it has reached its own full completion, and proceeds no farther. . . .

1 *Theologia Naturalis*, *Pars Prior*, § 22.

"Whatever in this way, in its existence, proceeds no farther, is called by Metaphysicians ὑφιστάμενον, and if to this be added the gift of intelligence or reason, then there exists a Person (*persona*).

"These things premised, let us see what there is in the nature of God thst justifies the designation of Three Persons. There is certainly in God a boundless power of action, and therefore evidence of His being a wholly singular Substance. We can also discover a triple activity, which completes that power; a triple activity, which not only exists, as it presupposes a power of action, but subsists also, as it is neither a part, nor an adjunct, nor an operation of anything else.

"And now there belongs to this triple unlimited activity, by which the Divine power is completed, a consciousness of itself, and a sense alike of the past and the future. It is therefore intelligent, and therefore a Person.

"Since there are three activities of this kind in God, or in the Divine Nature, which is an unlimited power of action, it follows that there are in it Three Persons, which by a threefold unlimited operation complete and exercise that unlimited power.

"Since in every created being, endowed with intelligence, the power of working, understanding, loving, cannot be completed except by one operation, or by one activity; it follows, that in every finite being there can only be one person.

"There is therefore a Trinity of Persons in God, which proceeds from his Infinite Nature as such: which was the thing proposed for demonstration."[1]

NOTE IV., p. 48.

Kant defines Rationalism, as distinguished from Naturalism and Supernaturalism, in the following terms: "He who interprets natural religion as morally necessary, i. e. as Duty, may also be called (in matters of faith) *Rationalist.* When such an one denies the reality of all supernatural Divine revelation, he is called *Naturalist;* if now he allows this, but maintains that to know it and accept it as real is not a necessary requisite to Religion, he could be called a *pure Rationalist;* but if he holds a faith in the same to be necessary to all Religion, he would have to be called, in matters of faith, a pure *Supernaturalist.*"[2] In the text, the term is used in

1 *Philosophiæ Wolfianæ Consensus cum Theologia*, Francofurti et Lipsiæ, 1737. This volume forms the third part of the *Philosophiæ Leibnitianæ et Wolfianæ usus in Theologia*, of which the first part was published in 1728, and the second in 1732. The third part is extremely rare. The two former parts were reprinted in 1749.

2 *Religion innerhalb der Grenzen der blossen Vernunft* (*Werke, ed.* Rosenkranz, x. p. 185). For different senses in which the term *Rationalist* has been used, see

a somewhat wider extent than that of the above definition. It is not necessary to limit the name of *Rationalist* to those who maintain that Revelation as a whole is unnecessary to religion; nor to those whose system is based solely on moral principles. There may be a partial as well as a total Rationalism: it is possible to acknowledge in general terms the authority of Scripture, and yet to exercise considerable license in rejecting particular portions as speculatively incomprehensible or morally unnecessary. The term is sometimes specially applied to the Kantian school of theologians, of whom Paulus and Wegscheider are representatives. In this sense, Hegel declares his antagonism to the Rationalism of his day;[1] and Strauss, in his controversies with the naturalist critics of the Gospels, frequently speaks of their method as "Rationalism." In the sense in which the term is employed in the text, Hegel and Strauss are themselves as thoroughly rationalists as their opponents. Even Schleiermacher, though a decided antagonist of the naturalist school, is himself a partial Rationalist of another kind; for with him the Christian Consciousness, i. e. the internal experience resulting to the individual from his connection with the Christian community, is made a test of religious truth almost as arbitrary as the Moral Reason of Kant. On the strength of this self-chosen criterion, Schleiermacher sets aside, among other doctrines, as unessential to Christian belief, the supernatural conception of Jesus, the facts of his resurrection, ascension, and the prediction of his future judgment of the world; asserting that it is impossible to see how such facts can be connected with the redeeming power of Christ.[2] Indeed, in some of the details of his system, he falls into pure Rationalism; as in his speculations on the existence of Angels, good and evil, on the Fall of Man, on eternal Punishment, on the two Natures of Christ, and on the equality of the Persons in the Holy Trinity.

The so-called Spiritualism of the present day is again only Rationalism disguised; for feeling or intuition is but an arbitrary standard, resting solely on the personal consciousness, and moreover must be translated into distinct thought, before it can be available for the purposes of religious criticism.

NOTE V., p. 48.

Thus Wegscheider represents the claim of the Rationalists. "They claim for sound reason the power of deciding upon any religious doctrine

Wegscheider, *Instit. Theol.* § 10; Rose, *State of Protestantism in Germany*, Introd. p. xvii. second edition; Kahnis, *Internal History of German Protestantism*, p. 169, Meyer's translation.

1 *Geschichte der Philosophie* (*Werke*, XIII. p. 96).

2 *Christliche Glaube*, § 97, 99.

whatsoever, derived from a supposed supernatural revelation, and of determining the argument for it to be made out, only according to the laws of thought and action implanted in reason."— *Inst. Theol.* § 10. See also Röhr, *Briefe über den Rationalismus*, p. 31.

NOTE VI., p. 51.

"Wherefore if it is not fitting in God to do anything contrary to justice or good order, it does not pertain to His freedom or goodness or will to let the sinner go unpunished, who does not pay to God, that of which he has robbed Him."— Anselm, *Cur Deus Homo*, i. 12. "For the voluntary satisfaction of sin, and (or) the exaction of punishment from him who makes no satisfaction, hold in the same universe their own place and fair order. And if the Divine wisdom should not make application of these, where sin is striving to disturb right order, the orderly beauty of that very universe which God ought to control, would be violated and disfigured, and God would seem to be deficient in his own administration. These two (suppositions) being as impossible as they are contrary to the fitness of things, either satisfaction or punishment is the necessary consequence of sin." *Ibid.* i. 15. "If therefore, as is evident, it is from men that the celestial state is to be made complete,— and this cannot be done unless the aforesaid satisfaction be made, which none *can* make but God, and none *ought*, but man,— then, as a necessary consequence, it must be made by God-man."— *Ibid.* ii. 6. Compare Alex. ab Ales. *Summa Theologiæ*, p. iii. Memb. 7, where the same argument is concisely stated.

NOTE VII., p. 51.

Anselm, *Cur Deus Homo*, l. ii. c. 16.

NOTE VIII., p. 51.

Anselm, *Cur Deus Homo*, l. i. c. 5.

NOTE IX., p. 51.

"God is in such way merciful, that He is also at the same time just; mercy does not exclude, in Him, the eternal rule of justice, but there is in Him a perfect and admirable mingling of mercy and justice; therefore, without an equivalent price, sin could not, in the judgment of God, have been remitted to man, and the Divine justice have been unimpaired.

There remained, therefore, no other remedy, than for the Son of God himself to assume human nature, and in it and through it to make satisfaction. God ought not, man could not."—J. Gerhard, *Loci Theologici, De Persona et Officio Christi*, c. 8.

NOTE X., p. 51.

"Because a mere creature could not have endured the immense weight of God's wrath, due to the sins of the whole world."—Chemnitz, *De duabus Naturis in Christo*, c. 11.

NOTE XI., p. 52.

Such is the demand of Anselm's interlocutor, which he himself undertakes to satisfy. "That I may understand on the ground of a reasonable necessity that all those things ought to be, which the Catholic faith teaches us to believe concerning Christ."—*Cur Deus Homo*, L. I. c. 25. To arguments founded on this principle the judicious remarks of Bishop Butler may be applied: "It may be needful to mention that several questions, which have been brought into the subject before us, and determined, are not in the least entered into here: questions which have been, I fear, rashly determined, and perhaps with equal rashness contrary ways. For instance, whether God could have saved the world by other means than the death of Christ, consistently with the general laws of his government."[1]

NOTE XII., p. 52.

"In what did this satisfaction consist? Was it that God was angry, and needed to be propitiated like some heathen deity of old? Such a thought refutes itself by the very indignation which it calls up in the human bosom."—Jowett, *Epistles of St. Paul*, vol. ii. p. 472. "Neither *can* there be any such thing as vicarious atonement or punishment, which, again, is a relic of heathen conceptions of an angered Deity, to be propitiated by offerings and sacrifices."—Greg, *Creed of Christendom*, p. 265. "The religion of types and notions can travel only in a circle from whence there is no escape. It is but an elaborate process of self-confutation. After much verbiage it demolishes what it created, and having begun by assuming God to be angry, ends, not by admitting its own gross mistake, but by asserting *Him* to be changed and reconciled."—Mackay, *Progress of the Intellect*, vol. ii. p. 504. Compare Wegscheider, *Inst. Theol.* § 141.

[1] *Analogy*, Part II. Ch. 5.

NOTE XIII., p. 52.

"For what is more unjust, than that an innocent one be punished instead of the guilty, especially when the guilty are themselves before the tribunal, and can themselves be punished?"—F. Socinus, *Prælect. Theol.*, c. xviii. "That each should have his exact due is *just*—is the best for himself. That the consequence of his guilt should be transferred from him to one that is innocent (although that innocent one be himself willing to accept it), whatever else it be, is not *justice*."—Froude, *Nemesis of Faith*, p. 70. Compare Newman, *Phases of Faith*, p. 92; Greg, *Creed of Christendom*, p. 265. A similar objection is introduced, and apparently approved, by Mr. Maurice, *Theological Essays*, p. 139.

NOTE XIV., p. 52.

"There is no one who cannot, with the utmost justice, pardon and remit injuries done to himself, and debts contracted to himself, without having received any real satisfaction. Therefore, unless we mean to allow less to God than is allowed to men themselves, we must confess that God might justly have pardoned our sins without having received any real satisfaction for them."—F. Socinus, *Prælect. Theol.* c. xvi.

"Now it is certainly required of us, that if our brother only *repent*, we should forgive him, even though he should repeat his offence seven times a day. On the same generous maxim, therefore, we cannot but conclude that the Divine being acts towards us."—Priestley, *History of Corruptions*, vol. i. p. 151. "Every good man has learnt to forgive, and when the offender is penitent, to forgive freely—without punishment or retribution: whence the conclusion is inevitable, that God also forgives, as soon as sin is repented of.'—Newman, *The Soul*, pp. 99, 100. "Was it that there was a debt due to Him, which must be paid ere its consequences could be done away? But even 'a man's' debt may be freely forgiven."—Jowett, *Epistles of St. Paul*, vol. ii. p. 472. Compare also Maurice, *Theol. Essays*, p. 138, and Garve, quoted by Röhr, *Briefe über den Rationalismus*, p. 442.

NOTE XV., p. 52.

"Pecuniary penalties, therefore, can be paid for another, because one person's money can be made another's; as when any one pays money, as a penalty, for some other person, then he for whom it is paid is tacitly, in reality, first presented with the money, and is considered to have paid it himself. But the death, or any bodily distress, of one person, cannot be made another's." — F. Socinus, *Prælect. Theol.* c. xviii. "Since money is, as the jurists say, something real, and so can be transferred from one to another. But punishments, and the deserts of men's sins from the law of God, are something personal, and moreover of such sort that they perpetually adhere to him who suffers them, and cannot be transferred to another." — F. Socinus, *Christianæ Religionis Institutio.* (*Opera*, 1656. vol. i. p. 665.) "This original guilt . . . . . . cannot, so far as we see by the light of the law of Reason within us, be abolished by any one else, for it is no *transmissible* obligation, which, like a pecuniary debt (where it is indifferent to the creditor whether the debtor pay it himself or another pay it for him), can be transferred to another, but the most personal of all personal ones, — the guilt of sin, which only the guilty can bear, not the innocent, be he ever so generous as to be willing to undertake it."— Kant, *Religion innerhalb der Grenzen der blossen Vernunft*, p. 84, ed. Rosenkranz. Compare Coleridge, *Aids to Reflection*, p. 249, ed. 1839. His argument is chiefly an expansion of Kant's.

Note XVI., p. 53.

Wilberforce, *Doctrine of the Incarnation*, pp. 44, 45; 4th edition. The germ of this theory may perhaps be found in Damascenus, *De Fide Orthod.* lib. iii. c. 6. See Dorner, *Lehre von der person Christi*, p. 115. It also partially appears, in a form more adapted to the realistic controversy, in Anselm, particularly in his treatise *De Fide Trinitatis et de Incarnatione Verbi*, written to refute the theological errors of the nominalist Roscelin. In modern times, a similar theory has found favor with those philosophers of the Hegelian school, who, in opposition to the development represented by Strauss, have undertaken the difficult task of reconciling the philosophy of their master with historical Christianity. In this point of view it has been adopted by Schaller in his "Der historische Christus und die Philosophie," and by Göschel in his "Beiträge zur Speculativen Philosophie von Gott und dem Menschen und von dem Gottmenschen." For an account of these theories see Dorner, p, 462, 477. A similar view is maintained by Marheineke, *Grundlehren der Christlichen Dogmatik*, § 338, and by Dorner himself, *Lehre von der Person Christi*, p. 527.

Note XVII., p. 54.

"Item sequitur quod aliquid de essentia Christi erit miserum et damnatum, quia illa natura communis existens realiter in Christo et in damnato erit damnatum, quia in Juda."—Occam, *Logica*, P. I. c. 15.

Note XVIII., p. 56.

"Religion is (subjectively considered) the acknowledgment of all our duties as divine commands."—Kant, *Religion innerhalb der Grenzen der blossen Vernunft*, p. 184. ed. Rosenkranz. In the same spirit, Fichte says, "Since all religion sets forth God only as a moral lawgiver, all that is not commanded by the moral law within us, is not His, and there is no means of pleasing Him, except by the observance of this same moral law."—*Versuch einer Kritik aller Offenbarung* (*Werke*, v. p. 127). This is exactly the theory of Religion which is refuted in anticipation by Bishop Butler (*Analogy*, P. II. ch. I.), as the opinion of those who hold that the "only design" of Revelation "must be to establish a belief of the moral system of nature, and to enforce the practice of natural piety and virtue."

Note XIX., p. 56.

Kant, *Religion innerhalb der Grenzen der blossen Vernunft*, pp. 184, 186.

Note XX., p. 56.

"Prayer, as an inward *formal* worship of God, and on that account considered as a means of grace, is a superstitious delusion."—*Ibid.*, p. 235.

Note XXI., p. 56.

"A hearty wish to please God in all our conduct,—*i. e.* the disposition, accompanying all our actions, to do them as in the service of God,—is the *spirit of prayer*, which can and ought to be in us 'without ceasing.' But to clothe this wish in words and forms (be it only inwardly, even), can, at the utmost, only carry with it the value of a means for the repeated quickening of that disposition in ourselves, but can have no immediate relation to the divine favor; also on that account cannot be a universal duty, because a means can only be prescribed to him who needs it for certain ends."—Kant, *Religion u. s. w.* p. 235.—Cf. Fichte, *Kritik aller Offenbarung*, p. 127. For an account of a similar view advocated in Scotland in the last century, by Dr. Leechman and others, see Combe's *Constitution of Man*, ch. ix. Subsequent writers have repeated the above theory in various forms, and in various spirits, but all urging the same objection, from the supposed unchangeable nature of God. See Schleiermacher, *Christliche Glaube*, § 147, and his sermon "Die Kraft des Gebetes," *Predigten*, I. p. 24; Strauss, *Glaubenslehre*, II. p. 387; Foxton, *Popular Christi-*

anity, p. 113; Parker, *Theism, Atheism, and Popular Theology*, p. 65; Emerson, *Essay on Self-Reliance;* and a remarkable passage from Greg's *Creed of Christendom*, quoted in Lecture VI. p. 147. Some valuable remarks on the other side will be found in two writers, usually opposed to each other, but for once united in vindicating the religious instincts of mankind from the perversions of a false philosophy. See F. W. Newman, *The Soul*, p. 118, and "Correspondence of R. E. H. Greyson, Esq," p. 218 (Am. Ed.). Kant's theory is ably criticized by Drobisch, *Grundlehren der Religionsphilosopie*, p. 267.

NOTE XXII., p. 56.

Thus Fichte lays it down, as one of the tests of a true Revelation, that it must not countenance an *objective Anthropomorphism* of God. In illustration of this canon, he says, "If we can really determine God by our feelings, can move him to sympathy, to compassion, to joy, then is He not the Unchangeable, the Only-sufficient, the Only-blessed, then is He determinable by something else than by the moral law; then can we hope to move Him, by moaning and contrition, to proceed otherwise with us, than the degree of our morality may have deserved. All these sensuous representations of divine attributes must not, therefore, be pronounced objectively valid; it must not be left doubtful, whether such be essentially the nature of God (Gott *an sich*), or whether he is willing to allow us so to think of it, in behoof of our sensuous needs."[1] On this principle, he considers the notions of a Resurrection and a Day of Judgment as having a merely subjective validity.[2] In another passage, he speaks of the representation of God under conditions of time, as "a gross Anthropomorphism;"[3] apparently not seeing that the notion of unchangeableness is at least as much one of time, and therefore of Anthropomorphism, as that of compassion or joy. In a similar spirit, a later writer observes: "With the great importance so often attached to the personality of God, is quite too easily mingled the interest of Anthropopathism and Anthropomorphism."[4] In another passage, Fichte says: "He who says, Form for thyself no idea of God, says, in other words, Make for thyself no idol; and his command has for the mind the same significance as the ancient Mosaic commandment had for the senses: Thou shalt make to thyself no graven image."[5] These words may perhaps have suggested the cognate remarks

1 *Versuch einer Kritik aller Offenbarung* (*Werke*, V. p. 135).

2 *Versuch einer Kritik aller Offenbarung* (*Werke*, V. p. 136, 137).

3 *Ibid.*, p. 109.

4 Baur, *Christliche Gnosis*, p. 705.

5 *Gerichtliche Verantwortung* (*Werke*, V. p. 267). In like manner, Herder says,

of Professor Jowett: "It would be little better than idolatry to fill the mind with an idea of God which represented Him in fashion as a man. And in using a figure of speech, we are bound to explain to all who are capable of understanding, that we speak in a figure only, and to remind them that logical categories may give as false and imperfect a conception of the Divine nature in our own age, as graven images in the days of the patriarchs."[1] If by *logical categories* are meant analogical representations formed from the facts of human consciousness, this passage may be so interpreted as to imply either an important truth, or a dangerous error. If interpreted to mean that such representations of God cannot be regarded as adequate expressions of His absolute and infinite nature, it states a truth, the importance of which can hardly be over-estimated; but if it be meant, as Fichte undoubtedly meant, to signify that mental no less than bodily images, are, regarded from a human point of view, false and idolatrous, the author would do well to tell us what we can substitute in their place. "We may confidently challenge all natural Theology," says Kant, "to name a single distinctive attribute of the Deity, whether denoting intelligence or will, which, apart from Anthropomorphism, is anything more than a mere word, to which not the slightest notion can be attached, which can serve to extend our theoretical knowledge."[2] Kant, however, attempts to avoid the conclusion to which this admission necessarily leads; — namely, that Anthropomorphism, in this sense of the term, is the indispensable condition of all human theology. As regards the charge of idolatry, it is best answered in the words of Storr: "The image of God we have not made for ourselves, but God has placed it before us."[3] The very commandment which forbids the representation of God by a bodily likeness, does so by means of two other human representations, that of a mental state, and that of a consequent course of action. "Thou shalt not make to thyself any graven image; for I the Lord thy God am a jealous God, and visit the sins of the fathers upon the children." The Satire of Xenophanes has been repeated by modern critics in a manner which deprives it entirely of its original point. Thus Mr. Theodore

"Therefore when we speak of God, better (have) no images! In philosophy, as in the law of Moses, this is our first commandment" — *Gott. Einige Gespräche über Spinoza's System.* (*Werke*, VIII. p. 228.)

1 *Epistles of St. Paul*, Vol. ii. p. 404.

2 *Kritik der praktischen Vernunft*, p. 282, ed. Rosenkranz. Compare the remarkable words of Jacobi (*Von den göttlichen Dingen*, *Werke*, III. p. 418, 422). "We confess, accordingly, to an Anthropomorphism inseparable from the conviction that man bears in him the image of God; and maintain that besides this Anthropomorphism, which has always been called Theism, is nothing but Atheism or Fetichism."

3 *Annotationes quædam Theologicæ*, p. 10.

Parker says, "A Beaver or a Reindeer, if possessed of religious faculties, would also conceive of the Deity with the limitations of its own personality, as a Beaver or a Reindeer."[1] The satire loses its entire force, when transferred from bodily forms to mental attributes. In imagining a Beaver or a Reindeer with a personal consciousness, we so far imagine him as resembling man, notwithstanding the difference of bodily form. The sarcasm, therefore, amounts to no more than this: that human consciousness in another body would be subject to the same limits of religious thought as in its present one. The latest specimen of this kind of would-be philosophy is furnished by Professor Baden Powell, in his "Christianity without Judaism," p. 108. "It is not one of the least remarkable of these Anthropomorphisms," he says, "that (as in former instances) the disclosure of the Divine purposes is made under the figure of Jehovah entering into a *covenant* with his people, — an idea specially adapted to a nation of the lowest moral capacity." One would have thought that the fact that this image was selected by God Himself, as the symbol of His relation to His chosen people (to say nothing of its repetition in the New Testament), might have insured its more respectful treatment at the hands of a Clergyman. But Mr. Powell, in his zeal for "Christianity without Judaism," seems to forget that Judaism, as well as Christianity, was a Revelation from God.

Note XXIII., p. 58.

This remark may seem at first sight not so appropriate in relation to Kant as to some other advocates of a similar theory, such, for instance, as Mr. Greg, whose remarks on prayer are quoted in Lecture VI. p. 147. For Kant, in language at least, expressly denies that any temporal consecution can be included in the conception of God.[2] But, in truth, this denial is and must be merely verbal. For the moral law, in Kant's own theory, is regarded as a divine command because it is conceived as a perpetual obligation, binding upon all human acts; and the perpetuity of the obligation, in relation to successive acts, necessarily implies the idea of Time. Thus God in relation to man, as a moral Governor, is necessarily manifested under the condition of time; and this manifestation is the only philosophical representation of God which the Kantian philosophy recognizes as valid. Indeed, if Time be, as Kant maintains, a necessary form of human consciousness, the language which speaks of a Being existing out of time can have no significance to any human thinker.

1 *Discourse of Matters pertaining to Religion*, p. 100.

2 *Religion innerhalb der Grenzen der blossen Vernunft*, p. 57, ed. Rosenkranz.

Note XXIV., p. 58.

Xenophanes, apud Clem. Alex. *Stromata*, V. p. 601:

"But if oxen and lions had hands like ours, and fingers,
Then would horses like unto horses, and oxen to oxen,
Paint and fashion their god-forms, and give to them bodies
Of like shape to their own, as they themselves too are fashioned."

[As translated in *Morrison's Ritter's Hist. Anc. Phil.*, vol. I., p. 431.]

Note XXV., p. 62.

Plato, *Republic*, IV. p. 433.

Note XXVI. p. 62.

Advancement of Learning. (*Works*, ed. Montagu, vol. ii. p. 303.)

Note XXVII., p. 63.

Versuch einer Kritik aller Offenbarung, Königsberg, 1792, 2d Ed. 1793. (Fichte's *Werke*, V. p. 9.) A few specimens of the criticisms hazarded in this work will be sufficient to show the arbitrary character of the method on which it proceeds. The author assumes that God is determined entirely and solely by the moral law as conceived by man; and that Religion, therefore, must consist solely in moral duties.[1] Hence he lays down, among others, the following criteria, without satisfying which, no revelation can be accepted as of divine origin.

There must have been a moral necessity for it at the time of its publication (p. 113).

It must not draw men to obedience by any other motive than reverence for God's holiness. Hence it must not contain any prospect of future reward or punishment (p. 115).

It must not communicate any knowledge attainable by the natural reason (p. 122).

It must contain only such moral rules as may be deduced from the principle of the practical reason (p. 124).

It must not promise any supernatural aids to men in the performance of their duty (p. 129).

Kant's own work, *Religion innerhalb der Grenzen der blossen Vernunft*,

1 *Werke*, V. pp. 42, 55.

Königsberg, 1793, is based on a similar principle; and many of his conclusions are identical with those of Fichte. He agrees with his disciple in maintaining that no doctrine can be received on the authority of Revelation, without the concurrent testimony of Reason; [1] and that a moral life is the only duty which God can require of a man.[2] Hence he defines Religion as "the acknowledgment of all our duties as divine commands;" and asserts that there can be no special duties towards God distinct from our moral obligations to our fellow-men.[3] In accordance with these principles, he advocates, and in some instances applies, a method of Scripture interpretation, which consists in forcing every available doctrine and precept into a so-called moral significance, and rejecting as unessential whatever will not bear this treatment.[4] Thus, in the fifty-ninth Psalm, the enemies of David are interpreted to mean the evil passions which he wished to overcome.

The narrowness of Kant's fundamental assumption, even as regards the human side of religion only, is pointed out by Willm, *Histoire de la Philosophie Allemande*, vol. ii. p. 47: "By regarding religion as chiefly a means of promoting morality, Kant has too much limited its divine mission; he has forgotten that religion must besides be a source of consolation and of hope, in the midst of the ills of the present life; and that by powerful motives and lofty meditations it must come to the succor of frail humanity, that it must serve as a support in the double struggle that we have to sustain against temptation to evil and against suffering." See also Drobisch, *Grundlehren der Religionsphilosophie*, p. 264, who adopts a similar ground of criticism.

NOTE XXVIII., p. 65.

"In the exposition of the pure conception it has yet further been declared, that it is the absolute divine conception itself; so that in truth there would not be the relation of an *application*, but the logical process is the immediate exhibition of God's self-determination to Being."—Hegel, *Logik*. (*Werke*, V. p. 170.) In like manner his disciple Marheineke says, "Only as *subsumed* into this Idea, and *sublated*[5] in it, is the human spirit capable of knowing God. His true self-exalting to God by thinking, is however,

1 *Werke*, X. p. 228.
2 *Ibid*. p. 122.
3 *Ibid*. p. 184.
4 *Ibid*. pp. 98, 130.
5 ["This sublating has the double meaning of *tollere* and of *conservare*, and indicates the taking up and the retaining under a higher point of view, etc."—*Chalybaeus's Hist. of Speculative Philosophy, transl. by Edersheim*, p. 351: *Edinburgh*, 1854.] — TRANS.

ever at the same time, a being-exalted, the insertion of the human thinking of God into the divine thinking of God."[1] Such passages are instructive as showing the only conditions under which, according to the admission of its ablest advocates, a Philosophy of the Absolute is attainable by human thought. In reference to these lofty pretensions, Sir William Hamilton justly speaks of "the scheme of pantheistic omniscience, so prevalent among the sequacious thinkers of the day."[2]

NOTE XXIX., p. 65.

"Besides God there *exists*, truly and in the proper sense of the word, nothing at all but *knowledge;* and this knowledge is the divine Existence itself, absolutely and immediately, and in so far as we are knowledge, are we, in the deepest root of our being, the divine Existence."— Fichte, *Anweisungen zum seligen Leben* (*Werke*, V. p. 448). "Man, rational being in general, is ordained to be a complement of the phenomenal world; out of him, out of his activity, is to develop itself all that is wanting to the totality of the revelation of God, since nature receives, indeed, the whole divine substance, but only in the Real: rational being is to express the image of the same divine Nature, as it is in itself, accordingly, in the Ideal."— Schelling, *Vorlesungen über die Methode des Academischen Studium*, p. 18. "God is infinite, I finite — these are false expressions, forms not fitted to the idea, to the nature of the case. . . . . . . God is the movement to the finite, and thereby as sublation of the same to himself; in the *I* as the self-sublating as finite, God regresses to himself, and is only God as this regress."— Hegel, *Vorlesungen, über die Philosophie der Religion* (*Werke*, XI. p. 194). "Man's knowledge of God is, according to the essential communion, a common knowledge; *i. e.*, man has knowledge of God, only in so far as God has knowledge of Himself; this knowledge is God's self-consciousness; but just so is it, too, His knowledge of man; and God's knowledge of man is man's knowledge of God."— *Ibid.* XII. p. 496. "Rational knowledge of truth is, first of all, as a knowledge of God, knowledge through God, knowledge in his Spirit and through it. By finite, relative thinking, God, who is nothing finite and relative, cannot be thought and known. On the contrary, in the knowledge, the *I* is out beyond

1 *Grundlehren der Christlichen Dogmatik*, § 21. In another passage of the same work (§ 84) he says, "As God in the knowledge of Himself does not have Himself *extra se*, and as the self-knowing is no other than the known, but rather the Spirit, unity and essence of both, so is the idea of the Absolute the absolute idea, and as such the stand-point of all knowledge and all science."

2 *Discussions*, p. 787.

itself, and the subjectivity of the isolated consciousness of itself, — it is in God, and God in it." Marheineke, *Grundlehren der Christlichen Dogmatik*, § 115.

Rationalism here takes up a common ground with Mysticism, and the logical process of the Hegelians becomes identical with the ecstatic intuition of the Neo-Platonists. Compare the language of Plotinus, Enn. VI. L. ix. c. 9. "It (the soul) may then see itself . . . . . . becoming God, or rather being God." In the same strain sings the "Cherubic Wanderer," Angelus Silesius:

> "In God is nothing known: He is the only One:
> What we in Him do know, that we ourselves must be."[1]

For an exactly similar doctrine, asserted in the Hindu Vedas, see Dr. Mill's *Observations on the application of pantheistic principles to the criticism of the Gospel*, p. 159.

NOTE XXX., p. 65.

Hegel, in his Lectures on the Philosophy of Religion, thus interprets the history of Christ. "The truth . . . . . . which men have reached in this entire history is this: that the idea of God has for them a certainty; that the Human is immediate, present God; and indeed, in such wise, that in this history, as the spirit apprehends it, the exhibition of the process pertains to that, which constitutes man, the spirit."[2] The view here obscurely intimated is more explicitly stated by his disciple, Strauss, whose theory is little more than the legitimate development of his master's. In his *Christliche Glaubenslehre*, § 33, he sums up the result of the speculations of modern philosophy concerning the Personality of God, in the following words: "God being in himself the eternal Personality itself, has been forever bringing forth out from Himself his Other (or *alterum*) Nature, in order forever to return to Himself as self-conscious Spirit. Or, the Personality of God must not be thought of as single-personality, but as all-personality; instead of on our side personifying the absolute, we must learn to apprehend it as the endlessly Self-personifying." This view is still more plainly stated in a fearful passage of his *Leben Jesu*, § 151, which the reader will find quoted at length in Lecture V. p. 130. The critic of Strauss, Bruno Bauer, in his *Kritik der evangelischen Geschichte der Synoptiker*, § 91, adopts the same view, observing, "In general the religious

1 *Cherubinischer Wandersmann*, I. 285. Quoted by Strauss, *Christliche Glaubenslehre*, I. p. 531.

2 *Werke*, XII. p. 807.

consciousness is the Spirit estranged from itself;" and to this origin he ascribes the doctrine of Christ's Divinity: "The historical Christ is man, raised to heaven by the religious consciousness." Feuerbach, in his *Wesen des Christenthums*,[1] from a different point of view, arrives at a similar conclusion, maintaining that God is but the personification of the general notion of humanity. Emerson gives us occasional glimpses of the same philosophy. Thus in his "Christian Teacher" he explains the Divinity of Christ: "He saw that God incarnates himself in man, and evermore goes forth anew to take possession of his world. He said in this jubilee of sublime emotion: 'I am divine. Through me God acts; through me, speaks. Would you see God, see me; or see thee, when thou also thinkest as I now think.'"[2] And, in the "Over-Soul." in still more daring language, he says: "In all conversation between two persons, tacit reference is made as to a third party, to a common nature. That third party or common nature is not social; it is impersonal, is God."[3]

Another form of this deification of humanity is that of M. Comte, who agrees with Strauss and Feuerbach, in finding God only in the human race. This discovery is announced as the grand consummation of Positive Philosophy. "This final estimation condenses *l'ensemble* of positive conceptions in the single notion of one Being immense and eternal, Humanity, whose sociological destinies develop themselves always under the necessary preponderance of biological and cosmological fatalities. Around this veritable Great-Being, the immediate mover of every existence, individual or collective, our affections centre as spontaneously as our thoughts and our actions."[4] From this grand ideal of humanity. unworthy individuals of the race are excluded; but, "si ces producteurs de fumier ne font vraiment point partie de l'Humanité, une juste compensation vous prescrit de joindre au nouvel Etre-Suprême tous ses dignes auxiliaires animaux."[5] Such is the brilliant discovery which entitles its author, in his own modest estimate, to be considered as uniting in his own person the characters of St. Paul and Aristotle, as the founder at once of true religion and sound philosophy.[6]

1 See Ewerbeck, *Qu'est ce que la Religion d'après la nouvelle Philosophie Allemande*, pp 271, 390, 413.

2 *Essays* (Orr's Edition, 1851), p. 511.

3 *Ibid.*, p. 125.

4 *Catechisme Positiviste*, p. 19.

5 *Catechisme Positiviste*, p. 31. Thus, under the auspices of the positive philosophy, we return once more to the worship of the ibis, the ichneumon, and the cat. The Egyptians had the same reverence for their "dignes auxiliares animaux." "They deified no beast, but for some utility which they might get from it." — (Cicero, *De Natura Deorum*, I. 36.)

6 This exquisite passage must be quoted in the original to be properly appre-

"Oh, worthy thou of Egypt's wise abodes,—
A decent priest, where monkeys were the gods!"

NOTE XXXI., p. 66.

"The object of religion as of philosophy, is *eternal truth* in its very objectivity, God, and nothing but God, and the unfolding of God."—Hegel, *Philosophie der Religion* (*Werke*, XI. p. 21).

NOTE XXXII., p. 66.

"Thus is religion the divine Spirit's knowledge of Himself through the mediation of the finite Spirit."—Hegel, *Werke*, XI. p. 200. "Religion we have defined as the self-consciousness of God."—*Ibid.* XII. p. 191. Compare Marheineke, *Grundlehren der Christlichen Dogmatik*, § 420. "Religion is, accordingly, nothing at all but the existence of the divine Spirit in the human; but an existence, which is life, a life which is consciousness, a consciousness which, in its truth, is knowledge. This human knowledge is essentially divine; for it is, first of all, the divine Spirit's knowledge, and religion in its absoluteness."

NOTE XXXIII., p. 66.

"Logic is consequently to be conceived as the system of the pure reason, as the realm of pure thought. *This realm is truth unveiled and absolute.* We may therefore say, that it contains in itself the exhibition of God, as He is in His eternal essence before the creation of nature and a finite spirit."—Hegel, *Logik* (*Werke*, III. p. 33).

NOTE XXXIV., p. 66.

Clemens Alex. *Stromata*, i. 2. Πρῶτον μὲν, εἰ καὶ ἄχρηστος εἴη φιλοσοφία, εἰ εὔχρηστος ἡ τῆς ἀχρηστίας βεβαίωσις, εὔχρηστος.

ciated. "En appliquant aussitôt ce principe évident, je devais spontanément choisir l'angélique interlocutrice, qui, après une seule année d'influence objective se trouve, depuis plus de six ans, subjectivement associée à toutes mes pensées comme à tous mes sentiments. C'est par elle qui je suis enfin devenu, pour l'Humanité, un organe vraiment double, comme quiconque a dignement subi l ascendant féminin. Sans elle, je n'aurais jamais pu faire activement succéder le carrière de St. Paul à celle d'Aristote, en fondant la religion universelle sur la saine philosophie, après avoir tiré celle-ci de la science réelle."—*Préface*, p. xxii.

LECTURE II.

NOTE I., p. 69.

"Unless we have independent means of knowing that *God knows the truth, and is disposed to tell it to us,* his word (if we be ever so certain that it is really his word) might as well not have been spoken. But if we know, independently of the Bible, that God knows the truth, and is disposed to tell it to us, obviously we know a great deal more also. We know not only the existence of God, but much concerning his character. For, only by discerning that he has Virtues similar in kind to human Virtues, do we know of his truthfulness and his goodness. Without this *a priori* belief, a book-revelation is a useless impertinence."— F. W. Newman, *The Soul,* p. 58. With this *a priori* belief, it is obvious that a book-revelation is, as far as our independent knowledge extends, still more impertinent; for it merely tells us what we knew before. See an able criticism of this theory in the *Eclipse of Faith,* p. 73 sqq.

NOTE II., p. 71.

"Furthermore, since, for us, that falls under the sphere of the understanding, which a great many philosophers before us have declared to be within the province of the reason, we shall have for the highest kind of intelligence a position unattained by them; and we shall define it as that by which finite and infinite are seen in the eternal, but not the eternal in the finite or in the infinite." — Schelling, *Bruno,* p. 163. (Compare p. 69.) "But there are still other spheres, which can be observed, — not merely those which are confined to a relativity of finite to finite, but those, too, wherein the divine in its absoluteness is in the consciousness." — Hegel, *Philosophie der Religion* (*Werke,* XI. p. 196). In like manner, Mr. Newman speaks of the Soul as "the organ of specific information to us," respecting things spiritual;[1] and Mr. Parker says, "that there is a connection between God and the soul, as between light and the eye, sound and the ear, food and the palate, etc."[2]

NOTE III., p. 71.

"This substance, simple, primitive, must comprise the *perfections* in eminent degree, contained in the derivative substances, which are its

1 *The Soul,* p. 3. 2 *Discourse of Matters pertaining to Religion,* p. 130.

effects; thus it will have *power, knowledge, good-will* in perfection; that is, omnipotence, omniscience, supreme goodness. And as *justice*, taken generally, is nothing but goodness conformed to wisdom, there must also be in God a supreme justice."—Leibnitz, *Principes de la Nature et de la Grace*, § 9. "Being conscious that I have, personally, a little Love, and a little Goodness, I ask concerning it, as concerning Intelligence, — where did I pick it up? and I feel an invincible persuasion, that if I have some moral goodness, the great Author of my being has infinitely more. He did not merely make rocks, and seas, and stars, and brutes, but the human Soul also; and, *therefore*, I am assured he possesses all the powers and excellencies of that soul in an infinitely higher degree." — F. W. Newman, *Reply to the Eclipse of Faith*, p. 26. This argument, however true in its general principle, is liable to considerable error in its special applications. The remarks of Bishop Browne are worth consideration, as furnishing a caution on the other side. "To say that God is infinite in perfection, means nothing *real* and *positive* in him, unless we say, in a *kind* of perfection altogether inconceivable to us as it is in itself. For the multiplying or magnifying the greatest perfections whereof we have any direct conception or idea, and then adding our gross notion only of *indefinite* to them, is no other than heaping up together a number of *imperfections* to form a chimera of our imagination." — *Divine Analogy*, p. 171.

NOTE IV., p. 72.

Compare Wegscheider's definition of Mysticism, *Instit. Theol.* § 5. — "A near approach to superstition, or rather a species of it, is *mysticism;* or a belief in a particular faculty of the soul, ... by which it may reach even in this world an *immediate* intercourse with the Deity or with celestial natures, and enjoy *immediately* a knowledge of divine things."

NOTE V., p. 73.

Fichte, *Versuch einer Kritik aller Offenbarung.* (*Werke*, V. pp. 40, 115.) — The following remarks of Mr. Parker are another application of the same principle, substituting, however, as if on purpose to show the contradictory conclusions to which such a method of reasoning may lead, the conception of perfect love and future compensation, for that of a moral nature with no affections and no future promises. "This we know, that the Infinite God must be a perfect Creator, the sole and undisturbed author of all that is in Nature. . . . . Now, a perfect Motive for creation, — what will that be? It must be absolute Love, producing a desire to bless everything which He creates. . . . . If God be infinite, then He must make and administer the world from perfect motives, for a perfect purpose, and as a perfect means, — all tending to the ultimate and absolute blessedness of each thing He directly or mediately creates; the world must be administered so as to achieve that purpose for each thing. Else God has made some things from a motive and for a purpose not benevolent, or as a means not adequate to the benevolent purpose. These suppositions are at variance with the nature of the Infinite God. I do not see how this benevolent purpose can be accomplished unless all animals are immortal, and find retribution in another life." — *Theism, Atheism and the Popular Theology*, pp. 108, 109, 198.

Note VI., p. 73.

The nature of the case implies that the human mind is competent to sit in *moral* and *spiritual* judgment on a professed revelation, and to decide (if the case seem to require it) in the following tone. 'This doctrine attributes to God that which we should all call harsh, cruel, or unjust, in man: it is, therefore, intrinsically inadmissible.'" — Newman, *The Soul*, p. 58. For an able refutation of this reasoning, see the *Defence of the Eclipse of Faith*, p. 38.

Note VII., p. 73.

"To suppose the future volitions of moral agents not to be necessary events; or, which is the same thing, events which it is not impossible but that they may not come to pass; and yet to suppose that God certainly foreknows them, and knows all things; is to suppose God's Knowledge to be inconsistent with itself." — Edwards, *On the Freedom of the Will*, part 2 sect. 12.

Note VIII., p. 73.

"Let us suppose a great prince governing a wicked and rebellious people. He has it in his power to punish: he thinks fit to pardon them. But he orders his only and well-beloved son to be put to death, to expiate their sins, and to satisfy his royal vengeance. Would this proceeding appear to the eye of reason, and in the unprejudiced light of nature, wise, or just, or good?" — Bolingbroke, *Fragments or Minutes of Essays* (*Works*, vol. v. p. 289, ed. 1754). Compare Newman, *Phases of Faith*, p. 92. See also above Lecture I., note 13.

Note IX., p. 73.

"*Intellectually*, we of necessity hold that the highest human perfection is the best type of the Divine. . . . . Every good man has learnt to forgive, and when the offender is penitent, to forgive freely,—without punishment or retribution: whence the conclusion is inevitable, that God also forgives, as soon as sin is repented of."—Newman, *The Soul*, p. 99. "It may be collected from the principles of *Natural Religion*, that God, on the sincere repentance of offenders, will receive them again into favour, and render them capable of those rewards *naturally* attendant on right behaviour."—Warburton, *Divine Legation*, b. ix., ch. 2. Compare, on the other side, Magee on the Atonement, notes iv. and xxiv. See also above, Lecture I., note 14.

Note X., p. 73.

"A divine command is pleaded in vain, except it can be shown that the thing supposed to be commanded is not inconsistent with the law of nature; which, if God can dispense with in any one case, he may in all."—Tindal, *Christianity as old as the Creation*, p. 272, quoted and answered by Waterland, *Scripture Vindicated*, on Numbers xxi. 2, 3.

Note XI., p. 74.

Kant, *Streit der Facultäten*, p. 321, ed. Rosenkranz. Newman, *Phases of Faith*, p. 150. Parker, *Discourse of Matters pertaining to Religion*, p. 84.

Note XII., p. 74.

Tindal, apud Waterland l. c. Newman, *Phases of Faith*, p. 151.

Note XIII., p. 74.

Newman, *The Soul*, p. 60. Greg, *Creed of Christendom*, p. 8.

Note XIV., p. 75.

"The Absolute is that which is free from all *necessary* relation, that is, which is free from every relation *as a condition of existence;* but it may exist in relation, provided that relation be not a necessary condition of its existence; that is, provided that relation may be removed without affecting its existence." . . . "The Infinite expresses the entire absence of all limitation, and is applicable to the one Infinite Being in all his attributes." — Calderwood, *Philosophy of the Infinite*, pp. 36, 37. The definitions may be accepted, though they lead to conclusions the very opposite of those which the ingenious author has attempted to establish. The Absolute, as above defined, is taken in the first of the two senses distinguished by Sir W. Hamilton, *Discussions*, p. 14; and in this sense it is the necessary complement of the idea of the Infinite. The other sense, in which the Absolute is contradictory of the Infinite, is irrelevant to the present argument.

NOTE XV., p. 76.

"The *absolutely infinite* is what contains everything, or every perfection, which can exist or be conceived; that you are wont to call *infinite in perfection*. *Infinite*, e. g. predicated of *extension*, means what embraces all existing or conceivable extension." — Werenfels, *De Finibus Mundi Dialogus* (*Dissertationes*, 1716, vol. ii., p. 192). In the latter sense, Clarke speaks of the error of "imagining all Infinites to be equal, when in things disparate they manifestly are not so; an *infinite Line* being not only *not equal* to, but *infinitely less* than an *infinite Surface*, and an *infinite Surface* than *Space infinite in all Dimensions*."[1] This remark assumes that an infinite extension is a possible object of conception at all; whereas, in fact, the attempt to conceive it involves the same fundamental contradictions which accompany the notion of the Infinite in every other aspect. This is ingeniously shown by Werenfels, in the above Dialogue, p. 218. "D. But do you then think, that an infinite line cannot be conceived at all without contradiction? Ph. I do, indeed; and I cannot be drawn from this opinion, unless some one of you have a conclusive answer to this demonstration; but this, unless you lack the patience to listen, I will briefly propose anew. You see this line *b* ——— *a* ——— *c*. Let us suppose it to be infinite, and to be extended *ad infinitum* beyond the termini *b* and *c*. Let this line be divided at the point *a*. It is manifest that these parts are equal to one another, because each begins at the point *a* and is extended *ad infinitum*. Now, I ask you, Dædalus, are these two parts finite, or infinite? D. Finite. Ph. So an infinite would be composed of two finites; which is a contradiction. D. I confess my mistake. They are infinite. Ph. Now you fall into Scylla Thus parts would be equal to

1 *Demonstration of the Being and Attributes of God*, Prop. I.

a whole; for infinite is equal to infinite. Besides, you see, that each part is terminated at the point *a;* it is, therefore, not without ends and bounds. What say you to this, Polymathes? Po. I have an answer. Each of these parts is on the one side finite, — namely, at the point *a,* — on the other, infinite, because it is extended beyond *b* and *c ad infinitum.* Ph. Ingeniously, acutely, nothing more so. But I ask you, whether there is on either section of the infinite line an infinite number of such parts as the line *ab* and the line *ac?* Po. Yes. Ph. But is that number infinite, to which an equal can be added, and the double of which is not only conceivable, but really existent? If you answer yes, then an infinite number does not contain all units, but there can besides be conceived and added to it, as many units as it may not have. But if this be not a contradiction, then what is there, that is a contradiction? Po. But, what if either section of the given line consist of a finite number of parts of such magnitude as the line *ab?* Ph. Then the given line is finite; because two finite numbers added together, make a finite number; which was the thing to be proved." The contradictions thus involved in the notion of infinite magnitudes in space, are not solved by maintaining, with Spinoza and Clarke, that infinite quantity is not composed of parts;[1] for space with no parts is as inconceivable as space composed of an infinite number of parts. These contradictions sufficiently show that relative infinity, no less than absolute, is not a positive object of thought at all; the so-called *infinites* and *infinitesimals* of the mathematicians being in fact only negative expressions, denoting magnitudes which bear no relation to any assignable quantity, however great or small. They are thus apprehended only by reference to their inconceivability; being merely the expression of our inability to represent in thought a first or last unit of space or time. — See Leibnitz, *Théodicée Discours,* § 70. "We are embarrassed in the series of numbers, progressing *ad infinitum.* We conceive of a last term, of an infinite or an infinitesimal; but these are only fictions. Every number is finite and assignable, and the infinites and the infinitesimals signify nothing but magnitudes, which we may take as large or as small as we please, etc." — Compare Pascal, *Pensées,* Partie I. Art. II. "In short,

1 See Spinoza, *Epist.* XXIX, *Ethica,* P. I. Prop. xv.; and Clarke, *Demonstration,* Prop. 1. A curious psychological discrepancy may be observed in relation to this controversy. Spinoza maintains that quantity as represented in the imagination is finite, but that as conceived by the intellect it is infinite. Werenfels, on the contrary, asserts that the imagined quantity is infinite, the conceived finite. The truth is, that in relation to Space, which is not a general notion containing individuals under it, conception and imagination are identical; and the notions of an ultimate limit of extension and of an unlimited extension, are both equally self-contradictory from every point of view.

whatever be the motion, number, space, time, there is always a greater and a less; so that they all stand between nothing and infinity, being always infinitely removed from these extremes." Some ingenious reasoning on this question will be found in a note by Mosheim on Cudworth's *Intellectual System*, b. I. ch. V., translated in Harrison's edition of Cudworth, vol. II. p. 541; though the entire discussion is by no means satisfactory.

NOTE XVI., p. 76.

"By the Deity I understand a Being absolutely infinite, *i. e.*, a substance consisting of infinite attributes, each one of which expresses an eternal and infinite essence. *I say infinite absolutely, but not in its kind, for whatever is infinite in its kind only, of that we cannot affirm infinite attributes; but to the essence of that which is absolutely infinite, there pertains whatever expresses essence and involves no negation.*"— Spinoza, *Ethica*, P. I. Def. VI.

NOTE XVII., p. 76.

See Spinoza l. c.; Wolf, *Theologia Naturalis*, P. II. § 15; Kant, *Kritik der reinen Vernunft*, p. 450. ed. Rosenkranz; *Vorlesungen über die Metaphysik*, ed. Poelitz, p. 276; Schelling, *Vom Ich*, § 10. The assumption ultimately annihilates itself; for if any object of conception exhausts the universe of reality, it follows that the mind which conceives it has no existence. The older form of this representation is criticized by Hegel, *Encyclopädie*, § 36. His own conception of God, however, virtually amounts to the same thing. A similar view is implied in his criticism of Aristotle, whom he censures for regarding God as one object out of many. See *Geschichte der Philosophie, Werke*, XIV. p. 283.

NOTE XVIII., p. 76.

Geschichte der Philosophie, Werke, XV. p. 275. See also, *Philosophie der Religion, Werke*, XI. p. 24. *Encyklopädie*, § 19, 20, 21. Compare Schelling, *Philosophie und Religion*, p. 35, quoted by Willm, *Histoire de la Philosophie Allemande*, vol. iii. p. 301. Schleiermacher (*Christliche Glaube*, § 80) is compelled in like manner to assert that God must be in some manner the author of evil; an opinion which is also maintained by Mr. Parker, *Theism, Atheism, and the Popular Theology*, p. 119.

NOTE XIX., p. 76.

" A thing is said *to be finite in its kind,* which can be limited by another of the same nature; *e. g.* a body is called finite, because we always conceive of one greater."— Spinoza, *Ethica,* P. I. Def. II.

NOTE XX., p. 76.

See Aquinas, *Summa,* P. I. Qu. II. Art. 3; Qu. IX. Art. 1. "Actus simplicissimus," says Hobbes contemptuously, "signifieth nothing."[1] And Clarke in like manner observes, "Either the words signify nothing, or else they express only the perfection of his power."[2]

NOTE XXI., p. 76.

See Plato, *Republic,* II. p. 381; Aristotle, *Metaph.* VIII. 8, 15; Augustine, *Enarratio in Ps.* IX. ii. *De Trinitate,* XV. c. 15; Hooker, *E. P.* b. I. c. 5; Descartes, *Meditatio Tertia,* p. 22. ed. 1685; Spinoza, *Ethica,* P. I. Prop. xvii. Schol.; Hartley, *Observations on Man,* Prop. cxv.; Herder, *Gott, Werke,* VIII. p. 180; Schleiermacher, *Christliche Glaube,* § 54; Hegel, *Werke,* XIV. p. 290; Marheineke, *Grundlehren der Christlichen Dogmatik,* § 195. The conclusion, that God actually does all that he can do; and, consequently, that there is no possibility of free action in any finite being, can only be avoided by the admission, which is ultimately forced upon us, that our human conception of the infinite is not the true one. Müller (*Christliche Lehre von der Sünde,* II. p. 251, third edit.) endeavors to meet this conclusion by a counter-argument. He shows that it is equally a limitation of the divine Nature to suppose that God is compelled of necessity to realize in act everything which he has the power to accomplish. This argument completes the dilemma, and brings into full view the counter-impotences of human thought in relation to the infinite. We cannot conceive an Infinite Being as capable of becoming that which he is not; nor, on the other hand, can we conceive him as actually being all that he can be.

NOTE XXII., p. 77.

"Now it is sufficiently manifest, that a thing *existing absolutely* (*i. e.* not under relation), and a thing *existing absolutely as a cause,* are contry-

1 *Questions concerning Liberty, Necessity and Chance,* Animadversions, No. XXIV. See, on the other side, Bramhall, *Works,* vol. IV. p. 524.

2 *Demonstration,* Prop IV. See, on the other side, Hegel, *Geschichte der Philosophie, Werke,* XIV. p. 290.

dictory. The former is the absolute negation of all relation; the latter is the absolute affirmation of a particular relation. A cause is a *relative*, and what exists absolutely as a cause, exists absolutely under relation."—Sir W. Hamilton, *Discussions*, p. 34.

NOTE XXIII., p. 77.

That a belief in creation is incompatible with a philosophy of the Absolute, was clearly seen by Fichte, who consistently denounces it, as a Jewish and Heathenish notion and the fundamental error of all false Metaphysics. He even goes so far as to maintain that St. John, the only teacher of true Christianity, did not believe in the Creation, and that the beginning of his Gospel was designed to contradict the Mosaic narrative. See his *Anweisung zum seligen Leben* (*Werke*, v. p. 479). Compare Schelling, *Bruno*, p. 60, who regards the finite as necessarily coeternal with the infinite. So also Rothe, *Theologische Ethik*, § 40, asserts that the doctrine of a creation in time is inconsistent with the essential nature of God, as unchangeable and necessarily creative. Spinoza's attempted demonstration that one substance cannot be produced from another,[1] though in itself a mere juggle of equivocal terms, yet testifies in like manner to his conviction, that to deny the possibility of creation is an indispensable step to a philosophy of the Absolute. Cognate to these theories are the speculations of Hermogenes, mentioned by Tertullian, *Adv. Herm.* c. 2; and of Origen, *De Princ.* I. 2. 10. Of the latter, Neander well observes: "Here, therefore, there occurred to him those reasons against a beginning of creation generally, which must ever suggest themselves to the reflecting mind, which cannot rest satisfied with simple faith in that which to itself is incomprehensible. Supposing that to create is agreeable to the divine essence, how is it conceivable that what is thus conformable to God's nature should at any time have been wanting? Why should not those attributes which belong to the very essence of the Deity, His almighty power and goodness, be always active? A transition from the state of not-creating to the act of creation is inconceivable without a change, which is incompatible with the being of God."[2]

NOTE XXIV., p. 78.

Arist. *Metaph.* XIV. 9. [Ed. Gul. Duval, Paris, 1629.] "If it have aught as the object of intelligence, and something other than itself be thus supe-

1 *Ethica*, P. I. Prop. vi.

2 *Church History*, English translation, Vol. II. p. 281, Bohn's edition.

rior to it, it will not be the Best (for then it will be intelligence only potentially, not essentially); since it is in the act of intelligence that the excellence lies. . . . . Itself, therefore, it has as the object of intelligence, if indeed it is the Supreme; and the intelligence is intelligence of intelligence." Plotinus, on the other hand, shows that even self-consciousness, as involving a logical distinction between the subject and object, is incompatible with the notion of the Absolute. See *Enn.* V. l. VI. c. 2.

NOTE XXV., p. 78.

Plotinus, *Enn.*, III. l. IX. c. 3. "The Intelligence is now twofold, and objectifies itself; and it is wanting in somewhat because it has 'the Well' (τὸ εὖ) in the act of intelligence, not in the substance." *Enn.* V. l. VI. c. 2. "Being a duality it will not be the first, ... in itself it will properly be neither the intelligent nor the intelligible; for what is intelligible is so relatively to another." *Enn.* V. l. VI. c. 6. "Therefore there will again be a duality in the conscious intelligence; but that (the first or the Absolute) is nowise a duality." Cf. Porphyr. *Sent.* XV. "But if there be plurality in the intelligible, since there is a plurality, not unity, in the objects of the conscious intelligence, then of necessity there must be plurality in the essence of the intelligence. But unity (the One) is prior to plurality, so that of necessity it is prior to the intelligence." "The Absolute, as absolutely universal, is absolutely *one;* absolute unity is convertible with the absolute negation of plurality and difference; *the Absolute,* and *the Knowledge of the Absolute,* are therefore *identical.* But knowledge, or intelligence, supposes a plurality of terms — the plurality of subject and object. Intelligence, whose essence is plurality, cannot therefore be identified with the Absolute, whose essence is unity; and if known, the Absolute, *as known,* must be different from the Absolute, *as existing;* that is, there must be two Absolutes — an Absolute in knowledge and an Absolute in existence: which is contradictory."— Sir W. Hamilton, *Discussions*, p. 32.

NOTE XXVI., p. 78.

Clem. Alex. *Strom.* V. 12. p. 587. "Nor, indeed, would any one rightly call it a whole, for the whole is predicated of magnitude . . . . . nor can it be said to have parts, for the One is indivisible." Plotinus, *Enn.* V. l. VI. c. 5. "For of a thing that is absolutely one, how can you predicate the coming to itself, or the want of consciousness?" On this point, the earlier and later forms of Pantheism are divided against each other. Spinoza (*Eth.* P. I. Def. 6) defines the Deity as composed of an infinite number of attributes. "By the Deity I understand a Being absolutely infinite, *i. e.*, a substance consisting of infinite attributes, every one of which expresses eternal and infinite essence." Hegel, on the contrary, in his Lectures on the proofs of the existence of God, regards a plurality of attributes as incompatible with the idea of the Infinite. "Here (*i. e.* in the absolute unity of God) the plurality of predicates — which only subjectively are bound in unity, but in themselves would be distinguished, and so would come into opposition and into contradiction — shows itself as something false, and the *plurality* of determinations (in the notion of God) as an impertinent category."[1] The lesson to be learnt from both is the same. No human form of thought can represent the Infinite: — a truth which Spinoza attempts to evade by multiplying such forms to infinity, and Hegel by renouncing human thought altogether.

NOTE XXVII., p. 78.

That the Absolute cannot be conceived as composed of a plurality of attributes, but only as the one substance conceived apart from all plurality, is shown by Plotinus, *Enn.* V. l. VI., c. 3. "If it be said that nothing hinders this same (*i. e.* the First) being the Many, the answer must be, that these Many have an underlying One (One *Subject, ὑποκείμενον*); for the Many cannot exist, except there exist the One from which the Many must be derived, and in which the Many must exist . . . . . . and this One must be taken as in itself the only One.". . . .Compare Proclus, *Inst. Theol.* c. 1. "All plurality in some way partakes of Unity (or the One), for if not, then neither will the whole be One, nor each one of the many which make up the plurality; but of certain *entities* each will be a plurality, and this on to an infinite, and of these infinites each again will be an infinite plurality." To the same effect is the reasoning of Augustine, *De Trinitate,* vi. c. 6. 7. "In every body magnitude is one thing, color another, figure another. For the magnitude diminished, the color may remain the same, and the figure the same; and the figure changed, the body may be just as large and of just the same color; and whatever other things are predicated of the body, may exist together, and may be changed without change on the part of the rest. And thus the nature of the body is proved to be manifold, but in nowise simple. . . . . . But also in the soul since it is one thing to be ingenious, another to be dull, another to be acute, another to have a good memory; since desire is one thing, fear another, joy another, sorrow another; and since there can be found in the nature of the soul

1 *Werke*, XII. p. 419. See also *Encyklopädie*, § 28 (*Werke*, VI. p. 62).

some things without others, and some more, and some less, and these to a number beyond all computation; — it is manifest that the nature of the soul is not simple but manifold, for nothing simple is changeable; but every created being is changeable. But God indeed is said to be in various ways great, good, wise, happy, true, and whatever else is not unworthily predicable of Him; but his greatness is the same as his wisdom; for he is great, not in quantity, but in quality; and his goodness is the same as his wisdom and greatness, and his truth the same as all these; and with Him the being happy is not different from being great, or wise, or true, or good, or from being Himself." See also Aquinas, *Summa*, P. I. Qu. III. Art. 5, 6, 7. Schleiermacher, *Christliche Glaube*, § 50.

NOTE XXVIII., p. 79.

See Plato, *Republic*, II. p. 380, VI. p. 511, VII. p. 517; *Timæus*, p. 31. Aristotle, *Metaph.* XI. 8, 18: 10, 14; *Eth. Nic.* VII. 14, 8. Cicero, *Tusc. Quæst.* I. 29; *De Nat. Deor.* II. 11. Plotinus, *Enn.* II. 9, 1, III. 9, 3. V. 4. 1, VI. 5, 1: 9, 6. Proclus, *Inst. Theol.* c. i. xxii. lix. cxxxiii. Clemens Alex., *Strom.* V. p. 587. Origen, *De Princ.* I. 1, 6. Augustine, *De Civ. Dei*, VIII. 6: *De Trinitate*, VI. 6, VII. 1, XV. 5, 13. Aquinas, *Summa*, P. I. Qu. III. Art. 7, Qu. VII. Art. 2. Qu. XI. Art. 3. Leibnitz, *Monadologie*, § 39, 40, 47. Clarke, *Demonstration*, Prop. vi. vii. Schelling, *Vom Ich*, § 9; *Bruno*, p. 185. Rothe, *Theol. Ethik*, § 8.

NOTE XXIX., p. 79.

"Hence, therefore, it is evident, that nothing is called one or *unique*, except after some other has been conceived, which agrees with it. But since the existence of God belongs to his own essence, and of his essence we cannot form a universal idea, it is certain that he who calls God one or *unique*, can have no idea of God, or speaks improperly of Him."—Spinoza, *Epist.* L. Compare Schleiermacher, *Christliche Glaube*, § 56.

NOTE XXX., p. 80.

"For the expression, '*if it be possible*,' referred not merely to the power of God, but also to his justice; for, as to the power of God, all things are possible, whether just or unjust; but as to his justice, He being not only powerful, but just, not all things are possible, but only those which are just."—Origen *in St. Matt.* xxvi. 42; compare *c. Celsum*, III. 70. Origen speaks still more strongly in a remarkable fragment of the *De Principiis*, which has been preserved in the original: "In that beginning (i. e., at the creation) God determined (to create) as great a number of intelligent beings as might be sufficient; for we must say that the divine power was limited, nor under pretence of praise take away all limitation of it; for if the divine power were unlimited, then, necessarily, it did not have a consciousness of itself." The language of Hooker (*E. P.* b. I. ch. 2. § 3) is more cautious and reverent, but contains the same acknowledgment of what, from a human point of view, is limitation. "If, therefore, it be demanded why, God having power and ability infinite, the effects notwithstanding of that power are all so limited as we see they are; the reason hereof is the end which he hath proposed, and the law whereby his wisdom hath stinted the effects of his power in such sort, that it doth not work infinitely, but correspondently unto that end for which it worketh." Some excellent remarks on the limitation of man's faculties with regard to the Divine Attributes, will be found in Mr. Meyrick's sermon, *God's Revelation and Man's Moral Sense considered in reference to the Sacrifice of the Cross*, p. 14. See the Collection of Sermons on *Christian Faith and the Atonement*, Oxford, 1856.

NOTE XXXI., p. 80.

Thus Spinoza (*Ethica*, P. I. Prop. 26) says, "A thing which was determined to the doing of somewhat, was necessarily so determined by God;" and, carrying the same theory to its inevitable consequence, he consistently maintains (P. IV. Prop. 64) that the notion of evil only exists in consequence of the inadequacy of our ideas. Hegel in like manner (*Encykl.* § 35) reduces evil to a mere negation, which may be identified with good in the absolute. See also above, note 18, p. 231.

NOTE XXXII., p. 80.

Plato, *Rep.* II. p. 381. "Does He, then, change Himself into something better and nobler, or into something worse and baser than Himself? Necessarily, said he, into something better, for we cannot say that God is wanting in any good or noble quality. Exactly so; and that being the case, does it seem to you, that any one, whether God or man, would voluntarily make himself worse in any respect?" Compare Augustine, *In Joannis Evangelium*, Tract. XXIII. 9. "You do not find in God any changeableness, anything which is different now, from what it was a little while ago. For where you find difference, there has taken place a kind of death; for that is death, the not being what (one) was. Whatever therefore, undergoes this sort of death, whether from the better to the worse, or from the worse to the better, — that is not God." And so Jacobi (*Von den göttlichen Dingen, Werke*, III. p. 391) says of the system of Schelling: "Consider that the one only living and true God (Nature) cannot become greater or less, higher or lower; but that this God, equivalent to Nature or the Universe, remains, from eternity to eternity, ever one and the same, in quality and in quantity. It would, therefore, be absolutely impossible for Him to bring about any change in Himself, without being changeableness, *temporalness*, change itself. This changeableness, however, is, we are told, in its *root*, an *Unchangeable*, namely, the holy, ever-creating original force of the world; in its *fruit*, on the contrary, in the real world, an *absolutely changeable*, so that in each single determined *momentum* the All of beings is nothing. Accordingly, the creative word of the naturalistic God is incontestibly, *Let there be Nothing!* He calls forth Not-Being from Being; as the God of theism calls forth Being from Not-Being." Compare Sir W. Hamilton's criticism of Cousin, *Discussions*, p. 36; and see also above, note 23, p. 233.

NOTE XXXIII., p. 81.

"What," says Sir W. Hamilton, "is our thought of creation? It is not a thought of the mere springing of nothing into something. On the contrary, creation is conceived, and is by us conceivable, only as the evolution of existence from possibility into actuality, by the fiat of the Deity. . . . . And what is true of our concept of creation, holds of our concept of annihilation. We can think no real annihilation, — no absolute sinking of something into nothing. But as creation is cogitable by us, only as a putting forth of Divine power, so is annihilation by us only conceivable, as a withdrawal of that same power. All that is now *actually* existent in the universe, this we think and must think, as having, prior to creation, *virtually* existed in the Creator; and in imagining the universe to be annihilated, we can only conceive this, as the retractation by the Deity of an overt energy into latent power. In short, it is impossible for the human mind to think what it thinks existent, lapsing into absolute non-existence, either in time past or in time future."[1] With all deference to this great

[1] *Discussions*, p 620. Compare a remarkable passage in Herder's *Gott* (*Werke* VIII. p. 241) where the author maintains a similar view of the impossibility of conceiving creation from or reduction to nothing. But Herder is speaking as a professed defender of Spinoza. Sir W. Hamilton's system is in all its essential features the direct antagonist of Spinoza; and even in the present passage the apparently pantheistic hypothesis is represented as the result not of thought, but of an inability to think. Still it is to be regretted that the distinguished author should have used language liable to be misunderstood in this respect, especially as it scarcely accords with the general principles of his own system.

philosopher, I cannot help thinking that a different representation would have been more in harmony with the main principles of his own system. We cannot conceive creation at all, neither as a springing of nothing into something, nor as an evolution of the relative from the absolute; for the simple reason that the first terms of both hypotheses, nothing and the absolute, are equally beyond the reach of human conception. But while creation, as a *process in the act of being accomplished*, is equally inconceivable on every hypothesis, creation, as a *result already completed*, presents no insurmountable difficulty to human thought if we consent to abandon the attempt to apprehend the absolute. There is no difficulty in conceiving that the amount of existence in the universe may at one time be represented by A, and at another by $A + B$: though we are equally unable to conceive how B can come out of nothing, and how A, or any part of A, can become B while A remains undiminished. But the result, no less than the process, becomes self-contradictory, when we attempt to conceive A as absolute and infinite; for in that case $A + B$ must be something greater than infinity.

Note XXXIV., p. 83.

"Pantheism teaches that all is good, for all is only one; and that every appearance of what we call wrong is only an empty delusion. Hence its disturbing influence upon the life; for here, — turn about language as we may, and attach ourselves as we will to the faith that everywhere comes forth through the voice of conscience, — yet at bottom, if we remain true to the destructive principle of the pantheistic doctrine, we must do away with and declare null and void, the eternal distinction between good and evil, between right and wrong." — F. Schlegel, *Ueber die Sprache und Weisheit der Indier*, b. III. c. 2. (Werke, VIII. p. 324). "If it is God who thinks in me, my thought is absolute; not only am I unable to think otherwise than I do think, . . . but I can make no choice in my conceptions, approve or search after some, reject and shun others, all being necessary and perfect, all being divine; in fine, I become a machine for thinking, an intelligent machine, but irresponsible."— Bartholmèss, *Histoire des doctrines religieuses de la philosophie moderne*, Introduction, p. xxxvii. These necessary consequences of Pantheism are fully exhibited by Spinoza, *Ethica*, P. I. Prop. 26; P. II. Props. 32, 33, 34, 35; P. IV. Prop. 64. Hegel (*Werke*, XI. pp. 95, 208, 390) endeavors, not very successfully, to defend his own philosophy from the charge of Pantheism and its consequences. His defence amounts to no more than the assertion that God cannot be identified with the universe of finite objects, in a system in which finite objects have no real existence. Thus explained, the system is identical with Pantheism in the strictest sense of the term. All that is proved is, that it cannot with equal propriety be called Pantatheism.

NOTE XXXV., p. 83.

"The dialectic intellect, by the exertion of its own powers exclusively, can lead us to a general affirmation of the supreme reality of an absolute being. But here it stops. It is utterly incapable of communicating insight or conviction concerning the existence or possibility of the world, as different from Deity. It finds itself constrained to identify, more truly to confound, the Creator with the aggregate of his creatures, and, cutting the knot which it cannot untwist, to deny altogether the reality of all finite existence, and then to shelter itself from its own dissatisfaction, its own importunate queries, in the wretched evasion that of nothings no solution can be required: till pain haply, and anguish, and remorse, with bitter scoff and moody laughter inquire, — Are we then indeed nothings? — till through every organ of sense nature herself asks, — How and whence did this sterile and pertinacious nothing acquire its plural number? — *Unde, quæso, hæc nihili in nihila tam portentosa transnihilatio?* — and lastly: — What is that inward mirror, in and for which these nothings have at least relative existence?" — Coleridge, *The Friend*, vol. III. p. 213.

NOTE XXXVI., p. 83.

The limitation, *speculative* Atheism, is necessary; for the denial of the Infinite does not in every case constitute practical Atheism. For it is not under the form of the Infinite that the idea of God is distinctly presented in worship; and it is possible to adore a superior Being, without positively asking how far that superiority extends. It is only when we are able to investigate the problem of the relation between the infinite and the finite, and to perceive that the latter cannot be regarded as expressing the true idea of the Deity, that the denial of the infinite becomes atheism in speculation. On the alternative between Christianity and Atheism, some excellent remarks will be found in the *Restoration of Belief*, p. 248.

NOTE XXXVII., p. 84.

"Much stress is wont to be laid upon the limits of thought, and it is asserted that the limit cannot be transcended. In this assertion lies the unconsciousness, that even in fixing somewhat as limit, it has already been transcended. For a determination, a bound, is determined as limit, only in opposition to its *Other* (*alterum*), its *Unlimited;* the *Other* (the correlate), of a limit is *something beyond it.*" — Hegel, *Logik* (*Werke*, III. p. 136). Compare *Encyklopädie*, § 60 (*Werke*, VI., p. 121). In maintaining that a limit as such always implies something beyond, and, consequently, that the notion of a limited universe is self-contradictory, Hegel is unquestionably right; but he is wrong in attempting to infer from thence the non-limitation of thought. For that which is limited is not necessarily limited by something of the same kind; — nay, the very conception of *kinds* is itself a limitation. Hence the consciousness that thought is limited by something beyond itself, by no means implies that thought itself transcends that limit. A prisoner chained up feels that his motion is limited, by his inability to *move* into the space which he *sees* or *imagines* beyond the length of his chain. On Hegel's principles, he ought to know his inability by actually moving into it.

NOTE XXXVIII., p. 84.

These opposite limitations fall under the general law of the Conditioned enunciated by Sir W. Hamilton. "The mind is astricted to think in certain forms; and, under these, thought is possible only in the conditioned interval between two unconditioned contradictory extremes or poles, each of which is altogether inconceivable, but of which, on the principle of Excluded Middle, the one or the other is necessarily true."[1] The lamented author has left us only a few fragmentary specimens of the application of this canon to the vexed questions of metaphysical speculation, and the principal one of these, in some of its details, may be open to objections; but the truth of the principle itself is unquestionable; and its value, rightly applied, in confining the inquiries of philosophy within their legitimate boundaries, can hardly be estimated too highly.

NOTE XXXIX., p. 84.

"Every finite is, by virtue of its notion, bounded by its opposite; and absolute finiteness is a self-contradictory notion." — Fichte, *Grundlage der gesammten Wissenschaftslehre* (*Werke*, I., p. 185).

NOTE XL., p. 87.

Religion innerhalb der Grenzen der blossen Vernunft, p. 98, 122, 137. For the influence of Kant on the rationalist theology, see Rosenkranz, *Geschichte*

1 *Discussions*, p. 618.

der Kant'schen Philosophie, b. III. cap. 2. Amand Saintes, *Histoire du Rationalisme en Allemagne*, 1. II. ch. II. Kahnis, *History of German Protestantism*, translated by Meyer, p. 167.

Note XLI., p. 87.

Paulus, in the preface to his *Leben Jesu*, expressly adopts, though without naming the author, Kant's theory, that miracles are indifferent to religion, and that the whole essence of Christianity consists in morality. Consistently with these principles, he maintains (§ 2) that the historical inquirer can admit no event as credible which cannot be explained by natural causes. The entire details of the evangelical narrative are explained by this method. The miracles of healing were performed by medical skill, which Christ imparted to his disciples, and thus was enabled to heal, not by a word, but by deputy. Thus he coolly translates the words of the centurion, Matt. viii. 8, "If He would only give an order to one of His (disciples), to provide in His name for the healing." The feeding of the five thousand consisted merely in persuading the richer travellers to share their provisions with the poorer. The stilling of the tempest was effected by steering round a point which cut off the wind. Lazarus, and the widow's son of Nain, were both cases of premature interment. Our Lord's own death was merely a swoon, from which he was restored by the warmth of the sepulchre and the stimulating effect of the spices. Such are a few specimens of *historical inquiry*. The various explanations of Paulus are examined in detail, and completely refuted by Strauss. The natural hypothesis had to be annihilated, to make way for the mythical.

Note XLII., p. 87.

Wegscheider, though he expressly rejects Kant's allegorizing interpretations of Scripture (see *Institutiones Theologiæ*, § 25), agrees with him in maintaining the supreme authority of reason in all religious questions, and in accommodating all religious doctrines to Ethical precepts (*Præf.* p. viii. ix.). Accordingly, in the place of the allegory, he adopts the convenient theory of adaptation to the prejudices of the age; by which a critic is enabled at once to set aside all doctrines which do not harmonize with his theory. Among the doctrines thus rejected, as powerless for the true end of religion, and useless or even prejudicial to piety, are those of the Trinity, the Atonement, the Corruption of human nature, Justification, and the Resurrection of the body. See § 51.

NOTE XLIII., p. 87.

See his *Grund-und-Glaubens-Sätze der Evangelisch-Protestantischen Kirche,* p. 70 (2nd edition). This work of Röhr was principally directed against the Lutheran Symbolical books; but the Catholic Creeds are also included in his sweeping condemnations. Of the Apostles' Creed he observes: "Our age needs a more logically correct, and a more comprehensive survey of the pure evangelical faith than is afforded by the so-called Apostles' Creed, which is good for its immediate and ordinary purpose, but too short, too aphoristic, and too historical for that which is here proposed." (p. 49.) Of the Nicene and Athanasian Creeds he remarks in a note: "The Niceno-Constantinopolitan and the pseudo-Athanasian Creeds, with their decidedly anti-scriptural dogmas, are here altogether out of the question, however much they were admitted by the reformers, in all honesty and faith, as truly scriptural." Röhr agrees with Kant in separating the historical facts of Christianity from the religion itself (p. 157), and in maintaining that morality is the only mode of honoring God (p. 56). His proposed creed, from which everything "historical" is studiously excluded, runs as follows:

"There is one true God, proclaimed to us by his only-begotten Son, Jesus Christ. To this God, as the most perfect of all Beings, as the Creator, Sustainer, and Governor of the world, and as the Father and Instructor of men and of all rational spirits, the deepest veneration is due. This veneration is best rendered by active striving after virtue and righteousness, by zealous control of the inclinations and passions of our sensual and evilly-disposed nature, and by honest, entire fulfilment of our duty, according to the exalted example of Jesus, whereby we may assure ourselves of the aid of his divine Spirit. In the consciousness of the filial relation into which we thereby enter with him, we may, in earthly need, reckon with confidence on his fatherly help, in the feeling of our moral weakness and unworthiness, upon his grace and mercy assured to us through Christ, and in the moment of death be assured that we shall continue to exist immortally, and receive a recompense in a better life."

The celebrated *Briefe über den Rationalismus,* by the same author, have at least the merit of being an honest and logical exposition of Rationalist principles and their consequences, without disguise or compromise. The commendation, however, to which in this respect the work is partly entitled, cannot be extended to the concluding letter, in which the author endeavors to establish, for himself and his fellow rationalists, the right to discharge the spiritual functions, and subscribe to the confessions, of a church whose doctrines they disbelieve; and even to make use of their position to unsettle the faith of the young committed to their instruction.

Note XLIV., p. 87.

The character of Hegel's philosophy in this respect is sufficiently shown by Strauss, *Streitschriften*, Heft III. p. 57, sqq.

Note XLV., p. 87.

Vatke's *Religion des Alten Testamentes,* forms the first part of his *Biblische Theologie wissenschaftlich dargestellt;* Berlin, 1835. In the Introduction (§ 7, 12, 13) the author lays down a law of the development of religion as a process of the infinite spirit in self-revelation, according to the principles of the Hegelian philosophy. As a consequence of this law he maintains that it is impossible for an individual to raise himself, even by the aid of divine revelation, above the spiritual position of his age, or for a nation to rise or fall from its normal stage of religious cultivation (pp. 87, 181). By this canon the entire narrative of Scripture is made to stand or fall. The account of a primitive revelation and subsequent alienation from God, must be rejected, because the human consciousness must attain to perfection through a succession of progressive stages (p. 102). The book of Genesis has no historical value; and we cannot decide whether the patriarchs before Moses had any knowledge of the one true God (pp. 180, 181). Moses himself, as represented in the scriptural account, is altogether inconceivable; for he appears at a period when, according to the laws of historical development, the time was not yet ripe for him (p. 183). Much of the history of Moses must be regarded as a mythus, invented by the priests at a later period (p. 186). The political institutions attributed to him could not possibly have been founded by him (p. 211). The ceremonial laws are such as could neither have been discovered by an individual *nor made known by divine revelation* (p. 218). The Passover was originally a feast of the sun, in celebration of his entering into the sign Aries; which fully accounts for the offering of a male lamb (p. 492). As regards the decalogue, the second commandment must be considered as an interpolation of a later date; for it implies a higher degree of abstraction than could have been reached in the Mosaic age (p. 234). The lapses into idolatry recorded in the book of Judges, are highly improbable; for a whole people cannot fall back from a higher to a lower state of religious culture (p. 181). The books of Samuel betray their legendary origin by the occurrence of round numbers, and by the significant names of the first three kings (p. 289). The wisdom attributed to Solomon is irreconcilable with his subsequent idolatry; and the account must therefore be regarded as legendary (p. 309). Such are a few of the results of the so-called philosophy of history, exercised on the narrative of Scripture. The book is valuable in one respect, and in one only. It shows the reckless manner in which rationalism finds it necessary to deal with the sacred text, before it can be accommodated to the antisupernatural hypothesis. To those who believe that a record of facts as they are is more trustworthy than a theory of facts as they ought to be on philosophical principles, the very features which the critic is compelled to reject, become additional evidence of the truth of the scripture narrative.

NOTE XLVI., p. 87.

The Hegelian element of Strauss's *Leben Jesu* is briefly exhibited at the end of the book (§ 150). The body of the work is mainly occupied with various cavils, some of them of the very minutest philosophy, designed to invalidate the historical character of the Gospel narratives. Among these precious morsels of criticism, we meet with such objections as the following. That the name of the angel Gabriel is of Hebrew origin (§ 17). That the angel, instead of inflicting dumbness on Zacharias, ought to have merely reprimanded him (*ibid.*). That a real angel would not have proclaimed the advent of the Messiah in language so strictly Jewish (§ 25). That the appearance of the star to the magi would have strengthened the popular belief in the false science of astrology (§ 34). That John the Baptist, being an ascetic, and therefore necessarily prejudiced and narrow-minded, could not have considered himself inferior to one who did not practise similar mortifications (§ 36). That Jesus could not have submitted to the rite of baptism, because that rite symbolized a future Messiah (§ 49). That if there is a personal devil, he cannot take a visible form (§ 54). That it is improbable that Jesus, when he read in the synagogue, should have lighted on an apposite passage of the prophet Isaiah (§ 58). That Jesus could not have known that the woman of Samaria had had five husbands, because it is not probable that each of them had left a distinct image in her mind, and because a minute knowledge of the history of individuals is degrading to the prophetic dignity (§ 69). That it is impossible to understand "how he, whose vocation had reference to the depths of the human heart, should be tempted to occupy himself with the fish-frequented depths of the waters" (§ 71). That Jesus could not have ridden into Jerusalem on an ass whereon never man sat, because unbroken asses are difficult to manage (§ 110). That the resurrection of the dead is impossible, because the inferior principles, whose work is corruption, will not be inclined to surrender back the dominion of the body to its former master, the soul (§ 140). That the ascension of Christ is impossible, because a body which has flesh and bones cannot be qualified for a heavenly abode; because it cannot liberate itself from the laws of gravity; and because it is childish to regard heaven as a definite locality (§ 142). — It is not creditable to the boasted enlightenment of the age, that a work which can seriously urge such petty quibbles as these should have obtained so much reputation and influence. In studying the philosophy which has given birth to such consequences, we see a new verification of the significant remark of Clemens Alexandrinus: "The philosophy, which is according to the divine tradition, establishes and confirms providence; take this away, and the Saviour's economy appears to be a myth."[1] "Strauss, the Hegelian theologian," says Sir W. Hamilton, "sees in Christianity only a *mythus*. Naturally: for his Hegelian 'Idea,' itself a myth, and confessedly finding itself in everything, of course finds in anything a myth."[2] As the labors of Strauss on the Gospel narratives have been sometimes compared to those of Niebuhr on the history of Rome, it may be instructive to peruse the opinion of the great historian on the cognate theories of a few years' earlier date. "In my opinion," writes Niebuhr in 1818, "he is not a Protestant Christian, who does not receive the historical facts of Christ's earthly life, in their literal acceptation, with all their miracles, as equally authentic with any event recorded in history, and whose belief in them is not as firm and tranquil as his belief in the latter; who has not the utmost faith in the articles of the Apostles' Creed, taken in their grammatical sense; who does not consider every doctrine and every precept of the New Testament as undoubted divine revelation, in the sense of the Christians of the first century, who knew nothing of a Theopneustia. Moreover, a Christianity after the fashion of the modern philosophers and pantheists, without a personal God, without immortality, without human individuality, without historical faith, is no Christianity at all to me; though it may be very intellectual, very ingenious philosophy. I have often said that I do not know what to do with a metaphysical God, and that I will have none but the God of the Bible, who is heart to heart with us."[3]

Niebuhr did not live to witness the publication of the *Leben Jesu;* but the above passage is as appropriate as if it had been part of an actual review of that work.

NOTE XLVII., p. 87.

With Feuerbach's *Wesen des Christenthums* I am only acquainted through the French translation by M. Ewerbeck, which forms the prin-

[1] *Stromata*, I. ii. p. 296.
[2] *Discussions*, p. 787 [696, ed. 1852].
[3] *Life and Letters of B. G. Niebuhr* vol. II. p. 123.

cipal portion of the volume entitled *Qu'est-ce que la Religion d'après la nouvelle Philosophie Allemande.* The following extracts will sufficiently show the character of the work. "The grand mystery, or rather the grand secret of religion, is here: man objectifies his being, and after having objectified it, he makes himself the object of this new subject." (p. 129.) "God is the notion, the personified idea of personality. He is the apotheosis of the human person, the *I* without the *Thou*, the subjectivity separate from the universe; the self-sufficient egoity." (p. 219.) "God is the notion of kind, but the notion personified and individualized in its turn; He is the notion of kind or its essence, and this essence as universal entity, as comprising all possible perfections, as possessing all human qualities cleared of their limitations." (p. 271.) "Where religion expresses the relation between man and the human essence, it is good and humanitary. Where it expresses the relation between man and the human essence changed to a supernatural being, it is illogical, false, and carries in it the germ of all those horrors which have been desolating society for sixty centuries." (p. 340.) "Atheism is the fruit of the contradiction in the existence of God . . . . . . we are told that God exists really and not really at the same time, we have then a perfect right to cut the matter short with such an absurd existence, and to say: there is no God." (p. 350.) "From the preceding we infer, that the divine personality, of which man avails himself to attribute his own ideas and his own qualities to a superhuman being, is nothing but the human personality externalized to the *I*. It is this psychological act which has become the basis of the speculative doctrine of Hegel, which teaches, that the consciousness that man has of God is the consciousness that God has of man." (p. 390.) The occasional notes which the translator has added to this work are, if possible, still more detestable than the text. So much disregard of truth and decency as is shown in some of his remarks on Christianity has probably seldom been compressed into the same compass.

NOTE XLVIII., p. 89.

"Christ, who taught his disciples, and us in them, how to pray, propounded not the knowledge of God, though without that he could not hear us; neither represented he his power, though without that he cannot help us; but comprehended all in this relation, *When ye pray, say, Our Father.*"—Pearson on the Creed, article I.

LECTURE III.

NOTE I., p. 93.

"Whatever is for us *something* is so only so far as it is *not* something else; all *position* is possible only by *negation;* as indeed the word itself *define* means nothing else but *limit.*" —Fichte, *Gerichtliche Verantwortung* (*Werke*, V. p. 265). "The Finite exists in relation to its *Other* (*the other* of it, *alterum*), which is its negation, and puts itself there as its limit." "Hegel, *Encykl.* § 28 (*Werke*, VI. p. 63). Compare Plotinus, *Enn.* V. l. III. c. 12. "But that is the One itself, without the Something (i. e. not some one thing); for if it were the *some* one thing, then it would not be the One itself; for the One itself is prior to the Something."—*Enn.* VI. l. VII. c. 39. "For the Intelligence, if it is to exercise intelligence, must always apprehend difference and identity." . . . . .— Spinoza, *Epist.* 50. "This determination, therefore, does not belong to the (or a) thing in its own *esse*, but, on the contrary, belongs to its *non-esse.*" The canon, undeniable from a human point of view, that all consciousness is limitation, seems to have had some influence on modern philosophical theories concerning the Divine Nature. Thus Hegel maintains that God must become limited to be conscious of himself,[1] and defines Religion as the Divine Spirit's knowledge of himself, by means of the finite Spirit.[2]

NOTE II., p. 94.

"For being limited (finite) ourselves, it would be absurd for us to make some determination of the infinite, and thus endeavor to limit it, as it were, and comprehend it."—Descartes, *Principia*, I. 26. "The second reason of our short and imperfect notions of the Deity is, *the Infinity* of it. For this we must observe, That we can perfectly know and comprehend nothing, but as it is represented to us under some certain Bounds and Limitations. . . . Upon which account, what a loss must we needs be at, in understanding or knowing the Divine Nature, when the very way of our knowing seems to carry in it something opposite to the thing known. For the way of knowing is by defining, limiting, and determining; and the thing known is that of which there neither are, nor can be, any Bounds, Limits, Definitions, or Determinations."—South, *Animadversions upon Sherlock*, ch. II. p. 55. ed. 1693. "All our thinking is a limiting; and exactly in this respect

1 *Werke*, XI. p. 193. 2 *Ibid.*, p. 200.

is it called *apprehending;* i. e., comprehending something from out of a mass of *determinable;* so that there always may remain something outside the boundary-line, which has not been included (*imprehended*) within it,—and so does not belong to that which has been apprehended."—Fichte, *Gerichtliche Verantwortung* (*Werke*, V. p. 265). "What I apprehend (or have an idea of) becomes finite by my mere apprehending, and this, even by endless ascending, never comes to the infinite."—Fichte, *Bestimmung des Menschen* (*Werke*, II. p. 304). "The subject without predicate is, what in the appearance the thing is without attributes, what the thing is in itself, an empty, undetermined ground; it is the notion in itself, which only in the predicate gets a distinction and definiteness."—Hegel, *Logik*, Th. II. (*Werke*, V. p. 70). Compare *Philosophie der Religion* (*Werke*, XI. p. 30). *Encyklopädie* § 28, 29 (*Werke*, VI. p. 65).

NOTE III., p. 94.

The opposite sides of this contradiction are indicated in the following passages. Aristotle, *Phys.* III. 6, [10,] 13: "The Infinite . . . . is the whole potentially, but not actually." . . . . Compare *Metaph.* viii. [ix. Ed. Gul. Duval, Paris, 1629] 8, 16: "That, therefore, which is capable of being, may both be and not be; the same thing, therefore, is capable both of being and of not being. But that, which is capable of not being, may not be; and that, which may not be, is corruptible. . . . . Nothing, therefore, of things simply incorruptible, is potentially simply being." For a full discussion of the distinction between *potentiality* and *actuality* (the δύναμις and ἐντελέχεια or ἐνέργεια of Aristotle), see Trendelenburg on Arist. *De Anima*, p. 295. Compare Arist. *Metaph.* viii. [ix. Ed. Gul. Duval.] 6, 2: "It is *actuality* when a thing is really so, not as when we say *potentially.* For we say *potentially* as (of) the Hermes in the wood, and the half in the whole, because it might be taken out; and so, too, a learned man, of one who is not really versed in learning, if he have the capacity for learning." . . . . This distinction plays a part in the controversy between Bramhall and Hobbes, the former of whom says, "The nearer that anything comes to the essence of God, the more remote it is from our apprehension. But shall we, therefore, make potentialities and successive duration, and former and latter, or a part without a part (as they say), to be in God? Because we are not able to understand clearly the Divine perfection, we must not therefore attribute any imperfection to Him."[1] To this Hobbes replies, "Nor do I understand what derogation it can be to the divine perfection, to attribute to it potentiality, that is, in English,

1 *Works*, vol. IV. p. 158.

power."[1] "By *potentiality*," retorts Bramhall, "he understandeth 'power' or might; others understand possibility or indetermination. Is not he likely to confute the Schoolmen to good purpose?"[2] Hobbes concludes by saying, "There is no such word as potentiality in the Scriptures, nor in any author of the Latin tongue. It is found only in School divinity, as a word of art, or rather as a word of craft, to amaze and puzzle the laity."[3] This charge may be answered in the words of Trendelenburg. "In unfolding these notions, drawn forth from the very recess of philosophy, we are forced into such straits by the laxness and the poverty of the Latin tongue in matters pertaining to philosophy, that we must have recourse, for the sake of perspicuity, to scholastic terms."[4]

But to go from the word to the thing. The contradiction thus involved in the notion of the Infinite has given rise to two opposite representations of it; the one, as the affirmation of all reality; the other, as the negation of all reality. The older metaphysicians endeavored to exhaust the infinite by an endless addition of predicates; hence arose the favorite representation of God, as the *Ens perfectissimum*, or sum of all realities, which prevailed in the Wolfian Philosophy, and was accepted by Kant.[5] On the other hand, the post-Kantian metaphysicians perceived clearly that all predication is necessarily limitation, and that to multiply attributes is merely to represent the infinite under a variety of finite determinations. The consummation of this point of view was attained in the principle of Hegel, that pure being is pure nothing, and that all determinate being (Daseyn) is necessarily limited.[6] Hence his constant assertion that God cannot be represented by predicates.[7] Both schools of philosophy are right in what they deny, and wrong in what they affirm. The earlier metaphysicians were right in assuming that thought is only possible by means of definite conceptions; but they were wrong in supposing that any multiplication of such conceptions can amount to a representation of the infinite. The later metaphysicians were right in opposing this error; but they fell into the opposite extreme of imagining that by the removal of determinations the act of thought and its object could become infinite. In truth, a thought about nothing is no thought at all; and the rejection of determinations is simply the refusal to think. The

1 *Works*, ed. Molesworth, vol. V. p. 342.
2 *Works*, vol. IV. p. 425.
3 *Works*, ed. Molesworth, vol. IV. p. 299.
4 *In Arist. de Anima*, p. 295.
5 See Wolf, *Theologia Naturalis*, Pars II. § 6, 14; Kant, *Kritik der reinen Vernunft*, p. 450, ed. Rosenkranz.
6 See *Werke*, III. p. 73; IV. p. 26, 27; V. p. 70; VI. p. 63.
7 See *Werke*, VI. p. 65; XI. p. 31, 153; XII. p. 229, 418.

conclusion to be drawn from the entire controversy is, that the infinite, as such, is not an object of human thought.

Note IV., p. 95.

"The adding infinity to any idea or conception necessarily finite, makes up no other than a curious contradiction for a divine attribute. . . . You make up an attribute of knowledge or wisdom *infinitely finite;* which is as chimerical and gigantic an idea as an infinite human body."—Bp. Browne, *Divine Analogy,* p. 77. "Discovering conditions of the Unconditioned, inventing a possibility for the absolutely Necessary, and the being willing to construct it in order to be able to conceive of it, must immediately and most obviously appear to be an absurd undertaking."—Jacobi, *Ueber die Lehre des Spinoza* (*Werke,* IV. Abth. II. p. 153). "Thou art different from the finite, not only in degree, but in kind. They only make Thee by that upward gradation a greater man, and ever still only a greater man; but never God, the Infinite, the Immeasurable."— Fichte, *Bestimmung des Menschen* (*Werke,* II. p. 304).

Note V., p. 95.

"For, if we should suppose a man to be made with clear eyes, and all the rest of his organs of sight well disposed, but endued with no other sense; and that he should look only upon one thing, which is always of the same color and figure, without the least appearance of variety, he would seem to me, whatsoever others might say, to see, no more than I seem to myself to feel the bones of my own limbs by my organs of feeling; and yet those bones are always, and on all sides, touched by a most sensible membrane. I might perhaps say he were astonished, and looked upon it; but I should not say he saw it; it being almost all one for a man to be always sensible of one and the same thing, and not to be sensible at all." Hobbes, *Elem. Phil.* (Eng. Works), Sect. I. P. IV. c. 25, 5.

Note VI., p. 95.

The paradox of Hegel, if applied, where alone we have any data for applying it, to the necessary limits of human thought, becomes no paradox at all, but an obvious truth, almost a truism. Our conceptions are limited to the finite and the determinate; and a thought which is not of any definite object, is but the negation of all thinking. Hegel's error consists in mistaking an impotence of thought for a condition of existence. That pure being is in itself pure nothing, is more than we can be warranted in assuming; for we have no conception of pure being at all, and no means of judging of the possibility of its existence. The absurdity becomes still more glaring, when this pure nothing is represented as containing in itself a process of self-development, — when being and non-being, which are absolutely one and the same, are regarded at the same time as two opposite elements, which, by their union, constitute *becoming*, and thus give rise to finite existence. But this absurdity is unavoidable in a system which starts with the assumption that thought and being are identical, and thus abolishes at the outset the possibility of distinguishing between the impotence of thought and its activity.

Note VII., p. 96.

Über den Grund unseres Glaubens an eine göttliche Weltregierung (*Werke*, V. p. 186). In a subsequent work written in defence of this opinion, Fichte explains himself as meaning that existence, as a conception of sensible origin, cannot be ascribed to God.[1] That the conception of existence is, like all other human representations, incompetent to express the nature of the Absolute, has been frequently admitted, by philosophers and theologians. Thus, Plato describes the supreme good "as not existence, but as above existence, and superior to it in dignity and power:"[2] and his language is borrowed by Justin Martyr and Athanasius, to express the absolute nature of God;[3] Plotinus in like manner says that "the One is above being;"[4] and Schelling, the Plotinus of Germany, asserts that the Absolute in its essence is neither ideal nor real, neither thought nor being.[5] This position is perfectly tenable so long as it is confessed that the Absolute is not the object of theological or philosophical speculation, and, consequently, that the provinces of thought and existence are not coëxtensive. But without this safeguard, there is no middle course

1 *Appellation an das Publicum gegen die Anklage des Atheismus* (*Werke*, V. p. 220).

2 *Republic*, VI p. 509.

3 Justin, *Dial. c. Tryph.* c. 4. "Who is above all existence; unspeakable, ineffable, but the only Noble and Good.—Athanasius c. Gentes. c. 2. "Who is superior to all existence, and human intelligence, seeing that He is good and surpassing in moral beauty." Compare Damascenus, De Fide Orthod. I. 4. "He is none of the things that are; not so as not to be, but to be above all things that are, above being itself."

4 *Enn.* V. I. 10. τὸ ἐπέκεινα ὄντος τὸ ἕν. Compare Proclus, *Inst. Theol.* c. 115. "It is manifest that every god is above all the things mentioned, existence, and life, and mind."

5 *Bruno*, p 57. "The Absolute we have now defined as essentially neither ideal nor real, neither thinking nor being."

between an illogical theology and an atheistical logic. The more pious minds will take refuge in mysticism, and seek to reach the absolute by a superhuman process: the more consistent reasoners will rush into the opposite extreme, and boldly conclude that that which is inconceivable is also non-existent.

Note VIII., p. 96.

Sextus Empiricus, *Adv. Math.* VII. 311. "If the subject that knows is the whole, then there will be no object that is known; and it belongs to the most irrational of things, that there be that which knows, and there be *not*, that which is known."—Plotinus, *Enn.* V. III. 10. "It must be, then, that that which has intelligence, be in duality when it exercises intelligence, and that either one of the two be outside it, or that both be in it, and that intelligence always have to do with *alterity* (difference)."—Compare Hegel, *Philosophie der Religion* (*Werke*, XI. p. 167). "In the consciousness, so far as I have knowledge of an object, I know it as my *Other* (or the *Other* of me), and hence myself limited by it and finite."—Marheineke, *Grundlehren*, § 84. "But this comes to pass thus: in the absolute idea, in which science takes its stand-point, the subject is not different from the object, but just as it (i. e. the absolute idea) is the idea of the Absolute, as object, so also is the object in it, as the absolute idea, subject, and therefore the absolute idea is not different from God Himself."

Note IX., p. 97.

In exhibiting the two universal conditions of human consciousness, that of *difference between objects*, and that of *relation between object and subject*, I have considered each with reference to its more immediate and obvious application; the former being viewed in connection with the Infinite, and the latter with the Absolute. But at the same time it is obvious that the two conditions are so intimately connected together, and the ideas to which they relate so mutually involved in each other, that either argument might be employed with equal force in the other direction. For difference is a relation, as well as a limit; that which is one out of many being related to the objects from which it is distinguished. And the subject and object of consciousness, in like manner, are not only related to, but distinguished from, each other; and thus each is a limit to the other: while, if either of them could be destroyed, a conception of the infinite by the finite would be still impossible; for either there would be no infinite to be conceived, or there would be no finite to conceive it.

The three Laws of Thought, commonly acknowledged by logicians, those of Identity, Contradiction, and Excluded Middle, are but the above two conditions viewed in relation to a given notion. For in the first place, every definite notion, as such, is discerned in the two relations of identity and difference, as being that which it is, and as distinguished from that which it is not. These two relations are expressed by the Laws of Identity and Contradiction. And in the second place, a notion is distinguished from all that it is not (*A* from not-*A*), by means of the mutual relation of both objects to a common subject, the universe of whose consciousness is constituted by this distinction. This mutual relation is expressed by the Law of Excluded Middle.

NOTE X., p. 97.

"Though we cannot fully comprehend the Deity, nor exhaust the infiniteness of its perfection, yet may we have an idea or conception of a Being absolutely perfect; such a one as is nostro modulo conformis, 'agreeable and proportionate to our measure and scantling;' as we may approach near to a mountain, and touch it with our hands, though we cannot encompass it all round, and enclasp it within our arms."—Cudworth, *Intellectual System*, ch. 5 (vol. II. p. 518, ed. Harrison). "We grant that the mind is limited, but does it thence follow that the object of thought must be limited? We think not. We grant that the mind cannot *embrace* the Infinite, but we nevertheless consider that the mind may have a notion of the Infinite. No more do we believe that the mind, as finite, can only recognize finite objects, than we believe that the eye, because limited in its power, can only recognize those objects whose entire extension comes within the range of vision. As well tell us that because a mountain is too large for the eye of a mole, therefore the mole can recognize no mountain: as well tell us that because the world is too large for the eye of a man, therefore man can recognize no world, — as tell us that because the Infinite cannot be embraced by the finite mind, therefore the mind can recognize no Infinite."— Calderwood, *Philosophy of the Infinite*, p. 12. The illustrations employed by both authors are unfortunate. The part of the mountain touched by the hand of the man, or seen by the eye of the mole, is, *ex hypothesi*, as a part of a larger object, imperfect, relative, and finite. And the world, which is confessedly too large for the eye of a man, must, in its unseen portion, be apprehended, not by sight, but by some other faculty. If, therefore, the Infinite is too large for the mind of man, it can only be recognized by some other mind, or by some faculty in man which is not mind. But no such faculty is or can be assumed. In admitting that we do not recognize the Infinite in its entire extension, it is admitted that we do not recognize it *as infinite*. The attempted distinction is sufficiently refuted in the words of Bishop Browne. "If it is said that we may then *apprehend* God directly, though not *comprehend* him; that we may have a direct and immediate knowledge *partly*, and in some *degree;* and though not of his *Essence*, yet of the *Perfections* flowing from it: I answer, That all the Attributes and Perfections of God are in their real Nature as infinite as his very Essence; so that there can be no such thing as having a direct view of him in part; for whatever is in God is equally Infinite. If God is to be apprehended at all by any direct and immediate idea, he must be apprehended *as Infinite;* and in that very act of the mind, he would be *comprehended;* and there is no medium between apprehending an Infinite Being *directly* and *analogically*."[1]

NOTE XI., p. 100.

The brevity with which this argument is necessarily expressed in the text, may render a few words of explanation desirable. Of course it is not meant that no period of time can be conceived, except in a time equally long; for this would make a thousand years as inconceivable as an eternity. But though there is nothing inconceivable in the notion of a thousand years or any other large amount of time, such a notion is conceivable only under the form of a *portion of time*, having other time before and after it. An infinite duration, on the other hand, can only be conceived as having no time before or after it, and hence as having no relation or resemblance to any amount of finite time, however great. The mere conception of an indefinite duration, bounding every conceivable portion of time, is thus wholly distinct from that of infinite duration; for infinity can neither bound nor be bounded by any duration beyond itself.

This distinction has perhaps not been sufficiently observed by an able and excellent writer of the present day, in a work, the principal portions of which are worthy of the highest commendation. Dr. McCosh argues in behalf of a positive conception of infinity, in opposition to the theory of Sir W. Hamilton, in the following manner: "To whatever point we go out in imagination, we are sure that we are not at the limits of existence; nay, we believe that, to whatever farther point we might go, there would be something still farther on." "Such," he continues, "seems to us to be

1 *Divine Analogy*, p. 37. The author is speaking of our knowledge in a future state; but his arguments are more properly applicable to our present condition.

the true psychological nature of the mind's conviction in regard to the infinite. It is not a mere impotence to conceive that existence, that time or space, should cease, but a positive affirmation that they do not cease."[1]

To this argument it may be objected, in the first place, that this "something still farther on" is not itself primarily an object of conception, but merely the boundary of conception. It is a condition unavoidable by all finite thought, that whatever we conceive must be related to something else which we do not conceive. I think of a thousand years as bounded by a further duration beyond it. But if, secondarily, we turn our attention to this boundary itself, it is not then actually conceived as either limited or unlimited on its remoter side; we do not positively think of it as having no boundary; we only refrain from thinking of it as having a boundary. It is thus presented to us as *indefinite*, but not as *infinite*. And the result will be the same, if to our conception of a thousand years we add cycle upon cycle, till we are wearied with the effort. An idea which we tend towards, but never reach, is indefinite, but not infinite; for, at whatever point we rest, there are conditions beyond, which remain unexhausted.

In the second place, even if we could positively perceive this further duration as going on forever, we should still be far removed from the conception of infinity. For such a duration is given to us as bounding and bounded by our original conception of a thousand years; it is limited at its nearer extremity, though unlimited at the other. If this be regarded as infinite, we are reduced to the self-contradictory notion of infinity related to a time beyond itself. Is a thousand years, *plus* its infinite boundary, greater than that boundary alone, or not? If it is, we have the absurdity of a greater than the infinite. If it is not, the original conception of a thousand years, from relation to which that of infinity is supposed to arise, is itself reduced to a nonentity, and cannot be related to anything. This contradiction may be avoided, if we admit that our conception of time, as bounded, implies an apprehension of the indefinite, but not of the infinite.

But possibly, after all, the difference between Dr. McCosh's view and that of Sir W. Hamilton, may be rather verbal than real. For the subsequent remarks of the former are such as might be fully accepted by the most uncompromising adherent of the latter. "The mind seeks in vain to embrace the infinite in a positive image, but is constrained to believe, when its efforts fail, that there is a something to which no limits can be put." All that need practically be contended for by the supporters

1 *Method of the Divine Government*, p. 534, 4th edition.

of the negative theory is, first, that this inability to assign limits indicates directly only an indefiniteness in our manner of thinking, but not necessarily an infinity in the object about which we think; and, secondly, that our indirect *belief* in the infinite, whether referred to an impotence or to a power of mind, is not of such a character that we can deduce from it any logical consequences available in philosophy or in theology. The sober and reverent tone of religious thought which characterizes Dr. McCosh's writings, warrants the belief that he would not himself repudiate these conclusions.

NOTE XII., p. 100.

For the antagonist theories of a beginning of time itself, and of an eternal succession in them, see Plato, *Timæus*, p. 37, 38, and Aristotle, *Phys.* VIII. 1. The two theories are ably contrasted in Prof. Butler's *Lectures on the History of Ancient Philosophy*, vol. II. p. 185 sqq. Plato does not appear to regard the beginning of time as the beginning of material existence, but only of the sensible phenomena of matter. The insensible substratum of the phenomena seems to have been regarded by him as coeternal with the Deity.[1] It has been conjectured, indeed, that to this matter was attributed a perpetual existence in successive duration, as distinguished from the existence of the Deity, in a manner devoid of all succession.[2] This hypothesis perhaps relieves the theory from the apparent paradox of an existence *before* time (*before* being itself a temporal relation), but it cannot be easily reconciled with the language of Plato; and moreover, it only avoids one paradox by the introduction of another, — that of a state of existence out of time *contemporaneous* with one in time.

NOTE XIII., p. 100.

In Joann. Evang. Tract. XXXVIII. 10. "Discuss the changes of things, and you will find a past and a future; think of God, and you will find a present, in which neither past nor future is possible."—Compare *Confess.* XI. c. ii.; *Enarr.* in Ps. II. 7; *De Civ. Dei*, XI. 21. See also Cudworth, vol. II. p. 529, ed. Harrison; Herder, *Gott, Werke*, VIII. p. 139.

1 See *Timæus*, p 49—53. Plato's opinion however has been variously represented. For some account of the controversies on this point, see Mosheim's Dissertation, *De Creatione ex Nihilo*, translated in Harrison's edition of Cudworth, vol. III. p. 140; Brucker, *Historia Philosophiæ*, vol. p. 676. Compare also Professor Thompson's note, in Butler's *Lectures on the History of Ancient Philosophy*, vol. II. p. 189.

2 See Mosheim's note in Harrison's Cudworth, vol. II. p. 551.

NOTE XIV., p. 100.

De Consol. Philos. L. V. Pr. 6. "Eternity, therefore, is at once the entire and the perfect possession of interminable life."

NOTE XV., p. 100.

Summa, P. I. Qu. X. Art. 1. "In this way, therefore, eternity is made known by two things. First, by this, that what is in eternity is interminable, *i. e.*, without beginning and without end. Second by this, that eternity is without succession, existing at once in totality."—Compare Plotinus, *Enn.* III. 1. viii. c. 2. . . . . . "Always having the whole present, but not this thing now, and then another, but all at once."—Proclus *Inst., Theol.* c. 52. "All which is eternal exists at once in totality." Several historical notices relating to this theory are given by Petavius, *Theologica Dogmata*, De Deo, l. III. c. 4.

NOTE XVI., p. 101.

. . . . "Nor can eternity be defined by time, or have any relation to time."—Spinoza, *Ethica*, P. V. Prop. 23. "Eternity, in the pure sense of the word, can be explained by no duration of time, even supposing we take this as endless (*indefinite*). Duration is an undetermined continuation of existence, which in every moment bears with it a measure of transientness, of the future as of the past."—Herder, *Gott* (*Werke*, VIII. p. 140). "In so far as the *I* is eternal, it has no duration at all. For duration is thinkable only in relation to objects. We speak of an eternity [sempiternity] of duration (æviternitas) *i. e.* of an existence in *all* time, but eternity in the pure sense of the word (æternitas) is Being in *no* time." Schelling, *Vom Ich*, § 15. Cognate to, or rather identical with, these speculations, is the theory advocated by Mr. Maurice (*Theological Essays*, p. 422 sqq.), "that eternity is not a lengthening out or continuation of time; that they are generically different."

NOTE XVII., p. 101.

In the acute and decisive criticism of Schelling by Sir W. Hamilton, this objection is urged with great effect. "We cannot, at the same moment, be in the intellectual intuition and in common consciousness; we must therefore be able to connect them by an act of memory—of recollection. But how can there be a *remembrance* of the Absolute and its Intuition? As out of time, and space, and relation, and difference, it is admitted that the Absolute cannot be construed to the understanding. But as remembrance is only possible under the conditions of the understanding, it is consequently impossible to remember anything anterior to the moment when we awaken into consciousness; and the *clairvoyance* of the Absolute, even granting its reality, is thus, after the crisis, as if it had never been."—*Discussions*, p. 23.

NOTE XVIII., p. 101.

See Augustine, *In Joann. Evang.* Tract. XXXVIII. 10. "Think of God, you will find a present (an *Is*) in which the past and future cannot be. In order, therefore, that *you* also *may be*, transcend time. But who shall transcend time by his own powers? He will raise you to it, who said to the Father, "*I will that they also be with me where I am.*" This precept has found great favor with mystical theologians. Thus Eckart, in a sermon published among those of Tauler, says, "Nothing hinders the soul so much in its knowledge of God as time and place. Time and place are parts, and God is one; therefore, if our soul is to know God, it must know him above time and place."[1] And the author of the *Theologia Germanica*, c. 7: "If the soul shall see with the right eye into eternity, then the left eye must close itself and refrain from working, and be as though it were dead. For if the left eye be fulfilling its office towards outward things; that is, holding converse with time and its creatures; then must the right eye be hindered in its working; that is, in its contemplation."[2] So too Swedenborg, in his *Angelic Wisdom concerning Divine Providence*, § 48: "What is infinite in itself and eternal in itself is divine, can be seen, and yet cannot be seen by men: it can be seen by those who think of infinite not from space, and of eternal not from time; but cannot be seen by those who think of infinite and eternal from space and time."[3] In the same spirit sings Angelus Silesius:

"Mensch, wo du deinen Geist schwingst über Ort und Zeit,
So kannst du jeden Blick sein in der Ewigkeit."[4]

The modern German mysticism is in this respect nowise behind the earlier. Schelling says of his intuition of the Absolute, "The pure self-

1 *Life and Sermons of Dr John Tauler*, translated by Susanna Winkworth, p. 190.

2 *Theologia Germanica*, translated by Susanna Winkworth, p. 20.

3 English translation, p. 27.

4 *Cherubinischer Wandersmann*, I. 12. Quoted by Strauss, *Glaubenslehre*, II. p. 738.

consciousness is an act which lies beyond all time, and posits all time."[1] And again, "But since in the Absolute thinking is entirely one with the intuition, so will all things not merely as endless, by their conceptions, but eternal by their ideas, and without any relation, even of opposition, to time, and with absolute unity of potentiality and actuality, be expressed in it, as the highest unity of thought and intuition."[2] Schleiermacher (*Christliche Glaube*, § 52) endeavors to find something analogous to the Divine Eternity, in the timeless existence of the personal self, as the permanent subject of successive modes of consciousness. The analogy, however, fails in two respects; first, because the permanent self cannot be contemplated apart from its successive modes, but is discerned only in relation to them; and, secondly, because, though not itself subject to the condition of *succession*, it is still in time under that of *duration*. Kant truly remarks on all such mystical efforts to transcend time: "All solely on this account, that men may at last rejoice over an *eternal rest*, which makes out their imagined happy end of all things; properly an idea, along with which their understanding is gone, and all thinking itself comes to an end."[3]

NOTE XIX., p. 101.

This is directly admitted by Fichte, who says, in his earliest work, "How the infinite Mind may contemplate its existence and its attributes, we cannot know, without being the infinite Mind ourselves."[4] But of the two alternatives which this important admission offers, Fichte himself, in his subsequent writings, as well as his successors in philosophy, chose the wrong one. See above, Lecture I. note 29.

NOTE XX., p. 102.

"Look into the dictionaries for the usage of the words *Person, personality*, etc., ... all say, that these words designate something *peculiar or special under a certain appearance*; a subordinate idea, which does not belong to the Infinite." . . . . Herder, *Gott* (*Werke*, VIII. p. 199). "What then do you call personality and consciousness? that certainly which you have found in yourselves, which you have become acquainted with in yourselves, and have designated with this name. But the least attention

1 *System des Transcendentalen Idealismus*, p. 59 (*Werke*, III. p. 375).
2 *Bruno*, p. 58.
3 *Das Ende aller Dinge* (*Werke*, VII. p. 422).
4 *Versuch einer Kritik aller Offenbarung* (*Werke*, V. p. 42).

to your construction of this notion can teach you, that you absolutely do not and cannot have this thought without limitation and finiteness." Fichte, *Ueber göttliche Weltregierung* (*Werke*, V. p. 187). Schleiermacher, in like manner, in his second Discourse on Religion, offers a half apology for Pantheism, on the ground of the limitation implied in the notions of personality and consciousness.[1] And Strauss remarks: "As persons, we know ourselves only in distinction from other persons of the same kind, from whom we distinguish ourselves, and of course, too, as finite; it appears, consequently, that the notion of personality loses all significance beyond this province of the finite, and that a being, who has no other besides himself of his own kind, cannot be a person at all."—*Christliche Glaubenslehre*, I. p. 504.

NOTE XXI., p. 103.

De Trinitate, XV. c. 5. "Therefore if we say, eternal, immortal, incorruptible, wise, powerful, just, good, happy, spirit; of all these, the last only seems to be significant of substance, but the others qualities of this substance; but not so is it in that ineffable and simple nature. For what there seems to be said of qualities must be understood of substance or essence. For God is far from being called Spirit as to substance, and good as to quality; but both of these as to substance . . . . although in God justice is one with goodness, with happiness, and the being Spirit is one with being just and good and happy."—*Ibid.* VI. c. 4. Compare Aquinas, *Summa*, P. I. Qu. XL. Art. I: . . . . "Because the divine simplicity excludes the composition of form and matter, it follows, that in divine things, the abstract and the concrete is one with the Deity and God. And because the divine simplicity excludes the composition of subject and accident, it follows that the attributes of God are one with his essential being; and therefore wisdom and virtue are identical in God, because both are in the divine essence." See also above, Lecture II. note 27.

NOTE XXII., p. 103.

Plotinus, *Enn.* VII. l. ix. c. 6. "Whatever may be said to be wanting, is wanting in "*the Well*" (i. e., in perfectness of condition); . . . . so that goodness, so that will, is not predicable of the One; for the One transcends goodness; . . . . nor intelligence . . nor motion, for it is prior to intelligence, to motion." . . . . Spinoza, *Eth.* P. I. Prop. 17. Schol. "If intelligence belongs to the divine nature, it cannot be, as our intelligence,

1 *Werke*, I. pp. 269, 280.

posterior to or coëxistent with the objects of intelligence, since God is in causality prior to all things; but on the contrary reality and the formal essence of things is on that account such, because as such it exists objectively in the Divine Mind. . . . . Since, therefore, the Divine Intelligence is the one and the only cause of things, indeed (as we have shown) as much of their essence as of their existence, He Himself ought necessarily to differ from them as much in respect to essence as to existence. . . . . And yet the Intelligence of God is the cause both of the essence and of the existence of our intelligence; therefore the Intelligence of God, so far as it is conceived to constitute the divine essence, differs from our intelligence, in respect alike to essence and to existence." . . . . Compare P. I. Prop. 32. Cor. 1, 2, and P. II. Prop. 11. Cor., where Spinoza maintains that God is not conscious in so far as he is infinite, but becomes conscious in man; — a conclusion identical with that of the extreme Hegelian school, and, indeed, substantially the same with that of Hegel himself. See above, Lecture I, notes 29, 32.

Note XXIII., p. 104.

Anselm, *Monolog.* c. 66. "Without doubt, in all investigations into the essential being of the Creator, the deeper knowledge is reached, the greater the likeness to Him of the created thing, by which the investigation is made. . . . . Manifestly, therefore, as the rational mind alone among all created things can rise to the investigation of this essential being, this alone can avail to the discovery of it." Compare Aquinas, *Summa,* P. I. Qu. XXIX. Art. 3. "*Person* signifies that which is most perfect in all nature, or a subsistence in a rational nature. Hence, since all which belongs to perfection, must be attributed to God because his essence contains in itself all perfection, — it is fitting that this name *person,* be used of God, yet not in the same way in which it is used of creatures, but in a more excellent way; just as other names are ascribed to God, which are put by us upon created beings." And Jacobi, at the conclusion of an eloquent denunciation of the Pantheism of his own day, truly observes, "A being without self-being is entirely and universally impossible. But a self-being without consciousness, and again a consciousness without self-consciousness, without substantiality and at least an implied personality, is just as impossible; the one as well as the other is but empty words. And so God is not in being, He is, in the highest sense, the Not-being, if He is not a *Spirit;* and He is not a Spirit, if he is wanting in the fundamental quality of Spirit, self-consciousness, substantiality and personality."[1] In the same

[1] *Ueber eine Weissagung Lichtenberg's* (*Werke,* III. p. 240). Compare also the Preface to Vol. IV. p. xlv. .

spirit, and with a just recognition of the limits of human thought, M. Bartholmèss says, "He who refuses to take some traits of resemblance from the moral part of the world will be forced to take them from the physical part, the mathematical, the logical; he will make God after the image of the material world, — after the image of a geometrical magnitude or arithmetical, — after the image of a logical abstraction. Always, in lifting himself to the Creator, he will rest upon some part or other of the creation."[1] To the same effect, a distinguished living writer of our own country observes, "The worshipper carried through the long avenues of columns and statues, and the splendid halls of the ancient temple of Egyptian Thebes, was not conducted at last to a more miserable termination, when in the inner shrine he found one of the lower animals, than the follower of a modern philosopher, when conducted through processes, laws, and developments, to a divinity who has less of separate sensation, consciousness, and life, than the very brutes which Egypt declared to be its gods."[2]

NOTE XXIV., p. 104.

Pensées, P. I. Art. IV. § 6. In like manner, in another passage, Pascal says, "All bodies, the firmament, the stars, the earth, kingdoms, — are not equal to the most insignificant spirit; for such a spirit knows all these, and itself; but the body, nothing."[3]

The following spirited translation of Jacobi[4] is from the pen of Sir W. Hamilton, and occurs in the second of his *Lectures on Metaphysics*, just published. The entire Lecture from which it is taken constitutes a forcible and admirably illustrated argument to the same effect. "*Nature conceals God:* for through her whole domain Nature reveals only fate, only an indissoluble chain of mere efficient causes without beginning and without end, excluding, with equal necessity, both providence and chance. An independent agency, a free original commencement, within her sphere and proceeding from her powers, is absolutely impossible. Working without will, she takes counsel neither of the good nor of the beautiful; creating nothing, she casts off from her dark abyss only eternal transformations of herself, unconsciously and without an end; furthering with the same ceaseless industry decline and increase, death and life, — never producing what alone is of God and what supposes liberty, — the virtuous, the immortal. *Man reveals God:* for Man by his intelligence rises above nature, and in virtue of this intelligence is conscious of himself, as a

1 *Histoire des doctrines religieuses de la Philosophie Moderne*, Introduction, p. xli.

2 McCosh, *Method of the Divine Government* p. 461 (4th edition).

3 *Pensées* P. II. Art X. § 1.

4 *Von den göttlichen Dingen* (*Werke*, III. p. 425).

power not only independent of, but opposed to, nature, and capable of resisting, conquering, and controlling her. As man has a living faith in this power, superior to nature, which dwells in him, so has he a belief in God; a feeling, an experience of his existence. As he does not believe in this power, so does he not believe in God: he sees, he experiences naught in existence but nature, — necessity, — fate."—*Hamilton's Lectures on Metaphysics*. Am. Edition, p. 29.

NOTE XXV., p. 105.

Descartes, *Discours de la Méthode*, P. IV., *Principia*, P. I. § 7. That the Cartesian *cogito, ergo sum*, is not intended as a syllogism, in which thought and existence are two distinct attributes, but as a statement of the fact, that personal existence consists in consciousness, has been sufficiently shown by M. Cousin, in his Essay "Sur le vrai sens du *cogito, ergo sum*." The same view has been well stated by Mr. Veitch, in the introduction to his translation of the *Discours de la Méthode*, p. xxii. M. Bartholmèss (*Histoire des doctrines religieuses*, I. p. 23) happily renders *ergo* by *c'est-à-dire*. It must be remembered, however, that the *cogito* of Descartes is not designed to express the phenomena of reflection alone, but is coëxtensive with the entire consciousness. This is expressly affirmed in the *Principia*, P. I. § 9. "By the word *cogitatio* I understand all the objects of our consciousness. And so not only to understand, to will, to imagine, but also to perceive, — all are meant by *cogitare*." The dictum, thus extended, may perhaps be advantageously modified by disengaging the essential from the accidental features of consciousness; but its main principle remains unshaken; namely, that our conception of real existence, as distinguished from appearance, is derived from, and depends upon, the distinction between the one conscious subject and the several objects of which he is conscious. The rejection of consciousness, as the primary constituent of substantive existence, constitutes Spinoza's point of departure from the principles of Descartes, and, at the same time, the fundamental error of his system. Spinoza in fact transfers the notion of *substance*, which is originally derived from the consciousness of personality, and has no positive significance out of that consciousness, to the absolute, which exists and is conceived by itself, — an object to whose existence consciousness bears no direct testimony, and whose conception involves a self-contradiction.

NOTE XXVI., p. 105.

"*I am, that I am.* This decisive utterance establishes all. Its echo in the human soul is the revelation of God in it. What makes man man, i. e., makes him the image of God, is called *Reason.* This begins with the — I am. . . . . Reason without personality is non-entity, the like non-entity with that original cause, — which is All and not One, or One and None, the perfection of the imperfect, the absolutely Undetermined — called God by those who will have no knowledge of the true God, but yet shrink from denying Him — with the lips."—Jacobi, *Von den göttlichen Dingen* (*Werke*, III. p. 418).

NOTE XXVII., p. 106.

For notices of Schelling's philosophy in this respect, see Bartholmèss *Histoire des doctrines religieuses*, II. p. 116, and Willm, *Histoire de la Philosophie Allemande*, III. p. 318. "The school of Schelling," says Mme de Stael, "supposes that the individual perishes in us, but that the inward qualities, which we possess, reënter into the grand whole of the eternal creation. This immortality has a terrible resemblance to death."[1] Schelling's views on this point are more completely developed by his disciple Blasche, in his *Philosophische Unsterblichkeitlehre*, especially §§ 18, 55, 56, 72. The tendency of Hegel's teaching is in the same direction; the individual being with him only an imperfect and insignificant phase of the universal:[2] and a personal immortality, though not openly denied, seems excluded by inference; an inference which his successors have not hesitated to make.[3] Schleiermacher concludes his Second Discourse on Religion with these remarkable words: "The final aim of a religious life is not the immortality, which

1 *De l' Allemagne*, Partie III. ch. 7.

2 *Phänomenologie des Geistes*, Vorrede (*Werke*, II. p. 22).

3 See Michelet, *Geschichte der letzten Systeme der Philosophie*, II. p. 638. Strauss, in his *Christliche Glaubenslehre*, § 106—110, gives an instructive account of some of the speculations of recent German writers on this question; his own commentary being not the least significant portion. "Thereby indeed," he says "the *Ego* makes known its will to carry on to all eternity (i. e. not to take a step out from its own finiteness) not only its subjectivity in general, but the particular relations of this subjectivity." And again: "Only the nature of the species is infinite and inexhaustible; that of the individual can be only finite." His inquiry concludes with the well-known words, "The other world is, in all forms, the one foe, but in its form as the world to come, the last foe, which speculative criticism has to combat and if possible to overcome." And Feuerbach, another "advanced" disciple of the Hegelian school, has written an essay on Death and Immortality, for the purpose of showing that a belief in personal annihilation is indispensable to sound morality and true religion; that the opposite belief is connected with all that is "satanic" and "bestial;" and that temporal death is but an image of God, the "great objective negation:" and has indicated significantly, in another work, the philosophical basis of his theory, by an aphorism the direct contradictory to that of Descartes, "Cogitans nemo sum. Cogito, ergo omnes sum homines."

many wish for and believe in, or only pretend to believe in . . . . not that beyond time or rather after this time, but yet in time, but the immortality, which we can have immediate in this temporal life, — and which is a problem in the solution of which we are ever employed. In the midst of the finite to be one with the infinite, and be eternal in every instant, — that is the immortality of religion." And later, in his *Christliche Glaube,* § 158, while admitting that the belief in a personal immortality follows naturally from the doctrine of the twofold nature of Christ, he notwithstanding thinks it necessary to apologize for those who reject this belief on pantheistic principles: "For from this point of view, it may be alike maintained, on the one hand, that the consciousness of God makes up the essential nature of every life which in the higher sense is self-conscious or rational, on the other hand, however, that, while the Spirit in this productivity is essentially immortal, yet the individual soul is only a transient action of this productivity, and so is also essentially perishable. . . . . With such a renunciation of the continuation of personality, would a supremacy of the consciousness of God perfectly agree." Mr. Atkinson, from the side of materialism, arrives at a similar conclusion: "What more noble and glorious than a calm and joyful indifference about self and the future, in merging the individual in the general good, — the general good in universal nature."[1] And M. Comte comes forward with his substitute of "subjective immortality," i. e., being remembered by other people, as a far nobler and truer conception of a future life than that held by theologians.[2] But the most systematic and thoroughgoing exponent of this philosophy is Schopenhauer. With him, the species is the exhibition in time of the idea or real being, of which the individual is but the finite and transient expression.[3] In the same sense in which the individual was generated from nothing, he returns to nothing by death.[4] To desire a personal immortality is to desire to perpetuate an error to infinity; for individual existence is the error from which it should be the aim of life to extricate ourselves.[5] Judaism, which teaches a creation out of nothing, consistently asserts that death is annihilation; while Christianity has borrowed its belief in immortality from India, and inconsistently engrafted it on a Jewish stem.[6] The true doctrine however is not to be found in these, but in the Indian Vedas, whose superior wisdom can only be ascribed to the fact, that their authors,

1 *Letters on the Laws of Man's Nature and Development*, p. 189.
2 *Catéchisme Positiviste*, p. 169.
3 *Die Welt als Wille und Vorstellung*, II. p. 484, 487, 511.
4 *Ibid.*, p. 482, 498.
5 *Ibid.*, p. 494.
6 *Ibid.*, p. 489, 617.

living nearer, in point of time, to the origin of the human race, comprehended more clearly and profoundly the true nature of things.[1] As a relief from this desolating pantheism, it is refreshing to turn to the opposite language of Neander. "Man could not become conscious of God as his God, if he were not a personal spirit, divinely allied, and destined for eternity, an eternal object (as an individual) of God; and thereby far above all natural and perishable beings, whose perpetuity is that of the species, not the individual.[2]

NOTE XXVIII., p. 106.

We have great reason to find fault with the strange manner of some men, who are ever vexing themselves with the discussion of ill-conceived matters. They seek for that which they know, and know not that for which they seek."— Leibnitz, *Nouveaux Essais*, L. II. Ch. 21. § 14.

NOTE XXIX., p. 106.

See the acute criticism of the Kantian distinction between *things* and *phenomena*, by M. Willm, in his *Histoire de la Philosophie Allemande*, Vol. I. p. 177. "It is not necessary to admit, that what interposes between the objects and the reason alters and falsifies, so to say, the view of the objects; and it may be that the laws of the mind are at the same time the laws of things as they are. Hegel has justly said, that it were quite possible, that after having penetrated behind the scene, which is open before us, we should find nothing there; we may add, that it is possible, that this veil — which seems to cover the picture, and which we are striving to lift — may be the picture itself." Kant unquestionably went too far, in asserting that things in themselves *are not* as they appear to our faculties: the utmost that his premises could warrant him in asserting is, that we cannot tell whether they are so or not. And even this degree of skepticism, though tenable as far as external objects are concerned, cannot legitimately be extended to the personal self. I exist as I am conscious of existing; and this conscious self is itself the *Ding an sich*, the standard by which all representations of personality must be judged, and from which our notion of reality, as distinguished from appearance, is originally derived. To this extent Jacobi's criticism of Kant is just and decisive. "All our philosophizing is a struggle to get behind the form of the thing; i. e., to get to the thing itself; but how is this possible, since then we

1 *Ibid.*, p. 487. 2 *Life of Jesus Christ*, p. 399. (Bohn's edition.)

must get behind ourselves, behind all nature, — things, behind their origin?"[1]

NOTE XXX., p. 108.

The Intellectual Intuition of Schelling has been noticed above. See notes 16, 17, 18, pp. 77 sqq. The method of Hegel, in its aim identical with that of Schelling, differs from it chiefly in making thought, instead of intuition, the instrument of reaching the Absolute. As Schelling assumes the possibility of an intuition superior to time and difference, so Hegel postulates the existence of a logical process emancipated from the laws of identity and contradiction. The Understanding and the Reason are placed in sharp antagonism to each other. The one is a faculty of finite thinking, subject to the ordinary laws of thought: the other is a faculty of infinite thinking, to which those laws are inapplicable. Hence the principles of Identity, of Contradiction, and of Excluded Middle are declared to be valid merely for the abstract understanding, from which reason is distinguished by the principle of the Identity of Contradictories.[2] But this assertion, indispensable as it is to Hegel's system, involves more consequences than the author himself would be willing to admit. The important admission, that an infinite object of thought can only be apprehended by an infinite act of thinking, involves the conclusion, that the understanding and the reason have no common ground on which either can make itself intelligible to the other; for the very principles which to the one are a criterion of truth, are to the other an evidence of falsehood. Moreover, the philosophy which regards the union of contradictories as essential to the conceptions of the reason, is bound in consistency to extend the same condition to its judgments and deductions; for whatever is one-sided and partial in the analysis of a notion, must be equally so in those more complex forms of thought into which notions enter. The logic of the understanding must be banished entirely, or not at all. Hence the philosopher may neither defend his own system, nor refute his adversary, by arguments reducible to the ordinary logical forms; for these forms rest on the very laws of thought which the higher philosophy is supposed to repudiate. Hegel's own polemic is thus self-con-

1 *Ueber das Unternehmen des Kriticismus*, (*Werke* III. p. 176).

2 See *Logik*, B. II. c. 2; *Encyklopädie*, § 28, 115, 119, *Geschichte der Philosophie*, *Werke*, XV. p. 598. See also his attempt to rescue speculative philosophy from the assaults of skepticism, *Werke*, XIV. p. 511, 512. He charges the skeptic with first making reason finite, in order to overthrow it by the principles of finite thought. The defence amounts to no more than this: "The laws of thought are against me; but I refuse to be bound by their authority."

demned; and his attempted refutation of the older metaphysicians, is a virtual acknowledgment of the validity of their fundamental principles. If the so-called infinite thinking is a process of thought at all, it must be a process entirely *sui generis*, isolated and unapproachable, as incapable as the intuition of Schelling of being expressed in ordinary language, or compared, even in antagonism, with the processes of ordinary reasoning. The very attempt to expound it thus, necessarily postulates its own failure.

But this great thinker has rendered one invaluable service to philosophy. He has shown clearly what are the only conditions under which a philosophy of the Absolute could be realized; and his attempt has done much to facilitate the conclusion, to which philosophy must finally come, that the Absolute is beyond the reach of human thought. If such a philosophy were possible at all, it would be in the form of the philosophy of Hegel. And Hegel's failure points to one inevitable moral. All the above inconsistency and division of the human mind against itself, might be avoided by acknowledging the supreme authority of the laws of thought over all human speculation; and by recognizing the consequent distinction between positive and negative thinking, — between the lawful exercise of the reason within its own province, and its abortive efforts to pass beyond it. But such an acknowledgment amounts to a confession that thought and being are not identical, and that reason itself requires us to believe in truths that are beyond reason. And to this conclusion speculative philosophy itself leads us, if in no other way, at least by the wholesome warning of its own pretensions and failures.

NOTE XXXI., p. 108.

Tertullian, *De Carne Christi*, c. 5. "The Son of God was born; that awakens no shame, precisely because it is shameful; and the Son of God died; it is thoroughly credible, because it is absurd; He was buried and then rose again; it is certain, because it is impossible."

NOTE XXXII., p. 110.

See above, Lecture II., note 37.

NOTE XXXIII., p. 113.

Hooker, *E. P.* B. I. ch. ii. § 2. Compare the words of Jacobi, *An Fichte* (*Werke*, III., p. 7). "A God, who could be *known*, were no God at all."

LECTURE IV.

Note I., p. 114.

Thus Wegscheider, after expressly admitting (*Instit. Theol.* § 52) that the infinite cannot be comprehended by the finite, and that its idea can only be represented by analogy and symbol, proceeds to assert, with the utmost confidence, that the attributes of omnipotence and omniscience do not truly represent the internal nature of God (§ 69); that a plurality of persons in the Godhead is manifestly repugnant to reason, and that the infinite God cannot assume the nature of finite man (§ 92); that the fall of man is inconsistent with the divine attributes (§ 117); that repentance is the only mode of expiating sin reconcilable with the moral nature of God (§ 138); that the doctrine of Christ's intercession is repugnant to the divine nature (§ 143).

By a somewhat similar inconsistency, Mr. Newman, while fully acknowledging that we cannot have any perfect knowledge of an infinite mind, and that infinity itself is but a negative idea, yet thinks it necessary to regard the soul as a separate organ of specific information, by which we are in contact with the infinite; and dogmatizes concerning the similarity of divine and human attributes, in a manner which nothing short of absolute knowledge can justify. (See *The Soul*, pp. 1, 3, 34, 54, 58.) He compares the infinite to the "illimitable haziness" which bounds the sphere of distinct vision. The analogy would be serviceable to his argument, if we possessed two sets of eyes, one for clearness and one for haziness; one to be limited, and the other to discern the limitation. The hypothesis of a separate faculty of consciousness, whether called soul, reason, or intellectual intuition, to take cognizance of the infinite, is only needed for those philosophers who undertake to develop a complete philosophy of the infinite as such. But the success of the various attempts in this province has not been such as to give any trustworthy evidence of the existence of such a faculty.

Note II., p. 115.

See above, Lecture I., note 3.

Note III., p. 115.

See Mr. Rose's remarks on the reäction against the Wolfian demonstrative method. *State of Protestantism in Germany*, p. 206 (second edition).

NOTE IV., p. 116.

See Kant, *Kritik der reinen Vernunft*, p. 497. ed. Rosenkranz. This admission, rightly understood, need not be considered as detracting from the value of the speculative arguments as auxiliaries. All that is contended for is, that the foundation must be laid elsewhere, before their assistance, valuable as it is, can be made available. Thus understood, this view coincides with that expressed by Sir W. Hamilton, in the second of the *Lectures on Metaphysics*, shortly to be published, "that the phenomena of matter, taken by themselves (you will observe the qualification, taken by themselves), so far from warranting any inference to the existence of a God, would, on the contrary, ground even an argument to his negation, — that the study of the external world, taken with and in subordination to that of the internal, not only loses its atheistic tendency, but, under such subservience, may be rendered conducive to the great conclusion, from which, if left to itself, it would dissuade us." The atheistic tendency is perhaps too strongly stated; as the same phenomena may be surveyed, by different individuals, in different spirits and with different results; but the main position, that the belief in God is primarily based on mental, and not on material phenomena, accords with the view taken in the text.

NOTE V., p. 116.

Kant, *Kritik der r. V.*, p. 488. Compare Hume, *Dialogues concerning Natural Religion*, Part V. Kant's argument is approved by Hegel, *Philosophie der Religion* (*Werke*, XII. p. 37). The objection which it urges is of no value, unless we admit that man possesses an adequate notion of the infinite, as such. Otherwise the notion of power indefinitely great, which the phenomena certainly suggest, is, both theoretically and practically, undistinguishable from the infinite itself. This has been well remarked by a recent writer. See *Selections from the Correspondence of R. E. H. Greyson*, Am. Ed., p. 550.

NOTE VI., p. 116.

Jowett, *Epistles of St. Paul*, Vol. II. p. 406. Professor Jowett considers the comparison between the works of nature and those of art as not merely inadequate, but positively erroneous. He says, "As certainly as the man who found a watch or piece of mechanism on the seashore would conclude, 'here are marks of design, indications of an intelligent artist,' so certainly, if he came across the meanest or the highest of the works of nature, would he infer, 'this was not made by man, nor by any human art and skill.' He sees at first sight that the sea-weed beneath his feet is something different in kind from the productions of man."[1] But surely the force of the teleological argument does not turn upon the *similarity* of the objects, but upon their *analogy*. The point of comparison is, that in the works of nature, as well as in those of art, there is an adaptation of means to ends, which indicates an intelligent author. And such an adaptation may exist in an organized body, no less than in a machine, notwithstanding numerous differences in the details of their structure. The evidence of this general analogy is in nowise weakened by Professor Jowett's special exceptions.

NOTE VII., p. 116.

"When the spiritual man (as such) cannot judge, the question is removed into a totally different court from that of the Soul, the court of the critical understanding. . .The processes of thought have nothing to quicken the conscience or affect the soul." F. W. Newman, *The Soul*, p. 245 (second edition).— Yet he allows in another place (not quite consistently) that "pure intellectual error, depending on causes wholly unmoral, *may* and *does* perpetuate moral illusions, which are of the deepest injury to spiritual life." p. 169. Similar in principle, though not pushed to the same extreme consequences, is the theory of Mr. Morell, who says, "Reason up to a God, and the best you can do is to hypostatize and deify the final product of your own faculties; but admit the reality of an intellectual intuition (as the mass of mankind virtually do), and the absolute stands before us in all its living reality."[2] This distinction he carries so far as to assert that "to speak of logic, as such, being inspired, is a sheer absurdity;" because "the process either of defining or of reasoning requires simply the employment of the formal laws of thought, the accuracy of which can be in no way affected by any amount of inspiration whatever:"[3] and in another passage he maintains, to the same effect, that "the *essential* elements of religion in general, as of Christianity in particular, appertain strictly

1 This argument is substantially the same with that of Hume, *Dialogues concerning Natural Religion*, Part II. "If we see a house, we conclude, with the greatest certainty, that it had an architect or builder . . . But surely you will not affirm that the universe bears such a resemblance to a house, that we can with the same certainty infer a similar cause."

2 *Philosophy of Religion*, p. 39.

3 *Ibid.*, p. 173, 174.

to the intuitional portion of our nature, and may be realized in all their varied influence without the coöperation of any purely reflective processes."[1] Here he apparently overlooks the fact that the intuitive and reflective faculties invariably act in conjunction; that both are equally necessary to the existence of consciousness as such; and that logical forms are never called into operation, except in conjunction with the matter on which they are exercised.

NOTE VIII., p. 119.

In acknowledging Expiation as well as Prayer to be prompted by the natural feelings of men, I have no intention of controverting the opinion, so ably maintained by Archbishop Magee and Mr. Faber, of the divine origin of the actual rite of sacrifice. That the religious instincts of men should indicate the need of supplication and expiation, is perfectly consistent with the belief that the particular mode of both may have been first taught by a primitive revelation. That religion, in both its constituent elements, was communicated to the parents of the human race by positive revelation, seems the most natural inference from the Mosaic narrative.[2] Yet we may admit that the positive institution must from the first have been adapted to some corresponding instinct of human nature; without which it would be scarcely possible to account for its continuance and universal diffusion, as well as for its various corruptions. We may thus combine the view of Archbishop Magee with that exhibited by Dr. Thomson. *Bampton Lectures*, pp. 30, 48.

NOTE IX., p. 121.

That the mere feeling of dependence by itself is not necessarily religion, is shown by Hegel, *Philosophie der Religion* (*Werke* XII. p. 173). Speaking of the Roman worship of evil influences, Angerona, Fames, Robigo, etc., he rightly remarks that in such representations all conception of Deity is lost, though the feeling of fear and dependence remains. To the same effect is his sarcastic remark that, according to Schleiermacher's theory, the dog is the best Christian.[3] Mr. Parker (*Discourse of Religion*,

1 *Philosophy of Religion*, p. 193.

2 Even Mr. Davison, who contends for the human origin of the patriarchal sacrifices, which he regards as merely eucharistic and penitentiary, expressly admits the divine appointment of expiatory offerings. See his *Inquiry into the Origin of Primitive Sacrifice* (*Remains*, p. 121).

3 See Rosenkranz, *Hegel's Leben*, p. 346.

Ch. 1.) agrees with Schleiermacher in resolving the religious sentiment into a mere sense of dependence; though he admits that this sentiment does not, itself, disclose the character of the object on which it depends. Referred to this principle alone, it is impossible to regard religious worship as a moral duty.

NOTE X., p. 121.

See Kant, *Metaphysik der Sitten*, Abschn. II. (pp. 61, 71. ed. Rosenkranz.) His theory has been combated by Julius Müller, *Christliche Lehre von der Sünde*, B. I. c. 2. Compare also Hooker, *E. P.* I. ix. 2. Some excellent remarks to the same effect will be found in McCosh's *Method of the Divine Government*, p. 298 (fourth edition), and in Bartholmèss, *Histoire des doctrines religieuses de la philosophie moderne*, vol. i. p. 405.

NOTE XI., p. 122.

The theory which regards absolute morality as based on the immutable *nature* of God, must not be confounded with that which places it in his arbitrary *will*. The latter view, which was maintained by Scotus, Occam, and others among the schoolmen, is severely criticized by Sir James Mackintosh, *Dissertation on the Progress of Ethical Philosophy*, section III., and by Müller, *Christliche Lehre von der Sünde*, B. I. c. 3. The former principle is adopted by Cudworth as the basis of his treatise on Eternal and Immutable Morality. See B. I. c. 3. B. IV. c. 4.

NOTE XII., p. 122.

On the universality of expiatory rites, see Magee on the Atonement, note V. On their origin, see the same work, notes XLI., XLVI. to LI., LIV. to LVIII., and Mr. Faber's *Treatise on the Origin of Expiatory Sacrifice*.

NOTE XIII., p. 123.

Schleiermacher, *Christliche Glaube*, § 4.

NOTE XIV., p. 124.

Morell, *Philosophy of Religion*, p. 75. Mr. Morell here goes beyond the theory of his master, Schleiermacher. The latter (*Christliche Glaube*, § 4) admits that this supposed feeling of absolute dependence can never be completely attained in any single act of consciousness, but is generally suggested by the whole. Mr. Morell speaks as if we could be immediately conscious of our own annihilation, by a direct intuition of the infinite. Both theories are inadequate to prove the intended conclusion. That of Schleiermacher virtually amounts to a confession that the infinite is not a positive object of consciousness, but a mere negation suggested by the direct presence of the finite. That of Mr. Morell saves the intuition of the infinite, but annihilates itself; for if in any act of consciousness the subject becomes absolutely nothing, the consciousness must vanish with it; and if it stops at any point short of nothing, the object is not infinite.

NOTE XV., p. 125.

That this is the legitimate result of Schleiermacher's theory, may be gathered from a remarkable passage in the *Christliche Glaube*, § 8, in which the polytheistic and monotheistic feelings of piety are compared together. The former, he says, is always accompanied by a sensible representation of its object, in which there is contained a germ of multiplicity; but in the latter, the higher consciousness is so separated from the sensible, that the pious emotions admit of no greater difference than that of the elevating or depressing tone of the feeling. This seems to imply that, in Schleiermacher's opinion, to worship a God of many attributes, is equivalent to worshipping a plurality of Gods. And to those philosophers who make the Infinite in itself a direct object of religious worship, this identification is natural; for a God of many attributes cannot be conceived as infinite, and therefore in one sense partakes of the limited divinity of Polytheism. But, on the other hand, a God of no attributes is no God at all; and the so-called monotheistic piety is nothing but an abortive attempt at mystical self-annihilation. Some acute strictures on Schleiermacher's theory from this point of view will be found in Drobisch, *Grundlehren der Religionsphilosophie*, p. 84.

NOTE XVI., p. 126.

Schleiermacher himself admits (*Christliche Glaube*, § 33) that the theory of absolute dependence is incompatible with the belief that God can be moved by any human action. He endeavors, however, to reconcile this admission with the duty of prayer, by maintaining (§ 147) that the true Christian will pray for nothing but that which it comes within God's absolute purpose to grant. This implies something like omniscience in the true Christian, and something like hypocrisy in every act of prayer.

Note XVII., p. 126.

Schleiermacher (*Chr. Glaube*, § 49) attempts, not very successfully, to meet this objection, by maintaining that even our free acts are dependent upon the will of God. This is doubtless true; but it is true as an article of faith, not as a theory of philosophy: it may be believed, but cannot be conceived, nor represented in any act of human consciousness. The apparent contradiction implied in the coëxistence of an infinite and a finite, will remain unsolved; and is most glaring in the theories of those philosophers, who, like Schleiermacher (§ 54), maintain that God actually does all that he can do. The only solution is to confess that we have no true conception of the infinite at all. Schleiermacher himself is unable to avoid the logical consequence of his position. He admits (§ 80) that God's omnipotence is limited if we do not allow him to be the author of sin; though he endeavors to soften this monstrous admission by taking it in conjunction with the fact that God is also the author of grace.

Note XVIII., p. 128.

De Augmentis Scientiarum, L. III. c. 1. Compare Theophilus of Antioch, *Ad Autolycum*, I. 5. "As the soul in the human body is not seen, being invisible to men, but is made known through the movement of the body, so God cannot be seen by human and bodily eyes, but is discovered to human intelligence by His providence and His works."[1] And Athanasius, *Contra Gentes*, c. 35. "For often the workman is recognized in his works; as they say of the sculptor Phidias, that the symmetry and nice proportions of his works revealed him to the beholders, even when he was not present himself, so the order of the universe necessarily reveals the divine Creator, though He is invisible to mortal eyes." On the other hand, Hegel, *Philosophie der Religion* (*Werke*, XII. p. 395), insists on the necessity of knowing God as He is, as an indispensable condition of all Theology.

Note XIX., p. 128.

Justin. Mart. *Apol.* I. c. 6. "Indeed, *Father*, and *God*, and *Lord*, and *Master*, are not names, but only appellatives, derivatives from His benefits and His works."—Basil. *Adv. Eunom.* I. 12. "As to the conceit of having found out the very essential being of God,—what arrogance and pride

1 Compare a similar argument in Bishop Berkeley, *Minute Philosopher*, Dial. IV. § 4.

does it display! . . . for let us inquire of him, by what method he boasts of having made such a discovery? is it from the common conception? But this only suggests that God exists, not what is His essence."— Gregor. Nyssen. *Contr. Eunom.* Orat. XII. "Thus also of the maker of the world, — we know that He is, but we do not deny that we are ignorant of the mode of his being."— Cyril. Hieros. *Catech.* VI. 2. "For we do not point out what God is; but we candidly confess that we have no accurate knowledge of Him, for in things pertaining to God, it is great knowledge, to confess our ignorance."— Pascal, *Pensées*, Partie II. Art. III. § 5. "We know that there is an infinite, and we are ignorant of its nature. For example, we know that it is false, that numbers are finite; then it is true that there is an infinite in numbers. But we do not know what it is. It is false that it is even; equally so that it is uneven; for, in adding the unit, it does not change its nature; nevertheless it is a number. . . . . We may, then, well know that there is a God, without knowing, what He is." The distinction is strongly repudiated by Hegel, *Werke*, XII. p. 396. Cf. IX. p. 19. XIV. p. 219. In the last of these passages, he goes so far as to say, that to deny to man a knowledge of the infinite is the sin against the Holy Ghost. The ground of this awful charge is little more than the repetition of an observation in Aristotle's Metaphysics, that God is not envious, and therefore cannot withhold from us absolute knowledge.

NOTE XX., p. 129.

Advancement of Learning, p. 128. ed. Montagu. Compare *De Augmentis*, III. 2.

NOTE XXI., p. 130.

This argument is excellently drawn out in Sir W. Hamilton's forthcoming Lectures on Metaphysics, Lecture II. So Mr. F. W. Newman observes, acutely and truly, "Nothing but a consciousness of active originating Will in ourselves suggests, or can justify, the idea of a mighty Will pervading Nature; and to merge the former in the latter, is to sacrifice the Premise to the glory of the Conclusion." *The Soul*, p. 40 (second edition).

NOTE XXII., p. 130.

Arist. *Metaph.* 1. 5. "Xenophanes was the first . . . who, on surveying the universe, said that the One was God."— Cicero, *Acad. Quæst.* IV. 37. "Xenophanes said that the One was All, and that that was not changeable, and was God."—Apuleius, *Asclepius Herm. Trimeg.* c. 20. "For I do not expect that the Maker of all majesty, and the Father or Lord of all things can be called by one name, though that were made up of many; but that He be unnamed or rather all-named, since indeed he is One and All, so that necessarily, either all things be designated by his name, or He himself by the names of all things."—Lessing, as quoted by Jacobi, *Werke,* IV. p. 54. "The orthodox notions of the Deity are no more for me; I cannot enjoy them,—One and All. I know nothing else."—Schelling, *Bruno,* p. 185. "So the All is One, the One is All, both the same, not different."

Note XXIII., p. 132.

Clemens Alex. *Stromata,* V. 11. "If therefore . . . . we should in some way draw nigh to the intelligence of the Omnipotent, we should come to know, not what He is, but what He is not."—Augustin. *Enarr. in Psalm* lxxxv. 12. "God is ineffable; we more easily say what He is not, than what He is."—Fichte, *Bestimmung des Menschen* (*Werke,* II. p. 305). "Thou *willest,*—for thou wilt, that my free obedience have consequences unto all eternity; the act of Thy Will I do not apprehend, and only know, that it is not like my own."

Note XXIV., p. 132.

The distinction between *speculative* and *regulative* knowledge holds an important place in the philosophy of Kant; but his mode of applying it is the exact reverse of that adopted in the text. According to Kant, the idea of the absolute or unconditioned has a regulative, but not a speculative value: it cannot be positively apprehended by act of thought; but it serves to give unity and direction to the lower conceptions of the understanding; indicating the point to which they tend, though they never actually reach it. But the regulative character thus paradoxically assigned, not to thought, but to its negation, in truth belongs to the finite conceptions as actually apprehended, not to any unapprehended idea of the infinite beyond them. Every object of positive thought, being conceived as finite, is necessarily regarded as limited by something beyond itself; though this something is not itself actually conceived. The true purpose of this manifest incompleteness of all human thought, is to point out the limits which we cannot pass; not, as Kant maintains, to seduce us into vain attempts to pass them. If there is but one faculty of thought, that which Kant calls the Understanding, occupied with the finite only, there is an obvious end to be answered in making us aware of its limits, and warning us that the boundaries of thought are not those of existence. But if, with Kant, we distinguish the Understanding from the Reason, and attribute to the latter the delusions necessarily arising from the idea of the unconditioned, we must believe in the existence of a special faculty of lies, created for the express purpose of deceiving those who trust to it. In the philosophy of religion, the true regulative ideas, which are intended to guide our thoughts, are the finite forms under which alone we can think of the infinite God; though these, while we employ them, betray their own speculative insufficiency and the limited character of all human knowledge.

Note XXV., p. 132.

"The purport of these remarks is only this . . . . that, in the further progress of the investigations, the question cannot be, what and how God is constituted in Himself, but only *how we have to think of Him in relation to ourselves and the whole morally-natural world.* For by our faith it is not that the being of God is theoretically known, but only *His existence, in the special relation to the moral design of the world, is revealed for us, as morally constituted beings;* and this is in a double sense a purely relative knowledge, first by being limited to a determined nature of the subject that knows, and secondly by the determined relation of the object that is known. Hence it follows, that there is nothing to be said here of the knowledge of the essence, the quality of a Being, but only of a nearer determination of the *idea* of God, as *we* have to form it, from our point of view; in other words, we are to think of God only by means of *relations.*" Drobisch, *Grundlehren der Religionsphilosophie*, p. 189. — "The Scripture intimates to us certain facts concerning the Divine Being: but conveying them to us by the medium of language, it only brings them before us darkly, under the signs appropriate to the thoughts of the human mind. And though this kind of knowledge is abundantly instructive to us in point of sentiment and action; teaches us, that is, both how to feel, and how to act, towards God; — for it is the language that we understand, the language formed by our own experience and practice; — it is altogether inadequate in point of Science." Hampden, *Bampton Lectures*, p. 54 (second edition). — "We should rather point out to objectors that what is revealed is *practical*, and not speculative; — that what the Scriptures are concerned with is, not the philosophy of the Human Mind in itself, nor yet the philosophy of the Divine Nature in itself, but (that which is properly *Religion*) the *relation* and connection of the two Beings; — what God is *to us*, — what He has done and will *do* for us, — and what *we* are to be and to do, in regard to Him." Whately, *Sermons*, p. 56 (third edition). — Compare Berkeley, *Minute Philosopher*, Dial. VII. § II.

LECTURE V.

NOTE I., p. 136.

Analogy, Part I. Ch. VI.

NOTE II., p. 137.

"When he (the Skeptic) awakes from his dream, he will be the first to join in the laugh against himself; and to confess, that all his objections are mere amusement, and can have no other tendency than to show the whimsical condition of mankind, who must act, and reason, and believe; though they are not able, by their most diligent inquiry, to satisfy themselves concerning the foundation of these operations, or to remove the objections which may be raised against them." Hume, *Essay on the Academical Philosophy*, Part II.

NOTE III., p. 137.

See Plato, *Parmenides*, p. 129, *Philebus*, p. 14, *Sophistes*, p. 251, *Republic*, VII. p. 524. The mystery is insoluble, because thought cannot explain its own laws; for the laws must necessarily be assumed in the act of explanation. Every object of thought, as being one object, and one out of many, all being related to a common consciousness, must contain in itself a common and a distinctive feature; and the relation between these two constitutes that very diversity in unity, without which no thought is possible.

NOTE IV., p. 138.

"The *commerce* between soul and body is a reciprocal dependence of determination. Accordingly we ask in the first place, how is such a *commerce* possible between a thinking being and a body? . . . The foundation of the difficulty seems to lie here: The soul is an object of the inward sense, and the body an object of the outward. . . . . Now by no reason do we come to understand, how that which is an object of the internal sense, is to be a cause of that which is an object of the outward." *Kant's Vorlesungen über die Metaphysik*, (1821), p. 224.

NOTE V., p. 139.

"When we examine the idea which we have of all finite minds, we see no necessary connection between their volition and the movement of any body whatsoever; we see, on the contrary, that there is none at all, and can be none."—Malebranche, *Recherche de la Vérité*, L.VI. Part II. Ch. 3. "Man is, to himself, the most astonishing object of nature; for he cannot conceive what body is, and still less what is spirit, and least of all can he conceive how a body can be united with a spirit. That is the acme of his difficulties; and yet that is his own being."—Pascal, *Pensées*, Partie I. Art vi. § 26. "I am, to be sure, compelled to believe,—that is, to act as if I thought, that my tongue, my hand, my foot, can be put in motion by my will; but how a mere breath, a pressure of the intelligence upon itself, such as the will is, can be the principle of motion in the heavy earthly mass,—of that not only can I have no conception, but the mere assertion is, before the tribunal of the reflecting intelligence, nothing but sheer unintelligence."—Fichte, *Bestimmung des Menschen*, (*Werke*, II. p. 290.)—Spinoza, *Ethica*, III. 2, denies positively that such commerce can take place. "Neither can the body determine the mind to thought, nor the mind the body to motion, or to quiet, or to anything else."

NOTE VI., p. 139.

The theory of Divine Assistance and Occasional Causes was partially hinted at by Descartes, and more completely elaborated by his followers, De La Forge and Malebranche. See Descartes, *Principia*, L. II. § 36. De La Forge, *Traité de l'esprit de l'homme*, Ch. XVI. Malebranche, *Recherche de la Vérité*, L. VI. P. II. Ch. 3; *Entretiens sur la Metaphysique*, Ent. VII. Cf. Hegel, *Geschichte der Phil.* (*Werke*, XV. p. 330.) For Leibnitz's theory of a Preëstablished Harmony, see his *Systême nouveau de la Nature*, § 12—15, *Opera*, ed. Erdmann, p. 127; *Troisième Eclaircissement*, *Ibid.* p. 134; *Théodicée*, § 61, *Ibid.* p. 520. A brief account of these two systems, together with that of Physical Influx, which is rather a statement of the phenomenon, than a theory to account for it, is given by Euler, *Lettres à une Princesse d'Allemagne*, Partie II. Lettre 14. ed. Cournot; and by Krug, *Philos. Lexikon*; Art. *Gemeinschaft der Seele und des Leibes*. The hypothesis, that the commerce of soul and body is effected by means of a Plastic Nature in the soul itself, is suggested by Cudworth, *Intellectual System*, B. I. Ch. III. § 37, and further developed by Leclerc, *Bibliothèque Choisie*, II. p. 113, who supposes this plastic nature to be an intermediate principle, distinct from both soul and body. See Mosheim's note in Harrison's edition of Cudworth, Vol. 1. p. 248. See also Leibnitz, *Sur le Principe de Vie, Opera*, ed. Erdmann, p. 429; Laromiguière, *Leçons de Philosophie*, P. II. l. 9.

NOTE VII., p. 139.

These two analogies between our natural and spiritual knowledge are adduced in a remarkable passage of Gregory of Nyssa, *Contra Eunomium*, Orat. XII. Of the soul, and its relation to the body, he says: . . . . "We live in ignorance of all things, of ourselves first of all, and then of all other things. For who is there, that has come to a comprehension of his own soul? Who has a knowledge of its essence? whether it is material or immaterial? Whether purely incorporeal, or whether there be something corporeal in it? how it comes into being, how it is regulated? whence it enters the body, how it departs?" etc. (*Opera*, Paris. 1615. Vol. II. p. 321.) Of body as distinguished from its attributes, he says: "For if any one were to analyze, into its component parts, what appears to the senses, and, having stripped the subject of all its attributes, should strive to get a knowledge of it, as it is in itself, I do not see what would be left for the mind to contemplate at all. For once take away color, figure, weight, size, motion, relativity, each one of which is not of itself the body, and yet all of them belong to the body,—what will be left to stand for the body? Whoever, therefore, is ignorant of himself, how is he to have knowledge of things above himself?" *Ibid.* p. 322.

NOTE VIII., p. 139.

Essay on the Academical Philosophy, (Philosophical Works, Vol. IV. p. 182.)

NOTE IX., p. 140.

The difficulty is ingeniously stated by Pascal, *Pensées*, Partie I. Art II. "For is there anything more absurd, than to pretend, that in dividing ever a space, we come finally to such a division, that in dividing it in two, each of the halves remains invisible, and without any extension? I would ask those, who have this idea, if they clearly conceive how two invisibles touch each other; if everywhere, then they are only one thing, and consequently the two together are indivisible; and if not everywhere, then it is only in a part that they come in contact; then they have parts, and therefore they are not indivisible."

NOTE X., p. 142.

Kant's theory, that we know phenomena only, not things in themselves, is severely criticized by Dr. McCosh, *Method of the Divine Government*, p. 536 (4th edition). I have before observed that Kant has, in two points at least, extended his doctrine beyond its legitimate place; first, in maintaining that our knowledge of the personal self is equally phenomenal with that of external objects; and secondly, in dogmatically asserting that the thing in itself *does not* resemble the phenomenon of which we are conscious, Against the first of these statements it may be fairly objected, that my personal existence is identical with my consciousness of that existence; and that any other aspect of my personality, if such exists in relation to any other intelligence, is in this case the phenomenon to which my personal consciousness furnishes the real counterpart. Against the second, it may be objected, that if, upon Kant's own hypothesis, we are never directly conscious of the thing in itself, we have no ground for saying that it is unlike, any more than that it is like, the object of which we are conscious; and that, in the absence of all other evidence, the probability is in favor of that aspect which is at least subjectively true. But when these deductions are made, the hypothesis of Kant, in its fundamental position, remains unshaken. It then amounts to no more than this; that we can see things only as our faculties present them to us; and that we can never be sure that the mode of operation of our faculties is identical with that of other intelligences, embodied or spiritual. Within these limits, the theory more nearly resembles a truism than a paradox, and contains nothing that can be regarded as formidable, either by the philosopher or by the theologian.

In the same article, Dr. McCosh criticizes Sir William Hamilton's cognate theory of the relativity of all knowledge. With the highest respect for Dr. McCosh's philosophical ability, I cannot help thinking that he has mistaken the character of the theory which he censures, and that the objection which he urges is hardly applicable. He attempts to avail himself of Sir W. Hamilton's own theory of the veracity of consciousness. He asks, "Does not the mind in sense-perception hold the object to be a real object?" Undoubtedly; but reality in this sense is not identical with absolute existence unmodified by the laws of the percipient mind. Man can conceive reality, as he conceives other objects, only as the laws of his faculties permit; and in distinguishing reality from appearance, he is not distinguishing the related from the unrelated. Both appearance and reality must be given in consciousness, to be apprehended at all; and the distinction is only between some modes of consciousness, such as those of a dream, which are regarded as delusive, and others, as in a waking state, which are regarded as veracious. But consciousness, whatever may be its veracity, can tell us nothing concerning the identity of its objects with those of which we are not conscious.

Dr. McCosh, in the above criticism, also classes Professor Ferrier as a representative of the same school with Kant and Hamilton. This classification is, at least, questionable. Professor Ferrier's system more nearly approaches to the Philosophy of the Absolute than to that of the Relative. He himself distinctly announces that he undertakes "to lay down the laws, not only of *our* thinking and knowing, but of *all* possible thinking and knowing."[1] Such an undertaking, whether it be successful or not, is, in its conception, the very opposite of the system which maintains that our knowledge is relative to our faculties.

NOTE XI., p. 143.

See above, Lecture IV. note 25.

NOTE XII., p. 143.

"It is the same with other mysteries, where, for well regulated minds, there is always to be found an explanation, sufficient for *faith*, but never as much as is necessary for comprehension. The *what it is* (τί ἐστι) is sufficient for us; but the *how* (πῶς) is beyond our comprehension, and is not at all necessary for us."— Leibnitz, *Théodicée, Discours de la conformité de la Foi avec la Raison*, § 56.

NOTE XIII., p. 144.

"It is plain, that, in any communication from an Infinite Being to creatures of finite capacities, one of two things must happen. Either the former must raise the latter almost to His own level; or else He must suit the form of His communication to their powers of apprehension. . . . . If we turn to Scripture, however, we shall see how this matter is decided. In God's dealings with men we find 'wrath,' 'jealousy,' 'repentance,' and other affections, ascribed to the Divine Being. He is described as 'sitting on a throne;' His 'eyes' are said 'to behold the children of men;' not to mention other instances, which must suggest themselves to every one, in which God condescends to convey to us, not the very reality indeed, but something as near the reality as He sees it expedient for us to know." Professor Lee, *The Inspiration of Holy Scripture*, pp. 63, 64 (second edition).

1 *Institutes of Metaphysic*, p. 55.

NOTE XIV., p. 146.

Plato, *Sophistes*, p. 242. "But our Eleatic sect, from Xenophanes, and yet earlier, go through with their views, as if what we call all were in reality only one." — Sextus Empiricus, *Pyrrh. Hyp.* I. 225. "Xenophanes laid down the doctrine . . . . that the All was One." — Arist. *Metaph.* II. 4. 30. "For whatever is different from that which is, (entity), is not; so that, according to the view of Parmenides, it must of necessity be the case, that all things that are, are one, and that this is that which is (entity)." — Plato, *Parmenides*, p. 127. "How is it, Zeno, did you mean this, that if the things in being are many, then that these many must be like and unlike, and that this is impossible . . . . . did you not say so? Exactly so, said Zeno." — Arist. *Soph. Elench.* 10. 2. . . . . "Zeno thought that all things are one . . . ." — Arist. *De Cœlo* III. 1. 5. "For some of these did away altogether with the idea of generation and of dissolution; for they maintained that none of the things in existence really came into being, and perished, but that all this only appeared so to us." — Diog. Laert. ix. 24 (De Melisso). "It seemed to him, that the All was infinite, and unchangeable, and immovable, and one, like itself, and complete; and that motion was not real, but only apparent." Cf. Plato, *Theætetus*, p. 183. Compare Karsten, *Parmenidis Reliquiæ*, p. 157, 194. Brandis, *Commentationes Eleaticæ*, p. 213, 214.

NOTE XV., p. 146.

Plato, *Theæt.* p. 152. "I will tell you, — and this is no trifling talk, — that nothing is an independent unity, and that you can rightly attribute to nothing any quality whatsoever; but if you call a thing great, it will at once appear small, if heavy, light, and so in like manner of all, so that nothing is one or somewhat or of any quality soever; but, that by motion, change, mixture, all things together are only *becoming*, while we say wrongly that they *are;* for nothing ever really *is*, but all things are ever *becoming;* and herein are the philosophers agreed, Parmenides excepted." —Diogenes Laert. ix. 51. "He said (Protagoras) that the soul was nothing but perceptions."—Aristot. *De Xenophane, Zenone et Gorgia*, c. 5. (De Gorgia.) "He said that there was nothing in existence; and if there were anything, that it was not an object of knowledge; and that if there were anything in existence and an object of knowledge, it could not be made known to others." . . . . "What we call a *mind*, is nothing but a heap or collection of different perceptions, united together by certain relations, and supposed, though falsely, to be endowed with a perfect simplicity and identity." Hume, *Treatise of Human Nature*, Part IV. sect. 2.—" 'Tis confessed by the most judicious philosophers, that our ideas of bodies are nothing but collections formed by the mind of the ideas of the several distinct sensible qualities, of which objects are composed, and which we find to have a constant union with each other. . . . . The smooth and uninterrupted progress of the thought . . . . readily deceives the mind, and makes us ascribe an identity to the changeable succession of connected qualities." *Ibid.* sect. 3.

NOTE XVI., p. 146.

"We must come now to the great question, which M. Bayle has lately brought upon the tapis, — namely, whether a truth, and especially a truth of faith, can be subject to insolvable objections. . . . . He thinks that, in Theology, the doctrine of Predestination is of this nature, and in Philosophy that of Continuity (the *Continuum*) in space. These are in fact the two labyrinths, which have tried theologians and philosophers of all times. Libertus Fromodus, a theologian of Louvain, who has studied much the subject of Grace, and has also written a book, entitled *Labyrinthus de compositione Continui*, has well expressed the difficulties of each; and the famous Ochin has well represented what he calls *the Labyrinths of Predestination.*" Leibnitz, *Théodicée, Discours de la conformité de la Foi avec la Raison*, § 24. Compare Sir W. Hamilton's *Discussions*, p. 632.

NOTE XVII., p. 147.

See Bishop Browne's criticism of Archbishop King, *Procedure of the Understanding*, p. 15. "He hath unwarily dropped some such shocking expressions as these, *The best representations we can make of God are infinitely short of Truth.* Which God forbid, in the sense his adversaries take it; for then all our reasonings concerning Him would be groundless and false. But the saying is evidently true in a favorable and qualified sense and meaning; namely, that they are infinitely short of the real, true, internal Nature of God as He is in Himself." Compare *Divine Analogy*, p. 57. "Though all the Revelations of God are *true*, as coming from Him who is Truth itself; yet the truth and substance of them doth not consist in this, that they give us any new set of ideas, and express them in a language altogether unknown before; or that both the conceptions and terms are so immediately and properly adapted to the *true and real nature* of the things revealed, that they could not without great impropriety and even profaneness be ever applied to the things of this world. But the *truth* of them consists in this; that whereas the *terms* and *conceptions* made use of in those Revelations are strictly proper to things worldly and obvious;

they are from thence *transferred analogically* to the correspondent objects of another world with as much *truth* and *reality*, as when they are made use of in their first and most *literal* propriety; and this is a solid foundation both of a *clear* and *certain knowledge*, and of a *firm* and well grounded *Faith*."

NOTE XVIII., p. 147.

Augustin. *Confess.* l. XIII. c. 16. "For as Thou altogether art, so Thou alone knowest, — Thou, who art unchangeably, and knowest unchangeably, and willest unchangeably. And Thy essence knoweth and willeth unchangeably, and Thy knowledge is and willeth unchangeably, and Thy will is, and knoweth unchangeably. Nor doth it seem right in Thy sight, that, as the Light unchangeable knoweth itself, so It be known by the changeable being, that is enlightened by It."

NOTE XIX., p. 148.

See Hegel, *Philosophie der Geschichte, Werke*, IX. pp. 238, 298; *Philosophie der Religion, Werke*, XI. p. 356, XII. p. 119. Schleiermacher substantially admits the same facts, though he attempts to connect them with a different theory.[1] He considers that there is a pantheistic and a personal element united in all religions: and this is perhaps true of heathen religions subjected to the philosophical analysis of a later age; though it may be doubted whether both elements are distinctly recognized by the worshipper himself. But even from this point of view, the Jewish religion stands in marked contrast to both Eastern and Western heathenism. In the latter forms of religion, the elements of personality and infinity, so far as they are manifested at all, are manifested in different beings: this is observable both in the subordinate emanations which give a kind of secondary personality to the Indian Pantheism, and in the philosophical abstraction of a supreme principle of good, which connects a secondary notion of the infinite with the Grecian Mythology. The Jewish religion still remains distinct and unique, in so far as in it the attributes of personality and infinity are united in one and the same living and only God.

NOTE XX., p. 150.

"And the Father, who, indeed, in respect of us, is invisible and indeterminable, is known by His own Word; and being indeclarable, is declared

1 *Reden über Religion*, (*Werke*, I. pp. 401, 441.)

to us by the Word Himself. Again, it is only the Father that knoweth His Word; and that both these things are so hath the Lord manifested. And on this account the Son revealeth the knowledge of the Father by His own manifestation. For the knowledge of the Father is the manifestation of the Son; for all things are manifested by the Word. That therefore we might know, that it is the Son himself who hath come, that maketh known the Father to them that believe on Him, he said to his disciples: 'No man knoweth the Son but the Father, neither knoweth any man the Father but the Son, and he to whomsoever the Son will reveal Him.'" Irenæus, *Contr. Hœres.* IV. 6, 3. "Accordingly, therefore, the Word of God became incarnate, and lived in human form, that He might quicken the body, and that, as in the creation, He is known by His works, so also He might work in man, and manifest Himself everywhere, leaving nothing void of His divine nature and knowledge." Athanasius, *De Incarn. Verbi* c. 45. . . . . "The Son of God became incarnate . . . . in order that man might have a way to the God of man through the man-God. For He is the Mediator of God and man, the man Christ Jesus." . . . Augustin. *De Civ. Dei*, XI. 2.

Note XXI., p. 150.

"We who believe that God lived upon the earth, and that He took upon Him the lowliness of human form for the sake of man's salvation, are far from the opinion of those who think that God has no care for anything." Tertullian, *Adv. Marc.* II. 16.

Note XXII., p. 150.

It is only a natural consequence of their own principles, when the advocates of a philosophy of the Absolute maintain that the Incarnation of Christ has no relation to time. Thus Schelling says: "The theologians also expound, in like empiric manner, the Incarnation of God in Christ, — that God took upon Him human nature in a definite *momentum* of time, a thing impossible of conception, as God is eternally out of all time. The Incarnation of God is therefore an incarnation from eternity (a becoming 'manifest in the flesh' from all eternity) . . . . "[1] Hegel, in his Lectures on the Philosophy of History,[2] thus comments on the language of St. Paul: "*When the fulness of time was come, God sent forth his Son;* such is

[1] *Vorlesungen über die Methode des Academischen Studium*, p. 192. Fitche speaks to the same effect, *Anweisung zum seligen Leben* (*Werke*, V. p. 482).

[2] *Werke*, IX. p. 388.

the language of the Bible. That means nothing else than this: the self-consciousness had risen up to those *momenta*, which belong to the conception of the Spirit, and to the necessity of apprehending these *momenta* after an absolute method." This marvellous *elucidation* of the sacred text may perhaps receive some further light, or darkness, from the obscure passages of the same author, quoted subsequently in the text of this Lecture: and such is the explanation of his theory given by Baur, *Christliche Gnosis*, p. 715: "From the stand-point of speculative thought, the Incarnation is no single historical fact, once taken place, but an eternal determination of the essential nature of God, by virtue of which God only so far becomes man (in every individual man) as He is man from eternity. The sorrowful humiliation to which Christ made Himself subject as God-man, God bears at all times as man. The atonement achieved by Christ is not a fact which has come to pass in time, but an eternal reconciliation of God with Himself, and the resurrection and exaltation of Christ is only the regress of the Spirit to itself. Christ as man, as God-man, is man in his universality, not a particular individual, but the universal individual." It is no wonder that, to a philosophy of these lofty pretensions, the personal existence of Christ should be a question of perfect indifference.[1] From a similar point of view, Marheineke says: "The incarnation of God, apprehended in its possibility, is the real incarnation of divine truth, which is not only the thought of God, but also his very essence; and Divine and Human, though still different, are yet no longer separate." *Grundlehren der Christlichen Dogmatik*, § 312. It is difficult to see what distinction can be made, in these theories, between the Incarnation of Christ as Man, and His eternal Generation as the Son of God; and indeed these passages, and those subsequently quoted from Hegel, appear intentionally to identify the two.

NOTE XXIII., p. 151.

Encyklopädie, §§ 564, 566. For the benefit of any reader who may be disposed to play the part of Œdipus, I subjoin the entire passage in the original. The meaning may perhaps, as Professor Ferrier observes of Hegel's philosophy in general, be extracted by *distillation*, but certainly not by literal translation.

"Was Gott als Geist ist, — Dies richtig und bestimmt im Gedanken zu fassen, dazu wird gründliche Speculation erfordert. Es sind zunächst die

1 For a criticism of these pantheistic perversions of Christianity, see Drobisch, *Grundlehren der Religionsphilosophie*, p. 247. The consummation of the pantheistic view may be found in Blasche, *Philosophische Unsterblichkeitlehre*, § 51-53. Here the eternal Incarnation of God is exhibited as the perpetual production of men, as phenomenal manifestations of the absolute unity.

Sätze darin enthalten: Gott ist Gott nur in sofern er sich selber weiss; sein sich Sich-wissen ist ferner sein Selbstbewusstseyn im Menschen, und das Wissen des Menschen *von* Gott, das fortgeht zum Sich-wissen des Menschen *in* Gott.

Der absolute Geist in der aufgehobenen Unmittelbarkeit und Sinnlichkeit der Gestalt und des Wissens, ist dem Inhalte nach der an-und-für-sich-seyende Geist der Natur und des Geistes, der Form nach ist er zunächst für das subjective Wissen der *Vorstellung*. Diese giebt den Momenten seines Inhalts einerseits Selbstständigkeit und macht sie gegen einander zu Voraussetzungen, and *zu einander folgenden* Erscheinungen und zu einem Zusammenhang *des Geschehens* nach *endlichen Reflexionsbestimmungen*; anderseits wird solche Form endlicher Vorstellungsweise in dem Glauben an den Einen Geist und in der Andacht des Cultus aufgehoben.

In diesem Trennen scheidet sich die *Form* von dem *Inhalte*, und in jener die unterschiedenen Momente des Begriffs zu *besondern Sphären* oder Elementen ab, in deren jedem sich der absolute Inhalt darstellt, — α) als in seiner Manifestation bei sich selbst bleibender, Ewiger Inhalt; — β) als Unterscheidung des ewigen Wesens von seiner Manifestation, welche durch diesen Unterschied die Erscheinungswelt wird, in die der Inhalt tritt; — γ) als unendliche Rückkehr und Versöhnung der entäusserten Welt mit dem ewigen Wesen, das Zurückgehen desselben aus der Erscheinung in die Einheit seiner Fülle."

The passage which, though perhaps bearing more directly on my argument, I have not ventured to attempt to translate,[1] is the following, § 568.

"Im Momente der *Besonderheit* aber des Urtheils, ist dies concrete ewige Wesen das *Vorausgesetzte*, und seine Bewegung die Erschaffung der *Erscheinung*, das Zerfallen des ewigen Moments der Vermittlung, des einigen Sohnes, in den selbstständigen Gegensatz, einerseits des Himmels und der Erde, der elementarischen und concreten Natur, andererseits des Geistes als mit ihr im *Verhältniss* stehenden, somit *endlichen* Geistes, welcher als das Extrem der in sich seyenden Negativität sich zum Bösen verselbstständigt, solches Extrem durch seine Beziehung auf eine gegenüberstehende Natur und durch seine damit gesetzte eigene Natürlichkeit ist, in dieser als denkend zugleich auf das Ewige gerichtet, aber damit in äusserlicher Beziehung steht."

Görres, in the preface to the second edition of his *Athanasius*, p. ix., exhibits a specimen of a new Creed on Hegelian principles, to be drawn up by a general council composed of the more advanced theologians of the day. The qualifications for a seat in the council are humorously described,

1 [After what has been said by the author, both here and in the Lecture, on page 152, it were certainly unbecoming to attempt a translation for the American edition. — *Transl.*]

and the creed itself contains much just and pointed satire. It will hardly, however, bear quotation; for a caricature on such a subject, however well intended, almost unavoidably carries with it a painful air of irreverence.

NOTE XXIV., p. 152.

See especially *Phänomenologie des Geistes, Werke*, II. p. 557; *Philosophie der Geschichte, Werke*, IX. p. 387; *Philosophie der Religion, Werke*, XII. p. 247; *Geschichte der Philosophie, Werke*, XIV. p. 222, XV. p. 88.

NOTE XXV., p. 152.

The indecision of Hegel upon this vital question is *satisfactorily* accounted for by his disciple, Strauss. To a philosophy which professes to exhibit the universal relations of necessary ideas, it is indifferent whether they have actually been realized in an individual case or not. This question is reserved for the Critic of History. See *Streitschriften*, Heft III. p. 68. Dorner too, while pointing out the merits of Hegel's Christology, admits that the belief in a historical Christ has no significance in his system; and that those disciples who reject it carry out that system most fully. See *Lehre von der Person Christi*, p. 409.

NOTE XXVI., p. 153.

Philosophie der Religion, Werke, XII. p. 286. In another passage of the same work, p. 281, the Atonement is *explained* in the following language: "Therein only is the possibility of the atonement — that the *essential oneness of the divine and the human nature* becomes known; that is the necessary basis; man can know himself taken up into God, so far as God is not somewhat foreign to him, somewhat external, accidental, but when he, according to his essential being, his freedom and subjectivity, is taken up into God; but this is possible, only in so far as this subjectivity of human nature is in God Himself." Compare also p. 330, and *Phänomenologie des Geistes, Werke*, II. pp. 544, 572. *Philosophie der Geschichte, Werke*, IX. p. 405. *Geschichte der Philosophie, Werke*, XV. p. 100.

NOTE XXVII., p. 153.

Grundlehren der Christlichen Dogmatik, § 319, 320.

NOTE XXVIII., p. 154.

Ibid. §§ 325, 326. A similar theory is maintained, almost in the same language, by Rosenkranz, *Encyklopädie der theologischen Wissenschaften*, § 26, 27. The substance of this view is given by Hegel himself, *Werke*, IX. pp. 394, 457; XV. p. 89. Some valuable criticisms on the principle of it may be found in Dr. Mill's *Observations on the application of Pantheistic Principles to the Criticism of the Gospel*, pp. 16, 42.

NOTE XXIX., p. 155.

Leben Jesu, § 151. English Translation, Vol. III. p. 437. The passage has also been translated by Dr. Mill in his *Observations on the application of Pantheistic Principles*, etc. p. 50. I have slightly corrected the former version by the aid of the latter. A sort of anticipation of the theory may be found in Hegel's *Phänomenologie des Geistes*, *Werke*, II. p. 569.

NOTE XXX., p. 155.

"Only the Metaphysical, but in nowise the Historical, makes our salvation." Fichte, *Anweisung zum seligen Leben*, (*Werke*, V. p. 485). With this may be compared the language of Spinoza, Ep. XXI. "I say that it is not at all necessary to salvation to know Christ after the flesh; but of that eternal Son of God, the eternal Wisdom of God, which has manifested itself in all things, and especially in the human mind, and most of all in Christ Jesus, we must have a far different opinion."

LECTURE VI.

NOTE I., p. 161.

See above, Lecture IV. p. 104 and note 19.

NOTE II., p. 162.

Christliche Lehre von der Sünde, II. p. 156, third edition, (English Translation, II. p. 126.) The doctrine that the Divine Essence is speculatively made known through Christ, is a common ground on which theologians of the most opposite schools have met, to diverge again into most adverse conclusions. It is substantially the opinion of Eunomius;[1] and it has been maintained in modern times by Hegel and his disciple Marheineke, in a sense very different from that which is adopted by Müller. See Hegel, *Philosophie der Geschichte, Werke*, IX. p. 19. *Philosophie der Religion, Werke*, XII. p. 204, and Marheineke, *Grundlehren der Christlichen Dogmatik*, § 69.

NOTE III., p. 162.

See L. Ancillon, in the *Mémoires de l'Académie de Berlin*, quoted by Bartholmèss, *Histoire des Doctrines religieuses*, I. p. 268. On the parallel between the mystery of Causation and those of Christian doctrines, compare Magee on the Atonement, Note XIX. See also Mozley, *Augustinian Doctrine of Predestination*, p. 19, and the review of the same work, by Professor Fraser, *Essays in Philosophy*, p. 274.

NOTE IV., p. 162.

Seven different theories of the causal nexus, and of the mode of our apprehension of it, are enumerated and refuted by Sir W. Hamilton, *Discussions*, p. 611. His own, which is the eighth, can hardly be regarded as more satisfactory. For he resolves the causal judgment itself into the inability to conceive an absolute commencement of phenomena, and the consequent necessity of thinking that what appears to us under a new form had previously existed under others. But surely a cause is as much required to account for the change from an old form to a new, as to account for an absolute beginning. On the defects of this theory I have remarked elsewhere. See *Encyclopædia Britannica*, eighth edition, vol. XIV. p. 601. It has also been criticized by Dr. McCosh, *Method of the Divine Government*, p. 529, fourth edition; by Professor Fraser, *Essays in Philosophy*, p. 170 sqq.; and by Mr. Calderwood, *Philosophy of the Infinite*, p. 139 sqq.

NOTE V. p. 163.

That Causation implies something more than invariable sequence, though what that something is we are unable to determine, is maintained, among others, by M. Cousin, in his eloquent Lectures on the Philosophy of Locke. "Solely because one phenomenon succeeds another, and succeeds it constantly, — is it the cause of it? Is this the whole idea, which you form to yourself, of cause? When you say, when you think that the fire is the

[1] See Neander, vol. iv. p. 60, ed. Bohn.

cause of the fluid state of the wax, I ask you, if you do not believe, if the whole human race do not believe, that there is in the fire *a certain something, an unknown property,* — the determination of which is no point in question here, — to which you refer the production of the fluid state of the wax?" *Histoire de la Philosophie au XVIIIe. siècle,* Leçon xix. Engel speaks to the same effect in almost the same words. "In what we call, for example, force of attraction, of affinity, or of impulsion, the only thing known (that is to say, represented to the imagination and the senses) is the effect produced, namely, the bringing together of the two bodies attracted and attracting. No language has a word to express that *certain something,* (effort, *conatus, nisus*) which remains absolutely concealed, but which all minds necessarily conceive of as added to the phenomenal representation."[1] Dr. McCosh (*Method of the Divine Government,* p. 525,) professes to discover this *certain something,* in *a substance acting according to its powers or properties.* But, apart from the conscious exercise of free will, we know nothing of *power,* or *property,* save as manifested in its effects. Compare Berkeley, *Minute Philosopher,* Dial. VII. § 9. Herder, *Gott, Werke,* VIII. p. 224.

NOTE VI., p. 163.

That the first idea of Causation is derived from the consciousness of the exercise of power in our own volitions, is established, after a hint from Locke,[2] by Maine de Biran, and accepted by M. Cousin.[3] To explain the manner in which we transcend our own personal consciousness, and attribute a cause to all changes in the material world, the latter philosopher has recourse to the hypothesis of a necessary law of the reason, by virtue of which it disengages, in the fact of consciousness, the necessary element of causal relation from the contingent element of our personal production of this or that particular movement. This Law, the Principle of Causality, compels the reason to suppose a cause, whenever the senses present a new phenomenon. But this Principle of Causality, even granting it to be true as far as it goes, does not explain what the idea of a Cause, thus extended, contains as its constituent feature: it merely transcends personal causation, and substitutes an unknown *something* in its room. We do not attribute to the fire a consciousness of its power to melt the wax:

1 *Memoires de l'Académie de Berlin,* quoted by Maine de Biran, *Nouvelles Considérations,* p. 23.

2 *Essay,* B. II. Ch. 21 §§ 4, 5. A similar view is taken by Jacobi, *David Hume, oder Idealismus und Realismus,* (*Werke,* II. p. 201.)

3 See De Biran, *Oeuvres Philosophiques,* IV. p. 241, 273, Cousin, *Cours de l' Histoire de la Philosophie,* Deuxième Série, Leçon 19. *Fragments Philosophiques,* vol. IV.; Préface de la Premiere Edition.

and in denying consciousness, we deny the only positive conception of power which can be added to the mere juxtaposition of phenomena. The *cause*, in all sensible changes, thus remains a *certain something*. On this subject I have treated more at length in another place. See *Prolegomena Logica*, pp. 135, 309.

And even within the sphere of our own volitions, though we are immediately conscious of the exercise of power, yet the analysis of the conception thus presented to us, carries us at once into the region of the incomprehensible. The finite power of man, as an originating cause within his own sphere, seems to come into collision with the infinite power of God, as the originating Cause of all things. Finite power is itself created by and dependent upon God; yet, at the same time, it seems to be manifested as originating and independent. Power itself acts only on the solicitation of motives; and this raises the question, which is prior? does the motive bring about the state of the will which inclines to it; or does the state of the will convert the coincident circumstances into motives? Am I moved to will, or do I will to be moved? Here we are involved in the mystery of endless succession. On this mystery there are some able remarks in Mr. Mozley's *Augustinian theory of Predestination*, p. 2, and in Professor Fraser's *Essays in Philosophy*, p. 275.

Note VII., p. 163.

De Ordine, II. 18. Compare *Ibid.* II. 16. "of that Supreme God, who is better known by not knowing."

Note VIII., p. 163.

Enarratio in Psalmum LXXXV. 12. Compare *De Trinitate*, VIII. c. 2.

Note IX., p. 164.

F. Socinus, *Tractatus de Deo, Christo, et Spiritu Sancto.* (*Opera*, 1656, vol. I. p. 811). "But even from that alone, that God is openly taught to be one, it can justly be concluded, that he can be neither three nor two. For the One and the Three, or the One and the Two are opposed to each other. So that if God be three or two, he cannot be one."—Priestley, *Tracts in Controversy with Bishop Horsley*, p. 78. "They are therefore both *one* and *many* in the same respect, viz., in each being *perfect God.* This is certainly as much a contradiction as to say that Peter, James, and John, having each of them every thing that is requisite to constitute a complete man, are yet, all together, not *three men*, but only *one man.*"—F. W. Newman, *Phases of Faith*, p. 48. "If any one speaks of *three men*, all that he means is, 'three objects of thought, of whom each separately may be called man.' So also, all that could possibly be meant by *three Gods*, is 'three objects of thought, of whom each separately may be called God.' To avow the last statement, as the Creed does, and yet repudiate Three Gods, is to object to the phrase, yet confess to the only meaning which the phrase can convey."

NOTE X., p. 164.

Schleiermacher (*Christliche Glaube*, § 171), has some objections against the Catholic Doctrine of the Holy Trinity, conceived in the thorough spirit of Rationalism. In the same spirit Strauss observes (*Glaubenslehre*, I. p. 460), "Whoever has sworn to the *Symbolum Quicunque* has forsworn the laws of human thought." The sarcasm comes inconsistently enough from a disciple of Hegel, whose entire philosophy is based on an abjuration of the laws of thought. In one respect, indeed, Hegel is right; namely, in maintaining that the laws of thought are not applicable to the Infinite. But the true conclusion from this concession is not, as the Hegelians maintain, that a philosophy can be constructed independently of those laws; but that the Infinite is not an object of human philosophy at all.

NOTE XI., p. 165.

Paradise Lost, B. II. 667.

NOTE XII., p. 166.

Compare Anselm, *De Fide Trinitatis*, c. 7. "But if he denies that three can be predicated of one, and one of three, ... let him allow that there is something in God, which his intellect cannot penetrate, and let him not compare the nature of God, which is above all things, free from all condition of place and time and composition of parts, with things, which are confined to place and time, or composed of parts; but let him believe that there is something, in that nature, which cannot be in those things, and let him acquiesce in christian authority, and not dispute against it."

NOTE XIII., p. 166.

See the objections raised against this doctrine by Mr. F. W. Newman, *Phases of Faith*, p. 84. "The very form of our past participle (*begotten*)," he tells us, "is invented to indicate an event in the past time." The true difficulty is not grammatical, but metaphysical. If ordinary language is primarily accommodated to the ordinary laws of thought, it is a mere verbal quibble to press its literal application to the Infinite, which is above thought.

NOTE XIV., p. 166.

The parallel here pointed out may be exhibited more fully by consulting Bishop Pearson's Exposition of this Doctrine, *On the Creed*, Art. I., and the authorities cited in his notes.

NOTE XV., p. 166.

On this ground is established a profound and decisive criticism of Hegel's System, by Trendelenburg, *Logische Untersuchungen*, c. 2. "Pure being," he says, "is quiescence; so also is the Nothing (das Nichts); how is the active *Becoming* (active reality), the result of the union of two quiescent conceptions?" M. Bartholmèss in like manner remarks, "In turning thus the abstraction to reality, this system tacitly ascribes to abstract being virtues and qualities which belong only to a concrete and individual being; that is, to a simple being capable of spontaneous and deliberate action, of intelligence and of will. It accords all this to it, at the same time that it represents it, and with reason, as an impersonal being. This abstract being produces concrete beings, this impersonal being produces persons; it produces the one and the other, because thus the system directs!" *Histoire des Doctrines Religieuses*, II p. 277.

NOTE XVI., p. 167.

Schelling, *Bruno*, p. 168. "In the Absolute, all is absolute; if, therefore, the perfection of His Nature appears in the real as infinite Being, and in the ideal as infinite Knowing, the Being in the absolute is, even as the Knowing, absolute; and each, being absolute, has not, out of itself, an opposite in the other, but the absolute Knowing is the absolute Nature, and the absolute Nature the absolute Knowing."

NOTE XVII., p. 167.

Aquinas, *Summa*, P. I. Qu. XXXII. Art. 1. "It is impossible, by means of natural reason, to reach the knowledge of the Trinity of the Divine Persons. For it has been shown above, that a man can, by natural reason, arrive at the knowledge of God, only from what is created. . . . . But the creative power of God is common to the whole Trinity; whence it pertains to the unity of the essence, not to the distinction of the Persons. By natural reason, therefore, only those things can be known concerning God, which belong to the Unity of the Divine essence, not to the distinction of the Divine Persons." This wise and sound limitation should be borne in mind, as a testimony against that neoplatonizing spirit of modern times, which seeks to strengthen the evidence of the Christian Doctrine of the Trinity, by distorting it into conformity with the speculations of Heathen Philosophy. The Hegelian Theory of the Trinity is a remarkable instance of this kind. Indeed, Hegel himself expressly regards coincidence with neoplatonism as an evidence in favor of an idealist interpretation of Christian doctrines.[1] A similar spirit occasionally appears in influential writers among ourselves.

Note XVIII., p. 168.

For the objection, see *Catech. Racov.* De Persona Christi, Cap. 1. (Ed. 1609. p. 43.) "It is repugnant to sound reason. *In the first place*, because two substances, opposite in their properties, cannot unite so as to form one person; . . . . *then, too*, because two natures, each constituting a person, cannot come together so as to constitute one person."— Spinoza, *Epist. XXI.* "As to the additional view, given by some churches, that God assumed human nature, I have expressly declared, that I know not what they say; nay, to confess the truth, they seem to me to talk no less absurdly than if any one should say that a circle has assumed the nature of a square." Similar objections are urged by F. W. Newman, *The Soul*, p. 116, and by Theodore Parker, *Critical and Miscellaneous Writings*, p. 320, *Discourse of Matters pertaining to Religion*, p. 234.

Note XIX., p. 169.

One half of this dilemma has been exhibited by Sir W. Hamilton, *Discussions*, p. 609. sqq. It is strange however that this great thinker should not have seen that the second alternative is equally inconceivable; that it is as impossible to conceive the creation as a process of evolution from the being of the Creator, as it is to conceive it as a production out of nothing. This double impossibility is much more in harmony with the philosophy of the conditioned, than the hypothesis which Sir W. Hamilton adopts.

1 *Philosophie der Geschichte*, *Werke*, IX. p. 402.

Indeed, his admirable criticism of Cousin's theory (*Discussions*, p. 36,) contains in substance the same dilemma as that exhibited in the text. For some additional remarks on this point, see above, Lecture II. note 33.

NOTE XX., p. 169.

Pensées, Partie II. Art. I. § 1.

NOTE XXI., p. 171.

Greg, *Creed of Christendom*, p. 248. sqq. Compare the cognate passages from other Authors, quoted above, Lecture I. note 21.

NOTE XXII., p. 172.

For some remarks connected with this and cognate theories, see above, Lecture I. notes 21, 22, 23, Lecture III. notes 16, 18.

NOTE XXIII., p. 173.

"For since in general it is one thing to understand *the impossibility* of a thing, and a far different thing *not* to understand its *possibility;* so especially in those matters of which we are utterly ignorant, such as those which are not exposed to sense, the things are by no means forthwith impossible, the possibility of which we do not thoroughly understand. Therefore it does not become the philosopher to deny universally Divine efficiency in the created world, or to maintain as certain, that God Himself contributes nothing (immediately) either to the consecutive order of natural things, — as for instance the keeping up of each part or species, embraced in a genus of animals or of plants, — or to moral changes, — as for instance, the improvement of the human soul, — or to assert that it is altogether impossible for a revelation or any other extraordinary event to be brought about by Divine agency." Storr, *Annotationes quædam Theologicæ*, p. 5.

NOTE XXIV., p. 173.

"For since the force and power of nature, is the very force and power of God, and its laws and rules are the very decrees of God, it is in general a thing to be believed, that the power of nature is infinite, and that its laws are so made, as to extend to all things which are conceived by the

Divine mind. For, otherwise, what else is determined, than that God made nature so impotent, and appointed for it laws and rules so unproductive, that he is often to come anew to its aid, if He will have it so preserved that things may succeed according to wish; a thing which I conceive to be indeed most foreign to reason." Spinoza, *Tractatus Theologico-Politicus*, cap. VI. — "The latter, indeed (Supernaturalists), assume that God governs human affairs in general by a natural order, and that when this natural order can no longer satisfy His will, He comes in with remedial aid by the working of miracles; the former (Rationalists) decide that God, from eternity, so wisely arranged that all things should follow in a continuous series, that the things which occurred many ages ago, prepared and brought about what is occurring now, and that there should be no need of certain miracles, as a kind of intercalations." Wegscheider, *Instit. Theol.* § 12. From an opposite point of view to that of Spinoza, Herbart arrives at a similar conclusion. "Religion requires the view, that He who, as Father, has made provision for men, now in deepest silence leaves the race to itself, as having no part in it; without trace of any such feeling as might be likened to human sympathy, and indeed to egotism."[1] The simile of the calculating engine, acting by its own laws, is adduced by Mr. Babbage (*Ninth Bridgewater Treatise*, ch. 2), "to illustrate the distinction between a system to which the restoring hand of its contriver is applied, either frequently or at distant intervals, and one which had received at its first formation the impress of the will of its author, foreseeing the varied but yet necessary laws of its action throughout the whole of its existence;" and to show "that that for which, after its original adjustment, no superintendence is acquired, displays far greater ingenuity than that which demands, at every change in its law, the direct intervention of its contriver." Mr. Jowett, though rejecting the analogy of the machine, uses similar language: "The directing power that is able to foresee all things, and provide against them by simple and general rules, is a worthier image of the Divine intelligence than the handicraftsman 'putting his hand to the hammer,' detaching and isolating portions of matter from the laws by which he has himself put them together."[2]

NOTE XXV., p. 174.

"The reason why, among men, an artificer is justly esteemed so much the more skilful, as the machine of his composing will continue longer to move regularly without any further interposition of the workman, is

1 *Lehrbuch zur Einleitung in die Philosophie*, § 155 (*Werke*, I. p. 278).

2 *Epistles of St. Paul*, vol. II. p. 412.

because the skill of all *human* artificers consists only in composing, adjusting, or putting together certain movements, the principles of whose motion are altogether independent upon the artificer. . . . . But with regard to *God*, the case is quite different; because He not only composes or puts things together, but is himself the Author and continual Preserver of their original forces or moving powers. And consequently it is not a diminution, but the true glory of his workmanship, that *nothing* is done without his *continual government* and *inspection*." Clarke, *First Reply to Leibnitz*, p. 15.

NOTE XXVI., p. 174.

"I do not believe," says Theodore Parker, "there ever was a miracle, or ever will be; every where I find law, — the constant mode of operation of the infinite God."— *Some account of my Ministry*, appended to *Theism, Atheism, and the Popular Theology*, p. 263. Compare the same work, pp. 113, 188; and Atkinson, *Man's Nature and Development*, p. 241. The statement is not at present true, even as regards the material world: it is false as regards the world of mind: and were it true in both, it would prove nothing regarding the "infinite God." For the conception of law is, to say the least, quite as finite as that of miraculous interposition. Professor Powell, in his latest work, though not absolutely rejecting miracles, yet adopts a tone which, compared with such passages as the above, is at least painfully suggestive. "It is now perceived by all inquiring minds, that the advance of true scientific principles, and the grand inductive conclusions of universal and eternal law and order, are at once the basis of all rational theology, and give the death-blow to superstition." *Christianity without Judaism*, p. 11.

NOTE XXVII., p. 174.

This point has been treated by the author at greater length in the *Prolegomena Logica*, p. 135, and in the article *Metaphysics*, in the eighth edition of the *Encyclopædia Britannica*, vol. XIV. p. 600.

NOTE XXVIII., p. 176.

See McCosh, *Method of the Divine Government*, pp. 162, 166. The quotations which the author brings forward in support of this remark, from Humboldt and Comte, are valuable as showing the concurrence of the highest scientific authorities as to the facts stated. The religious application of these facts is Dr. McCosh's own, and constitutes one of the most instructive portions of his valuable work. The fact itself has been noticed and commented on with his usual sagacity by Bishop Butler, *Analogy*, Part II. c. 3. "Would it not have been thought highly improbable, that men should have been so much more capable of discovering, even to certainty, the general laws of matter, and the magnitudes, paths, and revolutions of the heavenly bodies, than the occasions and cures of distempers, and many other things, in which human life seems so much more nearly concerned, than in astronomy?"

NOTE XXIX., p. 176.

"There are domains of nature in which man's foresight is considerably extended and accurate, and other domains in which it is very limited, or very dim and confused. Again, there are departments of nature in which man's influence is considerable, and others which lie altogether beyond his control, directly or indirectly. Now, on comparing these classes of objects, we find them to have a cross or converse relation to one another. Where man's foreknowledge is extensive, either he has no power, or his power is limited; and where his power might be exerted, his foresight is contracted. . . . . He can tell in what position a satellite of Saturn will be a hundred years after this present time, but he cannot say in what state his bodily health may be an hour hence. . . . . We are now in circumstances to discover the advantages arising from the mixture of uniformity and uncertainty in the operations of nature. Both serve most important ends in the government of God. The one renders nature steady and stable, the other active and accommodating. Without the certainty, man would waver as in a dream, and wander as in a trackless desert; without the unexpected changes, he would make his rounds like the gin-horse in its circuit, or the prisoner on his wheel. Were nature altogether capricious, man would likewise become altogether capricious, for he could have no motive to steadfast action: again, were nature altogether fixed, it would make man's character as cold and formal as itself." McCosh, *Method of the Divine Government*, pp. 172, 174 (fourth edition).

NOTE XXX., p. 177.

The solution usually given by Christian writers of the difficulty of reconciling the efficacy of prayer with the infinite power and wisdom of God, I cannot help regarding, while thoroughly sympathizing with the purpose of its advocates, as unsatisfactory. That solution may be given in the language of Euler. "When a christian addresses to God, at this present moment, a prayer worthy of being granted, we must not imagine that this prayer reaches now, for the first time, the knowledge of God. He has already heard that prayer from all eternity; and since this compassionate Father has judged it worthy of being granted, He has arranged the world expressly in favor of this prayer in such manner, that its accomplishment may be a consequence of the natural course of events."[1] In other words, the prayer is foreseen and foreordained, as well as the answer. This solution appears to assume that the conception of law and necessity adequately represents the absolute nature of God, while that of contingence and special interposition is to be subordinated to it. The arrangements of God in the government of the world are fixed from all eternity, and if the prayer is part of those arrangements, it becomes a necessary act likewise. It is surely a more reverent, and probably a truer solution, to say that the conception of general law and that of special interposition are equally human. Neither probably represents, as a speculative truth, the absolute manner in which God works in His Providence; both are equally necessary, as regulative truths, to govern man's conduct in this life. In neither aspect are we warranted in making the one conception subordinate to the other. A similar objection may be urged against the theory which represents a miracle as the possible manifestation of a higher and unknown law. There is nothing in the conception of *law* which entitles it to this preëminence over other human modes of representation.

NOTE XXXI., p. 177.

Kant, though he attaches no value to miracles as evidences of a moral religion, yet distinctly allows that there is no sufficient reason for denying their possibility as facts or their utility at certain periods of the history of religion.[2] This moderation is not imitated by his disciple, Wegscheider, who says: "The belief in a *supernatural* and *miraculous*, and that too, an *immediate* revelation of God seems not well reconcilable with the ideas of a God eternal, always constant to Himself, omnipotent, omniscient and most wise."[3] Strauss, in like manner, assumes that the absolute cause never disturbs the chain of secondary causes by arbitrary acts of interposition; and therefore lays it down as a canon, that whatever is miraculous is unhistorical.[4]

1 *Lettres à une Princesse d' Allemagne*, vol. I. p. 357, ed. Cournot. Compare McCosh, *Method of the Divine Government*, p 222.

2 *Religion innerhalb der Grenzen der blossen Vernunft*, p. 99, edit. Rosenkranz.

3 *Instit. Theol.* § 12.

4 *Leben Jesu*, § 16.

Note XXXII., p. 178.

See, on the one side, Babbage, *Ninth Bridgewater Treatise*, ch. 8; Hitchcock, *Religion of Geology*, p. 290. The same view is also suggested as probable by Butler, *Analogy*, Part II. ch. 4. On the other side, as regards the limitations within which the idea of law should be applied to the course of God's Providence, see McCosh, *Method of Divine Government*, p. 155. Kant, *Religion innerhalb, u. s. w.* p. 102, maintains, with reason, that from a human point of view, a law of miracles is unattainable.

Note XXXIII., p. 180.

Sir William Hamilton, *Discussions*, p. 625.

LECTURE VII.

Note I., p. 182.

The Moral and Religious Philosophy of Kant, which is here referred to, is chiefly contained in his *Metaphysik der Sitten*, first published in 1785, his *Kritik der praktischen Vernunft*, in 1788, and his *Religion innerhalb der Grenzen der blossen Vernunft*, in 1793. For Kant's influence on the rationalist theology of Germany, see Rosenkranz, *Geschichte der Kant'schen Philosophie*, p. 323. sqq. Amand Saintes, *Histoire du Rationalisme en Allemagne*, L. II. ch. xi. Rose, *State of Protestantism in Germany*, p. 183 (2nd edition), Kahnis, *History of German Protestantism*, pp. 88, 167 (Meyer's Translation).

Note II., p. 183.

See *Metaphysik der Sitten*, pp. 5, 31, 52, 87, 92; *Kritik der praktischen Vernunft*, p. 224 (ed. Rosenkranz).

Note III., p. 183.

A similar view of the superiority of the moral consciousness over other phenomena of the human mind, as regards absolute certainty, seems to be held by Mr. Jowett. In reference to certain doubts connected with the Doctrine of the Atonement, he observes, "It is not the pride of human reason which suggests these questions, but the moral sense which He himself has implanted in the breast of each one of us."[1] It is difficult to see the force of the antithesis here suggested. The "moral sense" is not more the gift of God than the "human reason;" and the decisions of the former, to be represented in consciousness at all, require the coöperation of the latter. Even as regards our own personal acts, the intellectual conception must be united with the moral sense in passing judgment; and in all general theories concerning the moral nature of God or of man, the rational faculty will necessarily have the larger share.

NOTE IV., p. 183.

Kritik der reinen Vernunft, p. 631. ed. Rosenkranz. *Metaphysik der Sitten*, p. 31. *Religion innerhalb u. s. w.* p. 123.

NOTE V., p. 183.

Religion u. s. w. p. 123.

NOTE VI., p. 183.

Ibid. pp. 122, 184.

NOTE VII., p. 183.

Ibid. pp. 123, 133. Compare *Streit der Facultäten*, p. 304.

NOTE VIII., p. 184.

See above, Lecture III, p. 74.

NOTE IX., p. 185.

On the existence of necessary truths in morals, comparable to those of mathematics, see Reid, *Intellectual Powers*, Essay VI. ch. 6 (pp. 453, 454. ed. Hamilton).

1 *Epistles of St. Paul*, Vol. II. p. 468.

NOTE X., p. 186.

Compare Jacobi, *An Fichte, Werke,* III. pp. 35, 37. "Just as certainly as I possess reason, so certainly do I *not* possess along with it the perfection of life, I do *not* possess the fulness of the good and the true; and just as certainly as I do *not* possess this, *and know it,* just so certainly do I *know* there is a *higher* Being, and in Him I have my origin . . . . . I acknowledge, then, that I do not know the *Good in itself,* the *True in itself,* also that I have only a remote *foreboding* of it." That the moral providence of God cannot be judged by the same standard as the actions of men, see Leibnitz, *Théodicée, De la Conformité,* etc. § 32 (*Opera,* ed. Erdmann, p. 489).

NOTE XI., p. 187.

"Wherefore, inasmuch as our actions are conversant about things beset with many circumstances, which cause men of sundry wits to be also of sundry judgments concerning that which ought to be done; requisite it cannot but seem the rule of divine law should herein help our imbecility, that we might the more infallibly understand what is good and what evil. The first principles of the Law of Nature are easy; hard it were to find men ignorant of them. But concerning the duty which Nature's law doth require at the hands of men, in a number of things particular, so far hath the natural understanding even of sundry whole nations been darkened, that they have not discerned, no not gross iniquity to be sin. — Hooker, *E. P.*, I. xii. 2.

NOTE XII., p. 187.

This corresponds to the distinction drawn by Leibnitz, between *eternal* and *positive* truths of the reason. See *Théodicée, Discours de la Conformité,* etc. § 2 (*Opera,* Erdmann, p. 480). The latter class of truths, he allows, may be subservient to Faith, and even opposed by it, but not the former.

NOTE XIII., p. 189.

That it is impossible to conceive the Divine Will as absolutely indifferent, is shown by Müller, *Christliche Lehre von der Sünde,* I. p. 128. But on the other hand, we are equally unable to conceive it as necessarily determined by the laws of the Divine Nature. We cannot therefore conceive absolute morality either as dependent on, or as independent of, the Will of God. In other words, we are unable to conceive absolute morality at all.

NOTE XIV., p. 190.

See above, Lecture I, note 14.

NOTE XV., p. 190.

"Sin *contains* its own retributive penalty, as surely and as naturally as the acorn contains the oak. . . . . It is ordained to follow guilt by God—not as a Judge, but as the Creator and Legislator of the universe. . . . We can be redeemed from the punishment of sin only by being redeemed from its commission. Neither *can* there be any such thing as vicarious atonement or punishment. . . . If the foregoing reflections are sound, the awful, yet wholesome conviction presses on our minds, that *there can be no forgiveness of sins*."—Greg, *Creed of Christendom*, p. 265. "I believe God is a just God, rewarding and punishing us exactly as we act well or ill. I believe that such reward and punishment follow necessarily from His will as revealed in natural law, as well as in the Bible. I believe that as the highest justice is the highest mercy, so He is a merciful God. That the guilty should suffer the measure of penalty which their guilt has incurred, is justice."—Froude, *Nemesis of Faith*, p. 69.

NOTE XVI., p. 190.

See above, Lecture I, note 13.

NOTE XVII., p. 190.

See above, Lecture I, note 12.

NOTE XVIII., p. 190.

See Newman, *Phases of Faith*, p. 8. Compare Wegscheider, *Instit. Theol.* § 141.

NOTE XIX., p. 191.

Mr. Rigg justly observes of the theory of immediate forgiveness, as substituted for the Christian Atonement, "Let all men be told that 'God cannot be angry with any,' and that whatever may have been a man's sins, if he will but repent, there is no hindrance to God's freely forgiving him all, without the infliction of any punishment whatever, and without the need of any atonement or intercession. What would be the effect of such a proclamation? Would it make sin appear 'exceeding sinful?' Would it enhance our idea of the holiness of God? Would it not make sin appear a light and trivial thing, tolerated too easily by a 'good-natured' God, to be held as of much account by man?"[1] Wegscheider indeed actually urges this argument against the Christian doctrine, which it suits his purpose to represent as a scheme of unconditional forgiveness. "Experience teaches, that the belief, that even the most wicked man can easily obtain absolute remission of sins, has always done the greatest detriment to true virtue and integrity."—*Instit. Theol.* § 140.

NOTE XX., p. 191.

Such is, in fact, the theory of Kant. See *Religion innerhalb der Grenzen der blossen Vernunft*, p. 84. He does not, however, carry his principle consistently out, but admits a kind of vicarious suffering in a symbolical sense; the penitent being morally a different individual from the sinner. Even this metaphorical conceit is utterly out of place according to the main principles of his system.

NOTE XXI., p. 192.

Some excellent remarks on this point will be found in McCosh's *Method of the Divine Government*, p. 475 (4th edition).

NOTE XXII., p. 192.

"This natural indignation is generally moderate and low enough in mankind, in each particular man, when the injury which excites it doth not affect himself, or one whom he considers as himself. Therefore the precepts to *forgive* and to *love our enemies*, do not relate to that general indignation against injury and the authors of it, but to this feeling, or resentment, when raised by private or personal injury."—Butler, Sermon IX, *On Forgiveness of Injuries.*

NOTE XXIII., p. 193.

Thus Mr. Froude exclaims, "He! to have created mankind liable to fail—to have laid them in the way of a temptation under which He knew

[1] *Modern Anglican Theology*, p. 317.

they would fall, and then curse them and all who were to come of them, and all the world for their sakes!"—*Nemesis of Faith*, p. 11. This author omits the whole doctrine of the redemption, and treats the fall and the curse as if they were the sole manner of God's dealing with sinners. His objection, stripped of its violent language, is but one form of the universal riddle—the existence of Evil. A similar objection is urged by Mr. Parker, *Theism, Atheism, and the Popular Theology*, p. 64: and by Mr. Atkinson, *Letters on the Laws of Man's Nature and Development*, pp. 173, 174.

NOTE XXIV., p. 193.

Aristotle *Eth. Nic.* V. 10. "For of a thing, which is not limited, the rule is also unlimited, like the plumb-rule of Lesbian house-building, changing according to the form of the stone, and not remaining the same rule."

NOTE XXV., p. 193.

On this spirit of universal criticism, Augustine remarks: "But they are foolish, who say, 'Could not the wisdom of God otherwise deliver men, than by assuming human nature, and being born of a woman, and suffering all those things from sinners?' To whom, we say He could, but if He were to do otherwise, He would in like manner be displeasing to your folly."—*De Agone Christiano*, c. 11.

The following passage from the *Eclipse of Faith*, p. 125, is an excellent statement of the versatility of the "moral reason," or "spiritual insight," when set up as a criterion of religious truth. "Even as to that fundamental position,—the existence of a Being of unlimited power and wisdom (as to his unlimited *goodness*, I believe that nothing *but* an external revelation can absolutely certify us), I feel that I am much more indebted to those inferences from *design*, which these writers make so light of, than to any *clearness* in the imperfect intuition; for if I found—and surely this is the true test—the traces of design less conspicuous in the external world, confusion there as in the moral, and in both greater than is now found in either, I extremely doubt whether the faintest surmise of such a Being would have suggested itself to me. But be that as it may; as to their other cardinal sentiments,—the nature of my relations to this Being—his placability if offended,—the terms of forgiveness, if any,—whether, as these gentlemen affirm, he is accessible to all, without any atonement or mediator:—as to all this, I solemnly declare, that apart from external instruction, I cannot by interrogating my racked spirit, catch even a mur-

mur. That it must be faint indeed, in *other* men — so faint as to render the pretensions of the certitude of the internal revelation, and its independence of all external revelation, perfectly preposterous — I infer from this, — that they have, for the most part, arrived at diametrically opposite conclusions from those of these interpreters of the spiritual revelation. As to the articles, indeed, of man's immortality and a future state, it would be truly difficult for *my* 'spiritual insight' to verify *theirs;* for, according to Mr. Parker, his 'insight' affirms that man *is* immortal, and Mr. Newman's 'insight' declares nothing about the matter! Nor is my consciousness, so far as I can trace it, mine only. This painful uncertainty has been the confession of multitudes of far greater minds; they have been so far from contending that we have naturally a clear utterance on these great questions, that they have acknowledged the necessity of an external revelation; and mankind *in general*, so far from thinking or feeling such light superfluous, have been constantly *gaping* after it, and adopted almost any thing that but *bore the name.*

What, then, am I to think of this all-sufficient revelation from *within?*"

NOTE XXVI., p. 193.

For the Socinian theory of a limited foreknowledge in God, see Müller, *Christliche Lehre von der Sünde*, II. pp. 276, 288; Davison, *Discourses on Prophecy*, pp. 360, 367. A similar view is held by Rothe, *Theol. Ethik*, Vol. I. p. 118; and by Drobisch, *Grundlehren der Religionsphilosophie*, p. 209. For the opposite necessitarian theory, see Calvin, *Inst.* L. II. ch. 4. § 6; Edwards, *On the Freedom of the Will*, Part II. Sect. xii. quoted above, Lect. II. note 7; and in the authorities cited by Wegscheider, *Inst. Theol.*, § 65.

NOTE XXVII., p. 193.

That God's knowledge is not properly *foreknowledge*, as not being subject to the law of time, is maintained by Augustine, *De Civ. Dei*, XI. 21, *De Div. Quæst ad Simpl.* L. II. Qu. 2. § 2, and by Boethius, *De Consol. Phil.* L. V. Pr. 3-6. A similar view is taken by Wegscheider, *Inst. Theol.* § 65. As a speculative theory, this view is as untenable as the opposite hypothesis of an absolute foreknowledge and predestination. We can only say that we do not know that the Divine Consciousness is subject to the law of succession; not that we know that it is not. As a means of saving the infinity of God's knowledge, consistently with the free agency of man, the hypothesis becomes unnecessary, the instant we admit that the infinite is not an object of human conception at all. If this is once conceded, we need no hypothesis to reconcile truths which we cannot certainly know to be in antagonism to each other. We cannot assume the simultaneity of the divine consciousness; for we know nothing of the infinite, either in itself or in its relation to time. Nor, on the other hand, could we deduce the necessity of human actions from the fact of God's foreknowledge, even if the latter could be assumed as absolutely true; for we know not whether the conception of necessity itself implies a divine reality, or merely a human mode of representation.

NOTE XXVIII., p. 194.

Wegscheider (*Inst. Theol.* § 50) denies the possibility of prophecy, on the ground that a prediction of human events is destructive of freedom. In this he follows Kant, *Anthropologie*, § 35.

NOTE XXIX., p. 194.

"As it is certain that prescience does not destroy the liberty of man's will, or impose any necessity upon it, men's actions being not therefore future, because they are foreknown, but therefore foreknown, because future; and were a thing never so contingent, yet upon supposition that it will be done, it must needs have been future from all eternity: so is it extreme arrogance for men, because themselves can naturally foreknow nothing but by some causes antecedent, as an eclipse of the sun or moon, therefore to presume to measure the knowledge of God Almighty according to the same scantling, and to deny him the prescience of human actions, not considering that, as his nature is incomprehensible, so his knowledge may be well looked upon by us as such too; that which is past our finding out, and too wonderful for us."—Cudworth, *Intellectual System*, ch. V. (Vol. III. p. 19. ed. Harrison). "*We* may be unable to conceive how a thing not necessary in its nature can be foreknown—for *our* foreknowledge is in general limited by that circumstance, and is more or less perfect in proportion to the fixed or necessary nature of the things we contemplate: . . . but to subject the knowledge of God to any such limitation is surely absurd and unphilosophical, as well as impious."—Copleston, *Enquiry into the Doctrines of Necessity and Predestination*, p. 46.

NOTE XXX., p. 194.

Origen. apud Euseb. *Præp. Evang.* VI. 11. 36. And if we must say, that foreknowledge is not the cause of events, we will say what, though more paradoxical, is yet true, that the fact that the thing is to be, is the cause of its foreknowledge."—Leibnitz, *Theodicée*, § 37. "It is very easy to decide, that foreknowledge in itself adds nothing to the determination of the reality of future events, except that this determination is known; a thing which does not at all increase the determination, or the *futurition* (as it is called) of these events."—Clarke, *Demonstration of the Being and Attributes of God*, p. 96. "The certainty of Foreknowledge does not cause the certainty of things, but is itself founded on the reality of their existence. Whatever now is, it is *certain* that it is; and it was yesterday and from eternity as *certainly* true, that the thing *would be* to-day, as 'tis now *certain* that it *is*. This *certainty of events* is equally the same, whether it is supposed that the thing could be foreknown or not."

Note XXXI., p. 195.

See above, Lecture VI, p. 150, and note 27.

Note XXXII., p. 196.

This question is discussed at some length by Euler, *Lettres á une Princesse d'Allemagne*, Vol. I. p. 360. ed., Cournot.

Note XXXIII., p. 196.

"Sins are finite; between the finite and the infinite there is no proportion; therefore punishments also ought to be finite."—Sonerus apud Leibnitz. *Præf.*[1] The same argument is used by Blasche, *Philosophische Unsterblichkeitlehre*, § 4; as well as by Mr. Newman, *Phases of Faith*, p. 78, and by Mr. Froude, *Nemesis of Faith*, p. 17. The latter however entirely misrepresents Leibnitz's reply to the objection.

Note XXXIV., p. 197.

Thus Leibnitz replies to the objection of Sonerus: "Even, therefore, if we should concede that no sin is of itself infinite, yet it can with truth be said, that the sins of the damned are infinite in number; for they persist in sinning, through all eternity." The same argument is repeated in the

1 Published by Lessing, in his tract, *Leibnitz von den ewigen Strafen* (*Lessing's Schriften*, ed. Lachmann, Vol. IX. p. 154).

Theodicée, §§ 74, 133, 266. The reply which Mr. Froude attributes to Leibnitz, namely, that sin against an Infinite Being contracts a character of infinity, is merely noticed by him as "la raison vulgaire," urged, among others, by Ursinus. With Leibnitz's language may be compared that of Müller; "And since experience shows, that men *really resist* the holiest work of divine love, why should it be thought impossible, that this resistance against God may also, on the other side this earthly life, be ever again renewed, and thus carried forward into endless periods?"—*Christliche Lehre von der Sünde,* II. p. 601.

NOTE XXXV., p. 197.

Thus Mr. Newman says, "I saw that the current orthodoxy made Satan eternal conqueror over Christ. In vain does the Son of God come from heaven and take human flesh and die on the cross. In spite of him the devil carries off to hell the vast majority of mankind, in whom not misery only, but *Sin,* is triumphant for ever and ever."[1] And Mr. Parker, to the same effect, remarks, "I can never believe that Evil is a finality with God."[2] The remarks of Müller, in answer to similar theories, are worthy of consideration. "It seems incredible, according to what we have said, that the idea of the world is to reach its complete development with an *unsettled discord,* that opposition to the Divine will is to maintain itself in the will of any creature whatsoever. This difficulty, however, is solved by a correct conception of *punishment.* The opposition to the Divine will does not hold its ground, but is absolutely overcome, when the entire condition of the beings, in whom it is, is a penal condition; so that evil, being in restraint, is no longer able to disturb the pure harmony of the world glorified and transformed to the kingdom of God."[3]

NOTE XXXVI., p. 197.

See a short treatise by Kant, *Ueber das Misslingen aller Philosophischen Versuche in der Theodicée* (*Werke,* VII. p. 385). For a more detailed account of various theories, see Müller, *Christliche Lehre von der Sünde,* B. II. An able review of the difficulties of the question will be found in Mr. Mozley's *Augustinian Doctrine of Predestination,* p. 262 *seq.*

1 *Phases of Faith,* p. 78.
2 *Some Account of my Ministry.* See *Theism, Atheism,* etc., p. 261.
3 *Christliche Lehre von der Sünde,* II. p. 599.

Note XXXVII., p. 197.

The theory which represents evil as a *privation* or a *negation* — a theory adopted by theologians and philosophers of almost every shade of opinion, in order to reconcile the goodness of God with the apparent permission of sin, can only be classed among the numerous necessarily fruitless attempts of metaphysicians to explain the primary facts of consciousness, by the arbitrary assumption of a principle of which we are not and cannot be conscious, and of whose truth or falsehood we have therefore no possible guarantee. Moral evil, in the only form in which we are conscious of it, appears as the direct transgression of a law whose obligation we feel within us; and thus manifested, it is an act as real and as positive as any performed in the most rigid compliance with that law. And this is the utmost point to which human research can penetrate. Whether, in some absolute mode of existence, out of all relation to human consciousness, the phenomenon of moral evil is ultimately dependent on the addition or the subtraction of some causative principle, is a question the solution of which is beyond consciousness, and therefore beyond philosophy. To us, as moral agents, capable of right and wrong acts, evil is a reality, and its consequences are a reality. What may be the nature of the cause which produces this unquestionably real fact of human consciousness, is a mystery which God has not revealed, and which man cannot discover.

Note XXXVIII., p. 199.

Analogy, Part II. ch. 5. In another significant passage (Part I. ch. 2), Butler exhibits the argument from analogy as bearing on the final character of punishment. "Though after men have been guilty of folly and extravagance *up to a certain degree*, it is often in their power, for instance, to retrieve their affairs, to recover their health and character; at least in good measure; yet real reformation is, in many cases, of no avail at all towards preventing the miseries, poverty, sickness, infamy, naturally annexed to folly and extravagance *exceeding that degree*. . . . So that many natural punishments are final to him who incurs them, if considered only in his temporal capacity." — Compare Bishop Browne, *Procedure of the Understanding*, p. 351. "The difficulty in that question, *What proportion endless torments can bear to momentary sins?* is quite removed, by considering that the punishments denounced and threatened are not in themselves sanctions entirely arbitrary, as it is in punishments annexed to human laws; but they are withal so many previous warnings or declarations of the *inevitable* consequence and *natural* tendency of Sin in itself, to render us miserable in another world."

NOTE XXXIX., p. 200.

Kant (*Religion, u. s. w., Werke*, X. p. 45) objects to the doctrine of inherited corruption, on the ground that a man cannot be responsible for any but his own acts. The objection is carried out more fully by Wegscheider, who says, "Neither can the goodness of God allow, that by one man's sin, universal human nature be corrupted and depraved; nor can His wisdom suffer, that God's work, furnished from the beginning with surpassing endowments, be transformed in a little while, for the slightest cause, to quite another and a worse condition."—*Inst. Theol.* § 117. The learned critic does not seem to be aware that the principle of one of these arguments exactly annihilates that of the other; for if we concede to the first, that every man is born in the state of pristine innocence, we must admit, in opposition to the second, that God's work is destroyed by slight causes, not once only, but millions of times, in every man that sins. The only other supposition possible is, that sin itself is part of God's purpose—in which case we need not trouble ourselves to establish any argument on the hypothesis of the divine wisdom or benevolence.

NOTE XL., p. 200.

Aristotle, *Eth. Nic.* VII. 2. "But one may be at a loss to understand how a person, who takes a right estimate of things, can live without moral self-control. Some, therefore, say that a person, who had knowledge, could not live in such manner; for (as Socrates thought), if knowledge were within him, he could not be controlled by something else, and dragged about by it, like a slave."

NOTE XLI., p. 200.

For sundry rationalist objections to the doctrine of Justification by Faith, see Wegscheider, § 154, 155. He declares the whole doctrine to be the result of the *anthropopathic* notions of a rude age.

NOTE XLII., p. 201.

"Our notion of freedom does not, it is true, exclude motives of conscious action; but motives are not compulsory, but are always effectual only through the will; motives for the human will can therefore proceed from God, without man's being thereby forced, without his losing his freedom, and becoming a blind instrument of the higher power."—Drobisch,

Grundlehren der Religionsphilosophie, p. 272. In like manner, Mr. Mozley, in his learned and philosophical work on the Augustinian Doctrine of Predestination, truly says, "What we have to consider in this question, is not what is the abstract idea of freewill, but what is the freewill which we really and actually have. This actual freewill, we find, is not a simple but a complex thing; exhibiting oppositions and inconsistencies; appearing on the one side to be a power of doing anything to which there is no physical hindrance, on the other side to be a restricted faculty" (p. 102). Neither the Pelagian theory on the one side, nor the Augustinian on the other, took sufficient account of the actual condition of the human will in relation to external influences. The question was argued as if the relation of divine grace to human volition must consist wholly in activity on the one side and passivity on the other; — in the will of its own motion accepting the grace, or the grace by its irresistible force overpowering the will. The controversy thus becomes precisely analogous to the philosophical dispute between the advocates of freewill and determinism; the one proceeding on the assumption of an absolute indifference of the will; the other maintaining its necessary determination by motives.

Mr. Mozley has thrown considerable light on the true bearings of the predestinarian controversy; and his work is especially valuable as vindicating the supreme right of Scripture to be accepted in all its statements, instead of being mutilated to suit the demands of human logic. But it cannot be denied that his own theory, however satisfactory in this respect, leaves a painful void on the philosophical side, and apparently vindicates the authority of revelation by the sacrifice of the laws of human thought. He maintains that where our conception of an object is indistinct, contradictory propositions may be accepted as both equally true; and he carries this theory so far as to assert of the rival doctrines of Pelagius and Augustine, "Both these positions are true, if held together, and both false, if held apart."[1]

Should we not rather say that the very indistinctness of conception prevents the existence of any contradiction at all? I can only know two ideas to be contradictory by the distinct conception of both; and, where

[1] P. 77. To the same effect are his criticisms on Aquinas, p. 260, in which he says, "The will as an original spring of action is irreconcilable with the Divine Power, a second first cause in nature being inconsistent with there being only one First Cause." This assumes that we have a sufficient conception of the nature of Divine Power and of the action of a First Cause; an assumption which the author himself in another passage repudiates, acknowledging that "As an unknown premiss, the Divine Power is no contradiction to the fact of evil; for we must know what a truth is before we see a contradiction in it to another truth" (p. 276). This latter admission, consistently carried out, would have considerably modified the author's whole theory.

such a conception is impossible, there is no evidence of contradiction. The actual declarations of Scripture, so far as they deal with matters above human comprehension, are not in themselves contradictory to the facts of consciousness; they are only made so by arbitrary interpretation. It is nowhere said in Scripture that God so predestines man as to take from him all power of acting by his own will: — this is an inference from the supposed nature of predestination; an inference which, if our conception of predestination is indistinct, we have no right to make. *Man* cannot foreknow unless the event is certain; nor predestine without coërcing the result. Here there is a contradiction between freewill and predestination. But we cannot transfer the same contradiction to Theology, without assuming that God's knowledge and acts are subject to the same conditions as man's.

The contradictory propositions which Mr. Mozley exhibits, as equally guaranteed by consciousness, are in reality by no means homogeneous. In each pair of contradictories, we have a limited and individual fact of immediate perception, — such as the power of originating an action, — opposed to a universal maxim, not perceived immediately, but based on some process of general thought, — such as that every event must have a cause. To establish these two as contradictory of each other, it should be shown that in every single act we have a direct consciousness of being coërced, as well as of being free; and that we can gather from each fact a clear and distinct conception. But this is by no means the case. The principle of causality, whatever may be its true import and extent, is not derived from the immediate consciousness of our volition being determined by antecedent causes; and therefore it may not be applied to human actions, until, from an analysis of the mode in which this maxim is gained, it can be distinctly shown that these are included under it.[1]

By applying to Mr. Mozley's theory the principles advanced in the preceding Lectures, it may, I believe, be shown that, in every case, the contradiction is not real, but apparent; and that it arises from a vain attempt to transcend the limits of human thought.

NOTE XLIII., p. 201.

Analogy, Introduction, p. 10.

[1] I am happy to be able to refer, in support of this view, to the able criticism of Professor Fraser, in his review of Mr. Mozley's work. "The coëxistence," he says, "of a belief in causality with a belief in moral agency, is indeed incomprehensible; but is it so because the two beliefs are known to be contradictory, and not rather because causality and Divine Power cannot be fathomed by finite intelligence?"— *Essays in Philosophy*, p. 271.

LECTURE VIII.

Note I., p. 206.

F. W. Newman, *Phases of Faith*, p. 199; *Reply to the Eclipse of Faith*, p. 11.

Note II., p. 206.

"Christianity itself has thus practically confessed, what is theoretically clear, that an authoritative *external* revelation of moral and spiritual truth is essentially impossible to man."—F. W. Newman, *The Soul*, p. 59.

Note III., p. 206.

"In teaching about God and Christ, lay aside the wisdom of the wise; forswear History and all its apparatus; hold communion with the Father and the Son in the Spirit; from this communion learn all that is essential to the Gospel, and still (if possible) retain every proposition which Paul believed and taught. Propose them to the faith of others, *to be tested by inward and spiritual evidence only;* and you will at least be in the true apostolic track."—F. W. Newman, *The Soul*, p. 250.

Note IV., p. 207.

"This question of miracles, whether true or false, is of no religious significance. When Mr. Locke said the doctrine proved the miracles, not the miracles the doctrine, he admitted their worthlessness. They can be useful only to such as deny our internal power of discerning truth."—Parker, *Discourse of matters pertaining to Religion*, p. 170. Pascal, with far sounder judgment, says, on the other hand, "we must judge of the doctrine by the miracles, we must judge of miracles by the doctrine. The doctrine shows what the miracles are, and the miracles show what the doctrine is. All this is true, and not contradictory. . . . . . Jesus Christ cured the man who was born blind, and did many other miracles on the sabbath day; whereby he blinded the Pharisees, who said, that it was necessary to judge of miracles by the doctrine. . . . . . The Pharisees said: *This man is not of God, because he keepeth not the sabbath day.* The others said: *How can a man that is a sinner, do such miracles?* Which is the clearer?"[1] In like manner Clarke observes, "'T is indeed the miracles only, that prove the doctrine; and not the doctrine that proves the miracles. But then in order to this end, that the miracles may prove the doctrine, 'tis always necessary to be first supposed that the doctrine be such as is in its nature capable of being proved by miracles. The doctrine must be in itself *possible* and *capable to be proved*, and then miracles will prove it to be *actually and certainly* true.[2] The judicious remarks of Dean Trench are to the same effect, "When we object to the use often made of these works, it is only because they have been forcibly severed from the whole complex of Christ's life and doctrine, and presented to the contemplation of men apart from these; it is only because, when on his head are 'many crowns,' one only has been singled out in proof that He is King of kings, and Lord of lords. The miracles have been spoken of as though they borrowed nothing from the truths which they confirmed, but those truths everything from the miracles by which they were confirmed; when, indeed, the true relation is one of mutual interdependence, the miracles proving the doctrines, and the doctrines approving the miracles, and both held together for us in a blessed unity, in the person of Him who spake the words and did the works, and through the impress of highest holiness and of absolute truth and goodness, which that person leaves stamped on our souls; — so that it may be more truly said that we believe the miracles for Christ's sake, than Christ for the miracles' sake."[3]

NOTE V., p. 207.

Foxton, *Popular Christianity*, p. 105. On the other hand, the profound author of the *Restoration of Belief*, with a far juster estimate of the value of evidence, observes, "Remove the supernatural from the Gospels, or, in other words, reduce the evangelical histories, by aid of some unintelligible hypothesis (German-born), to the level of an inane jumble of credulity, extravagance, and myth-power (whatever this may be), and then Christianity will go to its place, as to any effective value, in relation to humanizing and benevolent influences and enterprises; — a place, say, a few degrees above the level of some passages in Epictetus and M. Aurelius. . . .

1 *Penseés*, Partie II. Art. xvi. § i. 5, 10. Whatever may be thought of the evidence in behalf of the particular miracle on the occasion of which these remarks were written, the article itself is worthy of the highest praise, as a judicious statement of the religious value of miracles, supposing their actual occurrence to be proved by sufficient testimony.

2 *Evidence of Natural and Revealed Religion*, Prop. xiv.

3 *Notes on the Miracles of our Lord*, p. 94 (fifth edition).

The Gospel is a Force in the world, it is a force available for the good of man, not because it is Wisdom, but because it is Power. . . . But the momentum supplied by the Gospel is a force which disappears — which is utterly gone, gone for ever, when Belief in its authority, *as attested by miracles*, is destroyed."—Pp. 290, 291, 292. To the same effect are the excellent remarks with which Neander concludes his *Life of Jesus Christ*. "The end of Christ's appearance on earth corresponds to its beginning. No link in its chain of supernatural facts can be lost, without taking away its significance as a whole. Christianity rests upon these facts; stands or falls with them. By faith in them has the Divine life been generated from the beginning; by faith in them has that life in all ages regenerated mankind, raised them above the limits of earthly life, changed them from *glebæ adscripti* to citizens of heaven, and formed the stage of transition from an existence chained to nature, to a free, celestial life, far raised above it. Were this faith gone, there might, indeed, remain many of the *effects* of what Christianity has been; but as for Christianity in the true sense, as for a Christian Church, there could be none."—(English Translation, p. 487).

Note VI., p. 207.

Parker, *Some Account of my Ministry*, appended to *Theism, Atheism, and the Popular Theology*, p. 258.

Note VII., p. 207.

"All these criteria are the moral conditions under which alone it were possible for such a manifestation to be realized, conformably to the conception of a revelation; but by no means conversely — the conditions of an effect which could be realized only by God conformably to such a conception. In the latter case, they would — to the exclusion of the causality of all other beings — justify the conclusion, that *is* revelation; but, as it is, only this conclusion is justified; that *can* be a revelation."—Fichte, *Versuch einer Kritik aller Offenbarung* (*Werke* V. p. 146).

Note VIII., p. 208.

"*These* . . . were the outer conditions of the life of Christ, under which his public ministry and his personal character reached their destined development. It is not in that development *alone*, but in that development *under these conditions*, that the evidence will be found of his True

Origin and of his Personal Preëminence."—*The Christ of History*, by John Young, p. 33. "But this character, in its unapproachable grandeur, must be viewed in connection with the outward circumstances of the Being in whom it was realized,—in connection with a life not only unprivileged, but offering numerous positive hindrances to the origination, the growth, and, most of all, the perfection of spiritual excellence. In a Jew of Nazareth—a young man—an uneducated mechanic—moral perfection was realized. Can this phenomenon be accounted for? There is here, without doubt, a manifestation of humanity; but the question is, was this a manifestation of mere humanity and *no more?*"—*Ibid.* p. 251.[1]

NOTE IX., p. 209.

Newman, *The Soul*, p. 58.

NOTE X., p. 211.

Analogy, Part II. ch. 3.

NOTE XI., p. 214.

"Although some circumstances in the description of God's Firstborn and Elect, by whom this change is to be accomplished, may primarily apply to collective Israel [many others will admit of no such application. Israel surely was not the child whom a virgin was to bear; Israel did not make his grave with the wicked, and with the rich in his death; Israel scarcely reconciled that strangely blended variety of suffering and triumph, which was predicted of the Messiah]."—R. Williams, *Rational Godliness*, p. 56. In a note to this passage, the author adds, "I no longer feel confident of the assertion in brackets; but now believe that *all* the prophecies have primarily an application nearly contemporaneous." As a specimen of this application, we may cite a subsequent passage from the same volume, p. 169. "The same Isaiah sees that Israel, whom God had called out of Egypt, and whom the Eternal had denominated his first-born, trampled, captive, and derided; he sees the beauty of the

[1] The able and impressive argument of this little work is well worthy of the perusal of those who would see what is the real force of the Christian evidences, even upon the lowest ground to which skepticism can attempt to reduce them. Though far from representing the whole strength of the case, it is most valuable as showing what may be effected in behalf of Christianity, on the principles of its opponents.

sanctuary defiled, and the anointed priests of the living God degraded from their office, led as sheep to the slaughter, insulted by their own countrymen, as men smitten of God, cast off by Jehovah. Ah! he says, it is through the wickedness of the nations that Israel is thus afflicted; it is through the apostasy of the people that the priesthood is thus smitten and reviled; they hide their faces from the Lord's servant; nevertheless, no weapon that is formed against him shall prosper. It is a little thing that He should merely recover Israel, He shall also be a light to the Gentiles, and a salvation to the ends of the earth."

There are few unprejudiced readers who will not think the author's first thought on this subject preferable to his second. In the interpretation of any profane author, the perverse ingenuity which regards the Fifty-Third chapter of Isaiah (to say nothing of the other portions of the prophecy, which Dr. Williams has divorced from their context), as a description of the contemporaneous state of the Jewish people and priesthood, would be considered as too extravagant to need refutation. That such an interpretation should have found favor with thoroughgoing rationalists, determined at all hazards to expel the supernatural from Scripture, is only to be expected; and this may explain the adoption of this and similar views by a considerable school of expositors in Germany. But that it should have been received by those who, like Dr. Williams, hold fast the doctrine of the Incarnation of the Son of God, is less easily to be accounted for. If this greatest of all miracles be once conceded,—if it be allowed that "when the fulness of the time was come, God sent forth His Son, made of a woman;"—what marvel is it, that, while the time was still incomplete, a prophet should have been divinely inspired to proclaim the future redemption? Once concede the possibility of the supernatural at all, and the Messianic interpretation is the only one reconcilable with the facts of history and the plain meaning of words. The fiction of a contemporaneous sense, whether with or without a subsequent Messianic application, is only needed to get rid of direct inspiration; and nothing is gained by getting rid of inspiration, so long as a fragment of the supernatural is permitted to remain. It is only when we assume, *a priori*, that the supernatural is impossible, that anything is gained by forcing the prophetic language into a different meaning.

NOTE XII., p. 215.

Of this Eclectic Christianity, of which Schleiermacher may be considered as the chief modern representative, a late gifted and lamented writer has truly observed: "He could not effect the rescue of Christianity on these principles without serious loss to the object of his care. His efforts resemble the benevolent intervention of the deities of the classic legends, who, to save the nymph from her pursuer, changed her into a river or a tree. It may be that the stream and the foliage have their music and their beauty, that we may think we hear a living voice still in the whispers of the one and the murmurs of the other, yet the beauty of divine Truth, our heavenly visitant, cannot but be grievously obscured by the change, for 'the glory of the celestial is one, and the glory of the terrestrial is another.' Such ecclesiastical doctrines as contain what he regards as the essence of Christianity are received. All others, as being feelings embodied in the concrete form of dogmas, as man's objective conceptions of the divine, he considers as open to criticism. . . . . . Schleiermacher accounts as thus indifferent the doctrine of the Trinity, the supernatural conception of the Saviour, many of his miracles, his ascension and several other truths of the same class. This one reply, 'That doctrine makes no necessary part of our Christian consciousness,' stands solitary, like a Cocles at the bridge, and keeps always at bay the whole army of advancing queries. But surely it does constitute an essential part of our Christian consciousness, whether we regard the New Testament writers as trustworthy or otherwise. If certain parts of their account are myths, and others the expression of Jewish prejudice, and we are bidden dismiss them accordingly from our faith, how are we sure that in what is left these historians were faithful, or these expositors true representatives of the mind of Christ? Our Christian consciousness is likely to become a consciousness of little else than doubt, if we give credit to the assertion — Your sole informants on matters of eternal moment, were, every here and there, misled by prejudice and imposed upon by fable."[1]

NOTE XIII., p. 216.

For the objections of modern Pantheism against the immortality of the soul, See Lecture III., note 27. Of the resurrection of the body in particular, Wegscheider observes: "The resurrection of the body is so far from being reconcilable with the precepts of sound reason, that it is embarrassed with very many and the gravest difficulties. For, *in the first place*, it cannot be doubted that this opinion derived its origin from the lame and imperfect conceptions of men of defective culture; for such persons, being destitute of a just idea of the Divine being, are wont to imagine to themselves a life after death, solely after the nature of the earthly life. Hence it comes to pass, that, among barbarous nations, and also in the system of

1 *Essays and Remains of the Rev. Robert Alfred Vaughan*, Vol. I. p. 93.

Zoroaster, from which the Jews themselves seem to have drawn, that same doctrine is discovered. *Then, too,* the resurrection of the body, taught in the books of the New Testament, which, even from the apostolic age, was condemned by not a few, is seen to be so closely connected with the mythical opinions of the Messiah, and the story of Jesus restored to life, that it cannot be judged of and explained by any other method than those myths themselves. . . . . . *Moreover,* the idea is manifestly not in agreement with a God most holy and good, that man, who cannot pass a real life without the body, is to have this body restored to him after many thousands of years. . . . . Induced by these reasons, and others of scarcely less weight, we think that Jesus, wherever he is said to have taught the resurrection of the body, humored the opinions of his countrymen; or, rather, the disciples of Jesus . . . . falsely ascribed to Him an opinion of their own."[1] Concerning angels and spirits, one of the most significant specimens of modern Sadduceeism may be found in Dr. Donaldson's "Christian Orthodoxy Reconciled with the Conclusions of Modern Biblical Learning," p. 347, sqq. He holds, with regard to intermediate Intelligences, the same view which Wegscheider suggests with regard to the Resurrection, namely, "that our Lord, in his dealings with the Jews, rather acquiesced in the established phraseology than sanctioned the prevalent superstition."[2] He adds that, "in many respects, our Lord seems to have approved and recommended" the views of the Sadducees; though "he could not openly adopt a speculative truth, which was saddled with an application diametrically opposed to the cardinal verity of his religion."[3] It is obvious that, by this method of exposition, "Christian Orthodoxy" may mean anything or nothing. Any doctrine which this or

1 *Institutiones Theologicæ*, § 195.

2 P. 363. That is to say, it is boldly maintained that our Lord, in order to humor the prejudices of the Jews of that day, consented to lend his authority to the dissemination of a religious falsehood for the deception of posterity. This monstrous assertion is stated more plainly by Spinoza, *Tractatus Theologico-Polit.* c. 2. "Indeed He accommodated His forms of thought to every one's principles and opinions. For instance, when He said to the Pharisees, *And if Satan cast out Satan, he is divided against himself, how then can his kingdom stand?* he meant only to convict the Pharisees on their own principles, not to teach the doctrine of demons." In like manner, Schleiermacher (*Christliche Glaube*, § 42) asserts that Christ and his Apostles possibly adopted the popular representations, as we speak of fairies and ghosts. On the other side, it is justly urged by Storr (*Doctrina Christiana*, § 52), that our Lord employed the same language privately with his disciples. as well as publicly with the people; e. g. Matt. xiii. 39, xxv. 41; Mark iv. 15; Luke xxii. 31. See also Mosheim's note, translated in Harrison's edition of Cudworth, Vol. II. p. 631; Neander, *Life of Christ*, p. 157 (Eng. Tr.); Lee, *Inspiration of Holy Scripture*, p. 69 (second edition).

3 Pp. 372, 373.

that expositor finds it convenient to reject, may be set aside as a concession to popular phraseology; and thus the teaching of Christ may be stripped of its most essential doctrines by men who profess all the while to believe in His immanent Divinity and Omniscience. Strauss arrives at a similar conclusion, though, of course, without troubling himself about Scriptural premises. "It is, therefore, not enough to leave undecided, with Schleiermacher, the possibility of such beings as angels, and only to fix so much as this, that we have neither to take account of them in our conduct, nor to expect further revelations of their nature; rather is it the case, that, if the modern idea of God and the world is correct, there cannot be any such beings any where at all."[1] In the same spirit Mr. Parker openly maintains that "Jesus shared the erroneous notions of the times respecting devils, possessions, and demonology in general;"[2]—a conclusion which is at least more logical and consistent than that of those who acknowledge the divine authority of the Teacher, yet claim a right to reject as much as they please of his teaching.

NOTE XIV., p. 216.

Greg, *Creed of Christendom*, Preface, p. xii.

NOTE XV., p. 216.

The theory which represents the human race as in a constant state of religious progress, and the various religions of antiquity as successive steps in the education of mankind, has been a favorite with various schools of modern philosophy. Hegel, as might naturally be expected, propounds a theory of the necessary development of religious ideas, as determined by the movements of the universal Spirit.[3] It is true that he is compelled by the stern necessities of chronology to represent the polytheism of Greece and Rome as an advance on the monotheism of Judea;[4]

1 *Christliche Glaubenslehre*, § 49. To the same effect are his remarks on Evil Spirits, § 54 Among the earlier rationalists, the same view is taken by Röhr, *Briefe über den Rationalismus*, p. 35.

2 *Discourse of matters pertaining to Religion*, p 176.

3 See *Philosophie der Geschichte*, *Werke*, IX. p. 14. *Philosophie der Religion*, *Werke*, XI. p. 76, 78.

4 See his *Philosophie der Religion*, *Werke*, XI p. 82. XII. p. 45. The superiority of the Greek religion appears to consist in its greater acknowledgment of human freedom, and perhaps in being a step in the direction of Pantheism See *Werke*, XII 92, 125. Of the Roman religion, he says that it contained in itself all the elements of Christianity, and was a necessary step to the latter. Its evils sprang

and perhaps, if we regard the Hegelian philosophy as the final consummation of all religious truth, this *retrograde progress* may be supported by some plausible arguments.[1] Another form of the same theory is that of Comte, who traces the progress of humanity through Fetichism, Polytheism, and Monotheism, to culminate at last in the Positive Religion, which worships the idea of humanity, including therein the auxiliary animals.[2] In theories of this kind, the distinction between progress and mere fluctuation depends upon the previous question, Whence, and Whither? What was the original state of religious knowledge in mankind, and what is the end to which it is advancing? If Pantheism or Atheism is the highest form of religious truth, every step in that direction is unquestionably progressive; if otherwise, it is not progress, but corruption.

The previous question is clearly stated by Theodore Parker. "From what point did the human race set out, — from civilization and the true worship of one God, or from cannibalism and the deification of nature? Has the human race fallen or risen? The question is purely historical, and to be answered by historical witnesses. But in the presence, and still more in the absence, of such witnesses, the *a priori* doctrines of the man's philosophy affect his decision. Reasoning with no facts is as easy as all motion *in vacuo*. The analogy of the geological formation of the earth — its gradual preparation, so to say, for the reception of plants and animals, the ruder first, and then the more complex and beautiful, till at last she opens her bosom to man, — this, in connection with many similar analogies, would tend to show that a similar order was to be expected in the affairs of men — development from the lower to the higher, and not the

from the depth of its spirit (XII pp. 181, 184). The best commentary on this assertion may be found in Augustine, *De Civ. Dei*, Lib. VI.

1 Among the *imperfections* of Judaism, Hegel includes the fact that "it did not make men conscious of the identity of the human soul with the Absolute and its absorption therein (die Anschauung und das Bewusstseyn von der Einheit der Seele mit dem Absoluten, oder von der Aufnahme der Seele in den Schooss des Absoluten ist noch nicht erwacht, *Werke*, XII p. 86). In another place (p 161) he speaks of it as the religion of obstinate, dead understanding. Vatke (*Biblische Theologie*, p. 115) carries the absurdity of theory to its climax, by boldly maintaining that the later Judaism had been *elevated* by its conflict with the religions of Greece and Rome, and thus prepared to become the precursor of Christianity. The Hegelian theory is also adopted by Baur, as representing the law of development of Christian doctrines. The historical aspects of the doctrine are to be regarded as phases of a process, in which the several forms are determined one by another, and all are united together in the totality of the idea. See especially his *Christliche Lehre von der Versöhnung*, p. 11, and the preface to the same work, p. vi.

2 *Cours de Philosophie Positive*, Leçons, 52, 53, 54. Compare *Catechisme Positiviste*, pp. 31, 184, 243.

reverse. In strict accordance with this analogy, some have taught that man was created in the lowest stage of savage life; his Religion the rudest worship of nature; his Morality that of the cannibal; that all of the civilized races have risen from this point, and gradually passed through Fetichism and Polytheism, before they reached refinement and true Religion. The spiritual man is the gradual development of germs latent in the natural man." [1]

It is to be regretted that Professor Jowett has partially given the sanction of his authority to a theory which it is to be presumed he would not advocate to the full extent of the above statement. "The theory of a primitive religion common to all mankind," he tells us, "has only to be placed distinctly before the mind, to make us aware that it is the baseless fabric of a vision; there is one stream of revelation only — the Jewish. But even if it were conceivable, it would be inconsistent with facts. The earliest history tells nothing of a general religion, but of particular beliefs about stocks and stones, about places and persons, about animal life, about the sun, moon, and stars, about the divine essence permeating the world, about gods in the likeness of men appearing in battles and directing the course of states, about the world below, about sacrifices, purifications, initiations, magic, mysteries. These were the true religions of nature, varying with different degrees of mental culture or civilization." [2] And in an earlier part of the same Essay, he says, "No one who looks at the religions of the world, stretching from east to west, through so many cycles of human history, can avoid seeing in them a sort of order and design. They are like so many steps in the education of mankind. Those countless myriads of human beings who know no other truth than that of religions coëval with the days of the Apostle, or even of Moses, are not wholly uncared for in the sight of God." [3]

It would be unfair to press these words to a meaning which they do not necessarily bear. We will assume that by the "earliest history," profane history alone is meant, in opposition to the Jewish Revelation; and that the author does not intend, as some of his critics have supposed, to deny the historical character of the Book of Genesis, and the existence of a primitive revelation coëval with the creation of man. Even with this

1 *Discourse of Matters pertaining to Religion*, p. 68, 69. A similar view is advocated by Mr. Newman, *Phases of Faith*, p 223, and by Mr. Greg, *Creed of Christendom*, p. 71. Mr. Parker does not distinctly adopt this view as his own. but he appears to regard it as preferable to the antagonist theory, which he speaks of as supported by a "party consisting more of poets and dogmatists than of philosophers."

2 *Epistles of St. Paul*, Vol. II. p. 395.

3 *Ibid.*, p. 386.

limitation, the evidence is stated far too absolutely. But the words last quoted are, to say the least, incautious, and suggest coincidence in a favorite theory of modern philosophy, equally repugnant to Scripture and to natural religion. Two very opposite views may be taken of the false religions of antiquity. The Scriptures invariably speak of them as corruptions of man's natural reason, and abominations in the sight of God. Some modern writers delight to represent them as instruments of God's Providence, and steps in the education of mankind. This view naturally belongs to that pantheistic philosophy which recognizes no Deity beyond the actual constitution of the world, which acknowledges all that exists as equally divine, or, which is the same thing, equally godless; but it is irreconcilable with the belief in a personal God, and in a distinction between the good which He approves and the evil which He condemns. But men will concede much to philosophy who will concede nothing to Scripture. The sickly and sentimental morality which talks of the "ferocious" God of the popular theology,[1] which is indignant at the faith of Abraham,[2] which shudders over the destruction of the Canaanites,[3] which prides itself in discovering imperfections in the law of Moses,[4] is content to believe that the God who could not sanction these things, could yet create man with the morality of a cannibal, and the religion of a fetish-worshipper, and ordain for him a law of development through the purifying stages which marked the civilization of Egypt and Babylon and Imperial Rome. Verily this unbelieving Reason makes heavy demands on the faith of its disciples. It will not tolerate the slightest apparent anomaly in the moral government of God; but it is ready, when its theories require, to propound a scheme of deified iniquity, which it is hardly exaggeration to designate as the moral government of Satan.

We must believe, indeed, that in the darkest ages of idolatry, God "left not himself without witness;" we must believe that the false religions of the world, like its other evils, are overruled by God to the purposes of His good Providence. But this does not make them the less evils and abominations in the sight of God. Those who speak of the human race as under a law of vegetable development, forget that man has, what vegetables have not, a moral sense and a free will. It is indeed impossible, in our present state of knowledge, to draw exactly the line between the sins and the misfortunes of individuals, to decide how much of each man's history is due to his own will, and how much to the circumstances in which he is placed. But though Scripture, like philosophy, offers no com-

1 Parker, *Theism, Atheism, and the Popular Theology*, p. 103, 104.
2 Parker, *Discourse of Religion*, p. 214. Newman, *Phases of Faith*, p. 150.
3 Parker, *Discourse*, p. 87. Newman, *Phases*, p. 151.
4 Parker, *Discourse*, p. 204, 223. Greg, *Creed of Christendom*, p. 75.

plete solution of the problem of the existence of evil, it at least distinctly points out what the true solution *is not*. So long as it represents the sin of man as a fall from the state in which God originally placed him, and as a rebellion against a divine command; so long as it represents idolatry as hateful to God, and false religion as a declension towards evil, not as a progress towards good; — so long it emphatically records its protest against both the self-delusion which denies that evil exists at all, and the blasphemy which asserts that it exists by the appointment of God.

Note XVI., p. 219.

"It is an obvious snare, that many, out of such abundance of knowledge, should be tempted to forget at times this grand and simple point — that all *vital* truth is to be sought from Scripture alone. Hence that they should be tempted rather to combine systems for themselves according to some proportion and fancy of their own, than be content neither to add nor diminish anything from that which Christ and his Apostles have enjoined; to make up, as it were, a cento of doctrines and of precepts; to take from Christ what pleases them, and from other stores what pleases them (of course the best from each, as it appears to their judgment, so as to exhibit the most perfect whole); taking e. g. the blessed hope of everlasting life from Jesus Christ, but rejecting his atonement; or honoring highly his example of humanity, but disrobing Him of his divinity; or accepting all the comfortable things of the dispensation of the Spirit, but refusing its strictness and self-denials; or forming any other combination whatsoever, to the exclusion of the *entire* Gospel: thus inviting Christian hearers, not to the supper of the king's son, but to a sort of miscellaneous banquet of their own; 'using their liberty,' in short, 'as an occasion' to that *natural* disposition, which Christ came to correct and to repair.

" Now that by such methods, enforced by education and strengthened by the best of secondary motives, men may attain to an excellent proficiency in morals, I am neither prepared nor disposed to dispute. I am not desirous of disputing that they may possess therein an excellent religion, as opposed to Mahometanism or Paganism. But that they possess the true account to be given of their stewardship of that one talent, The Gospel itself, I do doubt in sorrow and fear. I do doubt whether they 'live the life that now is,' as St. Paul lived it, 'by the faith of the Son of God;' by true apprehension of the things that He suffered for us, and of the right which He has purchased to command us in all excellent qualities and actions; and further, of the invisible but real assistance which he gives us towards the performance of them." Miller, *Bampton Lectures*. p. 169 (third edition).

NOTE XVII., p. 219.

"Thus in the great variety of religious situations in which men are placed, what constitutes, what chiefly and peculiarly constitutes, the probation, in all senses, of some persons, may be the difficulties in which the evidence of religion is involved: and their principal and distinguished trial may be, how they will behave under and with respect to these difficulties." Butler, *Analogy*, Part II. ch. 6.

NOTE XVIII., p. 221.

I do not mean by these remarks to deny the possibility of any progress whatever in Christian Theology, such for instance, as may result from the better interpretation of Holy Writ, or the refutation of unauthorized inferences therefrom. But all such developments of doctrine are admissible only when confined within the limits so carefully laid down in the sixth Article of our Church. "Holy Scripture containeth all things necessary to salvation: so that whatsoever is not read therein, nor may be proved thereby, is not to be required of any man, that it should be believed as an Article of the Faith, or be thought requisite or necessary to salvation." Within these limits, the most judicious theologians have not hesitated to allow the possibility of progress, as regards at least the definite statement of Christian doctrine. Thus Bishop Butler remarks: "As it is owned the whole scheme of Scripture is not yet understood; so, if it ever comes to be understood, before the *restitution of all things*, and without miraculous interpositions, it must be in the same way as natural knowledge is come at: by the continuance and progress of learning and liberty; and by particular persons attending to, comparing, and pursuing intimations scattered up and down it, which are overlooked and disregarded by the generality of the world."[1] And a worthy successor to the name has pointed out the distinction between true and false developments of doctrine, in language based upon the same principle: "Are there *admissible developments* of doctrine in Christianity? Unquestionably there are. But let the term be understood in its legitimate sense or senses to warrant that answer; and let it be carefully observed how much, and how little, the admission really involves. All varieties of real development, so far as this argument is concerned, may probably be reduced to two general heads, *intellectual* developments, and *practical* developments, of Christian doctrine. By 'intellectual developments,' I understand *logical inferences* (and that whether for

[1] *Analogy*, Part II. ch. 3.

belief or practical discipline), from doctrines, or from the comparison of doctrines; which, in virtue of the great dialectical maxim, must be true, if legitimately deduced from what is true. 'Practical developments' are the *living, actual, historical results* of those true doctrines (original or inferential), when considered as influential on all the infinite varieties of human kind; the doctrines embodied in action; the doctrines modifying human nature in ways infinitely various, correspondently to the infinite variety of subjects on whom they operate, though ever strictly preserving, amid all their operations for effectually transforming and renewing mankind, their own unchanged identity. . . . In the former case, revealed doctrines may be compared with one another, or with the doctrines of 'natural religion;' or the consequences of revealed doctrines may be compared with other doctrines, or with their consequences, and so on in great variety: the combined result being what is called a System of Theology. What the first principles of Christian truth really are, or how obtained, is not now the question. But in all cases equally, no doctrine has any claim whatever to be received as obligatory on belief, unless it be either itself some duly authorized principle, or a logical deduction, through whatever number of stages, from some such principle of religion. Such only are legitimate developments of doctrine for the *belief* of man; and such alone can the Church of Christ — the Witness and Conservator of His Truth — justly commend to the consciences of her members. . . . But in truth, as our own liability to error is extreme, especially when immersed in the holy obscurity ("the *cloud* on the mercy-seat") of such mysteries as these, we have reason to thank God that there appear to be few doctrinal developments of any importance which are not from the first drawn out and delivered on divine authority to our acceptance."[1]

It is impossible not to regret deeply the very different language, on this point, of a writer in many respects worthy of better things; but who, while retaining the essential doctrines of Christianity, has, it is to be feared, done much to unsettle the authority on which they rest. "If the destined course of the world," says Dr. Williams, "be really one of providential progress, if there has been such a thing as a childhood of humanity, and if God has been educating either a nation or a Church to understand their duty to Himself and to mankind; it must follow, that when the fulness of light is come, there will be childish things to put away. . . . Hence, if the religious records represent faithfully the inner life of each generation, whether a people or a priesthood, they will be, in St. Paul's phrase, *divinely animated*, or with a divine life running through them; and every writing, divinely animated, will be useful; yet they *may*, or rather,

1 W. A. Butler, *Letters on the Development of Christian Doctrine*, pp. 55—58.

they *must* be cast in the mould of the generation in which they are written; their words, if they are true words, will express the customs of their country, the conceptions of their times, the feelings or aspirations of their writers; and the measure of knowledge or of faith to which every one, in his degree, had attained. And the limitation, thus asserted, of their range of knowledge, will be equally true, whether we suppose the shortcoming to be, on an idea of *special* Providence, from a particular dictation of sentiment in each case; or whether, on the more reasonable view of a *general* Providence, we consider such things permitted rather than directed; the natural result of a grand scheme, rather than a minute arrangement of thoughts and words for each individual man. It may be, that the Lord writes the Bible, on the same principle as the Lord builds the city; or that He teaches the Psalmist to sing, in the same sense as He teaches his fingers to fight; thus that the composition of Scripture is attributed to the Almighty, just as sowing and threshing are said to be taught by Him; for every part played by man comes from the Divine Disposer of the scene."[1]

It is the misfortune of this sort of language, that it suggests far more than it directly asserts, and probably more than the author intends to convey. Dr. Williams probably does not mean to imply that we are no more bound by the authority of Scripture in matters of religion than by the primitive practice in sowing and threshing, or that we are as much at liberty to invent new theological doctrines as new implements of husbandry. But if he does not mean this, it is to be regretted that he has not clearly pointed out the respects in which his comparison does not hold good.

NOTE XIX., p. 222.

Summa, P. I. Qu. II. Art. 2.

NOTE XX., p. 222.

See Archbishop King's *Discourse on Predestination*, edited by Archbishop Whately, p. 10. A different, and surely a more judicious view, is taken by a contemporary Prelate of the Irish Church, whose earlier exposition of the same theory[2] probably furnished the foundation of the Archbishop's discourse. "Though," says Bishop Browne, "there are literally

1 *Rational Godliness*, pp. 291, 292. A similar view is maintained by Mr Morell, *Philosophy of Religion*, p. 183, and is criticised by Professor Lee, *Inspiration of Holy Scripture*, p. 147.

2 In his Letter in answer to Toland's *Christianity not mysterious*.

speaking no such passions in God as Love or Hatred, Joy or Anger, or Pity; yet there may be *Inconceivable Perfections* in Him some way *answerable* to what those passions are in us, under a due regulation and subjection to reason. It is sure that in God those perfections are not attended with any degree of natural disturbance or moral irregularity, as the passions are in us. Nay, Fear and Hope, which imply something *future* for their objects, may have nothing answerable to them in the divine Nature to which everything is *present*. But since our reasonable affections are real dispositions of the Soul, which is composed of Spirit as well as Matter; we must conclude something in God *analogous* to *them*, as well as to our *Knowledge* or *Power*. For it cannot be a thought unworthy of being transferred to him, that he really *loves* a virtuous and *hates* a vicious agent; that he is *angry* at sinners; *pities* their moral infirmities; is *pleased* with their innocence or repentance, and *displeased* with their transgressions; though all these Perfections are in Him accompanied with the utmost *serenity*, and never-failing *tranquillity*."[1] With this may be compared the language of Tertullian (*Adv. Marc.* II. 16), "All which He suffers after His own manner, even as man after his."

NOTE XXI., p. 223.

Compare the remarks of Hooker, *E. P.* I. 3. 2. "Moses, in describing the work of creation, attributeth speech unto God. . . . Was this only the intent of Moses, to signify the infinite greatness of God's power by the easiness of his accomplishing such effects, without travail, pain, or labor? Surely it seemeth that Moses had herein besides this a further purpose, namely, first to teach that God did not work as a necessary but a voluntary agent, intending beforehand and decreeing with himself that which did outwardly proceed from him. Secondly, to shew that God did then institute a law natural to be observed by creatures, and therefore according to the manner of laws, the institution thereof is described, as being established by solemn injunction."

NOTE XXII., p. 224.

"But they urge, there can be no proportion or similitude between Finite and Infinite, and consequently there can be no analogy. That there can

[1] *Divine Analogy*, pp 45, 46. King's Theory is also criticized more directly by the same author in the *Procedure of the Understanding*, p. 11. Mr. Davison (*Discourses on Prophecy*, p. 513) has noticed the weak points in King's explanation; but with too great a leaning to the opposite extreme, which reasons concerning the infinite as if it were a mere expansion of the finite.

be no such proportion or similitude as there is between finite created beings is granted; or as there is between any material substance and its resemblance in the glass; and therefore wherein the *real ground* of this analogy consists, and what the degrees of it are, is as incomprehensible as the real Nature of God. But it is such an analogy as he himself hath adapted to our intellect, and made use of in his Revelations; and therefore we are sure it hath such a foundation in the nature both of God and man, as renders our *moral* reasonings concerning him and his attributes, solid, and just, and true."—Bp. Browne, *Procedure of the Understanding*, p. 31. The practical result of this remark is, that we must rest satisfied with a belief in the analogical representation itself, without seeking to rise above it by substituting an explanation of its ulterior significance or real ground.

Note XXIII., p. 224.

I am glad to take this opportunity of expressing, in the above words, my belief in the purpose and authority of Holy Scripture; inasmuch as it enables me to correct a serious misunderstanding into which a distinguished writer has fallen in a criticism of my supposed views — a criticism to which the celebrity of the author will probably give a far wider circulation than is ever likely to fall to the lot of the small pamphlet which called it forth. Mr. Maurice, in the preface to the second edition of his "Patriarchs and Lawgivers of the Old Testament," comments upon the distinction (maintained in the present Lectures and in a small previous publication), between *speculative* and *regulative* truths, in the following terms. "The notion of a revelation that tells us things which are not in themselves true, but which it is right for us to believe and to act upon as if they were true, has, I fear, penetrated very deeply into the heart of our English schools, and of our English world. It may be traced among persons who are apparently most unlike each other, who live to oppose and confute each other. . . . But their differences are not in the least likely to be adjusted by the discovery of this common ground. How the atmosphere is to be regulated by the regulative Revelation; at what degree of heat or cold this constitution or that can endure it; who must fix — since the language of the Revelation is assumed not to be exact, not to express the very lesson which we are to derive from it — what it does mean; by what contrivances its phrases are to be adapted to various places and times: these are questions which must, of course, give rise to infinite disputations; ever new schools and sects must be called into existence to settle them; there is scope for permissions, prohibitions, compromises, persecutions, to any extent. The despair which these must cause will probably drive numbers to ask for an infallible human voice, which shall regulate for each period that which the Revelation has so utterly failed to regulate."

Now I certainly believed, and believe still, that God is infinite, and that no human mode of thought, nor even a Revelation, if it is to be intelligible by the human mind, can represent the infinite, save under finite forms. And it is a legitimate inference from this position, that no human representation, whether derived from without or from within, from Revelation or from natural Religion, can adequately exhibit the absolute nature of God. But I cannot admit, as a further legitimate inference, that therefore "the language of the Revelation does not express the very lesson which we are to derive from it;" that it needs any regulation to adjust it to "this constitution or that;" that it requires "to be adapted to various places and times." For surely, if all men are subject to the same limitations of thought, the adaptation to their constitutions must be made already, before human interpretation can deal with the Revelation at all. It is not to the peculiarities which distinguish "this" constitution from "that," that the Revelation has to be adapted by man; but, as it is given by God, it is adapted already to the general conditions which are common to all human constitutions alike, which are equally binding in all places and at all times. I have said nothing of a revelation adapted to one man more than to another; nothing of limitations which any amount of intellect or learning can enable a man to overcome. I have not said that the Bible is the teacher of the peasant rather than of the philosopher; of the Asiatic rather than of the European; of the first century rather than of the nineteenth. I have said only that it is the teacher of man as man; and that this is compatible with the possible existence of a more absolute truth in relation to beings of a higher intelligence. We must at any rate admit that man does not know God as God knows Himself; and hence that he does not know Him in the fulness of His Absolute Nature. But surely this admission is so far from implying that Revelation does not teach the very lesson which we are to derive from it, that it makes that lesson the more universal and the more authoritative. For Revelation is subject to no other limitations than those which encompass all human thought. Man gains nothing by rejecting or perverting its testimony; for the mystery of Revelation is the mystery of Reason also.

I do not wish to extend this controversy further; for I am willing to believe that, on this question at least, my own opinion is substantially one with that of my antagonist. At any rate, I approve as little as he does of allegorical, or metaphysical, or mythical interpretations of Scripture: I believe that he is generally right in maintaining that "the most literal meaning of Scripture is the most spiritual meaning." And if there are points in the details of his teaching with which I am unable to agree, I believe that they are not such as legitimately arise from the consistent application of this canon.

Note XXIV., p. 225.

"There seems no possible reason to be given, why we may not be in a state of moral probation, with regard to the exercise of our understanding upon the subject of religion, as we are with regard to our behaviour in common affairs. . . . Thus, that religion is not intuitively true, but a matter of deduction and inference; that a conviction of its truth is not forced upon every one, but left to be, by some, collected with heedful attention to premises; this as much constitutes religious probation, as much affords sphere, scope, opportunity, for right and wrong behaviour, as anything whatever does."—Butler, *Analogy*, Part II. ch. 6.

Note XXV., p. 226.

Plato, *Rep*. VI. p. 486: "And this also it is necessary to consider, when you would distinguish between a nature which is philosophical, and one which is not.—What then is that?—That it takes no part, even unobserved, in any meanness; for petty littleness is every way most contrary to a soul that is ever stretching forward in desire to the whole and the all, to divine and to human."—Cicero, *De Off*. II. 2: "Nor is philosophy anything else, if you will define it, than the study of wisdom. But wisdom (as defined by ancient philosophers) is the knowledge of things human and divine, and of the causes in which these are contained."

Note XXVI., p. 226.

Plato, *Protag*. p. 343: "And these, having met together by agreement, consecrated to Apollo, in his temple at Delphi, as the first fruits of wisdom, those inscriptions which are in everybody's mouth, *Know thyself*, and *Nothing to excess*."—Compare Jacobi, *Werke*, IV.; Vorbericht, p. xlii.: "*Know thyself* is, according to the Delphian god and Socrates, the highest command, and, so soon as it becomes practical, man is made aware of this truth: without the Divine *Thou*, there is no human *I*, and without the human *I*, there is no Divine *Thou*."

NOTE XXVII., p. 226.

Clemens Alex. *Pædag.* III. 1: "It is, then, as it appears, the greatest of all lessons, to know one's self; for, if any one knows himself, he will know God."

NOTE XXVIII., p. 227.

"It is plain that there is a capacity in the nature of man, which neither riches, nor honors, nor sensual gratifications, nor anything in this world, can perfectly fill up or satisfy: there is a deeper and more essential want, than any of these things can be the supply of. Yet surely there is a possibility of somewhat, which may fill up all our capacities of happiness; somewhat, in which our souls may find rest; somewhat, which may be to us that satisfactory good we are inquiring after. But it cannot be anything which is valuable only as it tends to some further end. . . . As our understanding can contemplate itself, and our affections be exercised upon themselves by reflection, so may each be employed in the same manner upon any other mind. And since the Supreme Mind, the Author and Cause of all things, is the highest possible object to himself, he may be an adequate supply to all the faculties of our souls; a subject to our understanding, and an object to our affections."— Butler, Sermon XIV.

NOTE XXIX., p. 227.

"Christianity is not a religion for the religious, but a religion for man. I do not accept it because my temperament so disposes me, and because it meets my individual mood of mind, or my tastes. I accept it as it is suited to that moral condition in respect of which there is no difference of importance between me and the man I may next encounter on my path." *The Restoration of Belief*, p. 325.

NOTE XXX., p. 227.

"The Scripture-arguments are arguments of inducement, addressed to the whole nature of man — not merely to intellectual man, but to thinking and feeling man, living among his fellow men; — and to be apprehended therefore in their *effect* on our *whole* nature."— Hampden, *Bampton Lectures*, p. 92.—" There are persons who complain of the Word, because it is not addressed to some one department of the human soul, on which they set a high value. The systematic divine wonders that it is not a mere scheme of dogmatic theology, forgetting that in such a case it would address itself exclusively to the understanding. The German speculatists, on the other hand, complain that it is not a mere exhibition of the true and the good, forgetting that in such a case it would have little or no influence on the more practical faculties. Others seem to regret that it is not a mere code of morality, while a fourth class would wish it to be altogether an appeal to the feelings. But the Word is inspired by the same God who formed man at first, and who knows what is in man; and he would rectify not merely the understanding or intuitions, not merely the conscience or affections, but the whole man after the image of God." McCosh, *Method of the Divine Government*, p. 509.

INDEX OF AUTHORS.

Only those Authors are here given from whom passages are quoted.

VALUABLE

LITERARY AND SCIENTIFIC WORKS,

PUBLISHED BY

GOULD AND LINCOLN,

59 WASHINGTON STREET, BOSTON.

ANNUAL OF SCIENTIFIC DISCOVERY FOR 1859; or, Year-Book of Facts in Science and Art, exhibiting the most important Discoveries and Improvements in Mechanics, Useful Arts, Natural Philosophy, Chemistry, Astronomy, Meteorology, Zoology, Botany, Mineralogy, Geology, Geography, Antiquities, &c., together with a list of recent Scientific Publications; a classified list of Patents; Obituaries of eminent Scientific Men; an Index of Important Papers in Scientific Journals, Reports, &c. Edited by DAVID A. WELLS, A. M. With a Portrait of Prof. O. M. Mitchell. 12mo, cloth, $1.25.

VOLUMES OF THE SAME WORK for years 1850 to 1858 inclusive. With Portraits of Professors Agassiz, Silliman, Henry, Bache, Maury, Hitchcock, Richard M. Hoe, Profs. Jeffries Wyman, and H. D. Rogers. Nine volumes, 12mo, cloth, $1.25 per vol.

This work, issued annually, contains all important facts discovered or announced during the year.

☞ Each volume is distinct in itself, and contains *entirely new matter.*

INFLUENCE OF THE HISTORY OF SCIENCE UPON INTELLECTUAL EDUCATION. By WILLIAM WHEWELL, D. D., of Trinity College, Eng., and the alleged author of "Plurality of Worlds." 12mo, cloth, 25 cts.

THE NATURAL HISTORY OF THE HUMAN SPECIES; Its Typical Forms and Primeval Distribution. By CHARLES HAMILTON SMITH. With an Introduction containing an Abstract of the views of Blumenbach, Prichard, Bachman, Agassiz, and other writers of repute. By SAMUEL KNEELAND, Jr., M. D. With elegant Illustrations. 12mo, cloth, $1.25.

"The marks of practical good sense, careful observation, and deep research, are displayed in every page. The introductory essay of some seventy or eighty pages forms a valuable addition to the work. It comprises an abstract of the opinions advocated by the most eminent writers on this subject. The statements are made with strict impartiality, and, without a comment, left to the judgment of the reader." — *Sartain's Magazine.*

KNOWLEDGE IS POWER. A View of the Productive Forces of Modern Society, and the Results of Labor, Capital, and Skill. By CHARLES KNIGHT. With numerous Illustrations. American Edition. Revised, with Additions, by DAVID A. WELLS, Editor of the "Annual of Scientific Discovery." 12mo, cloth, $1.25.

☞ This is emphatically *a book for the people.* It contains an immense amount of important information, which everybody ought to be in possession of; and the volume should be placed in every family, and in every School and Public Library in the land. The facts and illustrations are drawn from almost every branch of skilful industry, and it is a work which the mechanic and artisan of every description will be sure to read with a RELISH.

CHAMBERS' WORKS.

CHAMBERS' CYCLOPÆDIA OF ENGLISH LITERATURE. A Selection of the choicest productions of English Authors, from the earliest to the present time. Connected by a Critical and Biographical History. Forming two large imperial octavo volumes of 700 pages each, double column letter press; with upwards of 300 elegant Illustrations. Edited by ROBERT CHAMBERS. Cloth, $5.00; sheep, $6.00; full gilt, $7.50; half calf, $7.50; full calf, $10.00.

This work embraces about one thousand Authors, chronologically arranged, and classed as poets, historians, dramatists, philosophers, metaphysicians, divines, etc., with choice selections from their writings, connected by a Biographical, Historical, and Critical Narrative; thus presenting a complete view of English Literature from the earliest to the present time. Let the reader open where he will, he cannot fail to find matter for profit and delight. The selections are gems — infinite riches in a little room; in the language of another, "A WHOLE ENGLISH LIBRARY FUSED DOWN INTO ONE CHEAP BOOK!"

☞ THE AMERICAN edition of this valuable work is enriched by the addition of fine steel and mezzotint engravings of the heads of SHAKSPEARE, ADDISON, BYRON; a full-length portrait of DR. JOHNSON; and a beautiful scenic representation of OLIVER GOLDSMITH and DR. JOHNSON. These important and elegant additions, together with superior paper and binding, and other improvements, render the AMERICAN far superior to the English edition.

W. H. PRESCOTT, THE HISTORIAN, says, "Readers cannot fail to profit largely by the labors of the critic who has the talent and taste to separate what is really beautiful and worthy of their study from what is superfluous."

"I concur in the foregoing opinion of Mr. Prescott." — EDWARD EVERETT.

"A popular work, indispensable to the library of a student of English literature." — DR. WAYLAND.

"We hail with peculiar pleasure the appearance of this work." — *North American Review.*

CHAMBERS' MISCELLANY OF USEFUL AND ENTERTAINING KNOWLEDGE. Edited by WILLIAM CHAMBERS. With elegant Illustrative Engravings. Ten volumes. Cloth, $7.50; cloth, gilt, $10.00; library sheep, $10.00.

"It would be difficult to find any miscellany superior or even equal to it. It richly deserves the epithets 'useful and entertaining,' and I would recommend it very strongly, as extremely well adapted to form parts of a library for the young, or of a social or circulating library in town or country." — GEO. B. EMERSON, Esq. — *Chairman Boston School Book Committee.*

CHAMBERS' HOME BOOK; or, Pocket Miscellany, containing a Choice Selection of Interesting and Instructive Reading, for the Old and Young. Six volumes. 16mo, cloth, $3.00; library sheep, $4.00; half calf, $6.00.

This is considered fully equal, and in some respects superior, to either of the other works of the Chambers in interest; containing a vast fund of valuable information. It is admirably adapted to the School or Family Library, furnishing ample variety for every class of readers.

"The Chambers are confessedly the best caterers for popular and useful reading in the world." — *Willis' Home Journal.*

"A very entertaining, instructive, and popular work." — *N. Y. Commercial.*

"We do not know how it is possible to publish so much good reading matter at such a low price. We speak a good word for the literary excellence of the stories in this work; we hope our people will introduce it into all their families, in order to drive away the miserable flashy-trashy stuff so often found in the hands of our young people of both sexes." — *Scientific American.*

"Both an entertaining and instructive work, as it is certainly a very cheap one." — *Puritan Recorder.*

"If any person wishes to read for amusement or profit, to kill time or improve it, get 'Chambers' Home Book.'" — *Chicago Times.*

CHAMBERS' REPOSITORY OF INSTRUCTIVE AND AMUSING PAPERS. With Illustrations. A New Series, containing Original Articles. Two volumes. 16mo, cloth, $1.75.

THE SAME WORK, two volumes in one, cloth, gilt back, $1.50.

IMPORTANT WORKS.

A TREATISE ON THE COMPARATIVE ANATOMY OF THE ANIMAL KINGDOM. By Profs. C. TH. VON SIEBOLD and H. STANNIUS. Translated from the German, with Notes, Additions, &c. By WALDO I. BURNETT, M. D., Boston. One elegant octavo volume, cloth, $3.00.

This is believed to be incomparably the best and most complete work on the subject extant; and its appearance in an English dress, with the additions of the American Translator, is everywhere welcomed by men of science in this country.

UNITED STATES EXPLORING EXPEDITION; during the years 1838, 1839, 1840, 1841, 1842, under CHARLES WILKES, U. S. N. Vol. XII. MOLLUSCA AND SHELLS. By AUGUSTUS A. GOULD, M. D. Elegant quarto volume, cloth, $5.00.

THE LANDING AT CAPE ANNE; or, THE CHARTER OF THE FIRST PERMANENT COLONY ON THE TERRITORY OF THE MASSACHUSETTS COMPANY. Now discovered, and first published from the ORIGINAL MANUSCRIPT, with an inquiry into its authority, and a HISTORY OF THE COLONY, 1624—1628, Roger Conant, Governor. By J. WINGATE THORNTON. 8vo, cloth, $1.50.

☞ "A rare contribution to the early history of New England." — *Mercantile Journal.*

LAKE SUPERIOR; Its Physical Character, Vegetation, and Animals. By L. AGASSIZ and others. One volume octavo, elegantly Illustrated, cloth, $3 50.

THE HALLIG; OR, THE SHEEPFOLD IN THE WATERS. A Tale of Humble Life on the Coast of Schleswig. Translated from the German of BIERNATSKI, by Mrs. GEORGE P. MARSH. With a Biographical Sketch of the Author. 12mo, cloth, $1.00.

As a revelation of an entire new phase in human society, this work strongly reminds the reader of Miss Bremer's tales, In originality and brilliancy of imagination, it is not inferior to those; — its aim is far higher.

THE CRUISE OF THE NORTH STAR; A Narrative of the Excursion made by Mr. Vanderbilt's Party in the Steam Yacht, in her Voyage to England, Russia, Denmark, France, Spain, Italy, Malta, Turkey, Madeira, &c. By Rev. JOHN OVERTON CHOULES, D. D. With elegant Illustrations, &c. 12mo, cloth, gilt backs and sides, $1.50; cloth, gilt, $2.00; Turkey, gilt, $3.00.

ILGRIMAGE TO EGYPT; embracing a Diary of Explorations on the Nile, with Observations Illustrative of the Manners, Customs, and Institutions of the People, and of the present condition of the Antiquities and Ruins. By Hon. J. V. C. SMITH, late Mayor of the City of Boston. With numerous elegant Engravings. 12mo, cloth, $1.25.

POETICAL WORKS.

COMPLETE POETICAL WORKS OF WILLIAM COWPER; with a Life and Critical Notices of his Writings. Elegant Illustrations. 16mo, cloth, $1 00.

POETICAL WORKS OF SIR WALTER SCOTT. Life and Illustrations. 16mo, cloth, $1.00.

MILTON'S POETICAL WORKS. With a Life and elegant Illustrations. 16mo, cloth, $1.00.

☞ The above Poetical Works, by standard authors, are all of uniform size and style, printed on fine paper from clear, distinct type, with new and elegant illustrations, richly bound in full gilt, and plain.

VALUABLE TEXT-BOOKS.

THE LECTURES OF SIR WILLIAM HAMILTON, BART., late Professor of Logic and Metaphysics, University of Edinburgh; embracing the METAPHYSICAL and LOGICAL COURSES; with Notes, from Original Materials, and an Appendix, containing the Author's Latest Development of his New Logical Theory. Edited by Rev HENRY LONGUEVILLE MANSEL, B. D., Prof. of Moral and Metaphysical Philosophy in Magdalen College, Oxford, and JOHN VEITCH, M. A., of Edinburgh. In two royal octavo volumes, viz.,

I. METAPHYSICAL LECTURES (*now ready*). Royal octavo, cloth.

II. LOGICAL LECTURES (*in preparation*).

☞ G. & L., by a special arrangement with the family of the late Sir William Hamilton, the Authorized American Publishers of this distinguished author's *matchless* LECTURES ON METAPHYSICS AND LOGIC, and they are permitted to print the same from advance sheets furnished them by the English publishers.

MENTAL PHILOSOPHY; Including the Intellect, the Sensibilities, and the Will. By JOSEPH HAVEN, Prof. of Intellectual and Moral Philosophy, Amherst College Royal 12mo, cloth, embossed, $1 50.

It is believed this work will be found pre-eminently distinguished.

1. The COMPLETENESS with which it presents the whole subject. Text-books generally treat of only *one class* of faculties; this work includes the *whole*. 2. It is strictly and thoroughly SCIENTIFIC. 3. It presents a careful analysis of the mind, as a whole. 4. The history and literature of each topic. 5. The latest results of the science. 6. The chaste, yet attractive style. 7. The remarkable condensation of thought.

Prof. PARK, of Andover, says: "It is DISTINGUISHED for its clearness of style, perspicuity of method, candor of spirit, acumen and comprehensiveness of thought."

The work, though so recently published, has met with most remarkable success; having been already introduced into a large number of the leading colleges and schools in various parts of the country, and bids fair to take the place of every other work on the subject now before the public.

THESAURUS OF ENGLISH WORDS AND PHRASES, so classified and arranged as to facilitate the expression of ideas, and assist in literary composition. New and Improved Edition. By PETER MARK ROGET, late Secretary of the Royal Society, London, &c. Revised and edited, with a List of Foreign Words defined in English, and other additions, by BARNAS SEARS, D. D., President of Brown University. A NEW AMERICAN Edition, with ADDITIONS AND IMPROVEMENTS. 12mo, cloth, $1.50.

This edition is based on the London edition, recently issued. The first American Edition having been prepared by Dr. Sears for *strictly educational purposes*, those words and phrases properly termed "vulgar," incorporated in the original work, were omitted. These expurgated portions have in the present edition, been *restored*, but by such an arrangement of the matter as not to interfere with the educational purposes of the American editor. Besides this, it contains important additions of words and phrases not in the English edition, making it in *all respects more full and perfect than the author's edition*. The work has already become one of standard authority, both in this country and in Great Britain.

PALEY'S NATURAL THEOLOGY. Illustrated by forty Plates, with Selections from the Notes of Dr. Paxton, and Additional Notes, Original and Selected, with a Vocabulary of Scientific Terms. Edited by JOHN WARE, M. D. Improved edition, with elegant newly engraved plates. 12mo, cloth, embossed, $1.25.

This work is very generally introduced into our best Schools and Colleges throughout the country. An entirely new and beautiful set of Illustrations has recently been procured, which, with other improvements, render it the best and most complete work of the kind extant.

WORKS FOR BIBLE STUDENTS.

KITTO'S POPULAR CYCLOPÆDIA OF BIBLICAL LITERATURE. Condensed from the larger work. By the Author, JOHN KITTO, D. D. Assisted by JAMES TAYLOR, D. D., of Glasgow. With over five hundred Illustrations. One volume, octavo, 812 pp. Cloth, $3.00; sheep, $3.50; cloth, gilt, $4.00; half calf, $4.00.

A DICTIONARY OF THE BIBLE. Serving, also, as a COMMENTARY, embodying the products of the best and most recent researches in biblical literature in which the scholars of Europe and America have been engaged. The work, the result of immense labor and research, and enriched by the contributions of writers of distinguished eminence in the various departments of sacred literature, has been, by universal consent, pronounced the best work of its class extant, and the one best suited to the advanced knowledge of the present day in all the studies connected with theological science. It is not only intended for ministers and theological students, but it is also particularly adapted to parents, Sabbath-school teachers, and the great body of the religious public.

THE HISTORY OF PALESTINE, from the Patriarchal Age to the Present Time; with Chapters on the Geography and Natural History of the Country, the Customs and Institutions of the Hebrews. By JOHN KITTO, D. D. With upwards of two hundred Illustrations. 12mo, cloth, $1.25.

☞ A work admirably adapted to the Family, the Sabbath, and the week-day School Library.

ANALYTICAL CONCORDANCE TO THE HOLY SCRIPTURES; or, the Bible presented under Distinct and Classified Heads or Topics. By JOHN EADIE, D. D., LL D., Author of "Biblical Cyclopædia," "Ecclesiastical Cyclopædia," "Dictionary of the Bible," etc. One volume, octavo, 840 pp. Cloth, $3.00; sheep, $3.50; cloth, gilt, $4.00; half Turkey morocco, $4.00.

The object of this Concordance is to present the SCRIPTURES ENTIRE, under certain classified and exhaustive heads. It differs from an ordinary Concordance, in that its arrangement depends not on WORDS, but on SUBJECTS, and the verses *are printed in full.* Its plan does not bring it at all into competition with such limited works as those of Gaston and Warden; for they select *doctrinal* topics principally, and do not profess to comprehend as this THE ENTIRE BIBLE. The work also contains a Synoptical Table of Contents of the whole work, presenting in brief a system of biblical antiquities and theology, with a very copious and accurate index.

The value of this work to ministers and Sabbath-school teachers can hardly be over-estimated; and it needs only to be examined, to secure the approval and patronage of every Bible student.

CRUDEN'S CONDENSED CONCORDANCE. A Complete Concordance to the Holy Scriptures. By ALEXANDER CRUDEN. Revised and Re-edited by the Rev. DAVID KING, LL. D. Octavo, cloth backs, $1.25; sheep, $1.50.

The condensation of the quotations of Scripture, arranged under the most obvious heads, while it *diminishes the bulk* of the work, *greatly facilitates* the finding of any required passage.

"We have in this edition of Cruden the *best* made *better.* That is, the present is better adapted to the purposes of a Concordance, by the erasure of superfluous references, the omission of unnecessary explanations, and the contraction of quotations, &c. It is better as a manual, and is better adapted by its price to the means of many who need and ought to possess such a work, than the former large and expensive edition."—*Puritan Recorder.*

A COMMENTARY ON THE ORIGINAL TEXT OF THE ACTS OF THE APOSTLES. By HORATIO B. HACKETT, D. D., Prof. of Biblical Literature and Interpretation, in the Newton Theol. Inst. ☞ A new, revised, and enlarged edition. Royal octavo, cloth, $2.25.

☞ This most important and very popular work has been thoroughly revised; large portions entirely re-written, with the addition of *more than one hundred pages of new matter;* the result of the author's continued, laborious investigations and travels, since the publication of the first edition.

IMPORTANT NEW WORKS.

CYCLOPÆDIA OF ANECDOTES OF LITERATURE AND THE FINE ARTS. Containing a copious and choice Selection of Anecdotes of the various forms of Literature, of the Arts, of Architecture, Engravings, Music, Poetry, Painting, and Sculpture, and of the most celebrated Literary Characters and Artists of different Countries and Ages, &c. By KAZLITT ARVINE, A. M., author of "Cyclopædia of Moral and Religious Anecdotes." With numerous Illustrations. 725 pp. octavo. Cloth, $3.00; sheep, $3.50; cloth, gilt, $4.00; half calf, $4.00.

This is unquestionably the choicest collection of *Anecdotes* ever published. It contains *three thousand and forty Anecdotes:* and such is the wonderful variety, that it will be found an almost inexhaustible fund of interest for every class of readers. The elaborate classification and Indexes must commend it especially to public speakers, to the various classes of *literary and scientific men*, *artists*, *mechanics*, and *others*, as a DICTIONARY *for reference*, in relation to facts on the numberless subjects and characters introduced. There are also more than *one hundred and fifty fine Illustrations.*

THE LIFE OF JOHN MILTON, Narrated in Connection with the POLITICAL, ECCLESIASTICAL, and LITERARY HISTORY OF HIS TIME. By DAVID MASSON, M.A., Professor of English Literature, University College, London. Vol. I, embracing the period from 1603 to 1639. With Portraits, and specimens of his handwriting at different periods. Royal octavo, cloth, $0.00.

This important work will embrace three royal octavo volumes. By special arrangement with Prof. Masson, the author, G. & L. are permitted to print from advance sheets furnished them, as the authorized American publishers of this magnificent and eagerly looked for work. Volumes *two* and *three* will follow in due time; but, as each volume covers a definite period of time, and also embraces distinct topics of discussion or history, they will be published and sold independent of each other, or furnished in sets when the three volumes are completed.

THE GREYSON LETTERS. Selections from the Correspondence of R. E. H. GREYSON, Esq. Edited by HENRY ROGERS, author of "Eclipse of Faith." 12mo, cloth, $1.25.

"Mr. Greyson and Mr. Rogers are one and the same person. The whole work is from his pen, and every letter is radiant with the genius of the author. It discusses a wide range of subjects, in the most attractive manner. It abounds in the keenest wit and humor, satire and logic. It fairly entitles Mr. Rogers to rank with Sydney Smith and Charles Lamb as a wit and humorist, and with Bishop Butler as a reasoner. Mr. Rogers' name will share with those of Butler and Pascal, in the gratitude and veneration of posterity." — *London Quarterly.*

"A book not for one hour, but for all hours; not for one mood, but for every mood; to think over, to dream over, to laugh over." — *Boston Journal.*

"The Letters are intellectual gems, radiant with beauty, happily intermingling the grave and the gay. — *Christian Observer.*

ESSAYS IN BIOGRAPHY AND CRITICISM. By PETER BAYNE, M. A., author of "The Christian Life, Social and Individual." Arranged in two Series, or Parts. 12mo, cloth, each, $1.25.

These volumes have been prepared by the author exclusively for his American publishers, and are now published in uniform style. They include nineteen articles, viz.:

FIRST SERIES: — Thomas De Quincey. — Tennyson and his Teachers. — Mrs. Barrett Browning. — Recent Aspects of British Art. — John Ruskin. — Hugh Miller. — The Modern Novel; Dickens, &c. — Ellis, Acton, and Currer Bell.

SECOND SERIES: — Charles Kingsley. — S. T. Coleridge. — T. B. Macaulay. — Alison. — Wellington. — Napoleon. — Plato. — Characteristics of Christian Civilization. — The Modern University. — The Pulpit and the Press. — Testimony of the Rocks: a Defence.

VISITS TO EUROPEAN CELEBRITIES. By the Rev. WILLIAM B. SPRAGUE, D. D. 12mo, cloth, $1.00; cloth, gilt, $1.50.

A series of graphic and life-like Personal Sketches of many of the most distinguished men and women of Europe, portrayed as the Author saw them in their own homes, and under the most advantageous circumstances. Besides these "pen and ink" sketches, the work contains the novel attraction of a *fac-simile of the signature* of each of the persons introduced.

VALUABLE WORKS

PUBLISHED BY

GOULD AND LINCOLN,

59 WASHINGTON STREET, BOSTON.

THE CHRISTIAN LIFE; SOCIAL AND INDIVIDUAL. By PETER BAYNE, M. A. 12mo, cloth, $1.25.

There is but one voice respecting this extraordinary book, — men of all denominations, in all quarters, agree in pronouncing it one of the most admirable works of the age.

MODERN ATHEISM; Under its forms of Pantheism, Materialism, Secularism, Development, and Natural Laws. By JAMES BUCHANAN, D. D., L. L. D. 12mo, cloth, $1.25.

" The work is one of the most readable and solid which we have ever perused." — *Hugh Miller in the Witness.*

NEW ENGLAND THEOCRACY. From the German of Uhden's History of the Congregationalists of New England, with an INTRODUCTION BY NEANDER. By MRS. H. C. CONANT, author of "The English Bible," etc. 12mo, cloth, $1.00.

A work of rare ability and interest, presenting the early religious and ecclesiastical history of New England, from authentic sources, with singular impartiality. The author evidently aimed throughout to do exact justice to the dominant party, and all their opponents of every name. The standpoint from which the whole subject is viewed is novel, and we have in this volume a new and most important contribution to Puritan History.

THE MISSION OF THE COMFORTER; with copious Notes. By JULIUS CHARLES HARE. With the NOTES translated for the AMERICAN EDITION. 12mo, cloth, $1.25.

THE BETTER LAND; or, The Believer's Journey and Future Home. By the Rev. A. C. THOMPSON. 12mo, cloth, 85 cts.

A most charming and instructive book for all now journeying to the " Better Land."

THE EVENING OF LIFE; or, Light and Comfort amidst the Shadows of Declining Years. By REV. JEREMIAH CHAPLIN, D. D. A new Revised, and much enlarged edition. With an elegant Frontispiece on Steel. 12mo, cloth, $1.00.

☞ A most charming and appropriate work for the aged, — large type and open page. An admirable " Gift" for the child to present the parent.

THE STATE OF THE IMPENITENT DEAD. By ALVAH HOVEY, D. D., Prof. of Christian Theology in Newton Theol. Inst. 16mo, cloth, 50 cts.

A WREATH AROUND THE CROSS; or, Scripture Truths Illustrated. By the Rev. A. MORTON BROWN, D. D. Recommendatory Preface, by JOHN ANGELL JAMES. With a beautiful Frontispiece. 16mo, cloth, 60 cts.

"'Christ, and Him crucified' is presented in a new, striking, and matter-of-fact light. The style is simple, without being puerile, and the reasoning is of that truthful, persuasive kind that 'comes from the heart, and reaches the heart.'" — *N. Y. Observer.*

WORKS FOR CHURCH MEMBERS.

THE CHRISTIAN'S DAILY TREASURY; a Religious Exercise for every Day in the Year. By Rev. E. TEMPLE. A new and improved edition. 12mo, cloth, $1.00.

☞ A work for every Christian. It is indeed a "Treasury" of good things.

THE SCHOOL OF CHRIST; or, Christianity Viewed in its Leading Aspects. By the Rev. A. R. L. FOOTE, author of "Incidents in the Life of our Saviour," etc. 16mo, cloth, 50 cts.

THE CHRISTIAN PASTOR; His Work and the Needful Preparation. By ALVAH HOVEY, D. D., Prof. of Theology in the Newton Theol. Inst. 16mo, pp. 60; flexible cloth, 25 cents; paper covers, 12 cents.

APOLLOS; or, Directions to Persons just commencing a Religious Life. 32mo, paper covers, cheap, for distribution, per hundred, $6.00.

THE HARVEST AND THE REAPERS. Home Work for All, and how to do it. By Rev. HARVEY NEWCOMB. 16mo, cloth, 63 cts.

This work is dedicated to the converts of 1858. It shows what *may* be done, by showing what has been done. It shows how much there is NOW to be done at home. It shows HOW to do it. Every man interested in the work of saving men, every professing Christian, will find this work to be for him.

THE CHURCH-MEMBER'S MANUAL of Ecclesiastical Principles, Doctrines, and Discipline. By Rev. WILLIAM CROWELL, D. D. Introduction by H. J. RIPLEY, D. D. Second edition, revised and improved. 12mo, cloth, 75 cts.

THE CHURCH-MEMBER'S HAND-BOOK; a Plain Guide to the Doctrines and Practice of Baptist Churches. By the Rev. WILLIAM CROWELL, D. D. 18mo, cloth, 38 cts.

THE CHURCH-MEMBER'S GUIDE. By the Rev. JOHN A. JAMES. Edited by J. O. CHOULES, D. D. New edition. With Introductory Essay, by Rev. HUBBARD WINSLOW. Cloth, 33 cts.

"The spontaneous effusion of our heart, on laying the book down, was: 'May every church-member in our land possess this book, and be blessed with all the happiness which conformity to its evangelical sentiments and directions is calculated to confer.'" — *Christian Secretary.*

THE CHURCH IN EARNEST. By Rev. JOHN A. JAMES. 18mo, cloth, 40 cts.

"Its arguments and appeals are well adapted to prompt to action, and the times demand such a book. We trust it will be universally read." — *N. Y. Observer.*

"Those who have the means should purchase a number of copies of this work, and lend them to church-members, and keep them in circulation *till they are worn out!*" — *Mothers' Assistant.*

CHRISTIAN PROGRESS. A Sequel to the Anxious Inquirer. By JOHN ANGELL JAMES. 18mo, cloth, 31 cts.

☞ One of the best and most useful works of this popular author.

"It ought to be sold by hundreds of thousands, until every church-member in the land has bought, read, marked, learned, and inwardly digested a copy." — *Congregationalist.*

"So eminently is it adapted to do good, that we feel no surprise that it should make one of the publishers' excellent publications. It exhibits the whole subject of growth in grace with great simplicity and clearness." — *Puritan Recorder.*

VALUABLE NEW WORKS.

GOD REVEALED IN NATURE AND IN CHRIST; including a Refutation of the Development Theory contained in the "Vestiges of the Natural History of Creation." By Rev. JAMES B. WALKER, author of "THE PHILOSOPHY OF THE PLAN OF SALVATION." 12mo, cloth, $1.00.

PHILOSOPHY OF THE PLAN OF SALVATION; a Book for the Times. By an AMERICAN CITIZEN. With an Introductory Essay by CALVIN E. STOWE, D. D. ☞ New improved and enlarged edition. 12mo, cloth, 75 cts.

YAHVEH CHRIST; or, The Memorial Name. By ALEXANDER MACWHORTER. With an Introductory Letter by NATHANIEL W. TAYLOR, D. D., Dwight Professor in Yale Theol. Sem. 16mo, cloth, 60 cts.

SALVATION BY CHRIST. A Series of Discourses on some of the most Important Doctrines of the Gospel. By FRANCIS WAYLAND, D. D. 12mo, cloth, $1.00; cloth, gilt, $1.50.

CONTENTS. — Theoretical Atheism. — Practical Atheism. — The Moral Character of Man. — The Fall of Man. — Justification by Works Impossible. — Preparation for the Advent. — Work of the Messiah. — Justification by Faith. — Conversion. — Imitators of God. — Grieving the Spirit. — A Day in the Life of Jesus. — The Benevolence of the Gospel. — The Fall of Peter. — Character of Balaam. — Veracity. — The Church of Christ. — The Unity of the Church. — Duty of Obedience to the Civil Magistrate (three Sermons).

THE GREAT DAY OF ATONEMENT; or, Meditations and Prayers on the Last Twenty-four Hours of the Sufferings and Death of Our Lord and Saviour Jesus Christ. Translated from the German of CHARLOTTE ELIZABETH NEBELIN. Edited by MRS. COLIN MACKENZIE. Elegantly printed and bound. 16mo, cloth, 75 cts.

THE EXTENT OF THE ATONEMENT IN ITS RELATION TO GOD AND THE UNIVERSE. By Rev. THOMAS W. JENKYN, D. D., late President of Coward College, London. 12mo, cloth, $1.00.

This work was thoroughly revised by the author not long before his death, exclusively for the present publishers. It has long been a standard work, and without doubt presents the most complete discussion of the subject in the language.

"We consider this volume as setting the long and fiercely agitated question as to the extent of the Atonement completely at rest. Posterity will thank the author till the latest ages for his illustrious argument." — *New York Evangelist.*

THE SUFFERING SAVIOUR; or, Meditations on the Last Days of Christ. By FRED. W. KRUMMACHER, D. D., author of "Elijah the Tishbite." 12mo, cloth, $1.25.

"The narrative is given with thrilling vividness, and pathos, and beauty. Marking, as we proceeded, several passages for quotation, we found them in the end so numerous, that we must refer the reader to the work itself." — *News of the Churches (Scottish).*

THE IMITATION OF CHRIST. By THOMAS A KEMPIS. With an Introductory Essay, by THOMAS CHALMERS, D. D. Edited by HOWARD MALCOM, D. D. A new edition, with a LIFE OF THOMAS A KEMPIS, by Dr. C. ULLMANN, author of "Reformers before the Reformation." 12mo, cloth, 85 cts.

This may safely be pronounced the best Protestant edition extant of this ancient and celebrated work. It is reprinted from Payne's edition, collated with an ancient Latin copy. The peculiar feature of this new edition is the improved page, the elegant, large, clear type, and the NEW LIFE OF A KEMPIS, by Dr. Ullmann.

VALUABLE WORKS.

FOOTSTEPS OF OUR FOREFATHERS; What they suffered and what they sought. Describing Localities, and Portraying Personages and Events, conspicuous in the Struggles for Religious Liberty. By JAMES G. MIALL. Containing thirty-six Illustrations. 12mo, cloth, $1.00.

MEMORIALS OF EARLY CHRISTIANITY; Presenting, in a graphic, compact, and popular form, Memorable Events of Early Ecclesiastical History, &c. By Rev. J. G. MIALL, author of "Footsteps of our Forefathers." With numerous Illustrations. 12mo, cloth, $1.00.

☞ The above, by Miall, are both exceedingly interesting and instructive works.

REPUBLICAN CHRISTIANITY; or, True Liberty, as exhibited in the Life, Precepts, and early Disciples of the Great Redeemer. By the Rev. E. L. MAGOON, D. D., author of "Proverbs for the People," &c. Second edition. 12mo, cloth, $1.25.

"The author has at his command a rich store of learning, from which he skilfully draws abundant evidence for the support of the positions he assumes." — *Puritan Recorder.*

THE PERSON AND WORK OF CHRIST. By ERNEST SARTORIUS, D.D., Konigsberg, Prussia. Translated by Rev. OAKMAN S. STEARNS, A. M. 18mo, cloth, 42 cts.

"A work of much ability, and presenting the argument in a style that will be new to most of American readers. It will deservedly attract attention." — *New York Observer*

CHRISTIANITY DEMONSTRATED; in four distinct and independent series of proofs; with an Explanation of the Types and Prophecies concerning the Messiah. By Rev. HARVEY NEWCOMB. 12mo, cloth, 75 cts.

THE SAINT'S EVERLASTING REST. By RICHARD BAXTER 16mo, cloth, 50 cts.

THE RELIGIONS OF THE WORLD, and their Relations to Christianity. By FREDERICK DENISON MAURICE, A. M., Professor of Divinity in King's College, London. 16mo, cloth, 60 cts.

THE CHRISTIAN WORLD UNMASKED. By JOHN BERRIDGE, A M., Vicar of Everton, Bedfordshire. With a Life of the Author, by Rev. THOMAS GUTHRIE, D. D., Minister of Free St. John's, Edinburgh. 16mo, cloth, 50 cts.

"The book," says DR. GUTHRIE, in his Introduction, "which we introduce anew to the public, has survived the test of years, and still stands towering above things of inferior growth, like a cedar of Lebanon. Its subject is all-important; in doctrine it is sound to the core; it glows with fervent piety; it exhibits a most skilful and unsparing dissection of the dead professor; while its style is so remarkable that he who could *preach* as Berridge has *written* would hold any congregation by the ears."

THE IMITATION OF CHRIST. By THOMAS A KEMPIS. Introductory Essay, by T. CHALMERS, D. D. Edited by the REV. HOWARD MALCOM, D. D. *Cheap edition.* 18mo, cloth, 38 cts.

GUIDO AND JULIUS. THE DOCTRINE OF SIN AND THE PROPITIATOR; or, the True Consecration of the Doubter. Exhibited in the Correspondence of two Friends. By FREDERICK AUGUSTUS O. THOLUCK, D. D. Translated from the German, by JONATHAN EDWARDS RYLAND, With an introduction by JOHN PYE SMITH, D. D. 16mo, cloth, 60 cts.

DR. JOHN HARRIS' WORKS.

THE GREAT TEACHER; or, Characteristics of our Lord's Ministry. By JOHN HARRIS, D. D. With an Introductory Essay by H. HUMPHREY, D. D. Sixteenth thousand. 12mo, cloth, 85 cents.

"DR. HARRIS is one of the best writers of the age; and this volume will not in the least detract from his well-merited reputation." — *American Pulpit.*

THE GREAT COMMISSION; or, the Christian Church constituted and charged to convey the Gospel to the World. A Prize Essay. With an Introductory Essay by W. R. WILLIAMS, D. D. Eighth thousand. 12mo, cloth, $1.00.

"This volume will afford the reader an intellectual and spiritual banquet of the highest order." — *Philadelphia Ch. Observer.*

THE PRE-ADAMITE EARTH. Contributions to Theological Science. By JOHN HARRIS, D. D. New and revised edition. 12mo, cloth, $1.00.

MAN PRIMEVAL; or, the Constitution and Primitive Condition of the Human Being. With a finely engraved Portrait of the Author. 12mo, cloth, $1.25.

PATRIARCHY; or, the Family, its Constitution and Probation. 12mo, cloth, $1.25.

This is the last of Dr. Harris' series entitled "Contributions to Theological Science."

SERMONS, CHARGES, ADDRESSES, &c., delivered by Dr. HARRIS in various parts of the country, during the height of his reputation as a preacher. Two elegant volumes, octavo, cloth, each, $1.00.

The immense sale of all this author's Works attests their intrinsic worth and great popularity.

DR. WILLIAMS' WORKS.

LECTURES ON THE LORD'S PRAYER. By WILLIAM R. WILLIAMS, D. D. Third edition. 12mo, cloth, 85 cts.

"We are constantly reminded, in reading his eloquent pages, of the old English writers, whose vigorous thought, and gorgeous imagery, and varied learning, have made their writings an inexhaustible mine for the scholars of the present day." — *Ch. Observer.*

RELIGIOUS PROGRESS; Discourses on the Development of the Christian Character. By WILLIAM R. WILLIAMS, D. D. Third edition. 12mo, cloth, 85 cts.

"His power of apt and forcible illustration is without a parallel among modern writers. The mute pages spring into life beneath the magic of his radiant imagination. But this is never at the expense of solidity of thought, or strength of argument. It is seldom, indeed, that a mind of so much poetical invention yields such a willing homage to the logical element." — *Harper's Monthly Miscellany.*

MISCELLANIES. By WILLIAM R. WILLIAMS, D. D. New and improved edition. *Price Reduced.* 12mo, cloth, $1.25.

☞ "Dr. Williams is a profound scholar and a brilliant writer." — *N. Y. Evangelist.*

BUNGENER'S WORKS.

THE PREACHER AND THE KING; or, Bourdaloue in the Court of Louis XIV.; being an Account of the Pulpit Eloquence of that distinguished era. Translated from the French of L. F. BUNGENER, Paris. Introduction by the Rev. GEORGE POTTS, D. D. *A new, improved edition,* with a fine LIKENESS and a BIOGRAPHICAL SKETCH OF THE AUTHOR. 12mo, cloth, $1.25.

THE PRIEST AND THE HUGUENOT; or, Persecution in the Age of Louis XV Translated from the French of L. F. Bungener. Two vols. 12mo, cloth, $2.25.

☞ This is not only a work of thrilling interest, — no fiction could exceed it, — but, as a Protestant work, it is a masterly production.

VALUABLE WORKS.

THE LIMITS OF RELIGIOUS THOUGHT EXAMINED. By HENRY LONGUEVILLE MANSEL, B. D., Prof. of Moral and Metaphysical Philosophy, Magdalen College, Oxford, Editor of Sir William Hamilton's Lectures, etc. etc. With the COPIOUS NOTES of the volume translated for the American Edition. 12mo, cloth, $1.25.

☞ This is a *masterly* production, and may be safely said to be one of the most important works of the day.

FIRST THINGS; or, The Development of Church Life. By BARON STOW, D. D. 16mo, cloth, 75 cts.

HEAVEN. By JAMES WILLIAM KIMBALL. With an elegant vignette title-page. 12mo, cloth, $1.00.

"The book is full of beautiful ideas, consoling hopes, and brilliant representations of human destiny, all presented in a chaste, pleasing and very readable style." — *N. Y. Chronicle.*

THE PROGRESS OF BAPTIST PRINCIPLES IN THE LAST HUNDRED YEARS. By T. F. CURTIS, Professor of Theology in the Lewisburg University, Pa., and author of "Communion," &c. 12mo, cloth, $1.25.

Eminently worthy of the attention, not only of Baptists, *but of all other denominations.* In his preface the author declares that his aim has been to draw a wide distinction between *parties* and *opinions.* Hence the object of this volume is not to exhibit or defend the Baptists, *but their principles.* It is confidently pronounced the best exhibition of Baptist views and principles extant.

THOUGHTS ON THE PRESENT COLLEGIATE SYSTEM in the United States. By FRANCIS WAYLAND, D. D. 16mo, cloth, 50 cents.

SACRED RHETORIC; or, Composition and Delivery of Sermons. By H. J. RIPLEY, D. D., Prof. in Newton Theol. Inst. To which is added, DR. WARE'S HINTS ON EXTEMPORANEOUS PREACHING. Second thousand. 12mo, cloth, 75 cts.

THE PULPIT OF THE REVOLUTION; or, The Political Sermons of the Era of 1776. With an Introduction, Biographical Sketches of the Preachers and Historical Notes, etc. By JOHN WINGATE THORNTON, author of "The Landing at Cape Anne," etc. 12mo, cloth. *In press.*

THE EIGHTEEN CHRISTIAN CENTURIES. By the Rev. JAMES WHITE, author of "Landmarks of the History of England." 12mo, cloth. *In press.*

THE PLURALITY OF WORLDS. A NEW EDITION. With a SUPPLEMENTARY DIALOGUE, in which the author's Reviewers are reviewed. 12mo, cloth, $1.00.

This masterly production, which has excited so much interest in this country and in Europe, will now have an increased attraction in the addition of the Supplement, in which the author's reviewers are triumphantly reviewed.

THE CAMEL; His Organization, Habits, and Uses, considered with reference to his introduction into the United States. By GEORGE P. MARSH, late U. S. Minister at Constantinople. 12mo, cloth, 63 cts.

This book treats of a subject of great interest, especially at the present time. It furnishes a more complete and reliable account of the Camel than any other in the language; indeed, it is believed that there is no other. It is the result of long study, extensive research, and much personal observation, on the part of the author, and it has been prepared with special reference to the experiment of domesticating the Camel in this country, now going on under the auspices of the United States government. It is written in a style worthy of the distinguished author's reputation for great learning and fine scholarship.

VALUABLE BIOGRAPHIES.

EXTRACTS FROM THE DIARY AND CORRESPONDENCE OF THE LATE AMOS LAWRENCE. With a brief account of some Incidents in his Life. Edited by his son, WM. R. LAWRENCE, M. D. With elegant Portraits of Amos and Abbott Lawrence, an Engraving of their Birthplace, an Autograph page of Handwriting, and a copious Index. One large octavo volume, cloth, $1.50; royal 12mo, cloth, $1.00.

A MEMOIR OF THE LIFE AND TIMES OF ISAAC BACKUS. By ALVAH HOVEY, Professor of Ecclesiastical History in Newton Theological Institution. 12mo, cloth, $1.25.

This work gives an account of a remarkable man, and of a remarkable movement in the middle of the last century, resulting in the formation of what were called the "Separate" Churches. It supplies an important deficiency in the history of New England affairs. For every Baptist, especially, it is a necessary book.

LIFE OF JAMES MONTGOMERY. By Mrs. H. C. KNIGHT, author of "Lady Huntington and her Friends," &c. Likeness and elegant Illustrated Title-Page on steel. 12mo, cloth, $1.25.

This is an original biography, prepared from the abundant but ill-digested materials contained in the seven octavo volumes of the London edition. The Christian public in America will welcome such a memoir of a poet whose hymns and sacred melodies have been the delight of every household.

MEMOIR OF ROGER WILLIAMS, Founder of the State of Rhode Island. By Prof. WILLIAM GAMMELL, A. M. 16mo, cloth, 75 cts.

PHILIP DODDRIDGE. His Life and Labors. By JOHN STOUGHTON, D. D. With an Introductory Chapter, by Rev. JAMES G. MIALL, Author of "Footsteps of our Forefathers," &c. With beautiful Illustrated Title-page and Frontispiece. 16mo, cloth, 60 cents.

THE LIFE AND CORRESPONDENCE OF JOHN FOSTER. Edited by J. E. RYLAND, with notices of Mr. FOSTER, as a Preacher and a Companion. By JOHN SHEPPARD. A new edition, two volumes in one, 700 pages. 12mo, cloth, $1.25.

"In simplicity of language, in majesty of conception, his writings are unmatched." — *North British Review.*

THE LIFE OF GODFREY WILLIAM VON LEIBNITZ. By JOHN M. MACKIE, Esq. On the basis of the German work of Dr. G. E. GUHRAUER. 16mo, cloth, 75 cts

"It merits the special notice of all who are interested in the business of education, and deserves a place by the side of Brewster's Life of Newton, in all the libraries of our schools, academies, and literary institutions." — *Watchman and Reflector.*

MEMORIES OF A GRANDMOTHER. By a Lady of Massachusetts. 16mo, cloth, 50 cts.

☞ "My path lies in a valley, which I have sought to adorn with flowers. Shadows from the hills cover it; but I make my own sunshine." — *Author's Preface.*

THE TEACHER'S LAST LESSON. A Memoir of MARTHA WHITING, late of the Charlestown Female Seminary, with Reminiscences and Suggestive Reflections. By CATHARINE N. BADGER, an Associate Teacher. With a Portrait, and an Engraving of the Seminary. 12mo, cloth, $1.00.

The subject of this Memoir was, for a quarter of a century, at the head of one of the most celebrated female seminaries in the country. During that period she educated more than *three thousand* young ladies. She was a kindred spirit to Mary Lyon.

WORKS FOR BIBLE STUDENTS.

NOTES ON THE GOSPELS. Designed for Teachers in Sabbath Schools and Bible Classes, and as an Aid to Family Instruction. By HENRY J. RIPLEY, Prof. in Newton Theol. Inst. With Map of Canaan. Cloth, embossed, $1.25.

NOTES ON THE ACTS OF THE APOSTLES. With a beautiful Map, illustrating the Travels of the APOSTLE PAUL, with a track of his Voyage from Cesarea to Rome. By Prof. HENRY J. RIPLEY, D. D. 12mo, cloth, embossed, 75 cts.

NOTES ON THE EPISTLE OF PAUL TO THE ROMANS. Designed for Teachers in Sabbath Schools and Bible Classes, and as an aid to Family Instruction. By HENRY J. RIPLEY. 12mo, cloth, embossed, 67 cts.

The above works by Prof. Ripley should be in the hands of every student of the Bible, especially every Sabbath-school and Bible-class teacher. They are prepared with especial reference to this class of persons, and contain a mass of just the kind of information wanted.

MALCOM'S NEW BIBLE DICTIONARY of the most important Names, Objects, and Terms, found in the Holy Scriptures; intended principally for Sabbath-School Teachers and Bible Classes. By HOWARD MALCOM, D. D., late President of Lewisburg College, Pa. 16mo, cloth, embossed, 60 cts.

☞ The former Dictionary, of which more than *one hundred thousand copies* were sold, is made the basis of the present work; yet so revised, enlarged, and improved, by the addition of new material, a greatly increased number of articles, new illustrations, etc., as to render it essentially a NEW DICTIONARY.

THE EVIDENCES OF CHRISTIANITY, as exhibited in the writings of its apologists, down to Augustine. By W. J. BOLTON, of Gonville and Caius College, Cambridge. 12mo, cloth, 80 cts.

HARMONY QUESTIONS ON THE FOUR GOSPELS, for the use of Sabbath Schools. By Rev. S. B. SWAIM, D. D. Vol. I. 18mo, cloth backs, 12½ cts.

The plan differs from all others in this, that it is based upon a HARMONY of the gospels. Instead of taking one of the gospels, — that of Matthew, for instance, — and going through with it, the author takes from ALL of the gospels those parts relating to the same event, and brings them together in the same lesson.

SABBATH-SCHOOL CLASS BOOK; comprising copious Exercises on the Sacred Scriptures. By E. LINCOLN. Revised and Improved by REV. JOSEPH BANVARD, author of "Topical Question Book," etc. 18mo, 12½ cts.

United testimony of Dr. Malcom, author of "Bible Dictionary," Dr. Stow, "Doctrinal Question Book," Dr. Hague, "Guides to Conversations on New Testament":

"It gives us pleasure to express our satisfaction with its design and execution. We think the work is well adapted to the end designed, having avoided, in a great degree, the evils of extreme redundance or conciseness."

LINCOLN'S SCRIPTURE QUESTIONS; with answers, giving, in the language of Scripture, interesting portions of the History, Doctrines, and Duties, exhibited in the Bible. 8½ cts. per copy; $1.00 per dozen.

☞ Where Bibles cannot be furnished to each scholar, this work will be found an admirable substitute, as the text is furnished in connection with the questions.

THE SABBATH-SCHOOL HARMONY; containing appropriate Hymns and Music for Sabbath Schools, Juvenile Singing Schools, and Family Devotion. By NATHANIEL D. GOULD. 12½ cts.

VALUABLE WORKS.

MOTHERS OF THE WISE AND GOOD. By JABEZ BURNS, D. D. 16mo, cloth, 75 cts.; cloth, gilt, $1.25.

☞ A sketch of the mothers of many of the most eminent men of the world, and showing how much they were indebted to maternal influence for their greatness and excellence of character.

MY MOTHER; or, Recollections of Maternal Influence. By a New England Clergyman. With a beautiful Frontispiece. 12mo, cloth, 75 cts.; cloth, gilt, $1.25.

A writer of wide celebrity says of the book: "It is one of those rare pictures painted from life with the exquisite skill of one of the *Old Masters*, which so seldom present themselves to the amateur."

THE EXCELLENT WOMAN, as Described in the Book of Proverbs With an Introduction by Rev. W. B. SPRAGUE, D. D. Containing twenty-four splendid Illustrations. Third thousand. 12mo, cloth, $1.00; cloth, gilt, $1.75; extra Turkey, $2.50.

☞ This elegant volume is an appropriate and valuable "Gift Book" for the husband to present the wife, or the child the mother.

THE SIGNET RING, AND ITS HEAVENLY MOTTO. From the German. Illustrated. 16mo, cloth, gilt, 31 cts.

☞ Seldom within so small a compass has such weighty teaching been presented with such exquisite and charming skill.

THE MARRIAGE RING; or, How to Make Home Happy. From the writings of JOHN ANGELL JAMES. Beautifully Illustrated edition. 16mo, cloth, gilt, 75 cts.

WORKS BY DR. TWEEDIE.

GLAD TIDINGS; or, the Gospel of Peace. A Series of Daily Meditations for Christian Disciples. By Rev. W. K. TWEEDIE, D. D. With an elegant illustrated title-page. 16mo, cloth, 63 cts.; cloth, gilt, $1.00.

A LAMP TO THE PATH; or, the Bible in the Heart, the Home, and the Market-place. With an elegant illustrated title-page. 16mo, cloth, 63 cts.; clo. gilt, $1.00.

SEED-TIME AND HARVEST; or, Sow Well and Reap Well. A Book for the Young. With an elegant illustrated title-page. 16mo, cloth, 63 cts.; cloth, gilt, $1.00.

☞ The above interesting works, by Dr. Tweedie, are of uniform size and style, and well adapted for "gift books."

GATHERED LILIES; or, Little Children in Heaven. By Rev. A. C. THOMPSON, Author of "The Better Land." 18mo, flexible cloth, 25 cts.; flexible cloth, gilt, 31 cts.; and cloth, gilt, 42 cts.

"My beloved has gone down into his garden to gather lilies." — *Song of Solomon.*

"In almost every household such a little volume as this will meet a tender welcome." — *N. Y. Evangelist.*

OUR LITTLE ONES IN HEAVEN. Edited by the Author of "The Aimwell Stories," &c. 18mo, cloth, 50 cts.; cloth, gilt, 75 cts.

This little volume contains a choice collection of pieces, in verse and prose, on the death and future happiness of young children.

SAFE HOME; or, the Last Days and Happy Death of Fannie Kenyon. With an Introduction by Prof. J. L. Lincoln, of Brown University. 18mo, flexible cloth cover, 25 cts.; gilt, 31 cts.

This is a delightful narrative of a remarkable little girl, and is recommended to the attention, particularly, of Sabbath Schools.

www.ingramcontent.com/pod-product-compliance
Lightning Source LLC
LaVergne TN
LVHW020121110826
845151LV00001B/234

* 9 7 8 1 4 2 5 5 4 1 5 1 4 *